Perspectives on Psychology

Perspectives on Psychology

INTRODUCTORY READINGS

EDITED BY

Ira S. Cohen

STATE UNIVERSITY OF NEW YORK AT BUFFALO

PRAEGER PUBLISHERS · NEW YORK

Published in the United States of America in 1975
by Praeger Publishers, Inc.
111 Fourth Avenue, New York, N.Y. 10003

Library of Congress Cataloging in Publication Data

Cohen, Ira S   1924–   comp.
   Perspectives on psychology.

   Includes bibliographies and index.
   1. Psychology—Addresses, essays, lectures.   I. Ti-
tle. [DNLM: 1. Behavior.   2. Psychology.   BF121
C676p]
BF149.C55   150'.8   73-8396
ISBN 0-275-51080-8
ISBN 0-275-88710-3 pbk.

Printed in the United States of America

Contents

Preface

THIS VOLUME was designed to provide a resource of supplementary readings for the introductory psychology course. Taken together the essays in this collection provide a readable, broad sample of the methods and findings of contemporary psychology and of some viewpoints, not always orthodox, on controversial issues. Some of the essays or research reports will help to illustrate significant points that are covered in most introductory psychology textbooks. Others will serve to focus attention on issues by exposing the student to writings that, at least superficially, seem to be incongruent with positions expounded in the basic text. In this way, the essays included here should serve effectively as stimuli for classroom discussion.

The challenge was to present a collection of supplementary readings that do not require training and vocabulary that is beyond the level of the beginning student yet, at the same time, do not compromise the intellectual honesty of the discipline. The aim was to tempt the student to look further at what psychology can mean for him/her as a disciplined inquiry into the study of human behavior.

These concerns resulted in a collection of readings that are in certain respects heterogeneous. Included are:

1. *Materials that are not usually considered part of social science professional literature,* but nonetheless cast an intelligent light on issues that are dealt with in the introductory psychology course. Thus, excerpts from the writings on the hatha-yoga raise questions about the usual distinction between the voluntary and the autonomic nervous systems; George Bernard Shaw's satirical attack on behaviorism raises questions about the experimental methodology of psychologists; Joyce's language in an excerpt from *Finnegans Wake* can be examined for its similarities with and differences from schizophrenic language, samples of which are also included.

2. *Materials written by behavior scientists, but addressed to an intelligent general readership.* An understanding of these materials should have no prerequisite of knowledge in psychology, yet the arti-

cles are authentic and authoritative. Thus, selections from Skinner's *Walden Two* illustrate the application of reinforcement theory to the development of a utopian society; Zimbardo's "Pirandellian Prison" points to the awesome potency of social role and social position in determining behavior in a prison; selections from Delgado's *Physical Control of the Mind* explore the accomplishments of research on the electrical stimulation of the brain and the prospects and limitations in applying this research to the control of people's behavior.

3. *Essays and articles addressed to an audience of behavior scientists who have a general interest in the subject matter* but are not specialists in the topics. As a consequence, the essays do not assume a level of sophistication nor draw upon a knowledge of vocabulary and conceptualizations with which the reader is not yet equipped. Thus, Rosenhan's article on insanity and mental hospitals was directed to scientists in general, and Harlow's on the nature of love to psychologists in general, rather than to specialists in each of these areas.

4. *A selection of research articles from the scientific journals.* Selections were carefully made to expose students to the kind of reports that are characteristic of psychological research. Samples were selected that are interesting, thought-provoking, and relatively free of the scientific language that to the novice can appear to be nothing more than jargon. Gardner and Gardner's "Teaching Sign Language to a Chimpanzee" and Darley and Latané's "Bystander Intervention in Emergencies" are examples of articles that meet these criteria.

Taken as a whole, these readings aim to provide a perspective on the broad scope of issues in contemporary psychology. The diverse viewpoints and the variety of sources are designed to pique the student's interest and, above all, should raise intelligent questions and provocative discussions. Without the latter, this effort will have fallen short of its mark.

I am grateful to the authors and publishers who were kind enough to permit the reprinting of their materials. In recognition of their cooperation, 50 per cent of the editor's royalties, after costs, will be contributed to the American Psychological Foundation.

IRA S. COHEN
Buffalo, New York
April 1975

To the Instructor

THE PRIMARY concern in compiling these materials was with teaching and "teachability." Therefore, the abiding criteria in the selection were the intrinsic interest of the essays, their likelihood to provoke discussion, the bridges that they draw with the standard text material, and their readability for the introductory student. Too often supplementary readings books ignore these obvious criteria. They characteristically include articles taken from professional journals and assume a level of sophistication that the reader has not yet reached, resulting in some students finding the experience more frustrating and of less interest than most of us teaching the course are willing to recognize.

The readings have been organized into sections that are congruent with the units in many introductory psychology textbooks. Nevertheless, since texts vary in the sequencing of materials, there will necessarily be some skipping around among these readings. Moreover, many of the readings will be relevant to more than one of the usual topics in the standard introductory course. For example, Meehl's article deals primarily with methodological issues (Part I), but has some interesting things to say about intelligence (Part II) and about punishment (Part III). In most cases, the more obvious cross-references are made in the headnotes for subsequent readings. But to facilitate assignments collateral to the basic text, the readings are numbered consecutively throughout the anthology. Also, the following index suggests selections that would be appropriate for a large number of basic psychology topics.

BASIC PSYCHOLOGY TOPICS

Topic	Selection Number	Author
History		
Functionalism; Wm. James	1	James
Psychoanalysis	22	Freud
Behaviorism	2	Shaw

Topic	Selection Number	Author
Methods		
Laboratory research	2	Shaw
Empiricism and the experimental method	3	Meehl
Physiological Foundations		
Brain research		
Electrostimulation of the brain	4	Delgado
Split-brain research	19	Pines
Sensory processes	5	Keller
Autonomic nervous system	6	Evans-Wentz
	11	Jonas
Species-specific behavior ("instincts")	7	Breland and Breland
Biological basis of sex-role behavior	24b	Weisstein
Developmental Processes		
Infancy and early childhood	8	McGraw
Development of sex-role behavior	24a	Kagan
	24b	Weisstein
Intellectual development	9	Sarason
Intelligence, nature-nurture	9	Sarason
	3	Meehl
Learning		
Reward and punishment (operant and	10	Skinner
classical conditioning)	3	Meehl
	2	Shaw
	7	Breland and Breland
Autonomic learning	11	Jonas
	6	Evans-Wentz
Learning of sex-roles	24a	Kagan
	24b	Weisstein
Cognitive Processes		
Memory	12	Brown and McNeill
Information-processing	12	Brown and McNeill
Language	13	Gardner and Gardner
Creativity and problem-solving	14	Rosner and Abt
Emotion and Motivation		
James-Lange theory of emotions	15	James
Autonomic responsivity	11	Jonas
Love and sex	16	Harlow
Maternal behavior	16	Harlow
Social motives	17	McClelland
Achievement motive	17	McClelland
Hunger	18	Goldman, Jaffa, and Schachter
Perception and Altered States of Awareness		
Perceptual effects of "split brain"	19	Pines
Extrasensory perception	20	McConnell
Perceptual effects of marihuana	21	Weil, Zinberg, and Nelson
Perception in limited sensory modalities	5	Keller
Personality and Personality Assessment		
Psychoanalytic theory	22	Freud
Humanistic personality theory	23	Maddi and Costa
Learning theory in personality	10	Skinner
Personality development: sex roles	24a	Kagan
	24b	Weisstein
The "normal" personality	27	McNeil

Topic	Selection Number	Author
Personality assessment: the interview	25	Kelly
Personality assessment: self-report inventory	26	Hathaway
Intelligence and race	9	Sarason
Intelligence and social class	3	Meehl
Behavior Disorders and Psychotherapy		
Normality-abnormality	27	McNeil
	28	Grier and Cobbs
	29	Rosenhan
The problem of "labeling"	29	Rosenhan
Cultural relativity in psychopathology	28	Grier and Cobbs
Schizophrenia	30a	Anonymous
	30b	Joyce
Drugs: marihuana	21	Weil, Zinberg, and Nelson
Psychotherapy	31	Rogers
Social Psychology		
Attitudes	32	Silverman and Shaw
Prejudice	32	Silverman and Shaw
	28	Grier and Cobbs
	9	Sarason
Bystander intervention	33	Darley and Latané
Obedience	34	Milgram
Sex roles	24a	Kagan
	24b	Weisstein
Social roles	35	Zimbardo
Prisons	35	Zimbardo

PART I

Psychology:
Its History and
Methods

1.

What Is Psychology?

WILLIAM JAMES

William James's *Principles of Psychology,* published in 1890, is a
landmark in the history of psychology. It played the critical role
in turning American psychology from the structural approach of
Wilhelm Wundt and E. B. Titchener, which explained conscious
processes in terms of the dimensions and attributes of the three
basic elements of the mind—sensations, images and feelings—to the
"functional," evolutionary approach he shared with John Dewey.
This approach was more concerned with adaptive processes and
adjustment to the environment.

In this excerpt from James's briefer version of his *Principles,*
he points to some philosophical problems of inquiry into states of
mind—problems such as the metaphysical nature of "free will"—and
argues that psychology must proceed as an objective, natural
science. He adds, however, that we have far to go before we can
present laws of behavior or systematic deductions in the manner of
some of the other natural sciences.

How does his conceptualization of the field of psychology
compare with the one offered in your textbook?

In the last chapter we handed the question of free-will over to 'metaphysics.' It would indeed have been hasty to settle the question absolutely, inside the limits of psychology. Let psychology frankly admit
that *for her scientific purposes* determinism may be *claimed,* and no
one can find fault. If, then, it turn out later that the claim has only a

From *Psychology: Briefer Course* by William James. Reprinted with permission of
Holt, Rinehart and Winston, Inc.

relative purpose, and may be crossed by counter-claims, the readjustment can be made. Now ethics makes a counter-claim; and the present writer, for one, has no hesitation in regarding her claim as the stronger, and in assuming that our wills are 'free.' For him, then, the deterministic assumption of psychology is merely provisional and methodological. This is no place to argue the ethical point; and I only mention the conflict to show that all these special sciences, marked off for convenience from the remaining body of truth, must hold their assumptions and results subject to revision in the light of each other's needs. The forum where they hold discussion is called metaphysics. Metaphysics means only an unusually obstinate attempt to think clearly and consistently. The special sciences all deal with data that are full of obscurity and contradiction; but from the point of view of their limited purposes these defects may be overlooked. Hence the disparaging use of the name metaphysics which is so common. To a man with a limited purpose any discussion that is over-subtle for that purpose is branded as 'metaphysical.' A geologist's purposes fall short of understanding Time itself. A mechanist need not know how action and reaction are possible at all. A psychologist has enough to do without asking how both he and the mind which he studies are able to take cognizance of the same outer world. But it is obvious that problems irrelevant from one standpoint may be essential from another. And as soon as one's purpose is the attainment of the maximum of possible insight into the world as a whole, the metaphysical puzzles become the most urgent ones of all. . . .

When, then, we talk of 'psychology as a natural science,' we must not assume that that means a sort of psychology that stands at last on solid ground. It means just the reverse; it means a psychology particularly fragile, and into which the waters of metaphysical criticism leak at every joint, a psychology all of whose elementary assumptions and data must be reconsidered in wider connections and translated into other terms. It is, in short, a phrase of diffidence, and not of arrogance; and it is indeed strange to hear people talk triumphantly of 'the New Psychology,' and write 'Histories of Psychology,' when into the real elements and forces which the word covers not the first glimpse of clear insight exists. A string of raw facts; a little gossip and wrangle about opinions; a little classification and generalization on the mere descriptive level; a strong prejudice that we *have* states of mind, and that our brain conditions them: but not a single law in the sense in which physics shows us laws, not a single proposition from which any consequence can causally be deduced. We don't even know the terms between which the elementary laws would obtain if we had them. This is no science, it is only the hope of a science. The matter of a science is with us. Something definite happens when to a certain brain-state a certain 'sciousness' corresponds. A genuine glimpse into what it is would be *the* scientific achievement, before which all past achievements would pale. But at present psychology is in the condition of physics before Galileo and the laws of motion, of chemistry before Lavoisier and the notion that mass is preserved in all reactions. The Galileo and the Lavoisier of psychology will be famous men indeed when they come, as come they some day surely will, or past successes are no index to the future. When they do come, however, the necessities of the case will make them 'metaphysical.' Meanwhile the best way in which we can facilitate their advent is to understand how great is the darkness in which we grope, and never to forget that the natural-science assumptions with which we started are provisional and revisable things.

2.

A Comment on
Psychological Experiments

GEORGE BERNARD SHAW

George Bernard Shaw, the great Irish playwright and essayist, was not at all reluctant to use his sharp pen to puncture the prevailing myths of the society in which he lived. In his plays, he commented, in his own way, on contemporary issues ranging from the role of women to the social class system in England. In this excerpt he describes the experiences of a naïve African girl who has run away from a missionary outpost to search for the God about whom she has been taught. Shaw takes the opportunity to mount a satirical attack on the work of Ivan Pavlov, the great Russian physiologist who is remembered today primarily for his research on the conditioning of the salivary response in dogs. More broadly, Shaw is criticizing the experimental-psychology approach to the development of knowledge about human behavior. Are his criticisms of psychological research well founded? Is it indeed true that the scientific study of behavior yields only findings that should have been obvious all along?

"SAY, BAAS" said the black girl: "are you the prophet that goes stripped and naked, wailing like the dragons and mourning like the owls?"

"I do a little in that line" he said apologetically. "Micah is my name: Micah the Morasthite. Can I do anything for you?"

"I seek God" she answered.

"And have you found Him?" said Micah.

Reprinted from George Bernard Shaw, *The Black Girl in Search of God and Some Lesser Tales*, Penguin Books Ltd., 1946. Reprinted with permission of the Society of Authors, on behalf of the Bernard Shaw Estate.

"I found an old man who wanted me to roast animals for him because he loved the smell of cooking, and to sacrifice my children on his altar."

At this Micah uttered such a lamentable roar that King Richard hastily took cover in the forest and sat watching there with his tail slashing.

"He is an impostor and a horror" roared Micah. "Can you see yourself coming before the high God with burnt calves of a year old? Would He be pleased with thousands of rams or rivers of oil or the sacrifice of your first born, the fruit of your body, instead of the devotion of your soul? God has shewed your soul what is good; and your soul has told you that He speaks the truth. And what does He require of you but to do justice and love mercy and walk humbly with him?"

"This is a third God" she said; "and I like him much better than the one who wanted sacrifices and the one who wanted me to argue with him so that he might sneer at my weakness and ignorance. But doing justice and shewing mercy is only a small part of life when one is not a baas or a judge. And what is the use of walking humbly if you don't know where you are walking to?"

"Walk humbly and God will guide you" said the Prophet. "What is it to you whither He is leading you?"

"He gave me eyes to guide myself" said the black girl. "He gave me a mind and left me to use it. How can I now turn on him and tell him to see for me and to think for me?"

Micah's only reply was such a fearful roar that King Richard fairly bolted and ran for two miles without stopping. And the black girl did the same in the opposite direction. But she ran only a mile.

"What am I running away from?" she said to herself, pulling herself up. "I'm not afraid of that dear noisy old man."

"Your fears and hopes are only fancies" said a voice close to her, proceeding from a very shortsighted elderly man in spectacles who was sitting on a gnarled log. "In running away you were acting on a conditioned reflex. It is quite simple. Having lived among lions you have from your childhood associated the sound of a roar with deadly danger. Hence your precipitate flight when that superstitious old jackass brayed at you. This remarkable discovery cost me twenty-five years of devoted research, during which I cut out the brains of innumerable dogs, and observed their spittle by making holes in their cheeks for them to salivate through instead of through their tongues. The whole scientific world is prostrate at my feet in admiration of this colossal achievement and gratitude for the light it has shed on the great problems of human conduct."

"Why didnt you ask me?" said the black girl. "I could have told you in twentyfive seconds without hurting those poor dogs."

"Your ignorance and presumption are unspeakable" said the old myop. "The fact was known of course to every child; but it had never been proved experimentally in the laboratory; and therefore it was not scientifically known at all. It reached me as an unskilled conjecture: I handed it on as science. Have you ever performed an experiment, may I ask?"

"Several" said the black girl. "I will perform one now. Do you know what you are sitting on?"

"I am sitting on a log grey with age, and covered with an uncomfortable rugged bark" said the myop.

"You are mistaken" said the black girl. "You are sitting on a sleeping crocodile."

With a yell which Micah himself might have envied, the myop rose and fled frantically to a neighboring tree, up which he climbed catlike with an agility which in so elderly a gentleman was quite superhuman.

"Come down" said the black girl. "You ought to know that crocodiles are only to be found near rivers. I was only trying an experiment. Come down."

"How am I to come down?" said the myop, trembling. "I should break my neck."

"How did you get up?" said the black girl.

"I dont know" he replied, almost in tears. "It is enough to make a man believe in miracles. I couldn't have climbed this tree; and yet here I am and shall never be able to get down again."

"A very interesting experiment, wasnt it?" said the black girl.

"A shamefully cruel one, you wicked girl" he moaned. "Pray did it occur to you that you might have killed me? Do you suppose you can give a delicate physiological organism like mine a violent shock without the most serious and quite possibly fatal reactions on the heart? I shall never be able to sit on a log again as long as I live. I believe my pulse is quite abnormal, though I cannot count it; for if I let go of this branch I shall drop like a stone."

"If you can cut half a dog's brain out without causing any reactions on its spittle you need not worry" she said calmly. "I think African magic much more powerful than your divining by dogs. By saying one word to you I made you climb a tree like a cat. You confess it was a miracle."

"I wish you would say another word and get me safely down again, confound you for a black witch" he grumbled.

"I will" said the black girl. "There is a tree snake smelling at the back of your neck."

The myop was on the ground in a jiffy. He landed finally on his back; but he scrambled to his feet at once and said "You did not take me in: dont think it. I knew perfectly well you were inventing that snake to frighten me."

"And yet you were as frightened as if it had been a real snake" said the black girl.

"I was not" said the myop indignantly. "I was not frightened in the least."

"You nipped down the tree as if you were" said the black girl.

"That is what is so interesting" said the myop, recovering his self-possession now that he felt safe. "It was a conditioned reflex. I wonder could I make a dog climb a tree."

"What for?" said the black girl.

"Why, to place this phenomenon on a scientific basis" said he.

"Nonsense!" said the black girl. "A dog cant climb a tree."

"Neither can I without the stimulus of an imaginary crocodile" said the professor. "How am I to make a dog imagine a crocodile?"

"Introduce him to a few real ones to begin with" said the black girl.

"That would cost a good deal" said the myop, wrinkling his brows. "Dogs are cheap if you buy them from professional dog-stealers, or lay in a stock when the dog tax becomes due; but crocodiles would run into a lot of money. I must think this out carefully."

"Before you go" said the black girl "tell me whether you believe in God."

"God is an unnecessary and discarded hypothesis" said the myop. "The universe is only a gigantic system of reflexes produced by shocks. If I give you a clip on the knee you will wag your ankle."

"I will also give you a clip with my knobkerry; so dont do it" said the black girl.

"For scientific purposes it is necessary to inhibit such secondary and apparently irrelevant reflexes by tying the subject down" said the professor. "Yet they also are quite relevant as examples of reflexes produced by association of ideas. I have spent twentyfive years studying their effects."

"Effects on what?" said the black girl.

"On a dog's saliva" said the myop.

"Are you any the wiser?" she said.

"I am not interested in wisdom" he replied: "in fact I do not know what it means and have no reason to believe that it exists. My business is to learn something that was not known before. I impart that knowledge to the world, and thereby add to the body of ascertained scientific truth."

"How much better will the world be when it is all knowledge and no mercy?" said the black girl. "Havnt you brains enough to invent some decent way of finding out what you want to know?"

"Brains!" cried the myop, as if he could hardly believe his ears. "You must be an extraordinarily ignorant young woman. Do you not know that men of science are all brains from head to foot?"

"Tell that to the crocodile" said the black girl. "And tell me this. Have you ever considered the effect of your experiments on other people's minds and characters? Is it worth while losing your own soul and damning everybody else's to find out something about a dog's spittle?"

"You are using words that have no meaning" said the myop. "Can you demonstrate the existence of the organ you call a soul on the operating table or in the dissecting room? Can you reproduce the operation you call damning in the laboratory?"

"I can turn a live body with a soul into a dead one without it with a whack of my knobkerry" said the black girl "and you will soon see the difference and smell it. When people damn their souls by doing something wicked, you soon see the difference too."

"I have seen a man die: I have never seen one damn his soul" said the myop.

"But you have seen him go to the dogs" said the black girl. "You have gone to the dogs yourself, havnt you?"

"A quip; and an extremely personal one" said the myop haughtily. "I leave you."

3.

Law and the Fireside Inductions: Some Reflections of a Clinical Psychologist

PAUL MEEHL

Paul Meehl is one of the outstanding psychologists of the last twenty years, a past president of the American Psychological Association and a winner of its Distinguished Scientific Contribution Award. More recently he has turned his attention to questions of religion, philosophy of science, and law. In the following article, he questions whether the methods used by psychologists (and therefore their answers) are necessarily more valid than those of legal scholars whose methods of inquiry are often based on a more "common sense" approach to the study of man. In this context, do you think your text makes too much of the scientific methodology in psychology? Does research have to be "experimental" in order to be "empirical" and "scientific"?

THE PSYCHOLOGY OF THE FIRESIDE

LAWMEN WILL immediately see the point of my title, but for social science readers I should explain. The phrase "fireside equities" is legalese for what the legal layman feels intuitively or commonsensically would be a fair or just result (see, e.g., Llewellyn, 1960). Sometimes the law accords with the fireside equities, sometimes not; and lawyers use the phrase with derisive connotation. Analogously, by the language "fireside inductions" I mean those commonsense empirical generalizations about human behavior which we accept on the culture's authority plus

Reprinted from *The Journal of Social Issues*, 1971, 27, pp. 65–100. Copyright 1971 by the Society for the Psychological Study of Social Issues and reproduced by permission.

introspection plus anecdotal evidence from ordinary life. Roughly, the phrase "fireside inductions" designates here what everybody (except perhaps the skeptical social scientist) believes about human conduct, about how it is to be described, explained, predicted, and controlled.

One source of conflict between the social scientist and practitioner of law–especially the legislator–is the former's distrust of common knowledge concerning human conduct and the latter's reliance upon this common knowledge. Such reliance is often associated among lawyers with doubts about the value of generalizations arising from systematic behavioral science research involving quantification and experimental manipulation in artificial situations. Reliance upon "what everyone knows" (simply by virtue of being himself a human being) was hardly critically scrutinized prior to the development of the experimental and statistical methods of contemporary social science. This historical fact provides a built-in preference for the commonsense knowledge of human behavior embodied in positive law. But psychologists mistakenly suppose that the lawyers' continued reliance upon the psychology of the fireside is wholly attributable to inertia, and these misunderstandings warrant consideration. Without being honorific or pejorative, I shall use "fireside inductions" to refer broadly to those expectations and principles, largely inchoate although partially embodied in proverbs and maxims (e.g., "The burnt child dreads the fire," "Blood is thicker than water," "Every man has larceny in his heart," "Power always corrupts") arising from some mixture of (a) personal anecdotal observations, (b) armchair speculation, (c) introspection, and (d) education in the received tradition of Western culture prior to the development of technical social science method. It is not clear where nonquantitative, nonexperimental but psychologically sophisticated ideas, such as those of contemporary psychoanalytic theory and therapy, should be classified, but for the moment I will set this aside.

With my fellow psychologists I share a considerable skepticism concerning the fireside inductions. Even universally held generalizations about the origins and control of human conduct should be subjected to (at least) *quantitative documentary* research and, where feasible, to systematic *experimental* testing. Obviously the degree of skepticism toward a dictum of commonsense psychology should increase as we move into those areas of social control where our efforts are hardly crowned with spectacular success. For example, there is no known system for the prevention or cure of crime and delinquency that is so strikingly successful that anyone can suggest we are doing so well at this social task that it is hardly necessary to call our techniques into question, absent specific research that casts doubt upon them (Meehl, 1970c). That the psychological presuppositions underlying the criminal law should be subjected to merciless armchair scrutiny and quantitative research is not said *pro forma,* but expresses a sincere conviction.

UNFAIR CONTROVERSIAL TACTICS SOMETIMES USED BY LAWYERS AND PSYCHOLOGISTS

Nor is this merely a platitude–"we need research"–that everyone accepts. One does come across rational, educated persons who disagree, at least when presented with concrete instances. I know, for instance, a very able law professor (formerly a practicing attorney) whose ignorance of the behavioral sciences was systematic and deliberate and who, although he regarded me highly as an individual intellect, made no secret that he thought most scientific research on law, such as quantitative studies of jury behavior, had little point. Over several months, I realized that he had a foolproof heads-I-win-tails-you-lose technique dealing with intellectual threats from the social sciences, to wit: If I introduced a quantitative-documentary or experimental study of some behavioral generalization having relevance to the law, the findings either accorded with his fireside inductions, or they did not. If they did, he typically responded, "Well, I suppose it's all right to spend the taxpayer's money researching that, although anybody could have told you so beforehand." If the results were *not* in harmony with the fireside mind-model, he refused to believe them! When I called this kind of dirty pool to his attention, he cheerfully admitted this truth about his debating tactics.

Without defending such illegitimate, systematic resistance to the inroads of behavior science data upon legal thinking, I direct my behavior sciences' brethren to some considerations that may render my law colleague's tactics less unreasonable than they seem at first glance. Some behavior scientists, particularly those ideologically tendentious and often completely uninformed with respect to the law, reveal a double standard of methodological morals that is the mirror image of my legal colleague's. They are extremely critical and skeptical about accepting, and applying in practical circumstances, fireside inductions but are willing to rely somewhat uncritically upon equally shaky generalizations purporting to be rigorous deliverances of modern behavior science. A shrewd lawyer, even though he might not know enough philosophy, logic of science, experimental method, or technical statistics to recognize just *what* is wrong with a particular scientific refutation of the fireside inductions, may nevertheless be right in holding to what he learned at his grandmother's knee or through practical experience, rather than abandoning it because, say, "Fisbee's definitive experiment on social conformity" allegedly shows the contrary.

Example: Punishment as a General Deterrent

Consider the threat of punishment as a deterrent, one of the most socially important and widely disputed issues relating behavior science to law. While I have not kept systematic records of my anecdotal material (fireside induction!), the commonest reaction of psychologists upon hearing of my interest in studying law and teaching in the Law School is a surprised "Well, Meehl, I have always thought of you as a hard-headed, dustbowl-empiricist, quantitatively-oriented psychologist —how can you be interested in that medieval subject matter?" When pressed for an explanation of why they consider law medieval, my behavior science colleagues generally mention the outmoded and primitive (sometimes they say "moralistic") reliance of the criminal law upon punishment, which "is out of harmony with the knowledge of modern social (or medical) science." This kind of rapid-fire sinking of the lawyer's ship quite understandably tends to irritate the legal mind. However, the same psychologist who says punishment doesn't deter relies on its deterrent effect in posting a sign in the departmental library stating that if a student removes a journal without permission, his privilege to use the room will be suspended but his use fee not returned. This same psychologist suspends his children's TV privileges when they fight over which channel to watch; tells the truth on his income tax form (despite feeling that the government uses most of the money immorally and illegally) for fear of the legal consequences of lying; and drives his car well within the speed limit on a certain street, having been informed that the police have been conducting speed traps there. It will not do for this psychologist to say that as a citizen, parent, professor, taxpayer, automobile driver, etc., he must make such judgments upon inadequate evidence, but when contemplating the legal order he must rely only on scientific information.

Psychologists and psychiatrists (especially the latter) say strange things when pressed to document their statement, often made with dogmatic assurance and an attitude of scientific superiority to the benighted legal profession, that the criminal law cannot deter. They say, for example, that the only way to control behavior is to get at its source or origin, rather than penalizing it; that capital punishment has been shown not to deter murderers; that experimental research on the behavior of infra-human animals has demonstrated that punishment is an ineffective mode of behavior control. These are the three commonest responses, along with a general overall flavor to think about crime "scientifically" instead of "in moralistic categories (e.g., *justice*)." I set aside this last as outside my province *qua* behavior scientist, although in my experience those who object to the introduction of ethical, theological, or juridical concepts in dealing with the problem of criminal conduct usually include some moral judgment upon present practices or upon society, frequently in a self-righteous manner They seem blissfully unaware of the elementary philosophical point that you either allow ethical categories into your discourse or not, and you cannot forbid them to your opponent and then use them polemically yourself. Karl Menninger's *The Crime of Punishment* (1969) contains a dreadful example, although a powerful and perceptive book in many respects. The book is full of moralizing and judgmental language about society, never the criminal offender. Why do the terms of ethical theory apply to social groups but not to individuals? Why is society blameworthy although (presumably) causally determined, and the individual not? Whether psychological determinism precludes all application of ethical terms is beyond the scope of this article, and Menninger does not appear to appreciate its philosophical difficulty. As a psychologist-citizen, I incline to agree with Spinoza (and our contemporary social critic Albert Ellis) that "blaming" behavior is one of the more useless human responses. Antisocial conduct should be approached as a problem of genetics, economics, and behavior engineering, because that orientation tends to minimize the intrusion of emotions into our problem solving, thereby fostering rationality. "Blame" words are emotion elicitors; their use tends to impair the cognitive functions of blamer, blamee, and interested third parties. Regrettably, practically all the words available to designate infractions of moral or legal rules, or persons disposed thereto, are blame laden; since society cannot articulate its legal processes without using the concept of a rule, of its violation, and of a rule violator. We could profitably dispense with words like heinous, dastardly, brutal, bloodthirsty, or wicked. But few would want a society whose legal system had no use for the words justice, fair, equal treatment, malicious intent, offender, obliged, or responsible. Avoiding affect-arousing "blame" words while retaining an axiological vocabulary adequate for the purposes of law is a terribly difficult task. But we can strive for consistency, and it is both inconsistent and unfair to forbid application of ethical descriptors to a burglar while freely applying condemnatory labels to society (= the rest of us) for our less-than-optimal treatment of his problem. Nor is such selective moralizing likely to induce the objective attitude that Menninger believes—I think rightly —would facilitate rationality and flexibility in our approach to crime control. If a psychiatrist tells a frightened shopkeeper, whose friend has recently been murdered by an armed bandit, that he, the shopkeeper, is wicked because he wrongly thinks of the bandit as wicked, his most probable reaction is to conclude that psychiatrists must be wicked, rather than to examine critically whether wickedness is a useful conceptual tool in thinking about law as a mode of social control. In addition to the mentioned inconsistency, Menninger advances the strange argument that lawyers should not invoke the concept "justice" in dealing with crime, because this concept is not used in surgery or bacteriology (1969, p. 17). Presumably this reasoning would preclude using concepts like unconscious wish or reaction formation, inasmuch as these notions are superfluous in metallurgy. When such fuzzy-headedness is retailed by a distinguished psychiatrist, can we wonder that lawyers, whose stock in trade is largely clarification of verbal inference, often view "mind experts" with contempt?

A well-known sociologist actually objected to the criminal law's reliance on (threatened) punishment as a deterrent on the ground that it does not work, since we find persons in jail who knew they would go there if convicted of crime! One can hardly understand the commitment of this low-level methodological mistake (pointed out repeatedly by criminologists and jurists, e.g., Andenaes, 1952, 1966) by a social scientist other than from ideological motives. That some persons commit crimes despite the criminal law, and that incarcerated burglars report verbally that they knew burglary was illegal, is as helpful in evaluating the deterrent effect of the criminal sanction as it would be to study the prophylactic effect of a drug by conversing with a sample of patients who had fallen ill despite its administration! When a law professor hears a psychologist, sociologist, or psychiatrist argue this way, it is hardly surprising that his regard for the logical incisiveness of social science thinking is not increased. The amazing thing is that there are actually scholarly monographs written, lectures delivered, and press releases made by university professors in the social or medical sciences which rely upon an argument whose structure is identical with the following: Medicine has always tried to prevent disease and death; but since people still get sick, and everybody finally dies, we can safely conclude that the medical sciences are a waste of time. Would anybody be impressed with this argument unless he had some sort of ideological axe to grind?

A more subtle mistake is inferring nondeterrency from the inefficacy of the threat of capital punishment (when compared with the threat of noncapital punishment) for murder. This is an instructive example of a little learning being a dangerous thing. One may know barely enough methodology to recognize the desirability of statistical study and experimental control, the necessity to make statistical significance tests between homicide rates in two jurisdictions, or in one jurisdiction before and after a change in the penalty for murder; but this minimal amount of social science sophistication is not always sufficient to recognize the limitations of such findings for generalizing about the effectiveness of the criminal sanction as a general deterrent. It is somewhat embarrassing to find that trained social scientists can make this higher-level mistake, so that a law professor (Andenaes, 1952, 1966) has to make—in ordinary language and without reliance upon technical psychometric concepts—a few elementary points which anyone familiar with learning theory, behavior genetics, and psychometric theory ought to arrive at with a little thought.

LEVELS OF SOPHISTICATION IN SOCIAL SCIENCE METHOD

This levels-of-sophistication question is of great importance in interdisciplinary work and in legal education. Any lawyer knows that having the more meritorious case does not guarantee winning it, a main interfering factor being skill of counsel. Differing levels of sophistication in any technical domain, even possession of a special vocabulary, often lead to misleading impressions as to who has the better of a theoretical or practical dispute. The parish priest can refute the theological objections of an unlettered Hausfrau parishioner. The priest, in turn, will lose a debate with the intellectual village atheist. C. S. Lewis will come out ahead of the village atheist. But when C. S. Lewis tangles with Bertrand Russell, it gets pretty difficult to award the prizes. This dialectical-upmanship phenomenon has been responsible for some of the friction between lawyers and social scientists, especially when the social scientist tendentiously presents what purport to be the findings of modern social science but is expressing the particular psychologist's, psychiatrist's, or sociologist's ethos or theoretical (ideological) prejudices. Undergraduate sophistication sufficiently questions the efficacy of criminal law sanctions as a deterrent (although some college-educated legislators appear to be naive about this!), and recognizes the desirability of adequate statistics on comparable jurisdictions or within the same jurisdiction before and after a change in severity (or certainty) of penalty. However, to understand threshold effects, asymptotes, second-order interactions, nonlinear dependencies, rate changes at different points on a growth function—considerations hardly profound or esoteric—already takes us beyond the level of sophistication of many social and medical writers who have addressed themselves to legal problems.

Example: Ineffectiveness of Capital Punishment

Consider the rapid-fire dismissal of the general idea that increasing a penalty will be effective on the ground that capital punishment is not effective (i.e., more effective than life imprisonment) as a general deterrent to murder. To draw such a general conclusion from this instance is illegitimate, but the levels-of-expertise problem requires a certain amount of social science know-how even to talk about difficulties in choosing a murder-rate index and calculating a significance test. (It takes more technical know-how to handle the data when time changes in the same jurisdiction are relied on. See, e.g., Campbell, 1969; Campbell & Ross, 1968; Glass, 1968; Ross, Campbell, & Glass, 1969.) Just a bit more sophistication takes into account problems of extreme values, curvilinearity, and the like involved in such a far-out deviation from social norms as murder. You do not need a PhD in Axiology or Social Psychology to know that murder is a crime *malum in se* rather than *malum prohibitum;* that (allowing for varying definitions) it is forbidden in all known societies, literate and preliterate; that it is regularly attended by strong moral disapprobation and severe legal penalties; that it is explicitly forbidden by all known recorded moral codes; that it is a crime of high deviation threshold, having a very low incidence compared with crimes against property, sexual offenses, and so forth. Given these facts, it may be safely assumed that we deal largely with individuals who are aberrated socially or psychiatrically (I do not mean insane or even formally diagnosable, see Livermore & Meehl, 1967; Livermore, Malmquist, & Meehl, 1968) or who were responding to extreme and unusual stresses in low-probability contexts. Futhermore, the alternative to capital punishment is life imprisonment, a sufficiently extreme penalty that, assuming a Benthamite rational calculation model, a person would not take a chance on this consequence appreciably more than on the death penalty if the probabilities of detection and conviction were other than small. We are comparing the deterrent effects of two penalties both of which are sufficiently far out on the hedonic continuum that their difference is probably not very great at the Benthamite calculational stage, *even when* such calculation occurs—presumably rarely in this crime. Evidently we cannot extrapolate, with any confidence at all, from "Capital punishment does not reduce murder rates" to "The notion of general deterrence in criminal law is empirically unsound."

Now the special-case question: Is capital punishment an efficacious general deterrent when operating (a) with less extreme personality deviates, and in a social context which (b) makes apprehension quasi-certain and (c) the penalty well publicized? That is, we inquire whether the threat of death as a sanction can be effective under conditions that come closer to the idealized Benthamite-calculus-user situation than is probably the case for most murderers or rapists. It is not easy to find examples, but the military setting is a pretty good one, and we have a fairly clear case in connection with the mass insubordination, defection, and mutiny of the French army during World War I. In 1917, following the collapse of the Nivelle offensive, morale in the French army was desperately low. The constant danger of death or horrible wounds, the obvious pointlessness of the attacks, and the overall conditions of daily existence must have provided a set of psychological instigations whose pervasiveness, intensity, and duration were beyond anything found in civilian life. In some units, refusals to obey orders had the full character of a mass mutiny and over half of the French army's divisions experienced such mutinies. In the Ninth Division, all three regiments formed a protest march in which they sang the *Internationale* and shouted, "We won't go up the line!"

> Not even units with the finest war records were immune from the profound discontent. . . . In one such army corps there was a large number of mutineers, who shut themselves in their huts or threatened to open fire on anyone who came near them. . . . Half of Petain's army therefore was mutinous [Barnett, 1965, p. 220].

Petain, who had replaced Nivelle, understood the instigations to mutiny and took appropriate steps to see that some (e.g., insufficient rest between attacks) did not occur. But he also recognized that the current emergency situation, in which half the army was mutinous, required drastic summary treatment. "I set about suppressing serious cases of indiscipline with utmost urgency [Barnett, 1965, p. 237]." Verdicts of guilty were passed on over 23,000 men, i.e., 1 in every 100 men in the field army on the Western front. Only 432 were sentenced to death and only 55 of these were actually shot, the remainder being sent to penal settlements in the colony. But of course every soldier and officer knew that the new commander was determined to punish mutineers, and the tiny number of executions were carefully dispersed and widely publicized. The general deterrence notion in criminal law presupposes knowledge (or, more precisely, belief) as to sanctions, and in civilian life such expectations doubtless vary a good deal. Petain saw the importance of making examples, writing:

> It is essential that the High Command impresses on all ranks that it is resolved on the strictest discipline and obedience, from top to bottom of the military structure. It must ruthlessly make examples where necessary and bring them to the knowledge of the army [Barnett, 1965, p. 226].

As the fireside inductions would predict, the mutinies ceased entirely and immediately. Presumably the efficacy of Petain's approach lay in some near-optimal combination of (a) reduced instigations to mutiny, or the hope thereof, under new command, (b) severity of the penalty, and (c) near certainty of detection. As for (c), in 1764 the great Italian criminologist Beccaria (1963) noted that the certainty of punishment is more important than its severity. Severity and certainty combined would predict a high efficacy of general deterrence. Persuasive anecdotal support comes from the area of narcotics law enforcement. Law-enforcement officers cannot get into the higher echelons of the drug traffic because the small-fry peddlers toward the terminal end of the chain cannot be effectively pressured by a prosecutor, under the usual threats and promises, to tell anything about the next level of the higher-ups. Peddlers have a solid conviction, amounting to a subjective certainty, that if they are known or strongly suspected to have turned stool pigeon, they will be killed by the organized international narcotics underworld (Lindesmith, 1965, p. 39). An Illinois state's attorney describes a defendant (from whom he was trying to get information about the pushers, sellers, and the higher-ups) as saying, "Well, what can you do? You can give me a couple of years. I have been there before. You can give me time. If I tell you and it gets out, I would be dead before the week is over." Here we have an example of what the underworld sees as a very serious offense, being a stool pigeon, punished with great severity (death) and with near certainty. Why as a psychologist should I dismiss this kind of evidence as worthless because it is not "scientific" but merely anecdotal? . . .

THE CONCEPTS EMPIRICAL, EXPERIMENTAL, QUANTITATIVE

Rational discussion of the law's reliance on the fireside inductions may be rendered needlessly difficult by an unfortunate semantic habit as to the honorific word "empirical." Since I have myself been fighting a running battle with my psychological associates for some years against this bad semantic habit, I would dislike to see it accepted by legal scholars. The following methodological equation, often implicit and unquestioned, is being taken over by lawyers from behavior science:

Empirical = Experimental-and-Quantitative = Scientific

This equivalence is objectionable on several grounds. It is epistemologically inaccurate since there is a great deal of the empirical (i.e., arising in or supported by observations or experiences, including introspective experiences) that is neither experimental nor quantitative. Furthermore, the middle term assumes a false linkage because (a) not all experimental research is quantitative and (b) not all quantitative research is experimental. Third, several disciplines (to which hardly anybody would refuse the term scientific) exhibit varying amounts of experimental manipulation conjoined with varying amounts of the qualitative/quantitative dimension, e.g., astronomy, ecology, comparative anatomy, botany, human genetics, paleontology, economics, meteorology, geography, historical geology, epidemiology, clinical medicine.

What is an experiment? I am not prepared to give an exactly demarcated definition of the term. Roughly, an experiment is a systematic, preplanned sequence of operations-cum-observations, the system of entities under study being relatively isolated from the influence of certain classes of causal factors; other causal factors being held quasi-constant by the experimenter; and still others manipulated by him, their values either being set for different individuals in the system or changed over time at the experimenter's will; and output is recorded at the time. Some (under Sir R. A. Fisher's influence) would add, but I would not, that remaining causally efficacious factors (known, guessed, or completely unidentified but assumed to exist) must be rendered noncorrelates of the manipulated variables by a randomizing procedure permitting their net influence to be estimated (statistical significance test).

This definition says nothing about apparatus, instruments, measurement, or even being in the laboratory. I disapprove of stretching the word "experiment" to include clinical or sociological research based upon ex post facto assessment processes, entering files of old data, naturalistic observations in the field or in public places, and so forth. But Campbell's "quasi-experiment" is useful to denote a subset of these possessing certain methodological features that render them relatively more interpretable (see Campbell, 1969). The word "experiment" has become invidious because biological and social scientists tend to denigrate nonexperimental sources of knowledge (such as clinical experience, analysis of documents, file data, or the fireside inductions). Then, by equating "experimental" with "empirical" with "scientific," they often imply that any knowledge source other than experimental is methodologically worthless (armchair speculation, appeal to authority, metaphysics, folklore, and the like). But the fireside inductions *are empirical*. No logician would hesitate to say this. Their subject matter is the domain of empirical phenomena, and one who invokes a fireside induction will, when pressed to defend it, appeal to some kind of experience which he expects the critic will share with him, whether personally or vicariously.

Even the traditional law review article which traces, say, the development of a juridical concept like "state action" or "substantive due process" through a historical sequence of appellate court opinions is empirical, since its subject matter is the verbal behavior, recorded in documents, of a class of organisms, and the researcher studies the changes in this verbal behavior over time. The presence of analytical discourse in such a traditional law review paper does not render it nonempirical, but to argue this is beyond the scope of the present paper (see Feigl & Meehl, in press; Meehl, 1970b; Skinner, 1969, Ch. 6).

There are important differences between the traditional law review article and the kind of article we expect to find in *Law and Society Review*. But we have some perfectly good words, more precise and less invidious, to characterize the difference. For a study of files or documents utilizing the statistical techniques of behavior science we can say simply "statistical," a straightforward word that means pretty much the same thing to most people and which is not loaded emotionally. If structural statistics (such as factor analysis or multidimensional scaling, see Meehl, 1954, pp. 11–14) are employed, we have the word "psychometric." Distinguishing the quantitative or statistical from the experimental dimension is particularly important in discussing methodology of research on law because—as in clinical psychology and personology—one research method in these fields is the application of statistical and psychometric techniques of analysis to documents (e.g., diaries, interview transcripts, jury protocols, Supreme Court opinions). It would be misleading to say that one "performs an experiment" if he plots a curve showing the incidence of concurring opinions over time in the behavior output of an appellate court, but it is equally misleading to say that a traditional law review article which draws no graphs and fits no mathematical functions but traces through a set of opinions over time with reference to the incidence of split votes and dissents, presented in ordinary text, is not empirical. Research does not cease to be empirical, or even behavioral, when it analyzes behavior products instead of the ongoing behavior flux itself.

Since the control of variables influencing a dependent variable is a matter of degree, situations arise in which one is in doubt as to whether the word "experiment" is applicable. But this is merely the familiar problem of drawing an arbitrary cut whose location matters little. For research designs methodologically more powerful than studying a slice of cross-sectional file data because we have changes over time in relation to a societal manipulation (e.g., amendment of a penal statute), we have the expression "quasi-experiment" (Campbell, 1969).

MENTAL TESTS AND SOCIAL CLASS: THE LEVELS-OF-SOPHISTICATION POINT EXEMPLIFIED

The sophistication-level effect is beautifully illustrated by the vexatious problem of interpreting socioeconomic differences on mental tests. I suppose the minimum sophistication level necessary in order even to put the interesting questions is that of understanding why and how intelligence tests were built and validated, including basic concepts of correlation, content-domain sampling, reliability, validity, developmental growth curves, etc., that one learns about in an elementary psychology class. Exposure to basic psychometric theory and multiple strands of validation data (Campbell & Fiske, 1959; Cronbach & Meehl, 1955; Jackson, 1969; Loevinger, 1957) should eliminate some common anti-test prejudices and excessive reliance upon anecdotal refutations. (*Example:* "I knew a kid with an IQ of 196 who became a bum.") I find it odd, by the way, that some lawyers will pronounce confidently to me about what intelligence tests do and do not measure, when the pronouncer could not so much as define I.Q., factor loading, or reliability coefficient. I cannot conceive myself asserting to a lawyer that "the Hearsay Rule is silly" without having at least taken a course or read a treatise on the law of evidence, where the rationale of the Rule and its exceptions was discussed. But I am uncomfortably aware that some psychologists permit themselves strong—usually negative—views about the law without knowing anything about it.

This bottom level of psychometric sophistication would suffice for an employer to consider using psychological tests in screening job applicants. At a higher level, one thinks about the social class bias in tests. If he stops there, relying upon the class-score correlations as definitive proof of test bias, he will perhaps avoid using tests, either because he may "miss" some good candidates (a poor reason, statistically) or from considerations of fairness, justice, equal opportunity (a good reason, provided his psychometric premise concerning bias is substantially correct). Moving one step higher in sophistication, we realize that the SES-IQ correlation is causally ambiguous, and that the limitations of statistical method for resolving this causal ambiguity are such that no analysis of file data can tell us what causes what. No one knows and, worse, no one knows how to find out to what extent the SES-IQ correlation is attributable to environmental impact and to what extent it is attributable to genetic influence. This causal ambiguity, while rather obvious (and clearly pointed out over 40 years ago in Burks & Kelley, 1928), is, as I read the record, somewhat above the sophistication level of many sociologists and psychologists, who talk, write, and design experiments on the (implicit) assumption that social class is entirely on the causal input side of the equation.

The terrible complexity of this problem cannot be discussed here, but I have treated it elsewhere (Meehl 1969, 1970a, 1971). I can briefly concretize it by reference to the Coleman Report (Coleman, Campbell, & Hobson, 1966) on equality of educational opportunity. In the course of an interdisciplinary discussion at the University of Minnesota branch of the Law and Society Association one law professor argued: Since the Coleman Report showed that the psychological characteristics of a student's peer group were more closely correlated with his measured ability and achievement than either the school's physical plant or the characteristics of the teaching staff, these "empirical data of behavior science" would indicate that the way to achieve equal educational opportunity should be mandatory busing to provide disadvantaged pupils with the presumably better stimulation from abler peers. Whatever the legal merits of mandatory busing in relation to de facto segregation, the methodological point is important and requires a level of psychometric sophistication a notch above my law colleague's. It is possible that the higher statistical correlation between peer-group attributes and student's academic level is attributable mainly to geographic selective factors mediated by the family's social class, rather than causal influence of peer-group stimulation. Parental intelligence, personality, and temperament factors are transmitted to the child in part genetically (no informed and unbiased person today could dispute this, but many social scientists are both uninformed and prejudiced against behavior genetics) and partly through social learning. If physical-plant characteristics and teacher characteristics are correlated with the biological and social inputs of the child's family only via the (indirect) economic-neighborhood-location and political (tax-use) factors, they will have a lower statistical relationship with the child's cognitive level than is shown by indicators of the cognitive level of other children attending the same neighborhood school. Roughly, peer-group attributes happen to be a better (indirect) measure of average family and neighborhood causal factors— genetic and environmental—than teacher or physical plant attributes. The differential correlation would reflect more a psychometric fact (about the factor loadings and reliabilities of certain measures) than a causal fact (about peer-group influence).

Whether one analyzes these data by inspecting a correlation table or by more complex statistical devices such as regression equations or analysis of covariance, neither the crude zero-order relationships, beta-weights, nor sums of squares tell us much about the direction of causal influence. We cannot infer whether social stimulation from other students is causally more efficacious than having better qualified teachers or a newer, better lighted, cleaner school building. The correlations with peer-group attributes cannot even tell us whether the impact upon a lower-IQ child of being in a classroom with more bright, dominant, articulate, and intellectually self-confident children does more harm than good.

In the opinion of Judge Skelley Wright in Hobson v. Hansen (1967) one cannot find a single sentence indicating recognition of this methodological problem. I do not suggest that awareness of it would have led to a different result. But a single sentence obiter would surely occur somewhere in his careful, scholarly opinion of 109 pages had the judge thought of it or counsel argued it in connection with the Coleman Report's significance. One may feel, as I do, that the problems of racial discrimination and educational disadvantagement are so grave that the society should lean over backwards—within limits set by principles of distributive justice to individuals—to change things, since we are confronted with a frightful combination of gross inequities and a major social emergency. Under such pressing circumstances the adoption and implementation of policy cannot await definitive solution of difficult scientific questions, especially when the kind of controlled experiment or even semi-controlled quasi-experiment (Campbell, 1969) capable of yielding clear answers cannot be performed and statistical techniques presently available are not adequate for the purpose of unscrambling causal influence. The Coleman Report shows that minority-group children receive substandard educational treatment, and I for one am willing to call that discriminatory, ipso facto. What concerns me here is the legal generalizability of a causal inference methodology. The kind of reliance upon social science data found in Hobson v. Hansen, lacking adequate clarification of the concept "unfair discrimination" in relation to correlational findings, might produce some untoward results in other contexts where the interpretative principles would be difficult to distinguish. And if judges should become cynical about the trustworthiness of what psychologists and sociologists assert, we might be faced with a judicial backlash against the social sciences. One can hardly blame Judge Wright for making a flat statement that intelligence tests do *not* measure innate intelligence, or for repeating the old chestnut that intelligence is "whatever the test measures [Hobson v. Hansen, 1967, p. 478]." The Coleman Report states flatly, with no hint that disagreement exists among psychologists on the highly technical and obscure issues involved, "recent research does not support [the] view" that intelligence tests measure more fundamental and stable mental abilities than achievement tests (Coleman et al., 1966, p. 292). "Ability tests are simply [*sic*] broader and more general measures of education" follows at the same locus, again without the faintest whiff of doubt or qualification to warn the legal reader that this is a complex and controversial issue. We read further, "The findings of this survey provide additional evidence that the 'ability' tests are at least as much affected by school differences as are the 'achievement' tests," the causal language "affected by" being again unqualified, with no mention made that some psychologists would interpret the parallelism of ability-score differences and achievement-score differences as suggesting that the achievement differences are not primarily due to school differences but to intelligence differences (an interpretation that would fit well with the report's other findings). It is well recognized among psychologists concerned with the ex post facto design's deficiencies that the report is dangerous reading for the nontechnically trained, because of its pervasive use of causal-sounding terms: influence, affect, depend upon, account for, independent effect (*sic*). This causal atmosphere cannot be counteracted by the brief methodological sections, which contain the usual caveats. One wonders whether the report's authors were really clear about what regression analysis can and cannot do (Guttman, 1941, pp. 286–292). I am not arguing the merits, except to show that an unresolved scientific controversy exists which we psychologists have no right to sweep under the rug when we talk or write for lawyers and judges. If we present a distorted picture even in a good cause, implying that certain technical matters are settled when in fact they are obscure and controversial, the powerful forces of the lawyers' adversary system will, sooner or later, ferret out the secret. Could we then complain if the findings of social science were treated with less respect than those of chemistry, geology, or medicine by less tractable, more wised-up judges?

Consider a nonracial example that I predict will arise in the near future. There is some correlation between the vocational interests of fathers and sons (Forster, 1931; Strong, 1943, 1957) and part of this correlation has a genetic basis (Carter, 1932; Vandenberg & Kelly, 1964; Vandenberg & Stafford, 1967). Nichols (1966, Table 2) also presents persuasive data which he under-interprets through neglect of the statistical power function (Cohen, 1962). This neglect, combined with his disappointment in the heritability coefficient as a precise, stable, clearly interpretable measure (see Elston & Gottesman, 1968; Fuller & Thompson, 1960, pp. 62–68; Hirsch, 1967, p. 423; Roberts, 1967, pp. 233–242) and his following the traditional practice of simply sorting results into "significant" and "nonsignificant," leads him to be baffled by sex patterns that should not baffle him and that are probably theoretically uninterpretable because they have no systematic meaning (except to a statistician interested in power functions). The "biggest" fact in Nichols's Table 2 is that 23 out of 24 (MZ–DZ) correlation differences are in the expected direction and respectable in size. Even with his large samples, an (MZ–DZ) difference less than around .14 Pearson r units will have less than 50% power $(1 - \beta)$. We ought not be surprised by sex differences in the pattern of significant variables under such circumstances. A sophisticated consideration of the question would involve a currently unstable area of social science method, where matters are murky and the social science establishment is maintaining a conspiracy of silence (see Bakan, 1966; Hogben, 1958; Lykken, 1968; Meehl, 1967; Rozeboom, 1960; and references cited therein). Whatever the merits, the point is that there exists a technical controversy which an appellate court justice with an MA in psychology would have difficulty following, let alone adjudicating. If the judge relies on expert testimony as to current accepted practice, he stands a good chance of being taken in by sincere diploma'd experts who will themselves be unaware how big a methodological storm is brewing. The discrepancy between Nichols's findings and the other twin studies provides a beautiful illustration of the levels-of-sophistication problem. Most law professors are just now learning about the significance test.

It will be 20 years or more before they learn what is wrong with it (Badia, Haber, & Runyon, 1970; Morrison & Henkel, 1970).

There is a sizable correlation between fathers' and sons' intelligence, the larger part of which is probably of biological origin (Burt, 1958, 1966, 1967; Erlenmeyer-Kimling & Jarvik, 1963—a short paper which alone almost suffices to prove the point; Fuller & Thompson, 1960, Ch. 7; Gottesman, 1963, 1968; Honzik, 1957; Jenkins & Paterson, 1961; Manosevitz, Lindzey, & Thiessen, 1969, Sections 5–6; Robinson, 1970; Shields, 1962; Thompson, 1967; Vandenberg, 1968; Waller, 1971; Whipple, 1940—thirty years old but still very much worth reading on this issue). Given these interest and ability correlations and other factors, the sons of physicians are more frequently admitted to medical schools than the sons of nonphysicians, and much more frequently than the sons of, say, unskilled laborers. Medical school selection committees allegedly have shown a preference for physicians' sons. To avoid this bias, some schools exclude father's occupation from the application blank, but a statistical association persists.

Suppose a WASP premedical student of proletarian origins brings an action against a state-supported medical school alleging occupational discrimination, offering in evidence the somewhat higher incidence of admission among physicians' sons. The school defends by showing that father's occupation does not appear on the application blank, and argues that selection is based upon a combination of premedical grades, scores on the Strong Vocational Interest Blank, and the Medical Aptitude Test. The student replies that the SVIB and Medical Aptitude Test are biased in favor of physicians' sons and, further, that both are generically biased against proletarians. If psychometric bias is defined ipso facto by tests yielding differences between groups identified socio-demographically (e.g., by parental occupation, father's income, neighborhood, race, religion) all such tests are biased. Pushed to the limit, the position is that, whatever may be the social or biological origins of individual differences in intellectual capacity, vocational interest, study habits, temperament, etc., any selection variable reflecting these differences and shown to be a correlate of parental occupation is discriminatory (in the sense of unfair).

Nor could this consequence be avoided by eliminating all use of psychological tests and relying solely upon undergraduate grades, inasmuch as the latter also correlate with father's occupation, education, and income. Point: The problem of interpreting correlations and the influence of "nuisance variables" is not a hairsplitting academic exercise, it is a major methodological stomach ache, arising in many legal contexts where social science findings are relevant to fair treatment or equal protection.

AWAY FROM THE FIRESIDE AND BACK AGAIN

The levels-of-sophistication problem has a time component reflecting the stage of scientific knowledge. We psychologists should be cautious when an alleged principle of modern behavioral science appears to conflict with the fireside inductions. There are some embarrassing instances of overconfident generalization and unjustified extrapolation which were subsequently corrected by movement back toward the fireside inductions. It would be worth knowing how often such back-to-the-fireside reversals have taken place, and whether there are features of subject matter or methodology that render the counter-fireside pronouncements of social science prone to reversal or modification. Sometimes psychologists seem to prefer negating the fireside inductions, especially those embedded in the received scholarly tradition (e.g., Aristotle should be beaten up wherever possible). For example, the experimental psychologists' revival of the constructs "curiosity" and "exploratory drive" seems strange to a nonpsychologist who has observed children or pets—or who remembers the opening sentence of Aristotle's *Metaphysics*, "All men by nature desire to know."

Consider three examples relevant to law as a means of social control. Traditional reliance upon punishment (aversive control) in socialization, both in suppressing antisocial conduct and in education, is horrifying to the contemporary mind. One reads about the execution of a fourteen-year-old for larceny in the 1700s, or Luther's description of his schooling, in which corporal punishment was not even confined to infractions of discipline, but was the standard procedure of instruction. If a child didn't give the right answer, he would be rapped on the knuckles with a rod. Research on white rats and, to a lesser extent, on human subjects led to the generalization that, by and large, punishment is a mode of behavior control inferior to reward (positive reinforcement). Thirty years ago, I was taught that the useful role of punishment was to suppress undesirable responses sufficiently (in the short run) so that alternative competing behaviors could occur, and the latter could then be positively reinforced. This is still a fair statement of the practical situation.

Following the publication of Skinner's epoch-making *The Behavior of Organisms* (1938), his student Estes's doctoral dissertation (1944), and especially Skinner's *Science and Human Behavior* (1953) and his Utopian novel *Walden Two* (1948), aversive control fell into extreme disfavor. These writings combined with the gruesome stories told to us clinical psychologists by adult neurotics about their aversively-controlled childhoods to produce a rejection of both the general deterrent and rehabilitative functions of the criminal law. But this could be an illicit extrapolation, conflating the rehabilitative and general deterrent functions of the criminal law under the generic rubric "punishment." Supporters of general deterrence need not assume the same psychological process operates on deterrable persons as that involved when punishment is unsuccessful in reforming convicts. Only punishment as a reformer even approximates the laboratory model of an aversive consequence following emission of the undesired response. Furthermore, the criminal sanction is rather more like withholding positive reinforcement (given elimination of flogging and similar practices from the penal system), both fines and imprisonment being deprivations. The distinction is becoming fuzzed up by experimental work with animals because manipulations such as "time out" (during which the instrumental act cannot be performed because the manipulandum is unavailable, or a stimulus signals that reinforcement will now be withheld) have aversive (punishing) properties. Having neither expertise nor space for the details, I refer the reader to Honig (1966), especially the chapter by Azrin and Holtz, which should be read asking, "To what extent do the current experimental findings refute, confirm, or modify the fireside inductions concerning punishment?" How would the psychologist classify a statutory provision that threatens to deprive the citizen of, say, money that the citizen had never learned to expect, e.g., the Agricultural Adjustment Act (see U.S. v. Butler, 1936, p. 81), where Mr. Justice Stone's dissent hinges partly on the semantics of coercion, which he argues must involve "threat of loss, not hope of gain." Can the experimental psychologist speak to this issue? I doubt it.

A second example concerns imitation. The folklore is that both humans and infrahumans learn by imitation. (The criminal law, as lawyers and psychologists agree, is invoked to handle trouble cases, where the normal processes of socialization have not been applied or have failed to work. I trust my selecting the notion of general deterrence as a fireside induction will not be misconstrued as a belief in its major socializing role, which I daresay no psychologist would care to defend.) Our policy concerning TV and movie presentation of social models of aggression or forbidden sexual behavior is influenced by our beliefs about imitation. Despite the related Freudian emphasis upon identification as a mechanism of character formation, when I was a student the tendency in academic psychology was to minimize the concept of imitation to the point of skepticism as to whether there was any such process at all. I was taught that the classic experiments of E. L. Thorndike on the cat (*circa* 1900) had demonstrated that, for infrahuman organisms at least, there was no learning by imitation. This alleged laboratory refutation was presented as an example of how scientific research had overthrown part of the folklore. The failure of

Thorndike's cats to learn one particular problem-box task, under his special conditions of drive and so forth, was overgeneralized to the broad statement, "Infrahuman animals cannot learn by imitation." The received doctrine of scientific psychology became so well entrenched that a well-designed experiment by Herbert and Harsh (1944) was largely ignored by the profession (see Barber, 1961). But beginning slightly earlier with Miller and Dollard's *Social Learning and Imitation* (1941), a book that cautiously reintroduced the concept and made important conceptual distinctions as to kinds of imitation, the subject came to be restudied, especially by developmental psychologists in relation to aggressive behavior (see, e.g., Bandura & Walters, 1963; Megargee & Hokanson, 1970). A recent article by John, Chesler, Bartlett, and Victor (1969) makes it probable that Thorndike's negative dictum at the turn of the century was just plain wrong, even for *Felis catus*. *Point:* A lawyer in 1930 might have lost a cocktail party debate with an animal psychologist, but the lawyer would have been closer to the truth.

A third area important in such legal contexts as presentence investigation is that of forecasting behavior probabilistically. The fireside inductions say that you should rely heavily upon the record of an individual's past conduct. As I have argued elsewhere (Meehl, 1970c), it may be that a naive judge will (over the long run) make better decisions than one who knows just enough psychology or psychiatry to rely on medical or social science experts' making an intensive study of the offender. The efficiency of actuarial prediction is almost always at least equal to, and usually better than, prediction based upon (purported) clinical understanding of the individual subject's personality (see references in Footnote 4 in Livermore, Malmquist, & Meehl, 1968; and Footnote 8 in Meehl, 1970c). Second, behavior science research itself shows that, by and large, the best way to predict anybody's behavior is his behavior in the past (known among my colleagues as Meehl's Malignant Maxim). Hence the naive judge's reliance on the fireside inductions may yield better results than the intermediate-level sophistication which knows enough to ask a psychologist's or psychiatrist's opinion, but does not know enough to take what he says *cum grano salis*, especially when clinical opinion conflicts with extrapolation from the offender's record.

The subtle interaction between levels of sophistication and the developing state of scientific knowledge is nicely illustrated by the Supreme Court's attitude toward statutes postulating inherited tendencies to mental deficiency and criminalism. In Buck v. Bell (1927) the Court upheld the constitutionality of an involuntary sterilization statute for mental defectives, in an opinion famous for Mr. Justice Holmes's "Three generations of imbeciles is enough." The opinion naturally does not display sophistication about the varieties of mental deficiency, such as the distinction between high-grade familial deficiency (usually nonpathological, being merely the low end of the normal polygenic distribution) and the Mendelizing or developmental anomaly varieties, characteristically yielding a lower IQ, relatively independent of social class, and presenting differing eugenic aspects since some of them have no discernible hereditary loading and others a clearcut one. Without entering into such technical issues in genetics, the court came to what I would regard as the right result (see Reed & Reed, 1965). In Skinner v. Oklahoma (1942) involuntary sterilization of a habitual criminal was disallowed, again a right result in my view. The fireside inductions that underlay Oklahoma's statute are perhaps as strong and widespread for criminal or "immoral" tendencies as for mental deficiency. But the scientific data on inherited dispositions are much stronger in the one case than in the other, and *that* much social science knowledge the Court did possess. Suppose that a more refined taxonomy of delinquents and criminals should enable us to discover that some persons disposed to antisocial behavior get that way in part on a genetic basis (see Footnote 10 in Meehl, 1970c), although in most delinquents the etiology is social. A modified form of the fireside inductions underlying Oklahoma's unconstitutional statute would then be defensible, and a properly redrafted statute combining habitual criminality as a legal category with psychogenetic categories or dimensions could be upheld on the same grounds as Virginia's sterilization statute. But the Court's new task would demand far more technical sophistication, especially given the ideological components that would saturate social scientists' opinions in the briefs, than was required for handling Buck v. Bell and Skinner v. Oklahoma.

DIRECT APPLICATION OF EXPERIMENTAL RESULTS TO LEGAL PROBLEMS: SOME RATIONAL GROUNDS FOR CAUTION

As a clinical practitioner who was trained at a hard-nosed, quantitatively-oriented, behavioristic psychology department (Minnesota has been called the "hotbed of dustbowl empiricism" by some of its critics), I sense a deep analogy between the problem faced by judge or legislator in balancing the fireside inductions against purportedly scientific psychological or sociological findings, and the perennial problem of how far we clinicians are entitled to rely upon our clinical experience, lacking (or apparently contradicting) experimental or quantitative research. For myself as clinician, I have not been able to resolve this dilemma in an intellectually responsible way, although I have been steadily conscious of it and engaged in theoretical and empirical research on it for over a quarter century. So I am hardly prepared to clean up the analogous dilemma for lawyers. However, dwelling on this analogy may enable me to offer some tentative suggestions. There is a similarity in the pragmatic contexts of law and clinical practice, in that something will be decided, with or without adequate evidence, good or bad, scientific or anecdotal. A judge cannot leave a case undecided—although a logician could point out that law, being an incomplete postulate set, renders some well-formed formulas undecidable.

Let us strip the concept "scientific experiment" to its essentials, as I have tried to do in a rough meaning stipulation *supra*. Forget the usual images of glass tubing and electronic equipment operated by bearded gents wearing white coats in a laboratory. What, for instance, is the purpose of gadgetry? Scientific apparatus performs one of two functions. Either it plays a role on the input side, contributing to the physical isolation of the system under study and to the control or manipulation of the variables, or it facilitates the recording of observations (output side). We conceive a situation space whose dimensions are all physical and social dimensions having behavioral relevance. In research on human subjects, this set of dimensions will include such minor variables as the material of the experimenter's desk, since in our society the social stimulus value of an oak desk differs from that of pine.

If we are studying the impact of a psychoanalytic interpretation and design an experiment to smuggle this real-life phenomenon into the laboratory, what happens? We move in the situation space from the ordinary-life context of psychotherapy to the experimental context. This movement is in the interest of locating the system studied more precisely, because in the ordinary-life, nonlaboratory situation, the values of certain variables known (or feared) to have an influence are neither assigned by the investigator nor measured by him (with the idea of their influence being removed statistically).

There is no mystery about this, no conflict between a scientific and nonscientific view of the subject matter. The problem presented is quite simple—it is the solution that presents complexities. In order either to eliminate certain causal variables, hold them constant, or manipulate them, or to measure them, we move to a different region of the situation space. By (a) eliminating, (b) fixing, (c) manipulating, or (d) measuring (and "correcting for") the input variables, we intend to test generalizations as to what influences what, generalizations we could not reach in the natural, field, nonexperimental situation. The price we pay is that these generalizations are only known to hold for the new region of the situation space; their application in the ordinary-life context is an extrapolation.

This untoward consequence of the experimental method does not flow from tendentious, polemic formulations polarizing a scientific against a nonscientific frame of reference (empirical versus armchair psychology). Such locutions are misleading, as they locate our methodological stomach ache in the wrong place. The problem can be stated in general terms within the scientific frame of reference. To concretize it: Suppose I am interested in the behavior of tigers. If I rely uncritically on anecdotes told by missionaries, hunters, native guides, etc., my evidence will suffer both on the input and output sides, i.e., from indeterminacy of the input and inaccuracy of the output. If I have accurate output data (e.g., carefully screened independent, convergent testimony by skeptical, reliable, scientifically-trained observers, use of telescopic camera recording, high-fidelity tapes of the tiger's vocalizations), I may be able by such means to take care of the recording-accuracy problem (although hardly the recording-completeness problem). But I will still be troubled by indeterminacy on the input side. I don't know all of the inputs to this tiger when I am photographing him at a distance. I do not know his inputs an hour earlier when he was invisible to me, and I have reason to believe that those previous inputs alter his momentary state and change his behavioral dispositions.

Suppose, to get rid of this uncertainty on the stimulus side, I capture my tiger and put him in a zoo or bring him to my animal laboratory. I eliminate the influence of variations in the chirping of a certain bird as part of the tiger's surround. There is a sense in which I now don't have to be concerned about birds chirping, the only birds that chirp in a proper psychological laboratory being those that the experimenter himself introduces. But there is another sense in which I should be worried about the influence of bird chirping. An average level and fluctuation of bird chirps is part of the normal ecology of tigers in the wild. If I want to extrapolate my laboratory findings to the behavior of wild tigers, this extrapolation is problematic. The background of bird chirps may have a quantitative impact upon the tiger's behavioral dispositions, and perhaps upon his second-order dispositions to acquire first-order dispositions (Broad, 1933; Meehl, 1972).

In research on human subjects, it is frequently found that the influence of variable x upon variable y is dependent upon values of variable z, called by statisticians an "interaction effect." Interaction effects regularly occur whenever the sensitivity of the experimental design suffices to detect them. It is not absurd to suppose that, in human social behavior, almost all interactions of all orders (for instance, the influence of variable v on the interaction effect of the variable z on the first-order influence of variable x on variable y) would be detected if our experiments were sufficiently sensitive. When we liquidate the influence of a variable, either by eliminating it through physical isolation or holding it fixed, we are in danger of wrongly generalizing from our experimental results to the natural, real-life setting.

Law-trained readers unfamiliar with social science statistical methods may have found the preceding rather abstract. Suppose I am a developmental psychologist interested in the deterrent effects of punishment and I argue that the sanctions of the criminal law are inefficacious, relying on "Fisbee's classic experiments on punishment in nursery-school children." In Table 3–1 I list differences that might be relevant in extrapolating from the laboratory study to the legal context.

One need hardly be obscurantist or anti-scientific in his sympathies in order to be nervous about extrapolation in the joint organism-situational space from the region of the left-hand column to that of the right as ground for repealing a statute penalizing larceny. In the foreseeable future, lawmakers will unavoidably rely upon a judicious mixture of experimental research, quasi-experiments, informal field observation, statistical analysis of file data, *and* the fireside inductions. The legislator, prosecutor, judge, and public administrator—like the clinical psychologist—cannot adopt a scientistic purist posture, "I will not decide or act until fully adequate standards of scientific proof are met by the evidence before me." The pragmatic context forces him to act. In these matters, not doing anything or not changing anything we now do is itself a powerful form of action. When the fireside inductions are almost all we have to go on, or when the fireside inductions appear to conflict with the practical consequences of extrapolated experimental research or psychological theory, it would be nice to have some sort of touchstone as to pragmatic validity, some quick and easy objec-

TABLE 3–1
EXTRAPOLATING FROM FISBEE TO REAL-LIFE

Experiment	Criminal Sanction Against Larceny
Four-year-olds	Adults
Mostly upper middle class	Mostly lower and lower middle class
Mostly biologically normal	Numerous genetic deviates in group
Time-span minutes or hours	Time-span months or years
Social context:Subject alone	Social context: Criminal peer-group inputs
Reward: Candy	Rewards: Money, prestige, women, autonomy, leisure, excitement
Punishment: Mild electric shock	Punishment: Deprivations of above rewards [Punishment more like non-reward or time-out than strictly aversive stimulus onset]
Punished response emitted; experimenter aims at reform	Punished response not emitted by most; law aims at general deterrence
Subject's perception of situation: Who knows?	Subject's perception of situation: Who knows?

tive basis for deciding where to place our bets. Unfortunately there is none. . . .

THE LAWMAKER'S DILEMMA

The legislator's, judge's, or administrator's situation is most comfortable when there is a sizable and consistent body of research, experimental and nonexperimental (file data and field observation data), yielding approximately the same results as the fireside inductions. While one may be scientifically skeptical even in this delightfully harmonious situation, in the pragmatic context of decision making, rule writing, policy adopting, etc., such rigorous skepticism can hardly lead to pragmatic vacillation. Some sort of action is required, and all we have goes in the same direction. The methodologically unsatisfactory situations can be divided into three groups, differing in degree rather than kind: (a) No quantitative or experimental evidence is available or readily collectable before action must be taken. Here we rely upon the fireside inductions, these being all we have. A healthy skepticism concerning the fireside inductions, engendered by the study of social science, makes us nonetheless uncomfortable. (b) We have a large-scale adequately conducted study in the field situation, supplemented by file data from different jurisdictions varying in relevant parameters (e.g., offense rate, community socioeconomic indices); these field-observation and file-data results accord with theoretical concepts developed experimentally on humans and infrahumans; but the conclusion conflicts with the fireside. Such a massive and coherent body of information should countervail the fireside inductions, even those with the admirable properties listed above. It seems difficult to dispute this, since by including file data from the nonlaboratory setting to which we wish to extrapolate, we are in effect comparing two sets of anecdotal data, one of which has the methodological advantage of being based upon records instead of relying upon our fallible and possibly biased memories of observations gathered nonsystematically as regards representativeness of persons and situations. *Example:* If statistics show that accuseds released without bail pending trial have such a low incidence of pretrial criminal offenses or failure to appear for trial that the bail system has negligible social utility (combined with its obvious inequity to the poor), our fireside inductions to the contrary should not countervail. But a nagging doubt persists, since other relevant statistics (e.g., ratio of reported felonies to arrests) tend to support the fireside induction that some fraction of these defendants have committed further crimes during their pretrial freedom, and we cannot accurately estimate this fraction (see the excellent paper by Tribe, 1970). A lively sense of the lawmaker's dilemma can be had by reading the Senate debate on the District of Columbia crime bill (*Congressional Record*, 1970). (c) The most difficult situation is that in which there is a collision between a fireside induction having several of the good properties listed above, and a smattering of social science research that is strong enough to give us pause about the fireside inductions, but not strong enough to convince us. Thus, the research may not be entirely consistent from one investigator to another; or it comes only from the experimental laboratory and consequently involves considerable extrapolation in the situation-space; or, if a large-scale quantitative nonexperimental survey, it has the causal-ambiguity and variable-unscrambling difficulties intrinsic to such studies (Meehl, 1969, 1971b). One hardly knows what to suggest in such collision situations except the social scientist's usual "more research is needed."

CONCLUSION

Unavoidably the law will continue to rely upon the fireside inductions. They should be viewed with that skepticism toward anecdotal evidence and the received belief system that training in the behavioral sciences fosters, but without intellectual arrogance or an animus against fireside inductions in favor of overvalued or overinterpreted scientific research. I can summarize my position in one not very helpful sentence since nothing stronger or more specific can be said shortly: In thinking about law as a mode of social control, adopt a healthy skepticism toward the fireside inductions, subjecting them to test by statistical methods applied to data collected in the field situation; but when a fireside induction is held nearly *semper, ubique, et ab omnibus* a similar skepticism should be maintained toward experimental research purporting, as generalized, to overthrow it.

REFERENCES

ANDENAES, J. General prevention: Illusion or reality? *Journal of Criminal Law, Criminology, and Police Science*, 1952, **43**, 176–198.

ANDENAES, J. The general preventive effects of punishment. *University of Pennsylvania Law Review*, 1966, **114**, 949–983.

AYLLON, T., & AZRIN, N. *The token economy.* New York: Appleton-Century-Crofts, 1968.

AZRIN, N., & HOLZ, W. C. In W. K. Honig (Ed.), *Operant behavior: Areas of research and application.* New York: Appleton-Century-Crofts, 1966.

BADIA, P., HABER, A., & RUNYON, R. P. (Eds.) *Research problems in psychology.* Reading, Mass.: Addison-Wesley, 1970.

BAKAN, D. The test of significance in psychological research. *Psychological Bulletin*, 1966, **66**, 423–437.

BANCROFT, H. H. *Popular tribunals.* San Francisco: History Company, 1887.

BANDURA, A., & WALTERS, R. H. *Social learning and personality develop-ment*. New York: Holt, Rinehart & Winston, 1963.
BARBER, B. Resistance by scientists to scientific discovery. *Science*, 1961, **134**, 596–602.
BARNETT, C. *The swordbearers: Supreme command in the First World War*. New York: Signet, 1965.
BECCARIA, C. B. *On crimes and punishments*. New York: Bobbs-Merrill, 1963 (Orig. published in 1764).
BROAD, C. D. *Examination of McTaggart's philosophy*. Cambridge, Eng.: Cambridge University Press, 1933.
BROWN, R. M. *The South Carolina regulators*. Cambridge: Harvard University Press, 1963.
BUCK v. BELL. *United States Reports*, 1927, **274**, 200–208.
BURKS, B., & KELLY, T. L. Statistical Hazards in nature-nurture investigation. *Twenty-seventh yearbook of the National Society for the Study of Education, nature and nurture, Part I: Their influence upon intelligence*. Bloomington: Public School Publishing, 1928.
BURT, C. The inheritance of mental ability. *American Psychologist*, 1958, **13**, 1–15.
BURT, C. The genetic determination of differences in intelligence: A study of monozygotic twins reared together and apart. *British Journal of Psychology*, 1966, **57**, 137–153.
BURT, C. The genetic determination of intelligence: A reply. *British Journal of Psychology*, 1967, **58**, 153–162.
CAMPBELL, D. T. Reforms as experiments. *American Psychologist*, 1969, **24**, 409–429.
CAMPBELL, D. T., & FISKE, D. W. Convergent and discriminant validation by the multitrait-multimethod matrix. *Psychological Bul'etin*, 1959, **56**, 81–105.
CAMPBELL, D. T., & ROSS, H. L. The Connecticut crackdown on speeding: Time-series data in quasi-experimental analysis. *Law and Society Review*, 1968, **3**, 33–53.
CARTER, H. D. Twin similarities in occupational interests. *Journal of Educational Psychology*, 1932, **23**, 641–655.
COHEN, J. The statistical power of abnormal-social psychological research: A review. *Journal of Abnormal and Social Psychology*, 1962, **65**, 145–153.
COLEMAN, J. S., CAMPBELL, E. Q., & HOBSON, C. *Equality of educational opportunity*. Washington: U.S. Government Printing Office, 1966.
Congressional Record, 1970, **116** (121), July 17, 1970.
COWLES, J. T. Food-tokens as incentives for learning by chimpanzees. *Comparative Psychology Monographs*, 1937, **14**, 1–96.
CRONBACH, L. J., & MEEHL, P. E. Construct validity in psychological tests. *Psychological Bulletin*, 1955, **52**, 281–302.
ELSTON, R. C., & GOTTESMAN, I. I. The analysis of quantitative inheritance simultaneously from twin and family data. *American Journal of Human Genetics*, 1968, **20**, 512–521.
ERLENMEYER-KIMLING, L., & JARVIK, L. F. Genetics and intelligence: A review. *Science*, 1963, **142**, 1477–1479.
ESTES, W. K. An experimental study of punishment. *Psychological Monographs*, 1944, **57** (Whole No. 263).
FEIGL, H., & MEEHL, P. E. The determinism-freedom and body-mind problems. In P. A. Schilpp (Ed.), *The philosophy of Sir Karl Popper*. Chicago: LaSalle, in press.

FORSTER, M. C. A study of father-son resemblance in vocational interests and personality traits. Unpublished doctoral dissertation, University of Minnesota, 1931.

FULLER, J. L., & THOMPSON, W. R. *Behavior genetics.* New York: John Wiley & Sons, 1960.

GLASS, G. V. Analysis of data on the Connecticut speeding crackdown as a time-series quasi-experiment. *Law and Society Review,* 1968, **3**, 55–76.

GOTTESMAN, I. I. Genetic aspects of intelligent behavior. In N. Ellis (Ed.), *Handbook of mental deficiency.* New York: McGraw-Hill, 1963.

GOTTESMAN, I. I. A sampler of human behavior genetics. In T. Dobzhansky, M. K. Hecht, & W. C. Steere (Eds.), *Evolutionary biology.* Vol. 2. New York: Appleton-Century-Crofts, 1968.

GOTTESMAN, I. I. Biogenetics of race and class. In M. Deutsch, I. Katz, and A. R. Jensen (Eds.), *Social class, race and psychological development.* New York: Holt, Rinehart & Winston, 1968.

GUTTMAN, L. An outline of the statistical theory of prediction. In P. Horst (Ed.), *The prediction of personal adjustment, SSRC Bulletin, No. 48.* New York: Social Science Research Council, 1941.

HERBERT, M. J., & HARSH, C. M. Observational learning by cats. *Journal of Comparative Psychology,* 1944, **37**, 81–95.

HIRSCH, J. (Ed.) *Behavior genetics analysis.* New York: McGraw-Hill, 1967.

HOBSON v. HANSEN. *Federal Supplement,* 1967, **269**, 401–519.

HOGBEN, L. *The relationship of probability, credibility, and error: An examination of the contemporary crisis in statistical theory from a behaviorist viewpoint.* New York: W. W. Norton, 1958.

HONIG, W. K. (Ed.) *Operant behavior: Areas of research and application.* New York: Appleton-Century-Crofts, 1966.

HONZIK, M. P. Developmental studies of parent-child resemblance in intelligence. *Child Development,* 1957, **28**, 215–228.

JACKSON, D. N. Multimethod factor analysis in the evaluation of convergent and discriminant validity. *Psychological Bulletin,* 1969, **72**, 30–49.

JENKINS, J. J., & PATERSON, D. G. (Eds.) *Studies in individual differences: The search for intelligence.* New York: Appleton-Century-Crofts, 1961.

JOHN, E. R., CHESLER, P., BARTLETT, F., & VICTOR, I. Observational learning in cats. *Science,* 1969, **159**, 1489–1491.

LINDESMITH, A. R. *The addict and the law.* Bloomington: Indiana University Press, 1965.

LIVERMORE, J. *Minnesota evidence: Minnesota practice manual 22.* Minneapolis: University of Minnesota General Extension Division, 1968.

LIVERMORE, J. M., & MEEHL, P. E. The virtues of M'Naghten. *Minnesota Law Review,* 1967, **51**, 789–856.

LIVERMORE, J. M., MALMQUIST, C. P., & MEEHL, P. E. On the justifications for civil commitment. *University of Pennsylvania Law Review,* 1968, **117**, 75–96.

LLEWELLYN, K. N. *The common law tradition: Deciding appeals.* Boston: Little, Brown, 1960.

LOEVINGER, J. Objective tests as instruments of psychological theory. *Psychological Reports,* 1957 (Whole Monograph Supplement 9).

LYKKEN, D. T. Statistical significance in psychological research. *Psychological Bulletin,* 1968, **70**, 151–159.

McCORMICK, C. T. *Handbook of the law of evidence.* St. Paul: West Publishing Company, 1954.

MANOSEVITZ, M., LINDZEY, G., & THIESSEN, D. *Behavioral genetics: Methods and research.* New York: Appleton-Century-Crofts, 1969.

MEEHL, P. E. *Clinical versus statistical prediction: A theoretical analysis and a review of the evidence.* Minneapolis: University of Minnesota Press, 1954.

MEEHL, P. E. Theory-testing in psychology and physics: A methodological paradox. *Philosophy of Science,* 1967, **34**, 103–115.

MEEHL, P. E. Letter in "Input." *Psychology Today,* 1969, **3** (6), 4.

MEEHL, P. E. Nuisance variables and the ex post facto design. In M. Radner and S. Winokur (Eds.), *Minnesota studies in philosophy of science.* Vol. 4. Minneapolis: University of Minnesota Press, 1970 (a).

MEEHL, P. E. Psychological determinism and human rationality: A psychologist's reaction to Sir Karl Popper's "Of Clouds and Clocks." In M. Radner and S. Winokur (Eds.), *Minnesota studies in philosophy of science.* Vol. 4. Minneapolis: University of Minnesota Press, 1970 (b).

MEEHL, P. E. Psychology and the criminal law. *University of Richmond Law Review,* 1970, **5**, 1–30. (c)

MEEHL, P. E. High school yearbooks: A reply to Schwarz. *Journal of Abnormal Psychology,* 1971, **77**, 143–48.

MEEHL, P. E. Specific genetic etiology, psychodynamics, and therapeutic nihilism. *International Journal of Mental Health,* 1972, **1**, 10–27.

MEGARGEE, E. I., & HOKANSON, J. E. (Eds.) *The dynamics of aggression.* New York: Harper & Row, 1970.

MENNINGER, K. A. *The crime of punishment.* New York: Viking Press, 1969.

MILLER, N. E., & DOLLARD, J. *Social learning and imitation.* New Haven: Yale University Press, 1941.

MORRISON, D. E., & HENKEL, R. E. (Eds.) *The significance test controversy.* Chicago: Aldine, 1970.

NEWMAN, K. J. Punishment and the breakdown of the legal order: The experience in East Pakistan. In C. J. Friedrich (Ed.), *Responsibiilty: Nomos III.* New York: Liberal Arts, 1960.

NICHOLS, R. C. The resemblance of twins in personality and interests. *National Merit Scholarship Reports,* 1966, **2** (Whole No. 8).

REED, E. W., & REED, S. C. *Mental retardation: A family study.* Philadelphia: Saunders, 1965.

ROBERTS, R. C. Some concepts and methods in quantitative genetics. In J. Hirsch (Ed.), *Behavior-genetic analysis.* New York: McGraw-Hill, 1967.

ROBINSON, D. N. (Ed.) *Heredity and achievement.* New York: Oxford University Press, 1970.

ROSS, H. L., CAMPBELL, D. T., & GLASS, G. V. The British crackdown on drinking and driving: A successful legal reform. Laboratory of Educational Research Paper No. 29, University of Colorado, May 1969.

ROZEBOOM, W. W. The fallacy of the null-hypothesis significance test. *Psychological Bulletin,* 1960, **57**, 416–428.

SHIELDS, J. *Monozygotic twins brought up apart and brought up together.* London: Oxford University Press, 1962.

SKINNER, B. F. *The behavior of organisms.* New York: Appleton-Century-Crofts, 1938.

SKINNER, B. F. *Walden two.* New York: Macmillan, 1948.

SKINNER, B. F. *Science and human behavior.* New York: Macmillan, 1953.

SKINNER, B. F. *Cumulative record.* New York: Appleton-Century-Crofts, 1968.

SKINNER, B. F. *The technology of teaching.* New York: Appleton-Century-Crofts, 1968.

SKINNER, B. F. *Contingencies of reinforcement: A theoretical analysis.* New York: Appleton-Century-Crofts, 1969.

SKINNER V. OKLAHOMA. *United States Reports,* 1942, **316,** 535–547.

STRONG, E. K., JR. *Vocational interests of men and women.* Stanford: Stanford University Press, 1943.

STRONG, E. K., JR. Interests of fathers and sons. *Journal of Applied Psychology,* 1957, **41,** 284–292.

THOMPSON, W. R. Some problems in the genetic study of personality and intelligence. In J. Hirsch (Ed.), *Behavior-genetic analysis.* New York: McGraw-Hill, 1967.

TRIBE, L. H. An ounce of detention: Preventive justice in the world of John Mitchell. *Virginia Law Review,* 1970, **56,** 371–407.

U.S. V. BUTLER. *United States Reports,* 1936, **297,** 1–88.

VALENTINE, A. *Vigilante justice.* New York: Reynal, 1956.

VANDENBERG, S. G. The nature and nurture of intelligence. In D. C. Glass (Ed.), *Genetics.* New York: Rockefeller University Press, 1968.

VANDENBERG, S. G., & KELLY, L. Hereditary components in vocational preferences. *Acta Geneticae Medicae et Gemellologiae,* 1964, **13,** 266–274.

VANDENBERG, S. G., & STAFFORD, R. E. Hereditary influences on vocational preferences as shown by scores of twins on the Minnesota Vocational Interest Inventory. *Journal of Applied Psychology,* 1967, **51,** 17–19.

WALLER, J. H. Social mobility: Father-son difference in social position related to difference in IQ score. *American Journal of Human Genetics,* 1971, in press.

WHIPPLE, G. M. (Ed.) Intelligence: Its nature and nurture. *39th yearbook of the National Society for the Study of Education.* Bloomington: Public School Publishing, 1940. 2 vols.

PART II

The Origins of Behavior: Physiological Bases and Developmental Processes

4.

Physical Control of the Mind

JOSE M. R. DELGADO

Jose Delgado is an eminent neurobiologist who has done pioneer
work in implanting electrodes and miniaturized radio transmitter-
receivers in the brains of cats, monkeys, and men. In this excerpt
he (1) differentiates between the brain as an organ and the mind as
a group of functions, (2) describes research on the electrostimulation
of the brain (abbreviated as ESB in the following materials), and
(3) points to the limitations of direct control of the brain. ESB is
fertile territory for science-fiction buffs, but Delgado suggests that it
is still fiction.

Some critics of ESB research have raised the specter of Orwellian
possibilities with the behavior and personality of unwilling victims
being controlled by a push-button. In view of the theoretical and
practical limits of ESB, are these concerns any greater than, or
different from, those evoked by other scientific innovations?

THE BRAIN DEFINED

IN CONTRAST with the difficulties and controversial issues encountered
in the attempt to characterize soul and mind, definition of the brain
is relatively easy. The brain, or cerebrum, is a material entity located
inside the skull which may be inspected, touched, weighed, and measured. It is composed of chemicals, enzymes, and humors which may
be analyzed. Its structure is characterized by neurons, pathways, and

From pp. 30–35, 140–49, and 190–95 in *Physical Control of the Mind* by Jose M.
R. Delgado. Copyright © 1969 by Jose M. R. Delgado. By permission of Harper
& Row, Publishers, Inc.

synapses which may be examined directly when they are properly magnified.

To function, the brain must be alive, meaning that the neurons are consuming oxygen, exchanging chemicals through their limiting surfaces, and maintaining states of electrical polarization interrupted by brief periods of depolarization; but even when it is dead—meaning that chemical and electrical phenomena are absent—the brain can still be recognized, preserved in Formalin, and dissected for examination of its anatomical structures. The brain is essentially a chemical and physical entity with many complex functions related to genetic and environmental influences. It functions as a part of the body, but it can survive independently for a limited period when appropriate circulation is provided.

Some of the brain's functions are recognized as mental activities, but other of its chemical, thermal, and electrical phenomena subserve physiological needs unrelated to the mind. One quality of the brain is that it may be considered in *static and material* terms, at least with respect to morphological, cytological, and chemical characteristics which are self-contained. In contrast, the mind is a *functional* entity which cannot be preserved in Formalin or analyzed under the microscope. It is not autonomous but depends on the cerebral reception of a temporal sequence of phenomena and a continuous exchange of information with the environment in order to function properly, as will be discussed later. The term "mind" is an abbreviation for the ill-defined group of mental activities. The existence of mind depends on the existence of a functioning brain, and without brain there is no mind. The contrary, however, is not true, and in the absence of mental manifestations, for example during deep anesthesia, several brain functions, such as maintenance of respiration, may still continue at physiological levels. The common usage of the terms "brain" and "mind" as equivalent may be acceptable provided we are aware of the points of contact and divergence of their respective meanings.

THE MIND AS A FUNCTIONAL ENTITY

The dynamic concept of the mind as a group of functions rather than as an object introduces a linguistic and grammatical dilemma which has been recognized by several authors. In languages with European roots, nouns are generally used to designate things which have a passive character (book, chair, table). Actions, movements, and dynamic processes are usually expressed by verbs (reading, running, eating). The fact that mind is considered as a noun and that its functions are expressed by verbs (thinking, willing, feeling) indicates a conceptual dichotomy which distorts general understanding. The mind should not be identified with other nouns like brain or heart: functions depend on, but should not be classified as, organs.

The mind or psyche, however, has been regarded as an organ comparable to other organs or systems such as the liver or kidney. A psychiatric dictionary states that "there is the organ called the psyche, which, like other organs, possesses its own form and function, its embryology, growth, and microscopic anatomy, physiology, and pathology. . . . The mind, like all other organs of the body, has its own local functions, and also those functions that are intimately associated with adjacent and distant organs. It is like the cardiovascular system in that it reaches all parts of the body." While most laymen as well as psychologists and philosophers would reject the concept that the mind is an organ, it is convenient to analyze the controversy briefly in order to clarify the ideas involved.

Organs such as the heart, the stomach, or the brain are tangible objects with a shape, structure, and chemical composition which can be identified even after the death of the host organism, when all normal functions have ceased. Mental functions do not form part of brain anatomy; they are related to cerebral physiology. The mind cannot be inspected visually; only its dynamic expression as behavioral performance is observable.

The functions of organs such as the heart are genetically determined. They are ready to start at the moment of birth, do not depend on environmental stimuli, and do not require learning. Mental activities have exactly contrary characteristics, and the development of their functional substratum within the brain depends essentially on extragenetic factors. This will be discussed later.

In biology, the physiology of structures cannot be completely ascertained from examination of the anatomy. For example, the circulation of the blood should be differentiated from the supporting organs such as the heart, arteries, and other parts of the cardiovascular system because blood pressure, flow, and circulation are dynamic concepts related to spatial and temporal changes in the blood as it moves through the vessels. The blood itself can be analyzed in order to discover its chemical and morphological properties, and this information will facilitate the understanding of its possible functions. It will not, however, explain the dynamics of circulation, which depends on the summation of systolic volume, heart rate, arterial elasticity, vasomotility, blood volume, blood viscosity, and many other factors, none of which are synonymous with circulation. In like manner, the mind should not be considered identical with its supporting organ, the brain. Information about the anatomy, physiology, and biochemistry of neurons will facilitate the understanding of mental manifestations because these activities depend upon cerebral functions. This information, however, will not fully explain mental dynamics because the mind is related not only to the structure of neurons but also to their spatial-temporal relations and to important extracerebral factors.

HETEROGENEOUS QUALITIES OF THE MIND

On previous pages, the mind has been referred to as a single entity, and it is very common in layman's language as well as in philosophical and scientific discussions to find that the mind is considered as a unit. In reality, however, mental activities such as talking, understanding, or problem solving not only have different sensory inputs and behavioral manifestations but depend on different cerebral structures and mechanisms. Even within a particular mental function there may be considerable anatomical and physiological specificity, as demonstrated by disturbances in speech recognition which may affect the written or the spoken word exclusively.

One of the main difficulties in attempts to define the mind is that we try to supply a common denominator for all mental manifestations, insisting upon similarities among entities which are basically unlike. Cats, monkeys, and men are homogeneous as mammals but heterogeneous as species, and many of the morphological and functional characteristics present in one group cannot be attributed to the others. Man, for example, does not enjoy catching and eating mice, nor are monkeys able to play chess. Unfortunately, some discussions about the mind concern elements as dissimilar as cats, monkeys, and men. It is only natural that agreement will be difficult if authors think that they are referring to the same subject—the mind—when one is considering free will, another consciousness, and still another creative writing. When consulting the literature we should not assume that different phenomena are equivalent merely because authors use the same words to identify them. We should remember that mental functions include a variety of heterogeneous phenomena.

One additional problem involves the dynamic quality of the mind. The heart can be taken out of an organism and stopped in order to study its valves, the thickness of its walls, or the shape of its cells, but we cannot remove the brain to study the mind because it vanishes; we cannot preserve intelligence in Formalin. The dynamic and temporal elements of mental activity are crucial and reflect the elusive and ever-changing qualities of the phenomenon.

The mind is so complex and heterogeneous that it is difficult to answer the classical questions, "What is the mind?" and "Where is the mind?" In my opinion, these questions are incorrectly stated. Present knowledge requires us to approach the problems in a new way and to rephrase them if we wish to progress in understanding. We should seek neither general nor total answers, but information about specific problems or fractions of problems. Today we are in an intellectual and technical position to ask, for example, which parts of the brain do—or do not—play a role in memory, problem solving, or visual recognition. Experiments may be designed and performed to investigate these subjects.

In my discussion of the physical exploration of the mind, I propose to examine the problem not in general, but in some detail, asking questions and presenting experimental data about modifications of pleasure, sensations, behavioral responses, and other manifestations of mental activities obtained by direct manipulation of the brain. . . .

PLEASURABLE EXCITATION OF THE ANIMAL BRAIN

It is surprising that in science as well as in literature more attention has been paid to suffering than to happiness. The central theme of most novels is tragedy, while happy books are hard to find; excellent monographs have been published about pain, but similar studies of pleasure are nonexistent. Typically, in the monumental *Handbook of the American Physiological Society,* a full chapter is devoted to pain, and pleasure is not even listed in the general subject index. Evidently the pursuit of happiness has not aroused as much scientific interest as the fear of pain.

In psychological literature the study of reward is well represented, but even there it has been considered a second-rate sensation and perhaps an artifact of a diminution of pain. It has been postulated that a truly "pleasant" sensation could not exist because organisms have a continuous tendency to minimize incoming stimuli. Pleasure was thus considered a subjective name for the diminution of drive, the withdrawal of a strong stimulation, or the reduction of pain. This "pain reduction" theory has been fruitful as a basis for psychological investigations, but it is gloomy to think that we live in a world of punishment in which the only reality is suffering and that our brain can perceive different degrees of pain but no real pleasure.

Interest in the earlier ideas of hedonism has been renewed by recent experimental studies. According to this theory, pain and pleasure are relatively independent sensations and can be evoked by different types of stimuli which are recognized by separate cerebral mechanisms. Behavior is considered to be motivated by stimuli which the organism tries to minimize (pain) or by stimuli which the organism tries to maximize (pleasure). The brain is thought to have different systems for the reception of these two kinds of inputs, and the psychological state of pleasure or reward can be determined not only by the termination of pain but also by the onset of primary pleasure. The discovery of two anatomically distinct mechanisms in the brain, one for punishment, as mentioned earlier, and one for reward, provides a physiological basis for the dualistic motivation postulated in hedonism.

The surprising fact is that animals of different species, including rats, cats, and monkeys, have voluntarily chosen to press a lever which provides electrical stimulation of specific cerebral areas. The demonstrations are highly convincing because animals which initially pressed a lever to obtain the reward of sugar pellets later pressed at similar or higher rates when electrical stimulation was substituted for food. These experiments showed conclusively that the animals enjoyed the electrical impulses which were delivered only at their own demand. Watching a rat or monkey stimulate its own brain is a fascinating spectacle. Usually each lever pressing triggers a brief 0.5 to 1.0-second brain stimulation which can be more rewarding than food. In a choice situation, hungry rats ran faster to reach the self-stimulation lever than to obtain pellets, and they persistently pressed this lever, ignoring food within easy reach. Rats have removed obstacles, run mazes, and even crossed electrified floors to reach the lever that provided cerebral stimulation.

Not all areas of the brain involved in pleasurable effects appear equally responsive. The highest lever-pressing rates (of up to a remarkable 5,000 times per hour) were recorded by animals self-stimulating in the posterior hypothalamus; excitation of rhinencephalic structures (of only about 200 times per hour) was considered moderately rewarding; and in sensory or motor areas, animals self-stimulated at merely a chance level (of 10 to 25 times per hour), and these areas were classified as neutral. As should be expected, when stimulation was shifted from rewarding areas to nuclei in the punishment system in the same animals, they pressed the lever once and never went back, showing that in the brain of the same animal there were two different groups of structures, one rewarding and the other aversive.

A systematic analysis of the neuroanatomical distribution of pleasurable areas in the rat shows that 60 per cent of the brain is neutral, 35 per cent is rewarding, and only 5 per cent may elicit punishing effects. The idea that far more brain is involved in pleasure than in suffering is rather optimistic and gives hope that this predominance of the potential for pleasurable sensations can be developed into a more effective behavioral reality.

Because of the lack of verbal communication with animals, any ideas about what kind of pleasure, if any, may be experienced during

ESB is a matter of speculation. There are some indications, however, that the perceived sensations could be related to anatomical differentiation of primary rewards of food and sex, because hungry animals self-stimulated at a higher rate in the middle hypothalamus, while administration of sexual hormones to castrated rats increased their lever pressing of more lateral hypothalamic points.

The controversial issue of how these findings in animals may relate to human behavior and the possible existence of areas involved in pleasure in the human brain has been resolved by the information obtained in patients with implanted electrodes.

HUMAN PLEASURE EVOKED BY ESB

On the basis of many studies during cerebral surgery, Penfield has said of anger, joy, pleasure, and sexual excitement in the human brain that "so far as our experience goes, neither localized epileptic discharge nor electrical stimulation is capable of awakening any such emotion. One is tempted to believe that there are no specific cortical mechanisms associated with these emotions." This statement still holds true for the cerebral cortex, but studies in human subjects with implanted electrodes have demonstrated that electrical stimulation of the depth of the brain can induce pleasurable manifestations, as evidenced by the spontaneous verbal reports of patients, their facial expression and general behavior, and their desire to repeat the experience. In a group of twenty-three patients suffering from schizophrenia, electrical stimulation of the septal region, located deep in the frontal lobes, produced an enhancement of alertness sometimes accompanied by an increase in verbal output, euphoria, or pleasure. In a more systematic study in another group of patients, further evidence was presented of the rewarding effects of septal stimulation. One man suffering from narcolepsia was provided with a small stimulator and a built-in counter which recorded the number of times that he voluntarily stimulated each of several selected points in his brain during a period of seventeen weeks. The highest score was recorded from one point in the septal region, and the patient declared that pushing this particular button made him feel "good" as if he were building up to a sexual orgasm, although he was not able to reach the end point and often felt impatient and anxious. His narcolepsia was greatly relieved by pressing this "septal button." Another patient with psychomotor epilepsy also enjoyed septal self-stimulation, which again had the highest rate of button pressing and often induced sexual thoughts. Activation of the septal region by direct injection of acetylcholine produced local electrical changes in two epileptic patients and a shift in mood from disphoria to contentment and euphoria, usually with concomitant sexual motivation and some "orgastic sensations."

Further information was provided by another group of sixty-five patients suffering from schizophrenia or Parkinson's disease, in whom a total of 643 contacts were implanted, mainly in the anterior part of the brain. Results of ESB were grouped as follows: 360 points were "Positive I," and with stimulation "the patients became relaxed, at ease, had a feeling of well-being, and/or were a little sleepy." Another 31 points were "Positive II," and "the patients were definitely changed . . . in a good mood, felt good. They were relaxed, at ease, and enjoyed themselves, frequently smiling. There was a slight euphoria, but the behavior was adequate." They sometimes wanted more stimulations. Excitation of another eight points evoked behavior classified as "Positive III," when "the euphoria was definitely beyond normal limits. The patients laughed out loud, enjoyed themselves, and positively liked the stimulation, and wanted more." ESB of another 38 points gave ambivalent results, and the patients expressed occasional pleasure or displeasure following excitation of the same area. From three other points, responses were termed "orgasm" because the patients initially expressed enjoyment and then suddenly were completely satisfied and did not want any more stimulation for a variable period of time. Finally, from about two hundred other points, ESB produced unpleasant reactions including anxiety, sadness, depression, fear, and emotional outbursts. One of the moving pictures taken in this study was very demonstrative, showing a patient with a sad expression and slightly depressed mood who smiled when a brief stimulation was applied to the rostral part of the brain, returning quickly to his usual depressed state, to smile again as soon as stimulation was reapplied. Then a ten-second stimulation completely changed his behavior and facial expression into a lasting pleasant and happy mood. Some mental patients have been provided with portable stimulators which they have used in self-treatment of depressive states with apparent clinical success.

These results indicate the need for careful functional exploration during brain surgery in order to avoid excessive euphoria or depression when positive or negative reinforcing areas are damaged. Emotional instability, in which the subject bursts suddenly into tears or laughter without any apparent reason, has been observed following some neurosurgical interventions. These major behavior problems might have been avoided by sparing the region involved in emotional regulation.

In our own experience, pleasurable sensations were observed in three patients with psychomotor epilepsy. The first case was V.P., a 36-year-old female with a long history of epileptic attacks which could not be controlled by medication. Electrodes were implanted in her right temporal lobe and upon stimulation of a contact located in the superior part about thirty millimeters below the surface, the patient reported a pleasant tingling sensation in the left side of her body "from my face down to the bottom of my legs." She started giggling and making funny comments, stating that she enjoyed the sensation "very much." Repetition of these stimulations made the patient more communicative and flirtatious, and she ended by openly expressing her desire to marry the therapist. Stimulation of other cerebral points failed to modify her mood and indicated the specificity of the evoked effect. During control interviews before and after ESB, her behavior was quite proper, without familiarity or excessive friendliness.

The second patient was J.M., an attractive, cooperative, and intelligent 30-year-old female who had suffered for eleven years from psychomotor and grand mal attacks which resisted medical therapy. Electrodes were implanted in her right temporal lobe, and stimulation of one of the points in the amygdala induced a pleasant sensation of relaxation and considerably increased her verbal output, which took on a more intimate character. This patient openly expressed her fondness for the therapist (who was new to her), kissed his hands, and talked about her immense gratitude for what was being done for her. A similar increase in verbal and emotional expression was repeated when the same point was stimulated on a different day, but it did not appear when other areas of the brain were explored. During control situations the patient was rather reserved and poised.

The third case was A.F., an 11-year-old boy with severe psychomotor epilepsy. Six days after electrode implantation in both temporal lobes, his fourth tape-recorded interview was carried out while electrical activity of the brain was continuously recorded and 5-second stimulations were applied in a prearranged sequence at intervals of about four minutes. The interviewer maintained an air of friendly interest thoughout, usually without initiating conversation. After six other excitations, point LP located on the surface of the left temporal lobe was stimulated for the first time, and there was an open and precipitous declaration of pleasure. The patient had been silent for the previous five-minute interval, but immediately after this stimulation he exclaimed, "Hey! You can keep me here longer when you give me these; I like those." He went on to insist that the ongoing brain tests made him feel good. Similar statements with an emphatic expression of "feeling good" followed eight of a total of sixteen stimulations of this point during the ninety-minute interview. Several of these manifestations were accompanied by a statement of fondness for the male interviewer, and the last one was accompanied by a voluptuous stretch. None of these manifestations appeared during the control prestimulation period of twenty-six minutes or during the twenty-two minutes when other points were excited. Statistical analysis of the difference between the frequency of pleasurable expressions before and after onset of stimulations proved that results were highly significant ($P <$ 0.001).

The open expressions of pleasure in this interview and the general passivity of behavior could be linked, more or less intuitively, to feminine strivings. It was therefore remarkable that in the next interview, performed in a similar manner, the patient's expressions of confusion about his own sexual identity again appeared following stimulation of point LP. He suddenly began to discuss his desire to get married, but when asked, "To whom?" he did not immediately reply. Following stimulation of another point and a one-minute, twenty-second silence, the patient said, "I was thinking—there's—I was saying *this* to you. How to spell 'yes'—y-e-s. I mean y-o-s. No! 'You' ain't y-e-o. It's this. *Y-o-u.*" The topic was then completely dropped. The monitor who was listening from the next room interpreted this as a thinly veiled wish to marry the interviewer, and it was decided to stimulate the same site again after the prearranged schedule had been completed. During the following forty minutes, seven other points were stimulated, and the patient spoke about several topics of a completely different and unrelated content. Then LP was stimulated again, and the patient started making references to the facial hair of the interviewer and continued by mentioning pubic hair and his having been the object of genital sex play in the past. He then expressed doubt about his sexual identity, saying, "I was thinkin' if I was a boy or a girl—which one I'd like to be." Following another excitation he remarked with evident pleasure: "You're doin' it now," and then he said, "I'd like to be a girl."

In the interpretation of these results it is necessary to consider the psychological context in which electrical stimulation occurs, because the personality configuration of the subject, including both current psychodynamic and psychogenetic aspects, may be an essential determinant of the results of stimulation. Expression of feminine strivings in our patient probably was not the exclusive effect of ESB but the expression of already present personality factors which were activated by the stimulation. The balance between drive and defense may be modified by ESB, as suggested by the fact that after one stimulation the patient said without apparent anxiety, "I'd like to be a girl," but when this idea was presented to him by the therapist in a later interview without stimulation, the patient became markedly anxious and defensive. Minute-to-minute changes in personality function, influenced by the environment and by patient-interviewer relations, may modify the nature of specific responses, and these variables, which are difficult to assess, must be kept in mind.

FRIENDLINESS AND INCREASED CONVERSATION
UNDER ELECTRICAL CONTROL

Human relations evolve between the two opposite poles of love and hate which are determined by a highly complex and little understood combination of elements including basic drives, cultural imprinting, and refined emotional and intellectual characteristics. This subject has so many semantic and conceptual problems that few investigators have dared to approach it experimentally, and in spite of its essential importance, most textbooks of psychology evade its discussion. To define friendliness is difficult although its identification in typical cases is easy, and in our daily life we are continuously evaluating and classifying personal contacts as friendly or hostile. A smiling face, attentive eyes, a receptive hand, related body posture, intellectual interest, ideological agreement, kind words, sympathetic comments, and expressions of personal acceptance are among the common indicators of cordial interpersonal relations. The expression of friendship is a part of social behavior which obviously requires contact between two or more individuals. A mutually pleasurable relation creates a history and provides each individual with a variety of optic, acoustic, tactile, and other stimuli which are received and interpreted with a "friendly bias." The main characteristic of love and friendship is precisely that stimuli coming from a favored person are interpreted as more agreeable than similar stimuli originating from other sources, and this evaluation is necessarily related to neuronal activity.

Little is known about the cerebral mechanisms of friendliness, but as is the case for any behavioral manifestation, no emotional state is possible without a functioning brain, and it may be postulated that some cerebral structures are dispensable and others indispensable both for the interpretation of sensory inputs as amicable and for the expression of friendship. Strong support for this idea derives from the fact, repeatedly proved in neurosurgery, that destruction of some parts of the brain, such as the motor and sensory cortices, produces motor deficits without modifying affective behavior, while ablation of the frontal lobes may induce considerable alteration of emotional personality. Further support has been provided by electrical stimulation of the frontal lobes, which may induce friendly manifestations.

In patient A.F., mentioned earlier in connection with pleasurable manifestations, the third interview was characterized by changes in the character and degree of verbal output following stimulation of one point in the temporal cortex. Fourteen stimulations were applied, seven of them through point RP located in the inferolateral part of the right frontal lobe cortex, and the other seven through contacts located on the cortex of the right temporal lobe and depth of the left and right temporal lobes. The interview started with about five minutes of lively conversation, and during the next ten minutes the patient gradually quieted down until he spoke only about five seconds during every subsequent two-minute period. Throughout the interview the therapist encouraged spontaneous expression by reacting compassionately, by joking with, urging, and reassuring the patient, and by responding to any information offered. The attitude never produced more than a simple reply and often not even that.

In contrast to this basic situation, there were six instances of sharp increase in verbal communication and its friendly content. Each of these instances followed within forty seconds after stimulation of point RP. The only exception was the last excitation of this point when the voltage had been changed. The increases in verbal activity were rapid but brief and without any consistency in subject material, which was typical for the patient. Qualification and quantification of the patient's conversation were made by analyzing the recorded typescript, which was divided into two-minute periods and judged independently by two investigators who had no knowledge of the timing or location of stimulations. Comparison of the two-minute periods before and after these stimulations revealed a verbal increase from seventeen to eighty-eight words and a greater number of friendly remarks, from six to fifty-three. These results were highly significant and their specificity was clear because no changes in verbalization were produced by stimulation of any of the other cerebral points. It was also evident that the evoked changes were not related to the interviewer's rather constant verbal activity. It was therefore concluded that the impressive increase in verbal expression and friendly remarks was the result of electrical stimulation of a specific point on the cortex of the temporal lobe.

CHARACTERISTICS AND LIMITATIONS
OF BRAIN CONTROL

The possibility of man's controlling the thoughts of other men has ranked as high in human fantasy as the control over transmutation of metals, the possession of wings, or the power to take a trip to the moon. Our generation has witnessed the accomplishment of so many nearly impossible tasks that today we are ready to accept almost anything. In the world of science, however, speculation and fantasy cannot replace truth.

There is already abundant evidence that ESB can control a wide range of functions, including motor activities and mental manifestations, in animals and in man. We know that by electrical stimulation of specific cerebral structures we can make a person friendlier or influence his train of thought. In spite of its spectacular potential, ESB has practical and theoretical limitations which should be delineated.

PREDICTABILITY

When we get into a car and press the starter, the motor will almost certainly begin to run in a few seconds. The brain, however, does not have the simplicity of a machine. When electrodes are introduced into a cerebral structure and stimulation is applied for the first time, we really cannot predict the quality, localization, or intensity of the evoked effects. We do not even know that a response will appear. This is especially true for complex structures, like the amygdaloid region, which have great functional multiplicity; but it is also the case in relatively simple areas like the motor cortex. The anatomical and functional variability of the brain are factors which hinder prediction of ESB results. The importance of these limiting factors is compounded by alterations in regional activity related to changes in local, general, and environmental circumstances. We know that certain functions are represented in specific cerebral structures, but the precise location of a desired target requires careful exploration, and implantation of only a few contacts may be rather disappointing. After repeated explorations of a selected area in several subjects, predictability of the observed responses in that area for that species can be assessed with a higher degree of confidence. Present information about functional mapping in most cerebral areas is still rather incomplete.

FUNCTIONAL MONOTONY

Electrical stimulation is a nonspecific stimulus which always activates a group of neurons in a similar way because there is no coded neural message or feedback carried to the stimulating source. The responses, therefore, are repeated in a monotonous way, and any variability is related to changes in the stimulated subject. This functional monotony rules out the possibility that an investigator could direct a subject toward a target or induce him, like a robot, to perform any complex task under remote-controlled orders.

Science fiction has already imagined men with intracerebral electrodes engaged in all kinds of mischief under the perverse guidance of radio waves sent by some evil scientist. The inherent limitations of ESB make realization of this fantasy very remote. The flexion of a limb can be radio controlled and an emotional state could also be set remotely, but the sequences of responses and adaptation to the environment depend on established intracerebral mechanisms whose complexity cannot be duplicated by ESB. Even if we could stimulate different points of the brain through twenty or thirty channels, it would be necessary to have sensory feedback and computerized calculations for the programing of simple spatiotemporal sequences. Induced performance of more complex acts would be far beyond available methodology. It should be clarified that I am talking about directing each phase of a response, and not about complex behavior such as lever pressing or fighting, which may be triggered by ESB but develops according to individual experiential circumstances which are beyond electrical control.

SKILLFUL PERFORMANCE

Many of the activities elicited by ESB certainly can be categorized as skillful. Pressing a lever, climbing a cage wall, and looking for a fight require good motor coordination and suitable processing of information. Walking on two feet, which has been repeatedly elicited in monkeys during stimulation of the red nucleus, is another example of refined coordination and equilibrium seldom observed in spontaneous behavior.

These facts demonstrate that ESB may result in different types of skillful performance, but it must be understood that these responses represent the manifestation of skills already familiar to the subject. Motor learning requires the reception of sensory inputs not only from the environment but also from the performing muscles, and a relatively lengthy process of motor training is required to perfect reactions related to each type of performance and to store the appropriate ideokinetic formulas in the brain for future reference and use. Much of the brain participates in learning, and a monotonous train of pulses applied to a limited pool of neurons cannot be expected to mimic its complexity. The acquisition of a new skill is theoretically and practically beyond the possibilities of electrical stimulation, but ESB can create the desire to perform certain acts which may be skillful.

INDIVIDUAL STABILITY

Personal identity and reactivity depend on a large number of factors accumulated through many years of experience interacting with genetic trends within the complexity of neuronal networks. Language and culture are among the essential elements of individual structure. All these elements cannot be substituted for by the delivery of electricity to the brain. Memories can be recalled, emotions awakened, and conversations speeded up by ESB, but the patients always express themselves according to their background and experience. It is possible to disturb consciousness, to confuse sensory interpretations, or to elicit hallucinations during excitation of the brain. It is also possible to induce fear, pleasure, and changes in aggressive behavior, but these responses do not represent the creation of a new personality—only a change in emotionality or reactivity with the appearance of manifestations closely related to the previous history of the subject.

ESB cannot substitute one personality for another because electricity cannot replicate or influence all the innumerable factors which integrate individual identity. Contrary to the stories of science fiction writers, we cannot modify political ideology, past history, or national loyalties by electrical tickling of some secret areas of the brain. A complete change in personality is beyond the theoretical and practical potential of ESB, although limited modification of a determined aspect of personal reactions is possible. In spite of important limitations, we are certainly facing basic ethical problems about when, why, and how some of these changes are acceptable, and especially about who will have the responsibility of influencing the cerebral activities of other human beings.

TECHNICAL COMPLEXITY

Electrical stimulation of the central nervous system requires careful planning, complex methodology, and the skillful collaboration of specialists with knowledge and experience in anatomy, neurophysiology, and psychology. Several prerequisites, including construction of the delicate multilead electrodes and refined facilities for stereotaxic neurosurgery, are necessary. The selection of neuronal targets and appropriate parameters of stimulation require further sophistication and knowledge of functional brain mapping as well as electronic technology. In addition, medical and psychiatric experience is necessary in order to take care of the patient, to interpret the results obtained, and to plan the delivery of stimulations. These elaborate requirements limit the clinical application of intracerebral electrodes which like other modern medical interventions depends on teamwork, equipment, and facilities available in only a few medical centers. At the same time, the procedure's complexity acts as a safeguard against the possible improper use of ESB by untrained or unethical persons.

FUNCTIONS BEYOND THE CONTROL OF ESB

We are in the initial steps of a new technology, and while it is difficult to predict the limits of unknown territory, we may suppose that cerebral manifestations which depend on the elaboration of complex information will elude electrical control. For example, reading a book or listening to a conversation involves reception of many messages which cannot be mimicked by ESB. A pattern of behavior which is not in the brain cannot be organized or invented under electrical control. ESB cannot be used as a teaching tool because skills such as playing the piano, speaking a language, or solving a problem require complex sensory inputs. Sequential behavior or even elemental motor responses cannot be synthetized by cerebral stimulation, although they are easily evoked if they have already been established in the excited area as ideokinetic formulas. Since electrical stimulation does not carry specific thoughts it is not feasible as a technique to implant ideas or direct behavioral performance in a specific context. Because of its lack of symbolic meaning, electricity could not induce effects comparable to some posthypnotic performances.

5.

. . . .

The Story of My Life

HELEN KELLER

Psychology textbooks discuss the sensory inputs required for normal development and usually emphasize vision and audition. Helen Keller could neither see nor hear, yet her remaining senses were so finely tuned that she could receive rich and detailed impressions of the world around her. The following segment from her autobiography reminds us of the significant potential available in our "other senses" (smell, taste, warmth, as examples).

MORE THAN once in the course of my story I have referred to my love of the country and out-of-door sports. When I was quite a little girl, I learned to row and swim, and during the summer, when I am at Wrentham, Massachusetts, I almost live in my boat. Nothing gives me greater pleasure than to take my friends out rowing when they visit me. Of course, I cannot guide the boat very well. Someone usually sits in the stern and manages the rudder while I row. Sometimes, however, I go rowing without the rudder. It is fun to try to steer by the scent of watergrasses and lilies, and of bushes that grow on the shore. I use oars with leather bands, which keep them in position in the oarlocks, and I know by the resistance of the water when the oars are evenly poised. In the same manner I can also tell when I am pulling against the current. I like to contend with wind and wave. What is more exhilarating than to make your staunch little boat, obedient to your will

Reprinted from *The Story of My Life* by Helen Keller. Copyright 1902. Reprinted with permission of Doubleday & Company, Inc.

and muscle, go skimming lightly over glistening, tilting waves, and to feel the steady, imperious surge of the water!

I also enjoy canoeing, and I suppose you will smile when I say that I especially like it on moonlight nights. I cannot, it is true, see the moon climb up the sky behind the pines and steal softly across the heavens, making a shining path for us to follow; but I know she is there, and as I lie back among the pillows and put my hand in the water, I fancy that I feel the shimmer of her garments as she passes. Sometimes a daring little fish slips between my fingers, and often a pond-lily presses shyly against my hand. Frequently, as we emerge from the shelter of a cove or inlet, I am suddenly conscious of the spaciousness of the air about me. A luminous warmth seems to enfold me. Whether it comes from the trees which have been heated by the sun, or from the water, I can never discover. I have had the same strange sensation even in the heart of the city. I have felt it on cold, stormy days and at night. It is like the kiss of warm lips on my face. . . .

It seems to me that there is in each of us a capacity to comprehend the impressions and emotions which have been experienced by mankind from the beginning. Each individual has a subconscious memory of the green earth and murmuring waters, and blindness and deafness cannot rob him of this gift from past generations. This inherited capacity is a sort of sixth sense—a soul-sense which sees, hears, feels, all in one.

I have many tree friends in Wrentham. One of them, a splendid oak, is the special pride of my heart. I take all my other friends to see this king-tree. It stands on a bluff overlooking King Philip's Pond, and those who are wise in tree lore say it must have stood there eight hundred or a thousand years. There is a tradition that under this tree King Philip, the heroic Indian chief, gazed his last on earth and sky.

I had another tree friend, gentle and more approachable than the great oak—a linden that grew in the dooryard at Red Farm. One afternoon, during a terrible thunderstorm, I felt a tremendous crash against the side of the house and knew, even before they told me, that the linden had fallen. We went out to see the hero that had withstood so many tempests, and it wrung my heart to see him prostrate who had mightily striven and was now mightily fallen. . . .

People who think that all sensations reach us through the eye and the ear have expressed surprise that I should notice any difference, except possibly the absence of pavements, between walking in city streets and in country roads. They forget that my whole body is alive to the conditions about me. The rumble and roar of the city smite the nerves of my face, and I feel the ceaseless tramp of an unseen multitude, and the dissonant tumult frets my spirit. The grinding of heavy wagons on hard pavements and the monotonous clangor of machinery are all the more torturing to the nerves if one's attention is not diverted by the panorama that is always present in the noisy streets to people who can see.

In the country one sees only Nature's fair works, and one's soul is not saddened by the cruel struggle for mere existence that goes on in the crowded city. Several times I have visited the narrow, dirty streets where the poor live, and I grow hot and indignant to think that good people should be content to live in fine houses and become strong and beautiful, while others are condemned to live in hideous, sunless tenements and grow ugly, withered and cringing. The children who crowd these grimy alleys, half-clad and underfed, shrink away from your outstretched hand as if from a blow. Dear little creatures, they crouch in my heart and haunt me with a constant sense of pain. There are men and women, too, all gnarled and bent out of shape. I have felt their hard, rough hands and realized what an endless struggle their existence must be—no more than a series of scrimmages, thwarted attempts to do something. Their life seems an immense disparity between effort and opportunity. The sun and the air are God's free gifts to all, we say; but are they so? In yonder city's dingy alleys the sun shines not, and the air is foul. Oh, man, how dost thou forget and obstruct thy brother man, and say, "Give us this day our daily bread," when he has none! Oh, would that men would leave the city, its splendor and its tumult and its gold, and return to wood and field and simple, honest living! Then would their children grow stately as noble trees, and their thoughts sweet and pure as wayside flowers. It is impossible not to think of all this when I return to the country after a year of work in town.

What a joy it is to feel the soft, springy earth under my feet once more, to follow grassy roads that lead to ferny brooks where I can bathe my fingers in a cataract of rippling notes, or to clamber over a stone wall into green fields that tumble and roll and climb in riotous gladness!

Next to a leisurely walk I enjoy a "spin" on my tandem bicycle. It is splendid to feel the wind blowing in my face and the springy motion of my iron steed. The rapid rush through the air gives me a delicious sense of strength and buoyancy, and the exercise makes my pulses dance and my heart sing. . . .

Museums and art stores are also sources of pleasure and inspiration. Doubtless it will seem strange to many that the hand unaided by sight can feel action, sentiment, beauty in the cold marble; and yet it is true that I derive genuine pleasure from touching great works of art. As my finger tips trace line and curve, they discover the thought and emotion which the artist has portrayed. I can feel in the faces of gods and heroes hate, courage and love, just as I can detect them in living faces I am permitted to touch. I feel in Diana's posture the grace and freedom of the forest and the spirit that tames the mountain lion and subdues the fiercest passions. My soul delights in the repose and gracious curves of the Venus; and in Barré's bronzes the secrets of the jungle are revealed to me.

A medallion of Homer hangs on the wall of my study, conveniently low, so that I can easily reach it and touch the beautiful, sad face with loving reverence. How well I know each line in that majestic brow—tracks of life and bitter evidences of struggle and sorrow; those sightless eyes seeking, even in the cold plaster, for the light and the blue skies of his beloved Hellas, but seeking in vain; that beautiful mouth, firm and true and tender. It is the face of a poet, and of a man acquainted with sorrow. Ah, how well I understand his deprivation—the perpetual night in which he dwelt—

> O dark, dark, amid the blaze of noon,
> Irrecoverably dark, total eclipse
> Without all hope of day!

In imagination I can hear Homer singing, as with unsteady, hesitating steps he gropes his way from camp to camp—singing of life, of love, of war, of the splendid achievements of a noble race. It was a wonderful, glorious song, and it won the blind poet an immortal crown, the admiration of all ages.

I sometimes wonder if the hand is not more sensitive to the beauties of sculpture than the eye. I should think the wonderful rhythmical flow of lines and curves could be more subtly felt than seen. Be this as it may, I know that I can feel the heart-throbs of the ancient Greeks in their marble gods and goddesses. . . .

Is it not true, then, that my life with all its limitations touches at many points the life of the World Beautiful? Everything has its wonders, even darkness and silence, and I learn, whatever state I may be in, therein to be content.

Sometimes, it is true, a sense of isolation enfolds me like a cold mist as I sit alone and wait at life's shut gate. Beyond there is light, and music, and sweet companionship; but I may not enter. Fate, silent, pitiless, bars the way. Fain would I question his imperious decree; for my heart is still undisciplined and passionate; but my tongue will not utter the bitter, futile words that rise to my lips, and they fall back into my heart like unshed tears. Silence sits immense upon my soul. Then comes hope with a smile and whispers, "There is joy in self-forgetfulness." So I try to make the light in others' eyes my sun, the music in others' ears my symphony, the smile on others' lips my happiness.

6.

Yoga Control of the Psychic Heat

W. Y. EVANS-WENTZ

The nervous system is comprised of two subsystems: the central
nervous system (the brain and spinal cord) and the peripheral nervous
system. The peripheral nervous system, in turn, is functionally
subdivided into the somatic nervous system and the autonomic
(sometimes called "involuntary") nervous system. Bodily functions
under the control of the autonomic nervous system—functions such
as the control of blood pressure, of glandular secretions, or of body
heat—are presumed not to be under voluntary control. Recently,
some psychologists have attempted to demonstrate, through the use
of biofeedback techniques, that it may be possible for people to
establish such voluntary control (see Selection 11). Yet oriental
philosophies have for many years contended that with special
training one could establish control over these "involuntary"
functions. In this excerpt from the Tibetan yoga (which is very
similar to parts of the Hindu hatha-yoga), the techniques for the
control of body heat are described. Do they seem plausible in terms
of your knowledge of the nervous system? How could you
account for their purported successes?

THE DOCTRINE of the Psychic-Heat is known to the Tibetans as *Tūmmō*,
signifying a peculiar bodily heat, or warmth of a psycho-physical character, generated by *yogic* means. According to the secret lore, the word
Tūmmō refers to a method of extracting *prāna*, from the inexhaustible
prānic reservoir in Nature, and storing it in the human-body battery

From *Tibetan Yoga and Secret Doctrines* by W. Y. Evans-Wentz. Published by
Oxford University Press, reprinted by permission of the publisher.

and then employing it to transmute the generative fluid into a subtle fiery energy whereby a psycho-physical heat is produced internally and made to circulate through the nerve-channels of the psychic nervous system.

This system, invisible to all save those possessed of clairvoyant vision, is the psychic counterpart of the physical nervous system. Its nerve-channels are called in Tibetan *tsas* and in Sanskrit *nādī*. Of these there are three of primary importance: the Median-Nerve (Tib. *Uma-tsa:* Skt. *Sushumnā-nādī*), extending through the centre of the spinal column; the Right-Nerve (Tib. *Roma-tsa:* Skt. *Pingalā-nādī*); and the Left-Nerve (Tib. *Kyangma-tsa:* Skt. *Idā-nādī*). The last two, like two serpents, are said to coil round the Median-Nerve to the right and to the left. Connected with these three are numerous subsidiary psychic-nerves by which the psycho-nervous energy (Tib. *Shugs:* Skt. *prāna*) is carried to each psychic nerve-centre (Tib. *khorlo:* Skt. *chakra*) and therein stored and thence distributed to every organ and part of the body. The system is described in more detail in *The Tibetan Book of the Dead*.

According to our text, in practising the art of *Tūmmõ*, the *yogin* must employ very elaborate visualizations, meditations, postures, breathings, directing of thought, training of the psychic-nerve system, and physical exercises. Our annotations are sufficiently numerous and detailed to serve as a commentary and to afford the student some practical guidance. But, as the Tibetan *gurus* emphasize, it is highly desirable for the neophyte, prior to beginning the practice of *Tūmmõ*, to obtain preliminary initiation and personal guidance from a master of the art.

A lengthy probationary period is usually necessary before the *yogin* can arrive at any assurance of success. At the outset, he must accustom himself to the minimum of clothing and avoid, as far as possible, resort to fire for warming the body. It is by their never wearing furs or woollen garments or seeking artificial external heat that the masters of the art are recognized. The *yogin* must also observe the strictest sexual continence, for it is chiefly upon the *yogically* transmuted sex energy that proficiency in *Tūmmõ* depends.

The actual practising must not be done inside or near the dwelling of a householder, but preferably in some place of hermitage, such as a remote mountain cave, far removed from localities where the air is made impure by smoke or the auric emanations of towns or villages. A *yogin* aiming at mastery of the art may remain in such solitary hermitage for a very long time and see no human being save the *guru*, who will appear at intervals to direct the *yogin's* progress. The beginner is advised to perform the *yogic* exercises in the early morning before sunrise, when Nature and the Earth's magnetic currents are apt to be the least disturbed. Once the art is mastered, it can be practised anywhere and at any time.

As progress is made in this science of *yogically* conserving and directing the physical, mental, and psychic energy of the human organism, the hermit *yogin* gradually develops the psycho-physical warmth. The subtle fiery energy, accompanied by a pleasant warmth, begins to pervade every atom of his body, and, little by little, he acquires the *yogic* power of enduring, with comfort, the most extreme cold, clad only in a single cotton cloth, or even entirely nude. Reference to this is made in *Tibet's Great* Yogī *Milarepa:*

> The warming breath of angels wear,
> As thy raiment pure and soft.

When the probationary training ends and the neophyte feels confident of success, the *guru* not infrequently tests him to judge of the degree of proficiency attained. The following account of such a testing is given by Madame David-Neel, whose interesting researches and experiences in the Orient, especially with respect to Tibetan mystics, parallel in many ways the editor's own:

'Upon a frosty winter night, those who think themselves capable of victoriously enduring the test are led to the shore of a river or lake. If all the streams are frozen in the region, a hole is made in the ice. A moonlight night, with a hard wind blowing, is chosen. Such nights are not rare in Tibet during the winter months.

'The neophytes sit on the ground, cross-legged and naked. Sheets are dipped in the icy water. Each man wraps himself in one of them and must dry it on his body. As soon as the sheet has become dry, it is again dipped in the water and placed on the novice's body to be dried as before. The operation goes on in that way until daybreak. Then he who has dried the largest number of sheets is acknowledged the winner of the competition.'

The size of the sheet varies. Some sheets are quite small, being little larger than the ordinary face towels; others are as big as large shawls. The rule requires that the *yogin* must have dried at least three of the wet sheets in order to be entitled to wear the insignia of proficiency in *Tūmmō*, namely, the single white cotton shirt or robe, on account of which he comes to be called, in Tibetan, a *Repa*, meaning 'Cotton-Clad One'. Mila-repa, the great Tibetan *Yogin*, as his name, meaning 'Mila, the Cotton-Clad One', indicates, mastered the art of *Tūmmō* under the guidance of his *guru* Marpa. Eight of Milarepa's advanced disciples, as stated in the first chapter of Milarepas' *Biography*, were also *Repas*. Other *Repas* are named in the appendix to the *Biography*.

In addition to the drying of wet sheets on the *yogin's* body, another test, to ascertain the degree of warmth which the *yogin* can generate, consists in making him sit naked in the snow, the quantity of snow melted under and round about him indicating his proficiency.

That there are at the present time adepts of *Tūmmō* in hermitage in Tibet, many of whom, being followers of Milarepa, are of the Order of Cotton-Clad Ones, is undoubtedly true. More than one European has occasionally caught glimpses of such ascetics, and well-authenticated accounts of their immunity to the arctic-like temperatures of the Tibetan winter are current throughout the high Himālayan countries.

Being a part of *Hatha Yoga*, *Tūmmō* appears to be known also to Hindus. I recall that during the summer of 1918 I had as traveling companions for a few weeks a group of naked Hindu ascetics, who had come, as I had, direct from the torrid plains of India. We met in Srinagar. Thence, in the midst of a moving throng of thousands of pilgrims from all parts of India, of both sexes and of many castes, we set out *en route* to the glacier-clad heights of the Himālayas of Kashmir, on the age-hallowed pilgrimage to the Cave of Amar-Nath, wherein the holy of holies is a natural *lingam* (phallus) of ice, sacred to Shiva, the Lord of the World.[1] A certain number of the ascetics donned no clothing, not so much as a loin-cloth, even when we had attained an altitude of ten thousand feet above sea-level, where the nights were freezingly cold and the glaciers and snowy peaks breathed down upon us their icy breath. A few of the ascetics, even when the glaciers were being traversed, were still unclad and remained so during the whole pilgrimage. Others, shortly before, or when the Cave was reached, wrapped about themselves thin cotton garments; whilst the least adept used blankets in which they had been carrying their meagre food supply.

At that time, I knew nothing of the Tibetan art of generating the extraordinary bodily warmth. Consequently I did not question these Hindu ascetics as to their remarkable *yogic* hardihood, attributing it to their being, as no doubt some of them were, masters of *Hatha Yoga*, which confers immunity to extremes of cold and also of heat.

At Rikhikesh, on the Ganges, I once witnessed a demonstration of the *yogic* immunity to extreme heat. A naked *yogin* at midday in the hot season sat on the shimmering sands of the river-shore surrounded by four glowing fires of heaped-up wood and dried cow-dung within only a few feet of his naked body, each fire being in one of the four cardinal directions. The unclouded midsummer sun, directly over his uncovered head, constituted the fifth fire in the *yoga*, called the *Pancha-*

---

[1] Shiva, as the personification of the forces in nature making for destruction, is the Lord of Regeneration, and so his symbol is the phallus, or male organ of generation, as it was of Osiris, the Egyptian deity associated with human fertility.

Dhūni ('Five-Fires'), which he was practising. Similar feats, proving *yogic* immunity from heat and from fire itself, have been witnessed and attested by Europeans, not only in India and Ceylon, but throughout the South Sea Islands and elsewhere, in connexion with the fire-walking ceremony. And in some of the *Tovil* (Devil-Dancing) Ceremonies of Ceylon fire is trodden upon and grasped by the devil-dancers without harm, in virtue of the use of *mantras* called 'fire-cooling *mantras*' (Sinhalese, *gini-sisil*). . . .

PRELIMINARY EXERCISE 1: VISUALIZING THE PHYSICAL BODY AS BEING VACUOUS

1. In the first of the preliminary exercises, Visualizing the Physical Body as Being Vacuous, proceed according to the practices which now follow.

2. At the outset, say the Prayer leading up to the communion with the Divine *Guru*.

3. Then imagine thyself to be the Divine Devotee Vajra-Yoginī, red of colour; as effulgent as the radiance of a ruby; having one face, two hands, and three eyes; the right hand holding aloft a brilliantly gleaming curved knife and flourishing it high overhead, cutting off completely all mentally disturbing thought-processes; the left hand holding against her breast a human skull filled with blood; giving satisfaction with her inexhaustible bliss; with a tiara of five dried human skulls on her head; wearing a necklace of fifty blood-dripping human heads; her adornments, five of the Six Symbolic Adornments, the cemetery-dust ointment being lacking; holding, in the bend of her arm, the long staff, symbolizing the Divine Father, the *Heruka;* nude, and in the full bloom of virginity, at the sixteenth year of her age; dancing, with the right leg bent and foot uplifted, and the left foot treading upon the breast of a prostrate human form; and Flames of Wisdom forming a halo about her.

4. (Visualize her as being thyself) externally in the shape of a deity, and internally altogether vacuous like the inside of an empty sheath, transparent and uncloudedly radiant; vacuous even to the finger-tips, like an empty tent of red silk, or like a filmy tube distended with breath.

5. At the outset, let the visualization be about the size of thine own body; then, as big as a house; then, as big as a hill; and, finally, vast enough to contain the Universe. Then concentrate thy mind upon it.

6. Next, gradually reduce it, little by little, to the size of a sesamum seed, and then to the size of a very greatly reduced sesamum seed, still

having all the limbs and parts sharply defined. Upon this, too, concentrate thy mind.

PRELIMINARY EXERCISE 2: VISUALIZING THE PSYCHIC NERVE-SYSTEM AS BEING VACUOUS

7. In the second of the preliminary exercises, Visualizing the Psychic Nerve-System as Being Vacuous, proceed according to the practices which now follow.

8. As extending through the centre of thy body (from the perineum to the Aperture of Brahma on the crown of the head),[2] thy body visualized as being the body of the Divine Yoginī, of normal size, imagine the median-nerve as possessing the following four characteristics: redness like that of a solution of lac,[3] brightness like that of the flame of a sesamum-oil lamp, straightness like that of the inner core of the plantain plant,[4] and hollowness like that of a hollow tube of paper. Let this visualization be about the size of a medium-sized arrow-reed.

9. Then, when that hath been done, expand the visualization to the size of a staff, then to the size of a pillar, then to the size of a house, then to the size of a hill, and, finally, make it vast enough to contain the Universe.

10. Meditate upon the median-nerve as pervading every part of the visualized body, even to the tips of the fingers.[5]

11. When the visualization is the size of a sesamum seed, meditate upon the median-nerve pervading it as being in thickness the one-hundredth part of the diameter of a hair (and hollow).

12. It hath been said,

"Create (or visualize) vacuity in that which is not clearly defined (because so minute);

"Create vacuity in that which cannot be caught hold of (by the eye, because invisible);

"Create vacuity in that which doth not rest (or is transitory)."[6]

---

[2] This is the highway for the circulation of the psychic forces of the human body.

[3] A dark red resin used in Oriental countries for making a brilliant red dye.

[4] A tropical plant allied to the banana, which contains a straight inner core, comparable to the median-nerve at the centre of the spinal column.

[5] But the median-nerve does not really pervade the body thus. This meditation exercise is for the purpose of helping the beginner in *yoga* to recognize the vacuity, or unsubstantiality, and, thereby, the unreality, of all component things, including the human form, each existing thing, alike, being the product of transitory phenomena.

[6] The first process of creating, or visualizing, vacuity has reference to material substance in its most minute organic aspects, barely visible to the human eye unaided by a microscope; the second, to matter in its invisible forms; the third, to the smallest particle of time mentally conceivable.

PRELIMINARY EXERCISE 3: VISUALIZING THE PROTECTIVE CIRCLE

13. In the third of the preliminary exercises, Visualizing (or Meditating upon) the Protective Circle, there are three parts: the Art of Posturing the Body; the Art of Breathing; and the Art of Directing Thought (or Mental Imagery).[7]

14. The first of these three, the Art of Posturing the Body, consisteth of the seven methods of making manifest all (psycho-physical) processes (or things).

15. In the Art of Breathing, one is to exhale the dead air thrice, then to press down the inhalation (to the very bottom of the lungs), then to raise the diaphragm a little so as to make the distended chest conform to the shape of a closed vessel (like an earthen pot) and to hold it thus as long as possible.

16. In the Art of Directing Thought (or Mental Imagery), one is to imagine, when the expiration is going out, that innumerable five-coloured rays are issuing from each of the hair-pores of the body and radiating over the whole world and filling it with their five-coloured radiances, and that when the inspiration is coming in they are re-entering the body through the hair-pores and filling the body.

17. Each of these (two complementary exercises) is to be performed seven times.

18. Then imagine that each of the rays is changed into the syllable *HŪM*, vari-coloured; and that while the expiration is going out the world is being filled with these *HŪMS*, and that when the inspiration is coming in, that one's body is being filled with them. Do this seven times.

19. Next imagine that the *HŪMS* are changed into Wrathful Deities, each having one face and two hands, the right hand held aloft, flourishing overhead a *dorje;* the left hand held in a menacing posture against the heart; the right leg bent and the left leg held tense; of very angry and fierce mien and of five colours, none of them larger than a sesamum seed.

20. As the expiration is going out, think of them as going out with it and filling the world.

---

[7] These three arts, namely, the *yogic* posturing of the body (Skt. *āsana*), the *yogic* disciplining and right directing of the breathing-process (Skt. *prāṇā-yāma*), and the *yogic* mastery of the thought-process (Skt. *dhāraṇā*) arouse in the *yogin* psychic virtues which shield him from worldly distractions and undesirable influences, and bestow upon him soundness of physical, mental, and spiritual health. Therefore they are called the "Protective Circle", as will be seen more clearly at the end of this section.

21. As the inspiration is being drawn in, and held, imagine them as coming in with it and filling the body.

22. Perform these two complementary exercises seven times each, making, in all (with the above), twenty-one exercises.

23. Then think that each of the hair-pores of thy body is filled with one of these Wrathful Deities, with his face turned outwards, and that all of them taken together constitute a coat of mail which thou art wearing.

7.

The Misbehavior of Organisms

KELLER BRELAND and MARIAN BRELAND

Breland and Breland, by the time this article was written, had
become successful commercial purveyors of conditioned operant
behavior. Using the techniques that Skinner had developed in the
animal laboratory and had suggested for the control of human
behavior in natural situations (see Selection 10), they had been able
to train a wide variety of animals to perform a remarkable number
of feats for displays in zoos, museums, fairs, and department stores.
But in this article they point to a number of instances in which
animals failed to maintain a specific learned response, and they
argue that instinctive behavior patterns seem to dominate the
behavior patterns that have been conditioned, that the behavior of
an animal cannot be understood without knowledge of its instinctive patterns (today often called "species-specific behavior") and its
evolutionary history. Does this mean that the concept of instinct
must be resurrected in contemporary psychology?

THERE SEEMS to be a continuing realization by psychologists that perhaps the white rat cannot reveal everything there is to know about behavior. Among the voices raised on this topic, Beach (1950) has
emphasized the necessity of widening the range of species subjected to
experimental techniques and conditions. However, psychologists as a
whole do not seem to be heeding these admonitions, as Whalen (1961)
has pointed out.

Perhaps this reluctance is due in part to some dark precognition of

Reprinted from *American Psychologist*, 1961, *16*, pp. 681–84. Copyright 1961 by
the American Psychological Association. Reprinted by permission.

what they might find in such investigations, for the ethologists Lorenz (1950, p. 233) and Tinbergen (1951, p. 6) have warned that if psychologists are to understand and predict the behavior of organisms, it is essential that they become thoroughly familiar with the instinctive behavior patterns of each new species they essay to study. Of course, the Watsonian or neobehavioristically oriented experimenter is apt to consider "instinct" an ugly word. He tends to class it with Hebb's (1960) other "seditious notions" which were discarded in the behavioristic revolution, and he may have some premonition that he will encounter this bête noir in extending the range of species and situations studied.

We can assure him that his apprehensions are well grounded. In our attempt to extend a behavioristically oriented approach to the engineering control of animal behavior by operant conditioning techniques, we have fought a running battle with the seditious notion of instinct.[1] It might be of some interest to the psychologist to know how the battle is going and to learn something about the nature of the adversary he is likely to meet if and when he tackles new species in new learning situations.

Our first report (Breland & Breland, 1951) in the *American Psychologist*, concerning our experiences in controlling animal behavior, was wholly affirmative and optimistic, saying in essence that the principles derived from the laboratory could be applied to the extensive control of behavior under nonlaboratory conditions throughout a considerable segment of the phylogenetic scale.

When we began this work, it was our aim to see if the science would work beyond the laboratory, to determine if animal psychology could stand on its own feet as an engineering discipline. These aims have been realized. We have controlled a wide range of animal behavior and have made use of the great popular appeal of animals to make it an economically feasible project. Conditioned behavior has been exhibited at various municipal zoos and museums of natural history and has been used for department store displays, for fair and trade convention exhibits, for entertainment at tourist attractions, on television shows, and in the production of television commercials. Thirty-eight species, totaling over 6,000 individual animals, have been conditioned, and we have dared to tackle such unlikely subjects as reindeer, cockatoos, raccoons, porpoises, and whales.

Emboldened by this consistent reinforcement, we have ventured further and further from the security of the Skinner box. However, in this cavalier extrapolation, we have run afoul of a persistent pattern of dis-

[1] In view of the fact that instinctive behaviors may be common to many zoological species, we consider *species specific* to be a sanitized misnomer, and prefer the possibly septic adjective *instinctive*.

comforting failures. These failures, although disconcertingly frequent and seemingly diverse, fall into a very interesting pattern. They all represent breakdowns of conditioned operant behavior. From a great number of such experiences, we have selected, more or less at random, the following examples.

The first instance of our discomfiture might be entitled, What Makes Sammy Dance? In the exhibit in which this occurred, the casual observer sees a grown bantam chicken emerge from a retaining compartment when the door automatically opens. The chicken walks over about 3 feet, pulls a rubber loop on a small box which starts a repeated auditory stimulus pattern (a four-note tune). The chicken then steps up onto an 18-inch, slightly raised disc, thereby closing a timer switch, and scratches vigorously, round and round, over the disc for 15 seconds, at the rate of about two scratches per second until the automatic feeder fires in the retaining compartment. The chicken goes into the compartment to eat, thereby automatically shutting the door. The popular interpretation of this behavior pattern is that the chicken has turned on the "juke box" and "dances."

The development of this behavioral exhibit was wholly unplanned. In the attempt to create quite another type of demonstration which required a chicken simply to stand on a platform for 12–15 seconds, we found that over 50% developed a very strong and pronounced scratch pattern, which tended to increase in persistence as the time interval was lengthened. (Another 25% or so developed other behaviors —pecking at spots, etc.) However, we were able to change our plans so as to make use of the scratch pattern, and the result was the "dancing chicken" exhibit described above.

In this exhibit the only real contingency for reinforcement is that the chicken must depress the platform for 15 seconds. In the course of a performing day (about 3 hours for each chicken) a chicken may turn out over 10,000 unnecessary, virtually identical responses. Operant behaviorists would probably have little hesitancy in labeling this an example of Skinnerian "superstition" (Skinner, 1948) or "mediating" behavior, and we list it first to whet their explanatory appetite.

However, a second instance involving a raccoon does not fit so neatly into this paradigm. The response concerned the manipulation of money by the raccoon (who has "hands" rather similar to those of the primates). The contingency for reinforcement was picking up the coins and depositing them in a 5-inch metal box.

Raccoons condition readily, have good appetites, and this one was quite tame and an eager subject. We anticipated no trouble. Conditioning him to pick up the first coin was simple. We started out by reinforcing him for picking up a single coin. Then the metal container was introduced, with the requirement that he drop the coin into the container. Here we ran into the first bit of difficulty: he seemed to have a great deal of trouble letting go of the coin. He would rub it up against the inside of the container, pull it back out, and clutch it firmly for several seconds. However, he would finally turn it loose and receive his food reinforcement. Then the final contingency: we put him on a ratio of 2, requiring that he pick up both coins and put them in the container.

Now the raccoon really had problems (and so did we). Not only could he not let go of the coins, but he spent seconds, even minutes, rubbing them together (in a most miserly fashion), and dipping them into the container. He carried on this behavior to such an extent that the practical application we had in mind—a display featuring a raccoon putting money in a piggy bank—simply was not feasible. The rubbing behavior became worse and worse as time went on, in spite of nonreinforcement.

For the third instance, we return to the gallinaceous birds. The observer sees a hopper full of oval plastic capsules which contain small toys, charms, and the like. When the S_D (a light) is presented to the chicken, she pulls a rubber loop which releases one of these capsules onto a slide, about 16 inches long, inclined at about 30 degrees. The capsule rolls down the slide and comes to rest near the end. Here one or two sharp, straight pecks by the chicken will knock it forward off the slide and out to the observer, and the chicken is then reinforced by an automatic feeder. This is all very well—most chickens are able to master these contingencies in short order. The loop pulling presents no problems; she then has only to peck the capsule off the slide to get her reinforcement.

However, a good 20% of all chickens tried on this set of contingencies fail to make the grade. After they have pecked a few capsules off the slide, they begin to grab at the capsules and drag them backwards into the cage. Here they pound them up and down on the floor of the cage. Of course, this results in no reinforcement for the chicken, and yet some chickens will pull in over half of all the capsules presented to them.

Almost always this problem behavior does not appear until after the capsules begin to move down the slide. Conditioning is begun with stationary capsules placed by the experimenter. When the pecking behavior becomes strong enough, so that the chicken is knocking them off the slide and getting reinforced consistently, the loop pulling is conditioned to the light. The capsules then come rolling down the slide to the chicken. Here most chickens, who before did not have this tendency, will start grabbing and shaking.

The fourth incident also concerns a chicken. Here the observer sees a chicken in a cage about 4 feet long which is placed alongside a miniature baseball field. The reason for the cage is the interesting part. At one end of the cage is an automatic electric feed hopper. At the other is an opening through which the chicken can reach and pull a loop on a bat. If she pulls the loop hard enough the bat (solenoid operated) will swing, knocking a small baseball up the playing field. If it gets past the miniature toy players on the field and hits the back fence, the chicken is automatically reinforced with food at the other end of the cage. If it does not go far enough or hits one of the players, she tries again. This results in behavior on an irregular ratio. When the feeder sounds, she then runs down the length of the cage and eats.

Our problems began when we tried to remove the cage for photography. Chickens that had been well conditioned in this behavior became wildly excited when the ball started to move. They would jump up on the playing field, chase the ball all over the field, even knock it off on the floor and chase it around, pecking it in every direction, although they had never had access to the ball before. This behavior was so persistent and so disruptive, in spite of the fact that it was never reinforced, that we had to reinstate the cage.

The last instance we shall relate in detail is one of the most annoying and baffling for a good behaviorist. Here a pig was conditioned to pick up large wooden coins and deposit them in a large "piggy bank." The coins were placed several feet from the bank and the pig required to carry them to the bank and deposit them, usually four or five coins for one reinforcement. (Of course, we started out with one coin, near the bank.)

Pigs condition very rapidly, they have no trouble taking ratios, they have ravenous appetites (naturally), and in many ways are among the most tractable animals we have worked with. However, this particular problem behavior developed in pig after pig, usually after a period of weeks or months, getting worse every day. At first the pig would eagerly pick up one dollar, carry it to the bank, run back, get another, carry it rapidly and neatly, and so on, until the ratio was complete. Thereafter, over a period of weeks the behavior would become slower and slower. He might run over eagerly for each dollar, but on the way back, instead of carrying the dollar and depositing it simply and cleanly, he would repeatedly drop it, root it, drop it again, root it along the way, pick it up, toss it up in the air, drop it, root it some more, and so on.

We thought this behavior might simply be the dilly-dallying of an animal on low drive. However, the behavior persisted and gained in strength in spite of a severely increased drive—he finally went through the ratios so slowly that he did not get enough to eat in the course of a day. Finally it would take the pig about 10 minutes to transport four coins a distance of about 6 feet. This problem behavior developed repeatedly in successive pigs.

There have also been other instances: hamsters that stopped working in a glass case after four or five reinforcements, porpoises and whales that swallow their manipulanda (balls and inner tubes), cats that will not leave the area of the feeder, rabbits that will not go to the feeder, the great difficulty in many species of conditioning vocalization with food reinforcement, problems in conditioning a kick in a cow, the failure to get appreciably increased effort out of the ungulates with increased drive, and so on. These we shall not dwell on in detail, nor shall we discuss how they might be overcome.

These egregious failures came as a rather considerable shock to us, for there was nothing in our background in behaviorism to prepare us for such gross inabilities to predict and control the behavior of animals with which we had been working for years.

The examples listed we feel represent a clear and utter failure of conditioning theory. They are far from what one would normally expect on the basis of the theory alone. Furthermore, they are definite, observable; the diagnosis of theory failure does not depend on subtle statistical interpretations or on semantic legerdemain—the animal simply does not do what he has been conditioned to do.

It seems perfectly clear that, with the possible exception of the dancing chicken, which could conceivably, as we have said, be explained in terms of Skinner's superstition paradigm, the other instances do not fit the behavioristic way of thinking. Here we have animals, after having been conditioned to a specific learned response, gradually drifting into behaviors that are entirely different from those which were conditioned. Moreover, it can easily be seen that these particular behaviors to which the animals drift are clear-cut examples of instinctive behaviors having to do with the natural food-getting behaviors of the particular species.

The dancing chicken is exhibiting the gallinaceous birds' scratch pattern that in nature often precedes ingestion. The chicken that hammers capsules is obviously exhibiting instinctive behavior having to do with breaking open of seed pods or the killing of insects, grubs, etc. The raccoon is demonstrating so-called "washing behavior." The rubbing and washing response may result, for example, in the removal of the exoskeleton of a crayfish. The pig is rooting or shaking—behaviors which are strongly built into this species and are connected with the food-getting repertoire.

These patterns to which the animals drift require greater physical output and therefore are a violation of the so-called "law of least effort." And most damaging of all, they stretch out the time required for reinforcement when nothing in the experimental setup requires them to do so. They have only to do the little tidbit of behavior to which they were conditioned—for example, pick up the coin and put it in the container—to get reinforced immediately. Instead, they drag the process out for a matter of minutes when there is nothing in the contingency which forces them to do this. Moreover, increasing the drive merely intensifies this effect.

It seems obvious that these animals are trapped by strong instinctive behaviors, and clearly we have here a demonstration of the prepotency of such behavior patterns over those which have been conditioned.

We have termed this phenomenon "instinctive drift." The general principle seems to be that wherever an animal has strong instinctive behaviors in the area of the conditioned response, after continued running the organism will drift toward the instinctive behavior to the detriment of the conditioned behavior and even to the delay or preclusion of the reinforcement. In a very boiled-down, simplified form, it might be stated as "learned behavior drifts toward instinctive behavior."

All this, of course, is not to disparage the use of conditioning techniques, but is intended as a demonstration that there are definite weaknesses in the philosophy underlying these techniques. The pointing out of such weaknesses should make possible a worthwhile revision in behavior theory.

The notion of instinct has now become one of our basic concepts in an effort to make sense of the welter of observations which confront us. When behaviorism tossed out instinct, it is our feeling that some of its power of prediction and control were lost with it. From the foregoing examples, it appears that although it was easy to banish the Instinctivists from the science during the Behavioristic Revolution, it was not possible to banish instinct so easily.

And if, as Hebb suggests, it is advisable to reconsider those things that behaviorism explicitly threw out, perhaps it might likewise be advisable to examine what they tacitly brought in—the hidden assumptions which led most disastrously to these breakdowns in the theory.

Three of the most important of these tacit assumptions seem to us to be: that the animal comes to the laboratory as a virtual *tabula rasa*, that species differences are insignificant, and that all responses are about equally conditionable to all stimuli.

It is obvious, we feel, from the foregoing account, that these assumptions are no longer tenable. After 14 years of continuous conditioning and observation of thousands of animals, it is our reluctant conclusion that the behavior of any species cannot be adequately understood, predicted, or controlled without knowledge of its instinctive patterns, evolutionary history, and ecological niche.

In spite of our early successes with the application of behavioristically oriented conditioning theory, we readily admit now that ethological facts and attitudes in recent years have done more to advance our practical control of animal behavior than recent reports from American "learning labs."

Moreover, as we have recently discovered, if one begins with evolution and instinct as the basic format for the science, a very illuminating viewpoint can be developed which leads naturally to a drastically revised and simplified conceptual framework of startling explanatory power (to be reported elsewhere).

It is hoped that this playback on the theory will be behavioral technology's partial repayment to the academic science whose impeccable empiricism we have used so extensively.

REFERENCES

BEACH, F. A. The snark was a boojum. *Amer. Psychologist,* 1950, 5, 115–124.

BRELAND, K., & BRELAND, M. A field of applied animal psychology. *Amer. Psychologist,* 1951, 6, 202–204.

HEBB, D. O. The American revolution. *Amer. Psychologist,* 1960, 15, 735–745.

LORENZ, K. Innate behaviour patterns. In *Symposia of the Society for Experimental Biology. No. 4. Physiological mechanisms in animal behaviour.* New York: Academic Press, 1950.

SKINNER, B. F. Superstition in the pigeon. *J. exp. Psychol.,* 1948, 38, 168–172.

TINBERGEN, N. *The study of instinct.* Oxford: Clarendon, 1951.

WHALEN, R. E. Comparative psychology. *Amer. Psychologist,* 1961, 16, 84.

8.

Major Challenges for Students of Infancy and Early Childhood

MYRTLE B. McGRAW

Most developmental psychologists (or "researchers of growth," as this author calls them) study such topics as sensory and motor development, cognitive and language development, child-rearing patterns, and the socialization of the child. McGraw suggests here that we need new theories and concepts in order to "develop to the maximum all potentials of the growing child" in a society that is undergoing change. For example, the concept of "critical periods" in learning has sometimes been used to argue against the feasibility of compensatory education programs. But are there not alternative ways of viewing "critical periods" that could answer this argument? Another example: Can we develop new theories on child-rearing out of the recent experiences with kibbutzim and other communal living arrangements?

IT IS not possible to pinpoint any particular ideologies or theories that have given rise to the present interest in early childhood development. The forces were many; they were complex and intertwined. Sputnik shocked the nation out of a state of educational complacency. The disparity of educational opportunities and achievements of children from differing socioeconomic and ethnic groups was brought to light. Then it was determined that children from less favorable environments entered school with educational handicaps already established. To alleviate this situation, the federal government set up Head Start

Reprinted from *American Psychologist*, 1970, *25*, pp. 754–56. Copyright 1967 by the American Psychological Association. Reprinted by permission.

programs. The outcome of the Head Start programs has led to the claim that even the prekindergarten period is too late—education begins in the cradle. Furthermore, since the body of knowledge doubles every 10 years, the amount of knowledge one must master favors an early beginning.

Clearly, the goal of this current wave of concern is to develop the optimum potentials of all children. The pressure is on learning, early learning. It seems clear that the infant and toddler are capable of learning a great deal, *if* the opportunities for learning are properly presented. It also seems evident that the principles of learning derived from laboratory studies of animals or college students are inadequate when it comes to dealing with rapid behavior development of the human infant. The prevailing notion is that these goals can be achieved by manipulation of the environments in which the child lives. To some extent these ideas are reinforced by experiments of the effects of "sensory deprivation," "prolonged isolation," and the comparative effects of "enriched and impoverished" environments. Such studies have been conducted on animals, children, and adults. Once again, the emphasis seems to be shifting to the environmental side of the scale, but it is not locked in with the old heredity-environment dichotomy. It is generally recognized now that nature-nurture are interdependent forces, and to try to separate them clouds inquiry. A few studies (Fowler, 1962; McGraw, 1935; Moore, 1960) have demonstrated that the performances of the young *in particular activities* can be advanced beyond normal expectancy. But we have not as yet learned how to develop to the maximum *all potentials of the growing child.* To do this we shall need new theories or concepts of development that transcend the established principles of learning.

CHALLENGE FOR THE RESEARCHERS OF GROWTH

The present corps of growth scientists are the legatees of a vast body of concepts, theories, and research strategies inherited from the "psychological establishment." Of course, the growth scientists will be drawn from many disciplines and from diverse areas of psychology, other than developmental. Already it is apparent that some dyed-in-the-wool experimentalists are selecting the human infant in preference to animals for special investigations. The challenge for all the students of growth—regardless of their scientific expertise and theoretical orientation—is to scan their legacy of knowledge and skills and to have the courage to rule out those theories and techniques that are not applicable to the study of a complex, ever-changing phenomenon, such as growth. Many experimentalists fail to take into account that their own preconceptions may operate as uncontrolled variables within a particular situation. Will the experimentalist, skillful in the manipulation of the variables and instruments of measurement, become able to recognize that the way the infant is held or positioned may also be a factor in the results obtained? Will the examiner be so focused on the toddler's response to the items set before him that he fails to detect that the child's wiggling and climbing off the chair and running toward the door is his way of saying that there is pressure on his bladder? Will researchers trained to use the IQ or just chronological age be able to devise strategies to evaluate a multiplicity of systems constantly in flux, each system influencing another and in different degrees? All growth and development is not in the form of accretion. The growth scientists will need to design methods that reveal the rises and falls, the pulsations and rhythms manifest in the growth of a given function. An understanding of these pulsations and rhythms may become promising guidelines for the development of optimum potentials of the growing child. Strategies developed in other disciplines (e.g., communication theories) may provide suggestive models for evaluating constantly changing phenomena, such as rapid growth during the early years. There is evidence that many of the current investigators (Endler, Boulter, & Osser, 1968) are alert to the problem, and that is the first step to improving methodologies.

THE CHALLENGE OF CULTURAL ACCEPTANCE OF SCIENTIFIC THEORIES

In the past, it has been traditional for scientists, especially those dealing with basic sciences, to be removed from the applied aspects of their findings. They were searching for fundamental truths, and whatever society did with [these] was none of their concern. On the other hand, many atomic physicists have begun to voice a sense of responsibility for the way society makes use of their knowledge. During this century we have been able to see how many psychological theories have been applied and misapplied to the matter of child rearing and education. If the periods of infancy and the early years are as important for total development as generally contended, then it is reasonable to expect the behavioral scientists to take some responsibility for the way in which their thoughts and theories are adopted into the cultural patterns of child management. Just how this can be done is not clear because it has never been systematically undertaken by any scientific discipline. The general public has faith in science and mass media and is quick to announce, "Science proves thus and so." Sometimes the misapplication of a theory may be ascribed to the use of a particular word, perhaps a word that was originally drawn from another discipline.

Let us consider for a moment some current thoughts that have the potential for creating parental anxiety. Take the question of "critical periods" as applied to learning. The concept was first used by embryologists. It was reinforced by Lorenz's (1935) study of imprinting. Recently, it has been emphasized in connection with studies of the effects of an impoverished environment. It has been asserted that if the impoverishment occurs at critical periods in development, then the damage done may be irreversible. Back in 1935, the writer applied the term "critical periods" to the acquisition of motor skills during infancy. If the agreed meaning of "critical periods" carries the idea that whatever is attained in development or learning must be achieved during a specified period, then the term should not be applied to normal behavioral growth. In the aforementioned instance, it was intended to signify that there are *opportune* times when specific activities can most economically be learned. If one misses that opportune time, then the methods of instruction should be altered for later learning of the same function. It is the irreversibility of damage done that adds emotion and fear to the "critical period" concept.

Just the amount of emphasis attached to certain concepts can also distort their meaning when adopted into the culture. Take, for example, the current emphasis on cognition. No investigator would contend that cognition operates independently of other aspects of learning. Yet, merely because it is the focus of investigative activity, cognition, like personality adjustment of old, is a kind of umbrella for all other goals: expose the child to the right knowledge, in the right way, and at the right time—then the job would be well done.

Perhaps most urgently of all, the growth scientists need to review the accepted principles of learning as they have been articulated and generally accepted. These principles of learning were determined largely by studies of animal subjects in laboratory situations and studies of children in the classroom. As stated above, there is every reason to suspect that they are not applicable to the process of growth taking place during infancy and during the early years. There is a pressing need for totally new guidelines for the benefit of those persons responsible for the management and socialization of the child from birth to three years of age. Obviously the most dominant force is change, change in the organism and change in behavior from day to day. Consistency in parental management does not mean setting up a pattern or rule and sticking to it. It means, rather, dealing with a child in a manner consistent with his developmental changes. To do this effectively requires knowledge, sensitivity, intuition, and flexibility. So the challenge is to orient mothers and teachers toward the concept of change, not toward stability in the ordinary sense. Parents should be taught to observe, to scan, and to detect the nonverbal as well as verbal signals of growth within the child and to design methods of instruction accordingly.

The United States may well be at the threshold of institutional reorganization for the care and education of the young. To develop maximum potentials of children of this age will require special preparation on the part of those responsible for this age group. They need to be not only knowledgeable but intuitive and observant. We have long adhered to the tradition that the biological parents are the ones best qualified to bring up young children. Whether we continue to follow that tradition or turn the education of the young over to specialists—kibbutz fashion—the personnel will require special preparation quite unlike that offered to elementary school teachers or even mothers of today.

The growth scientists are challenged to provide a theoretical frame of reference for the education of this crucial age group. And they are advised also to take account of the way in which their theories and pronouncements are adopted into the culture so that the growing child of today can confidently meet the social changes of the twenty-first century.

REFERENCES

ENDLER, N. S., BOULTER, L. R., & OSSER, H. *Contemporary issues in developmental psychology.* New York: Holt, Rinehart & Winston, 1968.

FOWLER, W. Teaching a two-year-old to read: An experiment in early childhood reading. *Genetic Psychology Monographs,* 1962, **66**, 181–283.

LORENZ, K. J. Der Kumpan in der Umwelt des Vogels. Der Artgenosse als auslösendes Moment sozialer Verhaltungsweisen. *Journal of Ornithology (Leipzig),* 1935, **83**, 137–213.

McGRAW, M. B. *Growth: A Study of Johnny and Jimmy.* New York: Appleton-Century, 1935.

MOORE, O. K. *Automated responsive environments.* Hamden, Conn.: Basic Education, Inc., 1960. (Film)

9.

Jewishness, Blackishness, and the Nature-Nurture Controversy

SEYMOUR B. SARASON

In 1969 Arthur Jensen published an article entitled "How Much Can We Boost IQ and Scholastic Achievement?" His article and the controversy that derived from it brought public attention once more to the question of whether heredity (nature) or environment (nurture) was the principal determinant of those primarily cognitive skills that we call intelligence. Jensen held that measured intelligence (IQ) is primarily genetically determined, that the difference between blacks and whites in IQ scores is probably genetic, and that therefore compensatory education programs like Head Start are doomed to fail.

For publishing this article, Jensen has been subjected to diatribes, threats of physical violence, and in some quarters ostracism, in some cases by people who neither read his article nor understood the nature of his analysis of the data. On the other hand, some perfectly valid arguments against his position have been voiced: that many of the studies on which he based his conclusions were methodologically defective, that there are studies that clearly show increments in IQ with improved environment, that IQ tests are culturally biased, and so on. Among the more interesting of these critiques is the following article by Seymour Sarason, who points out by comparing the Jewish and Black experiences that certain attitudinal and behavioral aspects of a group are not likely to change noticeably in a short period of time. Could we truly have expected, then, that compensatory education programs could undo in a short time what centuries have built up?

Reprinted from *American Psychologist*, November 1973, *28*, pp. 962–71. Copyright 1973 by the American Psychological Association. Reprinted by permission.

THOSE WHO have participated in the recent version of the nature-nurture controversy have, for the most part, neglected to confront the derivation of their time perspective in relation to social change in general and historically rooted group attitudes and performance in particular. As in past versions of the controversy, the issues have centered around personal and social values, methodology, the content of the measuring instruments, sampling problems, and genetic theories and laws, and the consequences of these issues for programs of social action. There seems to be recognition by all that social history is an important variable, that inequity and prejudice have been and are rampant, and that it is probably impossible at the present time to discuss the controversy in a dispassionate way. Within scientific circles it is an explosive issue, just as it is in the society at large. I assume that if a study were done asking people if they thought that future versions of controversy (say 20 or 40 years from now) would be conducted in a less explosive climate, almost all would reply in the negative. Indeed, many would probably predict a more explosive climate. If a similar study had been done 50 years ago when, after World War I, the nature-nurture controversy was once again peaking, far fewer people would have correctly predicted the present climate of social explosiveness in which the controversy is taking place. (At that time, interestingly enough, blacks were not central to the controversy. The inferiority of blacks was not then a burning issue, presumably because it was uncritically accepted by most people [white and black] as a fact which did not need to be labored. It was the flood of immigrant groups from Europe and Asia that brought together questions of national policy and the status of knowledge about the determinants of intellectual performance.) Today, sides have been taken and with a degree of partisanship that the passage of time will not easily change— a variant of my thesis that changes in attitude and performance of historically rooted groups are relatively immune to change except when viewed from a time perspective in which the basic measuring unit may be a century. When I say a century I do not mean it in a precise or literal way, but rather as a means to emphasize a time perspective far longer than that which we ordinarily adopt.

For a statement and description of my position convincingly to reflect my thinking requires that I be unusually personal and relatively unhindered by considerations of modesty, politeness, and that undefined criterion of "good taste." I shall talk about aspects of myself and my family not only because they are the "data" I know best, but because I assume (phenomenologically I *know*) that I am quite representative of Jews, possessed of all the ingredients that comprise Jewishness. What I have to say has been said, and far better, by other Jews. I justify going over old ground because, as the title of this article suggests, I wish to relate it to an important and fateful social and scientific issue. Here, too, I make no claim to originality, although I believe that I provide an emphasis that has been lacking in the scientific literature.

JEWISHNESS

I begin with my father, a simple, unassuming, relatively inarticulate man who spent a long working life as a cutter of children's dresses. He was not an impressive person. He did not read books, but he went to synagogue and obviously knew the Old Testament (in Hebrew) backward and forward. As he prayed, he kept the books open and turned the pages, but rarely did more than glance at them. He recited the prayers in a most undeviating, ritualistic manner. Beginning at age 8 or 9, having enrolled me in Hebrew school, he expected me to sit and pray with him. Of course, I did not understand what I was reading (or even why), and when from time to time my boredom and anger forced me to ask why the book could not be put into English, he never deemed the question worthy of a response.

He loved children and had a gentleness with them to which they responded, but my memory contains nothing that would support the notion that he had other than a primitive notion of children and learning. The early sources of my anger toward my father were many, but two are particularly relevant here. One concerns a leather-covered Oxford dictionary which I had not the strength to pick up until I was six or seven. I still have the dictionary, and when it comes to its weight I know whereof I speak. I never saw my father use that dictionary, and to me its presence was symbolic of his selfishness: Why did we have *that* around the house when we (I) needed other things? Why didn't we hide it, sell it, or throw it out? Occasionally I would peruse its pages, but the book was so large and heavy that even when I did not have to hold it, I could not comfortably use it. Related to this was our battle about the *New York Times*, which he bought and read every day. Why buy a newspaper that did not have funnies? How more selfish could a father be than to deprive his children of newspaper funnies, particularly on Sundays, when all other newspapers contained loads of them? I hated the *New York Times*, which, I need not tell you, I now read every day. I also have an aversion to funnies and truly cannot comprehend why my wife and daughter read them first when the local paper arrives—and sometimes even argue about who will read them first.

And then there were my older male cousins who, when I was in elementary school, were preparing to go to college. At that time I knew as much about college as I did about astronomy. There was a place called college and there were stars in the sky, and that exhausted my knowledge of both. But in the numerous meetings of the extended family that word *college* kept coming up in reverent and awesome tones. Cousin Leo was not going to any college, he was going to a place called Cornell and that showed (not to me) that Leo was smart because not many Jewish boys were *allowed* there. And if Leo did well there, as *of course* he would, he was then going to go to still another kind of college and become a doctor. Cousin Moey was a very smart fellow, too, and wasn't it too bad that he had to work during the day and go to college at night. Go to college at night! What kind of craziness was that? To me that meant he couldn't listen to the radio at night, those being the days when having a radio was still a novelty. It was during these early years that I kept hearing the phrase "He will make something of himself" applied to some of my relatives.

There was Leo's brother, Oscar, who was special. If I had available to me then the words I have now I would have described Oscar to my friends as smart-smart. That's the way the family regarded him. But Oscar posed a real problem because he played football, and extremely well. He was as good in football as he was in the classroom. That Oscar was on the small side was only one reason for family opposition to playing football. It was important because he might get "good and hurt," not be able to go to school, and maybe not even go to college. The more important point was that nice Jewish boys, particularly if they were smart-smart, didn't play football. That was for the gentiles (goys), who were by nature not smart; they were, instead, and again by nature, crudely physical and aggressive. Football was quintessentially goyish, and it was stupid for Jewish boys to compete in that arena. David may have slain Goliath, thanks to God, but that was in another world. Let's respect David, but let us not go so far as to identify with his actions! One Saturday morning I walked into my cousin's apartment—we lived upstairs, those being the days of extended families in restricted areas, and I use the word "restricted" in its geographical and discriminatory senses—and I heard my aunt yelling and screaming in Oscar's room. There was Oscar curled up womblike being pounded by my aunt at the same time that she was telling him and the world what she thought of a Jewish boy who was going to play football for his high school *on Saturday*. What had she done to deserve such punishment? What would *they* think? "They" referred to all her Jewish friends and neighbors who, she was sure, would both blame and sympathize with her on one of the worst fates a Jewish mother could experience. How could a mother stand by and watch her child, with such a "good head," go straight to hell? It was an awesome display of physical energy and verbal imagery—my Aunt Jennie was regarded by all as having no equal when it came to using and inventing the Yiddish equivalents of longshoreman language. When her physical energy was spent (the verbal flow never ceased), Oscar got up from the bed, collected his football suit, calmly but sweetly said good-bye, and went off to join the goyim in defense of the glory of Newark's Barringer High School. Needless to say, when he went to Brown, where he was quite a football player during the years when that college had its best teams, my aunt attended a number of games (*on Saturday*) because, I assume, she wanted to be on hand when her little boy would be near-fatally injured. He was no more than five feet nine inches tall and probably weighed no more than 170 pounds. Leonard Carmichael, who was then chairman of the Department of Psychology at Brown, once got Oscar aside and expressed concern that he could be injured and was, perhaps, wasting his time playing football when he could start making a career in psychology, in which Professor Carmichael had concluded Oscar had shown considerable aptitude.

Oscar was directly important in my life. Toward the end of the first semester of my first year in junior high school, Oscar, home from college for a few days, visited our family. He interrogated my mother about the courses I was taking and was horrified to learn that I was enrolled in the commercial curriculum, taking such courses as typing, junior business training, etc. He told my mother that if I stayed in the commercial curriculum I would not be admitted to college. My mother was aghast and took action. A few weeks later, at the beginning of the next semester, I found myself taking Latin, ancient history, and algebra.

I do not have to relate more anecdotes to make the point that being Jewish was inextricably interwoven with attitudes toward intellectual accomplishment. To separate the one from the other was impossible. This did not mean that being Jewish meant that one was smart or capable of intellectual accomplishments, but it meant that one had respect for such strivings. Respect is too weak a word to convey the force and role of these attitudes. It is like saying that we have respect for breathing. We did not have to learn these attitudes in any consciously deliberate way. We had no choice in the matter, just as we had no choice in choosing our parents. As children, we did not have to verbalize these attitudes to ourselves, we would not have known how. The word *attitudes* is a poor one to describe what and how we absorbed what we did. We learned those attitudes in as "natural" a way as learning to like lox and bagels, gefilte fish, or knishes.

How do we account for the strength and frequency of these aspects of Jewishness? Please note that I am not asking how to account for individuals like myself or my mother and father or my cousins, but rather why these aspects are characteristics of Jews as a group. This is, initially, at least, a cultural, not a psychological, question. It is a question which directs us, among other things, to history and tradition and requires the adoption of a time perspective quite different from what we ordinarily use when our focus is on a single individual or generation. Obviously, if these aspects of Jewishness have been manifested for generations and centuries, the outlines of an answer to my question become clear—and I do not confuse clarity of outline with complexity of the substantive answer. These aspects, when looked upon in the context of the sweep of social-cultural history, have always characterized Jewish life. Indeed, when one looks at my question from this time perspective, one ends up by asking another question: So what else is new? Or, one becomes intrigued by individual Jews who do not possess these characteristics, whose mental breathing apparatus inexplicably did not take in ingredients ever present in this social-cultural atmosphere.

The aspects of Jewishness I have thus far discussed are not understandable by looking only at the present or near past. That is an obvious point which needed to be said in order to make a second one: *These aspects have been and will continue to be immune to change in any short period of time, by which I mean a minimum of a century.* Leaving aside Hitler's "final solution" as well as other types of world catastrophes, I can think of no set of circumstances in which these aspects of Jewishness would disappear or be noticeably diluted in less than several or scores of generations. These circumstances could not be casual or indirect, they would have to be extremely potent and persistent. More of this later when I question the rationale behind the expectation that certain consequences of some aspects of blackishness can be changed noticeably in a decade or so, or that if blacks and whites differ on tests, one can ignore the relation of these differences to differences in the psychological core of blackishness and whiteishness, or that when you have equated a group of blacks and whites on an intelligence test or on a measure of academic achievement you have controlled for the most influential psychological determinants of intellectual performance in real life. (It's like saying that everybody is equal before the law, the person on welfare as well as the millionaire. There *is* a difference between facts and the truth.)

Now to another aspect of Jewishness to which I have alluded: the knowledge (it is not a feeling, it is phenomenologically a fact) that one is in a hostile world. This was crystal clear in my parents' and grandparents' generations. Their thinking went like this: Built into the mental core of every non-Jew is a dislike of and an enmity toward Jews. Yes, there were some nice Gentiles and up to a point you could trust and work with them, but let any conflict or dissension enter into the relationship and you would find that core of hatred asserting itself. It might not be verbalized, but, nonetheless, you could count on it. In the end, and there is always an end, you would get it in the neck—no ifs, ands, or buts. I have long felt that their resistance to mixed marriages— and the word *resistance* does not begin to convey the bitterness and strength of the feelings—was less a consequence of religion or clan-nishness than it was of the fear of physical injury to or destruction of one's child. To say they mistrusted the non-Jewish world is to reveal a genius for understatement. And if you tried to reason with them it was no contest because they could overwhelm you with history. They could marshall evidence from past centuries, as well as events in their own lives, with a rapidity, force, and cogency that doctoral students in history must fantasize about when they approach their orals. If you get a kick out of unproductive arguments I suggest you specialize in com-bating history with logic and goodwill—the kicks are endless. (If orthodox Jews are unavailable, try it with blacks, who have more kinship to Jews in this respect than they know.) If an aspect of you is poignantly and consciously rooted in history, you are not a candidate for attitude change. We would have had a more solid and realistic foundation for our efforts at social change if American social psychol-ogy had dealt with historically rooted, conscious attitudes of histor-ically rooted groups. At the very least, it might have provided a more realistic time perspective about the attainment of the goals of these efforts.

What about me and my generation who, unlike our parents and grandparents, were born in this country with its traditions of op-portunity and freedom? Did we possess the aspect of Jewishness that says this is a hostile world, even though "objectively" we grew up in a social environment radically different from that of previous genera-tions? The very fact that our family had been created in this country and not in a European one meant that it would be different from what went before. You could write for years about the differences and when you were all through and began to list the similarities you would soon be listing the aspect "This is a hostile world for Jews." Some anecdotes from my adult life: When in 1938 I applied for admission to graduate school the knotty question was whether or not I would lie about being Jewish. Those were the days when you were asked for your religion and a photograph. They also wanted to know your father's occupation. So if I told them my father was a cutter of children's dresses, that I was Jewish, plus the fact that I would be graduated from an unrec-ognized college (Dana College, renamed the University of Newark, housed then in the former Feigenspan Brewery) what would be my chances? The point is not what was objectively true but the strength of my feeling that my application would be read by people hostile to Jews. The strength of my feeling and its automatic and indiscriminate application were not justified, but it is the hallmark of historically rooted attitudes of historically rooted groups that there is a discrepancy between external conditions and subjective impressions. (This is true for blacks in regard to whites, as it is for the Irish in regard to the English, etc.) The fact that these attitudes receive periodic reinforcement is sufficient to maintain their strength and indiscriminateness. For example, why does a colleague of mine still have in his possession a letter written to him in 1939 by a most eminent person who was then chairman of the department of psychology of a prestigious university? I have seen the letter. It is a remarkable but not surprising document because it says that although my colleague had all the paper credentials to be admitted to the doctoral program, he should think hard about coming because, as a Jew, he would not be able to be placed in a teaching job. A list of names is given of Jewish students who finished their doctorates in that department but who could not get jobs. Come, the letter says, but only if you regard it as an "intellectual adventure" and not as preparation for a career. How complicated a theory do we need to understand why my colleague, like myself, generalized our expectation of discrimination indiscriminately?

I lived in a radically different world than my parents and grandparents. I differed from them in countless important ways, but I differed not at all from them in the possession of this aspect of Jewishness. When I was finishing graduate school in 1942, there were two other students, and good friends (Jorma Niven, Harry Older), who were also going into the job market. To avoid competition among us, we did not apply for jobs at the same colleges or universities. Jorma and Harry were not Jewish, but they understood what was at stake when I wondered whether on my vita I should note that I was Jewish and so avoid interviews at places that did not look kindly on Jews. The point of these anecdotes is not to say something about the external world or even my perception of it but rather the pervasiveness and strength of my psychological radar about Jewishness, a constantly tuned instrument that was always at work and always sighting "objects" about which I had to decide whether they were friend or foe. But why do I say *was?* It is as true of me today as it was then, and with far less justification. My external world has changed dramatically within my lifetime, it has changed even more in relation to my parents' world, and yet that radar continues to work as if the external world has not changed.

A year ago when I was at a social gathering at Yale's Hillel, the Rabbi told me, in confidence and with that all too familiar mixture of pride and fear, that approximately one-third of all students at Yale were Jewish. He did not have to put into words (or even bother to look at me to see if I understood his message) that this information should not be bandied about because it might arouse the envy and enmity of non-Jews. You might expect such an attitude in a rabbi but not in me, but such an expectation simply ignores what fine-tuned, efficient processes and mechanisms cultural transmission consists of, insuring that the most central aspects of our sense of identity are independent of choice and changes in our external world.

I have known scores of Jews of my generation who have visited Israel. They were heterogeneous in many respects so that if you administered to them every psychological test that has ever been standardized, I predict you would find that, intelligence tests and political attitudes aside, the scores would be distributed in a fairly normal fashion. With no exception, every one of them spontaneously described the feeling—compounded of surprise, disbelief, relief, and security—they had in response to the fact that "everyone there is Jewish." As one of them said in deep puzzlement: "Even though I knew everyone was Jewish, I found that I continued to ask myself whether this or that person was Jewish. It was very unsettling at times." There are some attitudinal radars that cannot be turned off, because they have no off-on switch. These visitors shared another reaction, this one compounded of respect, envy, and pride and put by one of them in this way: "They have no fear. They don't care what the rest of the world thinks and does. They are prepared to fight and they have no doubt who will win in the end." To the non-Israeli Jew, "in the end" meant and still means getting it in the neck; to the Israeli it means quite the reverse. It took several generations of Israeli sabras, with an assist from Hitler, to effect a change in attitude. Put more correctly: It took all of that for a millennia-old identification to reassert itself. It was all right now to identify with David because one had to, and like David, but unlike those at Masada, [one could expect that] the Goliath would be defeated. How strange this is to the American Jew. How strange it would be to the Israeli to learn about my reaction to an item in last week's *Yale Daily* that 50% of this year's Phi Beta Kappas were Jewish. He would have difficulty understanding my unreflective fear that this would not sit well in the minds of many non-Jews.

What about the younger generation of Jews in our society? Is this aspect of Jewishness in them or has it been eroded? As best as I can determine, this core of Jewishness is in them despite obvious changes in our society. When I asked a group of Jewish students about this, they looked at me as only smart-smart teen-agers can look at dumb-dumb professors, and one of them said: "In high school I read *The Wall*. There *was* the 1967 six-day war. And when I apply to medical school I know the chances of Jews have been decreased because they will take more minority people. How are we supposed to feel when we read that an African leader is sorry that Hitler did not win and that some black groups in our country seem to talk in the same way?" Toward the end of the discussion a young woman said, somewhat hostilely: "Because my parents were like you. What did *you* tell your daughter about going with or marrying a non-Jew?" A bull's-eye! Her comments recalled to me the time our family of three was about to leave our house to begin our first trip abroad. Just as we were ready to leave, my daughter (who then was 10) said she had forgotten something and went upstairs to get it. The "it" turned out to be a chain to which was attached a gold Star of David. No, my wife and I had not given it to her because we are not religious.[1] It had been given to her by a Catholic nun who was head of an agency to which I had been a consultant, but that is another story, albeit a quite relevant one.

Before continuing, let me summarize what I have tried to say:

1. There are certain attitudinal characteristics which are part of the core of Jewishness. What is notable is their frequency and strength.

2. These characteristics are a kind of "second nature," learned, absorbed, and inculcated with all the force, subtleness, and efficiency of the processes of cultural transmission.

3. To understand the frequency and strength of these characteristics requires a time perspective of centuries.

4. Similarly, these characteristics could not be extinguished or diluted in strength except over very long periods of time. What centuries have produced will not quickly change even under external pressures.

5. It is impossible to understand and evaluate intellectual performance of groups without taking account of each group's attitudes toward such activity. This is an obvious point to anyone who has engaged in clinical work, and it has received substantial support in the research literature, for example, the test anxiety literature. It is no less valid a point when one deals with the intellectual performance of historically rooted groups and their historically rooted attitudes. (Women's liberation groups, now and in the distant past, [have] understood this point quite well. The original title of this article was "Jewishness, Blackishness, Femaleness, and the Nature-Nurture Controversy.")

I have no difficulty accepting the notion that intelligence has its genetic components, nor do I have difficulty with the idea that dif-

---

[1] Jewishness, at least for many Jews in our society, is independent of religiousness, a fact which many rabbis keep complaining about, because they believe that when the two are experienced as independent, it will, over time, result in the disappearance of both. That they are experienced as independent was seen during the Israeli-Arab six-day war in 1967, as thousands of American Jews who had no interest in or commitment to Judaism spontaneously gave money for the support of Israel. The generosity of support is perhaps less relevant than the anxiety they felt about the threat to the continuation of Jewishness, not to the religion of their ancestors.

ferent groups may possess different patterns of abilities. It would require mental derangement of a most serious sort to deny that different groups get different scores on various tests of intelligence. But I have the greatest difficulty understanding how anyone can come to a definitive conclusion in these matters based on studies which assume that what culture and history have created can be changed in a matter of years or decades. What combination of ignorance and presumption, what kind of understanding of human history does one have to possess to accept the hypothesis that the central psychological core of *historically* rooted groups can markedly change in a lifetime? It is a fact that Jews as a group score high on intelligence tests, do well on achievement tests, and are disproportionately represented in the professions and academia. It may be true that this is in part a consequence of selective survival and breeding over the centuries. But if one invokes the law of parsimony (not for the purposes of denying a hypothesis or preventing anyone from pursuing a particular line of research) for the purpose of assigning weights to variables on the basis of what we know about culture, one must conclude that the transmission of Jewishness from generation to generation has been fantastically successful—a view of "success" understood but probably not shared by those approaching their deaths in the Nazi holocaust, the Spanish inquisition, and countless other Jew-murdering periods in history. My genes have a long history, an indisputable fact. My Jewishness also has a long history, another indisputable fact. At this point in time we know far more about my Jewishness than about my genes. When as a society we mount programs of social amelioration, I would prefer to act on the basis of the known, recognizing that I will not be alive to know the ultimate outcome.

BLACKISHNESS

What I have to say about "blackishness" has been foreshadowed by my description of certain aspects of Jewishness.[2] Jews and blacks share the characteristic "this is a hostile world." Some would argue that the sensitivity of blacks to anticipated hostility is stronger than it is in Jews. I am not sure this is the case, although some blacks and Jews would consider it self-evidently true. The more I talk to Jews about this, the more I am impressed by two things: how strong this aspect is and how much

---

[2] Obviously, I cannot talk about blackishness with the affective nuance and depth of knowledge and experience [with which] I can talk about Jewishness, nor is it necessary that I try or important that I cannot do justice to an equally complex cultural-psychological core. Sufficient for my purpose is that I pinpoint certain communalities and differences and their significance for the nature-nurture controversy.

they want to believe that it isn't strong. Their self-report about its workings is discrepant with its strength. I stick with this point because it is instructive about what happens when two historically rooted attitudes contradict each other: "This is a hostile world" and "this is a society free of prejudice." In any event, this aspect of blackishness (in white society) is historically rooted and will be immune to change except over a long, long period of time. Blacks, of course, are absolutely correct when they say that an equally long period of time will be required for whites to overcome *their* historically rooted attitudes toward blacks.

In our society, at least, blackishness has not had at its core unbounded respect for book learning and the acquisition of academically soaked, cognitive skills. Just as when the Jews in Egypt were slaves, did manual labor, and could only hope for survival and dream of freedom, so in black culture, intellectuality or bookishness (call it what you will) has been far from the top on the priority list. As groups, Jews and blacks could not be more far apart than on the degree to which their cultures are suffused with "intellectuality." On intelligence tests Jews get higher scores than blacks.[3] *From my perspective, the important question is not how to explain the difference but why the difference is not greater.* This reminds me of Goddard's description of the Kallikak culture and his use of it as proof of Kallikak mental inferiority passed on from generation to generation. From his description of that encapsulated culture, one might conclude that the Kallikaks were a biologically superior group, that is, anyone who could grow up and survive in that culture must have been extremely well endowed constitutionally.

Over the past century, more and more blacks have "made it" in the intellectual arena, but they have represented a very small percentage of all blacks. It is my impression that compared even to three decades

[3] There was a time (decades ago) when Jews, like blacks today, were viewed as being mentally inferior because of inferior genetic endowment. I am indebted to my colleague Edward Zigler (personal communication, 1973) for pointing out to me the anti-Jewish attitudes of the early eugenicists, particularly Galton and Pearson. In a manuscript he is preparing, Zigler states:

Pearson continually employed genetic arguments in his efforts to stem the immigration of Polish and Russian Jews into England, arguing that they were genetically inferior to the earlier settlers of the English nation. He concluded, "Taken on the average, and regarding both sexes, this alien Jewish population is somewhat inferior physically and mentally to the native population. . . .

The anti-Jewish attitude of the early eugenicists finally culminated in the complete bastardization of the eugenics movement in Nazi Germany, where the "final solution" of dealing with "races" of inferior genetic stock was to murder them in gas ovens. It is interesting to note that less than 50 years after Pearson's assertion of the genetic inferiority of the Jews, another distinguished Englishman, C. P. Snow, argued that in light of the large number of Jewish Nobel laureates, the Jews must be a superior people. We thus see how tenuous indeed are those assertions that a particular group is inferior or superior.

ago, more black children experience something akin to what I described of my childhood, but there is no basis at all for concluding that this has become a characteristic experience. What warrant is there in psychological theory and research that would lead to the expectation that the attitudinal core of blackishness could, under the most favorable conditions, be changed in less than scores of generations. And is there a psychologist who would argue that we have even remotely approximated "the most favorable conditions."

For me, the central question is how theories determine time perspective, that is, how one's conception of what man and society are determines one's time perspective about changing either? I have discussed this in connection with the problem of changing schools and creating new settings (Sarason, 1971, 1972). Two examples of what I mean: What if someone came to us and asked why we cannot teach children to read in 24 hours? Assuming that we knew the person to be sane and we could control the tendency to throw him out of our office, what would we say? It would probably take us 24 hours of uninterrupted talk to explain how children develop physically, mentally, and socially; the inevitable social and interpersonal context in which learning takes place; the complexity of motivation and its vicissitudes; the knowledge and cognitive skills that are necessary for the productive assimilation and use of symbols; and the problems that can be created when external pressures do not take developmental stages' readiness into account. Besides, we might ask this irritating ignoramus, Do you mean why can't we teach *a* child to read in 24 hours or do you mean a *group* of children in a classroom?

A second example: What if we went to a psychoanalyst friend and asked him really to level with us and explain how he justifies seeing *a* patient for one hour a day, four or five days a week, perhaps for two, three, four, or more years. Why does it take that long? "Do you really believe," we ask him, "that it takes that long to be helpful to someone? Aren't there quicker ways of giving help?" "Friend" (?), he replies, "there is much you do not understand." He then proceeds to summarize for us what the human organism is at birth, how its cognitive and affective equipment is organized and develops, the ways in which it becomes increasingly psychologically and physically differentiated, how it develops and utilizes a variety of coping mechanisms, the sources of inevitable internal and external conflict, the nature and strength of resistances to change, the relationship of all of this to the interpersonal dynamics of the nuclear family, and on and on depending on whether our psychoanalyst friend is summarizing Freud's *Introductory Lectures* or multivolumed collected works. (If he happens to be a true believer, we would also hear about parricide and the primal horde in the dawning history of mankind.) "Now," he would say, "you can begin to understand why psychoanalytic treatment takes so long. It is not that we desire to prolong it, but rather that our understanding of man requires it if we are to be able meaningfully to help somebody radically change accustomed ways of thinking and acting. Of course," he would admit, "you can help troubled people in a shorter period of time by focusing only on the elimination of symptoms, but that is not our goal, which is to illuminate for our patients their psychological core and its dynamics, and we are not always successful."

I do not have to labor the point that one's conception of a problem or process determines one's time perspective about how to influence or change it. The relationship may be grossly invalid either because one's conception is faulty, or one's time perspective poorly deduced, or both, but the fact remains that there is always a relationship. In my opinion, the failure or inability to confront this relationship in a systematic and realistic way is one of the most frequent sources of personal disillusionment and conflict, as it is also one of the central defects in most social science theorizing. Is it not amazing how many social scientists reacted to the Supreme Court desegregation decision in 1954 as if it really meant that desegregation was ended, or would be ended in a matter of a decade or so? Is it not equally amazing how many people really believed that if disadvantaged groups, like the blacks, were provided new and enriched educational experiences they would as a group blossom quickly in terms of conventional educational and intellectual criteria? Is it not pathetic how eager we were to believe that we possessed the knowledge to justify these expectations? What combination of ignorance and arrogance permitted people to proclaim that if we delivered the right kinds of programs and spent the appropriate sums of money we could quickly undo what centuries had built up? When the expectations that powered these efforts were obviously not being fulfilled, what permitted some people to conclude that perhaps the victim was in some ways different from (less endowed than) those in the dominant society? Why were they so ready to "blame the victim" instead of the thinking from which derived such an unrealistic time perspective? And again I must ask: What is there in man's history and in the corpus of social science knowledge which contradicts the statement that few things are as immune to quick changes as the historically rooted, psychological core of ethnic and racial groups? Jewishness and blackishness are products, among other things (and I assume there *are* other things), of social and cultural history, and their psychological cores will successfully resist short-term efforts aimed at changing them.

In one of his syndicated columns, William F. Buckley, Jr. (*New Haven Journal Courier,* March 20, 1969) has provided support of my thesis: needless to say, he does this unknowingly. Buckley quoted approvingly from an article by Ernest van den Haag:

> The heart of Mr. van den Haag's analysis, so critically useful at the present moment, should be committed to memory before the ideologists of racism take the Jensen findings and mount a campaign of I-told-you-soism with truly ugly implications. Van den Haag asked himself:
>
> Q. Suppose the average native intelligence of Negroes is inferior to that of whites. Would that mean that Negroes are inferior to whites?
> A. One may regard others as inferior to oneself, or to one's group, on the basis of any criterion, such as mating, eating, drinking or language habits, religious practices, or competence in sports, business, politics, art or finally, by preferring one's own type, quality or degree of intelligence, skin or hair color and so forth.
> By selecting appropriate criteria each group can establish the inferiority of others, and its own superiority. . . . The selection of criteria for superiority or inferiority is arbitrary, of course . . . I do not believe that intelligence is any more relevant to judgments of inferiority than, say, skin color is.
> If Negroes on the average turn out to have a genetically lower learning ability than whites in some respects, e.g. the manipulation of abstract symbols, and if one chooses this ability as the ranking criterion, it would make Negroes on the average inferior to some whites and superior to others. Suppose four-fifths of Negroes fall into the lower half of intelligence distribution. Chances are that, say, one-third of the whites will too. Hence, if intelligence is the criterion, the four-fifths of the Negro group would be no more "inferior" than the one-third of the white group. Judgments of inferiority among whites are rarely based solely on intelligence. There certainly are many people who do not rank high on intelligence tests but are, nonetheless, preferable, and preferred, to others who do. I know of no one who selects his associates—let alone friends—purely in terms of intelligence. God knows, we certainly do not elect to political office those who are most intelligent. I would conclude that whatever we may find out about Negro intelligence would not entail any judgment about general inferiority.

Buckley concluded the column with these words aimed at those who "by their dogmatic insistence on 'equality' at every level succeeded in persuading typical Americans to put far too great an emphasis on 'intelligence' ":

> Add to these observations the Christian point: namely that all men are equal in the truest sense of the word, and the findings of Dr. Jensen are placed in perspective. But it will take time to undo the damage brought by the ideologization of science during the reign of American liberalism.

It will take time to undo the damage! Mr. Buckley seems to have grasped the principle that historically rooted attitudes do not change quickly with time or evidence. He knows this to be true for political attitudes, that is, the liberal or conservative ideology. He knows this to be true of himself as a historically minded Catholic. If he cannot apply the principle to the nature and consequences of blackishness in our society, we should not be harsh, because it is a principle that unless rooted firmly in self-knowledge *as well as* knowledge of the force and processes of cultural transmission cannot be applied as a general principle.

Mr. Buckley's column was his answer to a study sponsored by the Anti-Defamation League of the B'nai Brith. It is understandable that he paid attention to the study and not to its sponsor. If he had asked why this Jewish group sponsored such a study, he would have gotten the conventional response: For obvious historical reasons, Jews are not indifferent to any form of religious, racial, or ethnic discrimination; if they do not defend *any* victim of discrimination, their own vulnerability to discrimination is increased; discrimination is a wound-producing act, the effects of which never heal in the lifetime of the victim. Mr. Buckley knows all this and knows it well. But what Mr. Buckley does not know, and what many Jews sense but would have difficulty conceptualizing and articulating, is that historically rooted discrimination (its causes and consequences) is immune to change by efforts based on our accustomed short-time perspective. I suspect that the guilt of whites in relation to blacks has less to do with acts of the past than with the intuitive feeling that black freedom is a long, long way off. I also suspect that the anger of blacks toward whites has the same source. The future is determining the present.

Why say all of this? The answer, which goes back 30 years to when I started work at the Southbury Training School, is suggested in two statements. First, if a neighbor's child had an IQ of 180 and strangled a dog to death, we would not say he did it *because* he had an IQ of 180. Second, if that neighbor's child had an IQ of 60, our prepotent response, *our act of discrimination,* would be to point to the IQ of 60 as the etiological agent without which the strangling would not have taken place.[4] This pernicious double-standard way of thinking, the

---

[4] We blame "bad" things on a low IQ, and we explain "good" ones by a high IQ, differences in language which are the hallmark of cultural influence. It is such a part of our thinking, it all appears so self-evident, that we cannot recognize the diverse ways in which these cultural influences work, for example, their self-fulfilling tendencies. For example, 25 years ago, Catherine Cox Miles, a long-time colleague of Lewis Terman, told me that nowhere in his write-up of his studies of "gifted" California boys and girls did Terman indicate the amount of time he spent helping his subjects get into college and graduate school, and obtain jobs. There was absolutely no chicanery involved. It was so self-evident to him that a high IQ was the cause of superior accomplishment that he could not recognize that he was an intervening variable, that is, that he, Lewis Terman, was a reflection and guardian of certain cultural values.

essence of discrimination, is so ingrained in us that when we recognize our logical error we feel helpless about how we should proceed to think and act. Life is so much easier when we, the experts, like most other people, can "blame the victim" for what he is and "is" means that he has a low IQ, and what more do we need to know to understand him? Why complicate our thinking by confronting the fact that the act of constructing and using tests is both a reflection and a determinant of cultural attitudes and deeply rooted ways of thinking which, as long as they go unrecognized, guarantee that facts will be confused with truth? Why get into these messy issues when you can talk about genetics? Of course, we should study the genetics of intelligence (high, low, black, white) but, unless I misread the history of genetics, productive theorizing about genotypes follows upon clearly described, stable phenotypes. In regard to the genetics of intelligence, we are far from the point at which we can say that we have a well-described, stable phenotype. The one thing we can say with assurance is that our concepts of intelligence are value laden, culture and time bound, and deficient in cross-cultural validity. *It has not even been demonstrated that the level of problem-solving behavior in nontest situations is highly correlated with the level of similar types of problem-solving processes in the standardized test situations* (Sarason & Doris, 1969). And, as I have tried to demonstrate in this article, relatively little attention has been paid either to the different ways in which attitudes toward intellectual activity are absorbed by and inculcated in us, or to how the presence or absence of these group attitudes has behind it the force of decades or centuries.

I began with a story about my father and I shall end with one. He was in the hospital recovering from an operation. I visited him on one day, and my brother visited him on the next. The nurse asked my father what work his sons did. When he told her that they were both professors of psychology, she semifacetiously asked him: "Mr. Sarason, how come *you* have two sons like *that?*" My sister reported that my father, without a moment's hesitation and with the most profound seriousness, replied: "Don't you know that smartness sometimes skips generations?" The nature and force of the processes of cultural transmission never skip generations, particularly when their ways have been finely honed over the centuries. They will not be quickly blunted. I excuse my father for not knowing this (although he may have known it). I cannot excuse this in the participants of the recent nature-nurture controversy. There is a point when one must regard the consequences of ignorance as sinful, and that point was reached for the advocates of nurture when they expected that the core of blackishness would quickly change; and it was reached by the advocates of nature when they concluded that the overall failure of compensatory programs demonstrated the significance of genetic factors on which new programs should be based. With friends like that, the blacks need not waste time worrying about enemies, a lesson Jews learned well over the centuries.

REFERENCES

SARASON, S. B. *The culture of the school and the problem of change.* Boston: Allyn & Bacon, 1971.

SARASON, S. B. *The creation of settings and future societies.* San Francisco: Jossey-Bass, 1972.

SARASON, S. B., & DORIS, J. *Psychological problems in mental deficiency.* (4th ed.) New York: Harper & Row, 1969.

PART III

Learning, Thinking, and Other Cognitive Processes

10.

On Freedom and Control
in a Utopian Community

B. F. SKINNER

In the novel *Walden Two* the eminent behaviorist B. F. Skinner
depicts a ⌊u⌉topian community constructed according to the principles of "behavioral engineering." These principles are simply the
systematic application of the techniques developed by Skinner and
his followers in the learning laboratory. They rely heavily on the
concept of reinforcement—the arrangement of circumstances so that
desired or acceptable behavior is rewarded ("reinforced") and thus
made more likely to recur in a similar situation.

The novel describes a three-day visit to the community by an
academic psychologist (Burris), a philosopher colleague (Castle),
and four of their friends. The workings of the community are
explained to them by its founder, Frazier, an old friend of Burris's.
In this excerpt, Castle, who has been skeptical for three days, has
just accused Frazier of being a "managerial Machiavelli," a "silent
despot." Frazier here responds with a discussion of the concepts of
freedom and control from the point of view of reinforcement theory.
(More recently, Skinner's *Beyond Freedom and Dignity* has elicited
reactions very much like Castle's.)

Do you find Frazier's arguments convincing? How would he
counter the argument raised by Meehl (see Selection 3) on the
efficacy of punishment in the modification of behavior?

"MR. CASTLE," said Frazier very earnestly, "let me ask you a question. I warn you, it will be the most terrifying question of your life.
What would you do if you found yourself in possession of an effective

Reprinted with permission of Macmillan Publishing Co., Inc., from *Walden Two*
by B. F. Skinner. Copyright 1948 by B. F. Skinner.

science of behavior? Suppose you suddenly found it possible to control the behavior of men as you wished. What would you do?"

"That's an assumption?"

"Take it as one if you like. *I* take it as a fact. And apparently you accept it as a fact too. I can hardly be as despotic as you claim unless I hold the key to an extensive practical control."

"What would I do?" said Castle thoughtfully. "I think I would dump your science of behavior in the ocean."

"And deny men all the help you could otherwise give them?"

"And give them the freedom they would otherwise lose forever!"

"How could you give them freedom?"

"By refusing to control them!"

"But you would only be leaving the control in other hands."

"Whose?"

"The charlatan, the demagogue, the salesman, the ward heeler, the bully, the cheat, the educator, the priest—all who are now in possession of the techniques of behavior engineering."

"A pretty good share of the control would remain in the hands of the individual himself."

"That's an assumption, too, and it's your only hope. It's your only possible chance to avoid the implications of a science of behavior. If man is free, then a technology of behavior is impossible. But I'm asking you to consider the other case."

"Then my answer is that your assumption is contrary to fact and any further consideration idle."

"And your accusations—?"

"—were in terms of intention, not of possible achievement."

Frazier sighed dramatically.

"It's a little late to be proving that a behavioral technology is well advanced. How can you deny it? Many of its methods and techniques are really as old as the hills. Look at their frightful misuse in the hands of the Nazis! And what about the techniques of the psychological clinic? What about education? Or religion? Or practical politics? Or advertising and salesmanship? Bring them all together and you have a sort of rule-of-thumb technology of vast power. No, Mr. Castle, the science is there for the asking. But its techniques and methods are in the wrong hands—they are used for personal aggrandizement in a competitive world or, in the cases of the psychologist and educator, for futilely corrective purposes. My question is, have you the courage to take up and wield the science of behavior for the good of mankind? You answer that you would dump it in the ocean!"

"I'd want to take it out of the hands of the politicians and advertisers and salesmen, too."

"And the psychologists and educators? You see, Mr. Castle, you can't have that kind of cake. The fact is, we not only can control human behavior, we must. But who's to do it, and what's to be done?"

"So long as a trace of personal freedom survives, I'll stick to my position," said Castle, very much out of countenance.

"Isn't it time we talked about freedom?" I [Burris] said. "We parted a day or so ago on agreement to let the question of freedom ring. It's time to answer, don't you think?"

"My answer is simple enough," said Frazier. "I deny that freedom exists at all. I must deny it—or my program would be absurd. You can't have a science about a subject matter which hops capriciously about. Perhaps we can never *prove* that man isn't free; it's an assumption. But the increasing success of a science of behavior makes it more and more plausible."

"On the contrary, a simple personal experience makes it untenable," said Castle. "The experience of freedom. I know that I'm free."

"It must be quite consoling," said Frazier.

"And what's more—you do, too," said Castle hotly. "When you deny your own freedom for the sake of playing with a science of behavior, you're acting in plain bad faith. That's the only way I can explain it." He tried to recover himself and shrugged his shoulders. "At least you'll grant that you *feel* free."

"The 'feeling of freedom' should deceive no one," said Frazier. "Give me a concrete case."

"Well, right now," Castle said. He picked up a book of matches. "I'm free to hold or drop these matches."

"You will, of course, do one or the other," said Frazier. "Linguistically or logically there seem to be two possibilities, but I submit that there's only one in fact. The determining forces may be subtle but they are inexorable. I suggest that as an orderly person you will probably hold—ah! you drop them! Well, you see, that's all part of your behavior with respect to me. You couldn't resist the temptation to prove me wrong. It was all lawful. You had no choice. The deciding factor entered rather late, and naturally you couldn't foresee the result when you first held them up. There was no strong likelihood that you would act in either direction, and so you said you were free."

"That's entirely too glib," said Castle. "It's easy to argue lawfulness after the fact. But let's see you predict what I will do in advance. Then I'll agree there's law."

"I didn't say that behavior is always predictable, any more than the weather is always predictable. There are often too many factors to be taken into account. We can't measure them all accurately, and we couldn't perform the mathematical operations needed to make a prediction if we had the measurements. The legality is usually an assumption—but none the less important in judging the issue at hand."

"Take a case where there's no choice, then," said Castle. "Certainly a man in jail isn't free in the sense in which I am free now."

"Good! That's an excellent start. Let us classify the kinds of determiners of human behavior. One class, as you suggest, is physical restraint—handcuffs, iron bars, forcible coercion. These are ways in which we shape human behavior according to our wishes. They're crude, and they sacrifice the affection of the controllee, but they often work. Now, what other ways are there of limiting freedom?"

Frazier had adopted a professorial tone and Castle refused to answer.

"The threat of force would be one," I said.

"Right. And here again we shan't encourage any loyalty on the part of the controllee. He has perhaps a shade more of the feeling of freedom, since he can always 'choose to act and accept the consequences,' but he doesn't feel exactly free. He knows his behavior is being coerced. Now what else?"

I had no answer.

"Force or the threat of force—I see no other possibility," said Castle after a moment.

"Precisely," said Frazier.

"But certainly a large part of my behavior has no connection with force at all. There's my freedom!" said Castle.

"I wasn't agreeing that there was no other possibility—merely that *you* could see no other. Not being a good behaviorist—or a good Christian, for that matter—you have no feeling for a tremendous power of a different sort."

"What's that?"

"I shall have to be technical," said Frazier. "But only for a moment. It's what the science of behavior calls 'reinforcement theory.' The things that can happen to us fall into three classes. To some things we are indifferent. Other things we like—we want them to happen, and we take steps to make them happen again. Still other things we don't like —we don't want them to happen, and we take steps to get rid of them or keep them from happening again.

"Now," Frazier continued earnestly, "if it's in our power to create any of the situations which a person likes or to remove any situation he doesn't like, we can control his behavior. When he behaves as we want him to behave, we simply create a situation he likes, or remove one he doesn't like. As a result, the probability that he will behave that way again goes up, which is what we want. Technically it's called 'positive reinforcement.'

"The old school made the amazing mistake of supposing that the reverse was true, that by removing a situation a person likes or setting up one he doesn't like—in other words by punishing him—it was possible to *reduce* the probability that he would behave in a given way again. That simply doesn't hold. It has been established beyond question. What is emerging at this critical stage in the evolution of society is a behavioral and cultural technology based on positive reinforcement alone. We are gradually discovering—at an untold cost in human suffering—that in the long run punishment doesn't reduce the probability that an act will occur. We have been so preoccupied with the contrary that we always take 'force' to mean punishment. We don't say we're using force when we send shiploads of food into a starving country, though we're displaying quite as much power as if we were sending troops and guns."

"I'm certainly not an advocate of force," said Castle. "But I can't agree that it's not effective."

"It's *temporarily* effective, that's the worst of it. That explains several thousand years of bloodshed. Even nature has been fooled. We 'instinctively' punish a person who doesn't behave as we like—we spank him if he's a child or strike him if he's a man. A nice distinction! The immediate effect of the blow teaches us to strike again. Retribution and revenge are the most natural things on earth. But in the long run the man we strike is no less likely to repeat his act."

"But he won't repeat it if we hit him hard enough," said Castle.

"He'll still *tend* to repeat it. He'll want to repeat it. We haven't really altered his potential behavior at all. That's the pity of it. If he doesn't repeat it in our presence, he will in the presence of someone else. Or it will be repeated in the disguise of a neurotic symptom. If we hit hard enough, we clear a little place for ourselves in the wilderness of civilization, but we make the rest of the wilderness still more terrible.

"Now, early forms of government are naturally based on punishment. It's the obvious technique when the physically strong control the weak. But we're in the throes of a great change to positive reinforcement—from a competitive society in which one man's reward is another man's punishment, to a cooperative society in which no one gains at the expense of anyone else.

"The change is slow and painful because the immediate, temporary effect of punishment overshadows the eventual advantage of positive reinforcement. We've all seen countless instances of the temporary effect of force, but clear evidence of the effect of not using force is rare. That's why I insist that Jesus, who was apparently the first to discover the power of refusing to punish, must have hit upon the principle by accident. He certainly had none of the experimental evidence which is available to us today, and I can't conceive that it was possible, no matter what the man's genius, to have discovered the principle from casual observation."

"A touch of revelation, perhaps?" said Castle.

"No, accident. Jesus discovered one principle because it had immediate consequences, and he got another thrown in for good measure."

I began to see light.

"You mean the principle of 'love your enemies'?" I said.

"Exactly! To 'do good to those who despitefully use you' has two unrelated consequences. You gain the peace of mind we talked about the other day. Let the stronger man push you around—at least you avoid the torture of your own rage. *That's* the immediate consequence. What an astonishing discovery it must have been to find that in the long run you could *control the stronger man* in the same way!"

"It's generous of you to give so much credit to your early colleague," said Castle, "but why are we still in the throes of so much misery? Twenty centuries should have been enough for one piece of behavioral engineering."

"The conditions which made the principle difficult to discover made it difficult to teach. The history of the Christian Church doesn't reveal many cases of doing good to one's enemies. To inoffensive heathens, perhaps, but not enemies. One must look outside the field of organized religion to find the principle in practice at all. Church governments are devotees of *power,* both temporal and bogus."

"But what has all this got to do with freedom?" I said hastily.

Frazier took time to reorganize his behavior. He looked steadily toward the window, against which the rain was beating heavily.

"Now that we *know* how positive reinforcement works and why negative doesn't," he said at last, "we can be more deliberate, and hence more successful, in our cultural design. We can achieve a sort of control under which the controlled, though they are following a code much more scrupulously than was ever the case under the old system, nevertheless *feel free.* They are doing what they want to do, not what they are forced to do. That's the source of the tremendous power of positive reinforcement—there's no restraint and no revolt. By a careful cultural design, we control not the final behavior, but the *inclination* to behave—the motives, the desires, the wishes.

"The curious thing is that in that case *the question of freedom never arises.* Mr. Castle was free to drop the matchbook in the sense that nothing was preventing him. If it had been securely bound to his hand he wouldn't have been free. Nor would he have been quite free if I'd covered him with a gun and threatened to shoot him if he let it fall. The question of freedom arises when there is restraint—either physical or psychological.

"But restraint is only one sort of control, and absence of restraint isn't freedom. It's not control that's lacking when one feels 'free,' but the objectionable control of force. Mr. Castle felt free to hold or drop the matches in the sense that he felt no restraint—no threat of punishment in taking either course of action. He neglected to examine his positive reasons for holding on or letting go, in spite of the fact that these were more compelling in this instance than any threat of force.

"We have no vocabulary of freedom in dealing with what we want to do," Frazier went on. "The question never arises. When men strike for freedom, they strike against jails and the police, or the threat of them—against oppression. They never strike against forces which make them want to act the way they do. Yet, it seems to be understood that governments will operate only through force or the threat of force, and that all other principles of control will be left to education, religion, and commerce. If this continues to be the case, we may as well give up. A government can never create a free people with the techniques now allotted to it.

"The question is: Can men live in freedom and peace? And the answer is: Yes, if we can build a social structure which will satisfy the needs of everyone and in which everyone will want to observe the supporting code. But so far this has been achieved only in Walden Two. Your ruthless accusations to the contrary, Mr. Castle, this is the freest place on earth. And it is free precisely because we make no use of force or the threat of force. Every bit of our research, from the nursery through the psychological management of our adult membership, is directed toward that end—to exploit every alternative to forcible control. By skillful planning, by a wise choice of techniques, we *increase* the feeling of freedom.

"It's not planning which infringes upon freedom, but planning which uses force. A sense of freedom was practically unknown in the planned society of Nazi Germany, because the planners made a fantastic use of force and the threat of force.

"No, Mr. Castle, when a science of behavior has once been achieved, there's no alternative to a planned society. We can't leave mankind to an accidental or biased control. But by using the principle of positive reinforcement—carefully avoiding force or the threat of force—we can preserve a personal sense of freedom."

Frazier threw himself back upon the bed and stared at the ceiling.

11.

. . . .

Visceral Learning

GERALD JONAS

The following article is excerpted from a book by Gerald Jonas, a journalist who displays the rare ability to write interestingly and authoritatively on scientific matters. (For another example, see Selection 19.)

Instrumental learning refers to the situation where a person responds in a number of ways until he hits on one that produces a desired reward. This successful response is then more likely to be repeated in future similar situations. (Simple operant learning, as illustrated in Selection 10, is a form of instrumental learning. Other illustrations of instrumental learning are: a cat that learns to un-latch a puzzle box to get at food; a child who learns that crying will gain his mother's attention; a worker who increases his production for monetary rewards.)

For years, psychologists assumed that visceral responses (re-sponses in the autonomic nervous system, in our glands and internal organs) could be conditioned only by the classical (Pavlovian) techniques, and not by the methods of instrumental learning. Jonas here tells of the work of Neal Miller and his attempts to demon-strate instrumental learning of nonvoluntary responses.

Could Miller's approach account for the yogic control of involuntary functions such as body temperature or blood pressure (see Selection 6)? Is there an equivalent of reward or feedback in the yoga procedure?

When you finish this article, try wiggling an ear in front of a mirror.

SCIENTISTS, DESPITE their passion for objectivity, are as dependent as anyone on subjective judgment when it comes to assessing their colleagues. In the summer of 1969, a fellow scientist referred to Dr. Neal E. Miller of the Rockefeller University in New York as "the best-known experimental psychologist in the country." Although Miller's name was hardly as familiar to the general public as that of the Harvard behavioral psychologist B. F. Skinner, the hyperbole was a tribute to Miller's standing in the professional community and a mark of the importance that scientists attached to his laboratory demonstration of a "new" behavioral phenomenon known as visceral learning. Miller had devoted thirty-five years to the study of how higher animals learn, and he was regarded as a leading theorist for the school of psychology that believes there are general "laws" governing all learning situations— from the hungry white rat searching for food in a maze to the college student cramming for a calculus exam. In his most recent series of experiments, he had shown that white rats could be taught to control many of the bodily functions that had long been regarded by almost everyone—scientists and nonscientists alike—as involuntary. Behind this achievement lay a controversial hypothesis about the nature of the nervous system and more than a decade of research by Miller and a long line of collaborators. In the crucial experiments, rats had learned to work for specific rewards by speeding up or slowing down heartbeat, raising or lowering blood pressure, and increasing or decreasing intestinal contractions. And there was good reason to believe that if rats could learn to modify these functions, so could human beings. This meant that people suffering from hypertension, spastic colon, irregular heartbeats, and other functional disorders might someday be taught to control their own symptoms—from the inside, as it were— without drugs, surgery, or the usual forms of physical therapy. Researchers who shared Miller's basic outlook were already investigating some of these practical applications. But the first experiments that Miller and his co-workers ran with human subjects only pointed up how much basic research remained to be done, and how little anyone really knew about the fundamental relationship of the brain, the body, and the outside world. . . .

Most people think of learning as a conscious mental process, a deliberate attempt to grasp an abstract principle ("The square of the hypotenuse is equal to the sum of the squares of the other two sides") or to master a special skill involving the so-called skeletal muscles of the limbs, the torso, and the head (driving a car, hitting a golf ball, singing on key). At first glance, visceral learning appears to be something else entirely. For example, the circulation of blood through the arteries and veins, even in a severe case of hypertension, produces no consciously perceived sensations. This means that before a person can even begin to learn to control his blood pressure he has to be provided with some kind of artificial feedback, through a monitoring device akin to the inflatable rubber cuff that physicians use to gauge blood pressure. The monitoring device can be rigged to let the patient know whenever his blood pressure drops significantly, but there is no way to make him *feel* what is happening inside his body. Learning to control the body's cardiovascular machinery under these conditions would be a little like learning to make love by correspondence course.

Despite these obvious difficulties, some of the subjects in Neal Miller's early experiments at Rockefeller University did learn to reduce their blood pressure on cue, though they were unable to explain what they had done or how they had done it. The subjects themselves compared their newly acquired skill to feats of bodily control reportedly performed by Indian yogis or by people in deep hypnotic trances. Miller found these parallels fascinating and definitely worth further investigation. But this did not mean he shared the view of his subjects that visceral learning was some kind of behavioral anomaly; in fact, his analysis of the phenomenon had already led him to the opposite conclusion; that the most interesting thing about visceral learning was its similarity to ordinary learning.

In objective terms, the lowest common denominator of all learning is a change in behavior resulting from an encounter with the outside world. In the case of the skeletal muscles, this process begins in early infancy; we observe infants making repeated passes at an offered rattle or shying away from an object that has been associated with an unpleasantly loud noise or bright light. But since we retain no memory of our own "basic training" in the use of the skeletal muscles, we tend to think of the learning process in terms of later, more sophisticated manifestations. For instance, we say that we are "starting from scratch" when we take up some new activity like driving a car or playing golf. No matter how helpless we may look and feel during our first lesson, however, we already have at our fingertips most of the tools we need. Years of experience in grappling with our environment have taught us that a little more tension in *these* fingers will give us a little better control *here*, and bending the wrist in *that* direction will provide a little more flexibility *there*. By contrast, our glands and internal organs are normally so well insulated from learning encounters that the average person goes through life with hardly any more control over his visceral functions than a newborn baby. If Miller was right, the human volunteers in his visceral-learning experiments were being thrust into a kind of second childhood, where they were discovering on their own what a few experimental psychologists had always contended in theory —that consciousness was "an unnecessary hypothesis" when one got down to the bare bones of the learning process. In other words, there was nothing strange about acquiring muscular skills without conscious control; it was simply learning on the most basic level.

Even Miller, however, had difficulty imagining what learning on this level might be like. One way to satisfy his curiosity would have been to use himself as a subject for a visceral-learning experiment. But he appeared to be a particularly unsuitable subject, since his heart rate and blood pressure were unusually steady. Besides, as the head of a major laboratory in which fifteen Ph.D.s and twelve technicians were working on a number of other important projects in addition to visceral learning—all supported by grants from the National Institute of Mental Health—Miller had only a limited amount of time to spare. So he looked around for some informal experiment that he could perform on himself outside the laboratory—something involving a simple skeletal response that was almost as far removed from the mainstream of human learning experiences as blood-pressure control. While his experimental subjects were working to control their glands and internal organs, Dr. Miller set out to teach himself to wiggle one of his ears without moving the other. . . .

Compared with other skeletal responses that have a high survival value—like running and reaching and grasping—the average person's control of his ear-wiggling apparatus is almost completely undeveloped. Many people are unable to wiggle their ears at all. Some, like Miller, are amused to discover during their childhood that they can wiggle both ears in unison. But wiggling one ear without moving the other is a surprisingly difficult feat of coordination that can be appreciated only by someone who has tried to master it. As an experimental psychologist known for his contributions to modern learning theory, Miller at least had a pretty good idea of what to expect. The problem, as he defined it for himself, was "to bring the wiggling response of the right ear under more specific stimulus control." While this formulation did not guarantee success, it was helpful in explaining to Mrs. Miller why her eminent husband could be found from time to time staring intently at his reflection in a bathroom mirror.

Miller could "tell" both his ears to wiggle in unison, and he knew that the muscles were responding correctly, because he could see the movement in the mirror and could also feel it. The fact that some people could wiggle their ears independently showed that it was physiologically possible to break this response down into a right and a left component, but Miller also knew that no one—not even an ear-wiggling virtuoso—could guide him toward this goal, for the simple reason that there are no commonly accepted cue words for the necessary muscular adjustments. The parents who have tried to teach a two-year-old child to blow his nose or to drink through a straw will recognize the problem; the child is born with the ability to blow air out through his nose and to suck air in through his mouth, but he has not yet learned to associate these actions with specific instructions. The would-be ear-wiggler may know the Latin name for every muscle and nerve in the head, but this will not help him if he has never learned to attach a physical response to the words.

For his personal training program in ear-control, Miller adopted a method of step-by-step instruction that he had used successfully with rats, dogs, and human beings in the visceral-learning experiments. This method—which is known as instrumental, or operant, conditioning—is based on the familiar observation that immediate rewards influence future behavior. Animal trainers, for example, know that a hungry dog will work for food. To teach a dog to sit up on the command "Beg!" the trainer tosses the animal a piece of food every time it makes the correct response. If the trainer is patient enough, the dog will eventually learn to do whatever is instrumental—from *its* point of view—in getting the reward. The dog will also learn to avoid certain actions if it is punished whenever it makes an incorrect response—the reward in this case being the cessation of punishment as soon as the incorrect response ceases. Experimental psychologists prefer to describe this whole training process in terms that do not require unverifiable hypotheses about what is going on inside the dog's head. They speak of a reward as "reinforcing" the connection between a response (sitting up) and a stimulus (the command "Beg!"). A "reinforced response" is simply one that is more likely to recur the next time the stimulus is repeated. Exactly how the reinforcing effect is achieved inside the learning organism is one of the great mysteries of the life sciences, but it is not hard to see what role the mechanism of reinforcement plays in the individual's daily life. There is a close parallel to the process of natural selection in the life of the species. In general, higher organisms tend to repeat those patterns of behavior which are instrumental in satisfying physical needs, avoiding pain, and relieving stress and tension in the nervous system. A white rat trying to escape an electric shock, a hungry dog sitting up on command, a baby reaching for a teething ring, a psychologist trying to prove a point by wiggling his ears—in all these cases the underlying mechanism of reinforcement is assumed to be the same. In laymen's terms, all four learners are working, whether they know it or not, for rewards.

Laymen and many scientists refer to the initial stages of the process as "trial-and-error" learning, but from the point of view of modern learning theory this is something of a misnomer. Each error leads only to the elimination of fruitless response and therefore to another trial; to get learning, you need successful trials, suitably reinforced. In fact, the most difficult part of the trainer's job can be waiting for the subject to perform the first correct response—or, if the response is quite an elaborate one, even some small part of it—so that a reward can be administered. This was what kept Miller in front of the bathroom mirror. According to his own understanding of the laws of learning, his chances of teaching himself to wiggle one ear were almost nil unless he could catch himself in the act—even the faintest flutter of independent movement would do—and immediately reinforce this spontaneous wiggle with a burst of self-congratulation. . . .

The image that stared back at Miller from the mirror was of a stocky, outdoorsy man, bald except for a white fringe behind the ears, with ruddy cheeks, a firm jaw, a broad nose, and deep-set green eyes, which did not need corrective lenses. Born in 1909, he was a member of what might be called the third generation of American behavioral scientists; he had been associated with Yale University for more than thirty years before moving to the Rockefeller University in 1966. Much of his career had been spent teaching white rats and other laboratory animals to make simple physical responses (pressing a bar, spinning a wheel) in order to earn concrete rewards (a pellet of food, a sip of water). Underlying this work was a modern theory of learning that began with an almost total rejection of the "introspective" approach of classical psychology.

The experimental psychologists of the early twentieth century, in aspiring to the methodological purity of physics and chemistry, turned their backs on all forms of inquiry that did not allow verification by other investigators. Since there was obviously no way to verify someone's account of his own thoughts and feelings, the systematic study of human consciousness—a touchstone of nineteenth-century psychology— was dropped from the syllabus. What replaced it was the systematic study of overt behavior. Thoughts and feelings were recognized as important only insofar as they found expression in observable activity. Still, implicit in this new approach, which came to be known as behaviorism, was a challenge to take over the subject matter of the old, introspective psychology by restating it in a set of purely "operational" definitions. Unlike a dictionary definition, an operational definition of a phenomenon does not necessarily describe or explain. Rather, it provides a lever for *manipulating* the phenomenon in a specified setting. For example, everyone knows what the sensation of fear is, and *Webster's New International Dictionary* (second edition) gives an adequate descriptive definition: "Painful emotion marked by alarm, extreme awe, or anticipation of danger." But a researcher interested in fear as a determinant of behavior needs something more concrete; he wants something he can observe directly and measure objectively. From this standpoint, the most useful information about psychological variables like fear has come from a stimulus-response analysis of behavior. A researcher working with white rats might make the following observation: When a rat is turned loose in a cage where it was previously given a strong electric shock through a metal grid in the floor, the rat scrambles about, trying to escape, even though the current in the grid has been turned off. Since the rat is not now receiving shock, it appears to be motivated by the fear of a second shock; presumably, the more frightened the rat, the harder it will try to escape. These statements sound reasonable; indeed, they verge on truism. What is important about them is that, taken together, they point to a prediction about future behavior that can be stated in strictly objective terms: the stronger the original shock, the more vigorous the animal's escape responses will become. This statement requires no subjective judgments; it can be proved or disproved by the use of a simple restraining harness that allows the investigator to measure the animal's pulling strength after it has received shocks of varying voltage. Of course there is bound to be a lower limit below which the shock is too weak to produce any observable effect on the rat's behavior, and there will also be an upper limit above which the shock is so strong that the animal simply freezes. But if the predicted correlation between shock strength and pulling strength does hold true over a clearly defined middle range, the researcher can assume that he is getting an objective fix on the subjective experience commonly called fear.

Once a particular operational definition is shown to be reliable within given limits, it can be used as a yardstick to measure other aspects of behavior. For example, the researcher may adapt the pulling-strength criterion to test the hypothesis that certain drugs, like alcohol, substantially weaken the fear response (as the colloquial phrase "Dutch courage" suggests). Or the researcher may use the criterion to determine whether an electric shock that is preceded by a warning buzzer produces stronger fear than a shock that comes without any warning. Eventually, from a small but carefully cross-checked body of data on the behavior of the frightened white rat, the researcher can advance to predictions about the behavior of the frightened human being.

Rigorous pursuit of this strategy has helped to liberate researchers from culture-bound dogmas and unexamined assumptions about behavior that had long masqueraded as "common sense." But scientists are only human, and the history of behavioral psychology in the United States offers a cautionary lesson in the pitfalls of objectivity.

Encouraged by their initial success in manipulating a few simple laboratory situations, some early behaviorists rushed to elevate a perfectly sound research strategy into a new intellectual dogma. All subjective phenomena that could not be operationally defined with the techniques then available were set aside. Before long, the failure of behaviorism to deal with such phenomena was taken as a sign not that the available techniques were inadequate but that the phenomena themselves were irrelevant, and in this way many of the mental processes that the scientists themselves prized most highly, including self-awareness, abstract reasoning, imagination, and creativity, were virtually excluded from serious consideration.

Among his colleagues Miller has a reputation for carrying out painstaking behavioral research in areas of major importance and for reporting his findings with precision and circumspection. Yet his attitude toward the shibboleths of modern behaviorism has been anything but doctrinaire. Unlike many of his predecessors and contemporaries, he can be refreshingly candid about the interplay of fact and theory in scientific research. "Pure empiricism is a delusion," he has written. "Gathering all the facts with no bias from theory is utterly impossible. Scientists are forced to make a drastic selection, either unconsciously on the basis of perceptual habits and the folklore and linguistic categories of the culture, or consciously on the basis of explicitly formulated theory." And in his technical articles, as if to remind himself (and the reader) of the tentative nature of all scientific theory, he goes out of his way to detail the particular assumptions on which he has proceeded and to present a brief critique of the strengths and weaknesses of his theoretical position. He will even offer odds on the likelihood that one of his assumptions will turn out to be incorrect: "Although I believe that the foregoing hypothesis has a considerably less than 50-per-cent chance of being correct," he wrote in one paper, "I do believe it is better at the present moment than any other single hypothesis." When he runs into unexpected trouble—as he has recently in replicating some of the early animal experiments in visceral learning—his reports to the scientific community are every bit as candid and precise as those dealing with his most successful work.

In the long run, Miller believes, the task of behavioral psychology is to lay the groundwork for a much broader science—"a unified science of human behavior," which will draw on the techniques and insights of physiology, zoology, biochemistry, anthropology, psychiatry, and cybernetics, among other disciplines—and he feels that the young scientists now emerging from the colleges and graduate schools take naturally to such a multidisciplinary approach. In 1966, to encourage this trend, Miller set up a laboratory of physiological psychology at Rockefeller. Typical of the young people working with him today is a twenty-nine-year-old researcher in the life sciences named Barry Dworkin, who brings to the visceral-learning project an impressive schooling in physiology, a thorough grounding in Freudian theory, and a knack for designing and building the complex electronic hardware that has become indispensable to the modern behavioral laboratory.

Miller readily admits that he does not consciously apply the insights of learning theory in his relationship with his graduate students. As he puts it, the job of teaching graduate students falls "halfway between the realm of art and the realm of science," since creative scientific research involves "complex motivations and responses that we know very little about." He adds, "You can try to sharpen the problems for your students and help them avoid blind alleys, but essentially you have to give them practice in learning things on their own. Unfortunately, there is a type of teacher who tends to put a ceiling on the development of his students by implying that they can never hope to learn as much as he has. It so happens that out of necessity—because I have such a wide range of interests and keep getting involved in new areas—I regularly expect my students to know more than I do about at least one field. And I expect them to be able to put this knowledge to work in the laboratory." One of his greatest rewards in teaching, Miller says, is to watch his students go on to make significant contributions to the scientific understanding of behavior. A young colleague of his sums up Miller's success as a teacher in tongue-in-cheek behavioral jargon: "Dr. Miller has been consistently reinforced for making unreasonable demands on his students." . . .

The goal of all science, as Miller sees it, is to account for the greatest number of facts with the fewest possible assumptions, in conformity with what is sometimes referred to as the Law of Parsimony. Philosophers know it as Ockham's razor: "Entities must not be unnecessarily multiplied," or, in layman's language: "Never accept a complicated explanation where a simpler one will do." Learning theory is an attempt to set down in one parsimonious package some of the regularities of behavior that experimental psychologists have observed in their laboratories over the years. Like the laws of physics, the laws of learning can be expressed in either prescriptive or statistical language, and they can be useful in comprehending situations far removed from the original laboratory context. Some of the laws seem to be nothing but elaborate paraphrases of common sense. To anyone who knows what a habit is, for instance, it will hardly come as a revelation that consistently rewarded behavior tends to be repeated. But other laws contradict what everyone "knows" from personal experience. According to learning theory, steady practice in itself will *not* lead to the strengthening of learned behavior. Just the opposite—there is no quicker way to extinguish a learned skill or habit than to practice it steadily in the absence of continued reinforcement. Most behaviorists even lean toward the view that there is no such thing as forgetting in the conventional sense. What appears to be the decay of certain memory traces with the passage of time may be an active weeding out, or unlearning, of stimulus-response connections that interfere with connections providing a higher payoff.

Most of the laws of learning were first worked out in carefully controlled experiments with white rats and other laboratory animals and then tested and confirmed with human subjects. The rationale for this procedure can be found in a key hypothesis of experimental psychology. In Miller's words, "all the psychological processes found in other mammals are likely also to be present in man." Some justification for this assumption comes from studies in comparative anatomy indicating that man's vertebrate ancestors built up a bigger and better nervous system through a process of accretion. New neural structures, instead of replacing the old, were literally piled on top of one another, culminating in the twin cerebral hemispheres that cap the human brain stem and spinal cord. As far as brain structure is concerned, rats and men have much in common—up to a point. The most distinctive part of the human brain is the neocortex, the layer of gray cells that covers the surface of the cerebral hemispheres. Man's greatly enlarged cortex is capable of processing far more information and organizing far more complicated tasks than the brain of any other animal, but from the anatomical evidence alone there is no way of knowing how closely the new cortical functions are related to the "old Adam" below. Does man behave like a lower-order mammal in certain ways and like a self-aware rational being in others? Is he literally divided against himself? Or can one coherent set of principles be found to account for the entire spectrum of human behavior, from the most primitive responses to the most advanced—from the reflex sneeze of the newborn infant to the abstract cognition of the poet or the mathematician?

Numerous attempts have been made to bring the same degree of order to the behavioral spectrum that the laws of physics brought to electromagnetism, but none of the proposed theories have won wide acceptance among experimental psychologists. Instead, over the years most researchers have settled for a less parsimonious explanation of the peculiarities of human nature. By postulating one or more radical jumps in the long chain of evolution leading to man, they feel justified in assigning radically different laws to the "lower" and "higher" levels of behavior. Not all psychologists divide the spectrum in exactly the same place or for exactly the same reasons. But there is near unanimity about the category of behavior that belongs at the bottom of the scale. In colloquial usage, the phrase "visceral reaction," or "gut reaction," refers to an automatic, unthinking, and therefore irremediably primitive response of the individual to his environment. It would be no exaggeration to say that this usage has been firmly endorsed by the modern life sciences. The great neuroanatomists of the nineteenth and early twentieth centuries set out to map the structure of the entire nervous system. They succeeded in laying bare the pathways that make up the so-called somatic nervous system, which provides a direct link between individual skeletal muscles and the higher brain centers. But the neural circuitry serving the internal organs and glands presented a different and more confusing picture. These organs and glands seemed to be linked to the higher brain centers only indirectly, through a series of ganglia, which one early researcher likened to a chain of "little brains." While the anatomical evidence was far from conclusive—considering the technical difficulties of the research involved—it happened to fit in with an already prevalent view that the viscera belonged to a lower, more primitive level of organization. For the moment, it seemed both logical and practical to treat this lower level as a separate entity—a bit of the "old Adam" that had somehow retained its autonomy when the higher brain centers were superimposed on it during a later stage of human evolution.

More recent research has shown that elaborate avenues of communication exist between the somatic network and the autonomic one. Yet modern textbooks continue to draw a sharp distinction between the two, and many psychologists have found it convenient to divide the behavioral spectrum along similar lines. As Miller puts it, a number of traditional beliefs have "coalesced" into an assertion that instrumental learning is possible only with those responses which are under the control of the somatic nervous system. The reasoning behind this assertion is not hard to follow. Every healthy member of every species enters life with a vast repertoire of unlearned stimulus-response connections, which produces what is known as instinctive behavior. No one has to teach a newborn infant to cry, or to suck a nipple, or to close his fingers around an object thrust into his palm. Crying, sucking, and grasping are innate reflexes—behavioral patterns wired into the nervous system and ready to be triggered into action by appropriate stimuli. Many reflexes—sucking, for one—have been observed in the human fetus. Others appear within the first few weeks after birth. Still others, like those having to do with reproduction, may not become operative until the organism matures. A simple reflex, such as the eye-blink that follows a touch on the cornea, may guard the organism against danger from the outside world. Reflexes may also be chained together in elaborate relays and feedback loops to help maintain optimal conditions within the body—the stable internal environment that the physiologist calls "homeostasis" and the layman calls "good health." Yet, no matter how varied the built-in repertoire, innate reflexes are based on stereotyped responses to predictable stimuli. And since the world keeps changing, the organism that is capable of modifying at least some of its behavioral units in the light of its own experience—that is, through instrumental learning—will have a greater chance of survival. Flexibility of this kind is the hallmark of most skeletal behavior. (The rat learns to press a lever with its paw to get a pellet of food; the infant learns to reach out for a teething ring; the racing-car driver learns to control his vehicle with a precision far beyond that attained by the average motorist.) But both science and common sense have long maintained that there is no room for instrumental learning in the blind interplay of visceral reflexes. By and large, homeostasis is maintained by involuntary, unconscious mechanisms, and when outside stimuli do interfere with these mechanisms the glands and internal organs seem to respond only in stereotyped patterns associated with strong emotion or psychosomatic illness: the blush of the shy lover, the intestinal spasm of the terrified soldier, the high blood pressure of the harried executive. It is usually taken for granted that the higher brain centers cannot alter such behavior except by the most indirect means: the frightened soldier can pray for courage or get drunk or remove himself from the battlefield, but he cannot simply turn off an intestinal spasm at will, the way he might raise or lower his arm. It is even possible to argue that a sharp break between the visceral functions and the cerebral control centers is a *necessary* biological development. In contrast to the endless flexibility of skeletal responses, the survival value of emotional behavior becomes apparent only when large numbers of visceral responses fire together—as in the familiar fear-alarm reaction that prepares an organism for a burst of instrumental activity. The release of adrenalin into the bloodstream at such moments is just one part of a general mobilization of bodily resources that is often described as "the flight-or-fight syndrome." According to the traditional argument, while an individual might occasionally find it convenient to exert voluntary control over a specific visceral organ, the frequent exercise of such control could seriously upset the homeostatic balance of the organism and so make it more vulnerable to outside dangers.

Of course, no amount of speculation about evolution could ever prove visceral learning to be impossible. But the arguments against it seemed so persuasive for so long that the great majority of behavioral scientists were effectively discouraged from looking into the matter more deeply. . . .

Miller's long-range program to teach rats and people to control their glands and internal organs was highly unorthodox in many ways, but his experimental strategy was solidly based on conventional learning theory and on the simple biological fact that the body's vital functions are never maintained at a perfectly constant level. Even when the organism is at rest, slight fluctuations occur from moment to moment in the heart rate, the body temperature, the diastolic blood pressure, and so forth. These spontaneous increases and decreases are normally of no significance, since they tend to cancel each other out, leaving a relatively stable baseline. But Miller reasoned that if certain fluctuations could be treated as responses and reinforced appropriately, learning would take place; for instance, if every decrease in diastolic pressure was rewarded, the baseline of the blood-pressure cycle would gradually shift downward as the organism tried to earn more and more rewards.

The key to success in instrumental training is knowing exactly when to reinforce and—equally important—when not to, and making this split-second decision can be difficult even with the more accessible skeletal responses. With a deeply buried visceral function like blood pressure, the technical problems proved to be of another order of magnitude entirely. To begin with, the monitoring system had to be absolutely safe and virtually painless, and it had to provide absolutely reliable feedback within a fraction of a second, because a reward delivered after even the slightest upward movement in diastolic pressure would act as a reward for increasing pressure, and a few such contradictory lessons could undermine the entire training program. Since the only known method of measuring blood pressure on a moment-to-moment basis involved the rather drastic means of placing a needle into an artery, Dworkin had to design and build a completely new system, working in collaboration with Miller and with Dr. Saran Jonas, an associate professor of clinical neurology at the New York University School of Medicine. The basic components included an inflatable pressure cuff; a servopump (to keep the cuff at the proper pressure); an oscilloscope and a polygraph machine (for recording all the data); and a panel of programing circuits, to regulate the rest of the apparatus. The first series of tests was conducted at Rockefeller University, using both healthy volunteers and people with mild hypertension. The results were so encouraging that the researchers decided to shift their base of operations to University Hospital, where, it was assumed, a pool of suitable hypertensive subjects would be available.

A typical training session lasted about an hour. The subject lay face up on a cot in a quiet, darkened room with the inflatable pressure cuff wrapped around his arm at the biceps, where the brachial artery—the major artery in the upper arm—runs close to the skin. Instead of a physician's stethoscope, a small microphone had been placed inside the cuff to pick up the sounds of blood pulsing through the partly constricted artery. Any physician could have translated these sounds into an approximate blood-pressure reading, but Dworkin's machine tracked the subject's diastolic pressure on a heartbeat-to-heartbeat basis—something that no physician could conceivably do. In addition, the machine monitored other vital functions, such as heart rate and respiration, through several small electrodes taped to different parts of the body; the signals from these electrodes were fed into separate channels of the polygraph, and a permanent record of the subject's internal behavior was traced in black ink on a roll of graph paper directly in front of the operator of the machine (but out of sight of the subject himself).

The basic strategy was to reward the subject whenever his diastolic pressure dropped to a level that had been arbitrarily selected as a criterion of therapeutic progress. The reward was nothing but an electronic tone that came on automatically to inform the subject that he was making the correct response. (To a sick person who desperately wants to get well, any indication of improvement, however small or transitory, should be an effective reinforcement.) Although each subject was told in advance that he was going to learn to lower his blood pressure, his only specific instructions at the start of the session were "Lie still, relax, and try to keep the tone on." The difficulty of this assignment depended entirely on the setting of the criterion. For example, the initial criterion might be set just below the subject's current baseline, so that a spontaneous drop of a millimeter or two would trigger a reinforcing tone. If the subject stayed below that setting for a while, the operator simply turned a knob to lower the criterion by four or five millimeters—which automatically shut off the tone until the subject's pressure fell to the new setting. While "chasing the tone" in this way, a few subjects managed to reduce their diastolic pressure by as much as fifteen millimeters in an hour. Since the heart rate remained unchanged, it looked as if the subjects had actually learned to control the reflex mechanisms responsible for dilating the miles and miles of blood vessels in the circulatory system.

The subjects themselves found it hard to accept the fact that anything so important could be accomplished without the direction, or even the knowledge, of their conscious minds. Perhaps because breathing is an internal function that can be controlled voluntarily, most of the subjects started adjusting their respiratory rate in order to improve their performance. Slow, deep, evenly spaced breathing seemed to be the most popular maneuver, but the polygraph record indicated that this had no more than a transitory effect on blood pressure. The subjects also tried to control their pressure through mental discipline of one kind or another. A few made an effort to think only calm, pleasant thoughts; others concentrated on listening to the tone and nothing else; still others tried to empty their minds of all thoughts and sensations, so that their bodies could take over. No one could say for sure whether such efforts had any influence on the learning process. One thing soon became clear, however: The dramatic reductions in blood pressure achieved in the early sessions were disappointingly short-lived, and it was impossible to prove that the gradually declining base-lines exhibited by some of the patients were not simply due to a "placebo effect"—a lessening of physical and mental tensions brought about by exposure to the experimental situation itself. The typical hypertensive subject whose diastolic reading dropped from 130 millimeters to 115 in a single hour on the cot would return a day or two later for his next session with a reading of 130, and he would repeat this sequence day after day without any lasting benefit. It was as if he had to relearn the lesson from scratch each time. Conceivably, the trouble lay in the fact that the subject's newly acquired control of his blood pressure was totally dependent on the feedback provided by the tone; as soon as the subject was unhooked from the machine, all possibility of selective reinforcement ceased. But since the upward and downward fluctuations in his diastolic pressure did not cease, this meant that he was performing the correct response thousands of times a day without further reinforcement. The outcome was quite predictable, according to learning theory. The subject's control was bound to keep fading (or "extinguishing," as the behaviorists say) unless some way could be found to monitor his blood pressure and provide suitable rewards *between* sessions. Since a portable version of Dworkin's cumbersome machine would not be feasible for a long time, one logical alternative was to try to teach the subjects to become more aware of increases and decreases on their own. With this additional skill, they might be able to cue themselves into a therapeutic response whenever their control started to fade, and reward themselves with the awareness of a job well done when their pressure returned to normal. . . .

Miller is one of a handful of experimental psychologists who have argued consistently (his colleagues might even say stubbornly) for what is known as a "global" view of man. He has always proceeded on the assumption that human behavior is all of a piece; that all responses to the environment, whether on a visceral or skeletal or cognitive level, are governed by the same basic laws—the laws of instrumental learning—and that the key to this is the continuous, multileveled integrative function performed by the human brain, which he once referred to, in an uncharacteristic burst of rhetoric, as the "greatest miracle in the universe."

"We no longer view the brain as merely an enormously complicated telephone switchboard, which is passive unless excited from without,"

Miller said on another occasion (his installation as president of the American Psychological Association for the 1960–1961 term). "The brain is a device for sorting, processing, and analyzing information. The brain contains sense organs which respond to states of the internal environment, such as osmotic pressure, temperature, and many others. The brain is a gland which secretes chemical messengers, and it also responds to such messengers, as well as to various types of feedback, both central and peripheral. A combination of behavioral and physiological techniques is increasing our understanding of these processes and their significance for psychology."

Almost a decade later, in a progress report on visceral learning published in the issue of *Science* for January 31, 1969, Miller took to task the legions of behavioral scientists who, without seriously investigating the matter, had simply assumed that instrumental learning on the visceral level was impossible. Looking over the evidence usually cited in support of this view, he could find nothing but "two incompletely reported exploratory experiments and a vague allusion to the Russian literature," and he concluded, "It is only against a cultural background of great prejudice that such weak evidence could lead to such a strong conviction." In Western culture, he wrote, the prejudice goes back at least as far as Plato's "invidious dichotomy" between the higher, rational soul in the head and the lower, appetitive souls in the body. "Since ancient times, reason and the voluntary responses of the skeletal muscles have been considered to be superior, while emotions and the presumably involuntary glandular and visceral responses have been considered to be inferior."

Scientists are obviously not immune to general cultural prejudices. But their experience in framing, testing, and, if necessary, discarding hypotheses makes it easier for them to accept the possibility that long-unchallenged habits of thought might be wrong. And, because of the great influence of science on contemporary thought, the laboratory demonstration of visceral learning can be expected to produce intellectual tremors far beyond its immediate range of application. On one level, the visceral-learning experiments directly challenge the assumptions that lie behind Western man's profound alienation from his own body. On another level, the work of Miller and other researchers in this field opens the door for a fresh look at some of the so-called higher mental processes, like consciousness and volition, which have up to now resisted a satisfactory behavioral formulation. . . .

Conventional English usage tells us that our behavior is "voluntary" when we are doing what we intend to do and "conscious" when we are fully aware of what we are doing. A moment's introspection, together with some minimal knowledge of physiology, however, reveals that nothing we do ever comes close to meeting these criteria. The behavior we call voluntary and conscious actually depends on a substratum of reflex actions, most of which—like the barrage of neural signals to and from the brain, the simultaneous flexing and relaxing of dozens of muscles, the intricate metabolic adjustments—occur without causing the slightest subjectively perceived sensation. This is not to say that there are no objective differences between the peristaltic contractions of a newborn baby's intestines and the exquisitely orchestrated finger movements of a neurosurgeon at work. But Miller argues that our efforts to comprehend these differences have been hampered by an uncritical acceptance of "folklore" categories such as conscious/ unconscious and voluntary/involuntary. "Just because we have certain word pairs in our language doesn't mean that they necessarily represent the best way to slice reality," he has said. "We may be dealing with what I call Monday-Tuesday-Wednesday definitions. If you define all the different things that happen on those days as Monday-things, Tuesday-things, and Wednesday-things, your definitions will be accurate as far as they go, but they won't help you much in understanding the events themselves." For Miller, the discovery of visceral learning—which cuts across all the existing categories—only emphasizes the confusion inherent in our traditional view of the higher mental processes. "Suppose I were to tell you that I'd achieved complete voluntary control of my ear-wiggling response," he says. "How would you go about verifying this statement? You'd probably begin by asking me to wiggle both ears, then just the right ear, then just the left. The acid test would be whether or not I could follow your instructions to the letter." In conventional terminology, with its subjective bias, the paradox is inescapable: To prove that his behavior is voluntary, a person must be able to respond on cue as if he had no free will at all. However, the confusion disappears if such responses are defined *operationally*. From an objective point of view, voluntary behavior is simply behavior that has been brought under the control of a special kind of stimulus—a stimulus with symbolic content, which is usually, but not necessarily, a verbal cue. As Miller puts it, "When we set out to make blood pressure voluntary, our task is done if we can arrange it so that whenever we say, 'Decrease,' the subject's pressure goes down, and whenever we say, 'Increase,' the subject's pressure goes up." By the same logic, blood-pressure control can be defined as "conscious" if the subject, in responding to instructions, can accurately report the changes that are occurring inside his body, and guide his subsequent responses accordingly.

The whole purpose of an operational definition is to pin down an elusive, hard-to-measure variable in terms of a more accessible phenomenon. Weather conditions, for example, are usually defined in terms of the behavior of certain instruments—thermometer, barometer, hygrometer. Although these instruments do not provide an exhaustive description of the weather, they give a picture that is detailed enough for most purposes. To the layman's eye, however, Miller's operational definition of "conscious control" seems to ignore precisely that detail which most people consider to be the essence of human consciousness. Our personal experience, supported by a cultural heritage of several millennia, assures us that somewhere inside the person seen by others there is an invisible core of being—a purely private self that observes, if it cannot always control, our actions and is ultimately free of all controls imposed on the organism from outside. Whether it makes any sense or not, that is what it *feels* like to be conscious, and any definition of "conscious control" that fails to mention such a feeling is like a weather report that fails to mention whether it is raining or sunny.

Miller concedes that there is almost certainly more to human consciousness than the ability to respond to and manipulate symbolic cues. "I'm not sure how to describe it, but there seems to be some kind of multi-sensory, total-field experience that helps us organize our most complex and flexible behavior." Yet this is still a far cry from the notion of an autonomous individual inside the behaving organism—a notion that Miller, as a behaviorist, cannot accept. In fact, he argues that the conscious control of behavior is itself a product of the gradual socialization of the human infant through instrumental conditioning. As a working hypothesis, Miller has assumed that the superiority of man's mental powers over those of his animal forebears can be explained without postulating any radically new behavioral principles. In his view, the really significant factors are man's innate ability to use symbolic cues and the possession of a much greater information-processing capacity. While the laws governing reinforcement presumably remain the same from rat to man, the superior resources available in the human nervous system make possible an incomparably greater flexibility in reinforcement schedules. This means, among other things, that a response can now be modified *before* it occurs through anticipated rewards and punishments. Miller points out that since symbols are created and transmitted by men in society, symbolic control of a response actually implies a kind of social control. At the same time, the use of symbolic cues places a premium on the ability of the organism to become conscious of its own responses. As Miller notes, there are only two visceral functions that are routinely subjected to socially determined schedules of reinforcement—urination and defecation—and these are the only visceral functions that are routinely brought under voluntary and conscious control. "The analysis may be somewhat over-simplified," Miller says, "but perhaps we can say that the average person does not have any specificity of feelings from the viscera because he hasn't learned the right labels for them, and perhaps he doesn't have the right labels because most visceral functions are not normally observed by other people, and so are not normally brought under social control. In other words, it may be that we are not conscious of these sensations *only* because we have not been trained to label them." . . .

Having spent more than a decade investigating a phenomenon that most of his colleagues were convinced did not exist, Miller now tends to be wary of the current public interest in visceral learning and in other medical applications of what has recently been called "biofeedback training." The danger he anticipates is that, as he said recently, "overoptimistic publicity will arouse impossible hopes for quick miracle cures, which will, in turn, lead to premature disillusionment with the whole approach." Characteristically, he counsels long-range optimism combined with extreme caution about the immediate future. . . . "For instance, even if our theory is perfectly correct we might still run into a situation where a patient is getting some specific benefit from a particular symptom and does not *want* to give it up. We're settling down now to the long and difficult task of determining exactly what the important variables are, and trying out new techniques—one by one—to overcome the obstacles we have already encountered."

When a research project reaches this frustrating stage, even as single-minded a scientist as Miller may feel the need for a little positive feedback to reassure him that he is still on the right track. The informal experiment in ear-wiggling served this purpose. After nearly a year of intermittent practice, Miller finally satisfied his own criterion of success: he learned to wiggle his right ear at will. In keeping with his standard operating procedure, he experimented with a number of different approaches to the problem. One approach called for him to focus his attention on the sensations on both sides of his face while he wiggled his ears, and then to try to imagine these sensations occurring on the right side only. He also tried to imagine the left side of his face as cold or numb, so that the ear on that side would be unable to wiggle. Miller was not very surprised when neither of these techniques worked. Nor did he expect to have much success simply willing a specific response into existence. His lifelong study of the learning process had convinced him that the only way to build a new physical habit was to take an already existing neural connection between brain and muscle and bring it under specific stimulus control through differential reinforcement. "I may have been prejudiced because it fitted in so well with my theory, but I found that the best technique was to stand in front of the mirror, where I could see what was happening, and then try to shape the response one small step at a time," Miller told me. "I'd start by trying to produce the most minute independent movement with my right ear. Then I'd try to increase it a little bit each day. If my left ear started to move at any time, I'd drop back until I was sure that only the right one was moving. Then I'd start increasing the movement again, little by little. Eventually . . ." Miller paused, and his face took on a look of intense concentration. His right ear began to twitch against the side of his head. His left ear seemed perfectly motionless. After about thirty seconds, he relaxed and broke into a wide grin. It was obvious that in this small matter, as in all scientific endeavors, success was its own reward.

12.

The "Tip of the Tongue" Phenomenon

ROGER BROWN and DAVID McNEILL

Psychological researchers, interested in the scientific study of behavior, attempt to base their conclusions on measurable observations that are obtained systematically and objectively. To meet these criteria, much psychological research is conducted in experimental laboratories, gaining objectivity and experimental control for what is lost by having less natural conditions. The final product of this kind of research study is presented in reports that typically appear in professional journals. So far in this collection of articles we have encountered a number of references to experimental research studies, but the reports themselves have been characteristically less formal than those that appear in the journals. We have not yet seen firsthand what a formal research report looks like. The following article is a good example. (Other examples may be found in Selections 18, 21, 29, 33, and in any of a host of psychology journals.)

Psychologists have found it useful to view cognitive processes such as memory in terms of "input" (what is selected for attention), "storage" (in something akin to a "memory bank"), and "retrieval" from storage. Brown and McNeill make use of this kind of "information-processing" model to account for a phenomenon that most of us have experienced.

Does their "dictionary" analogy (or model) make it easier for you to conceptualize what might be occurring when you have a word on the tip of your tongue? If so, then the model is useful. It would also be useful if it leads the researchers to think of aspects

Reprinted from *Journal of Verbal Learning and Verbal Behavior*, 1966, 5, pp. 325–27. Copyright 1966 by Academic Press, Inc., and reproduced by permission.

of the phenomenon that might have escaped them otherwise. Did that happen here?

Brown and McNeill refer to encoding in the "storage bank" by similarity of sound and similarity of meaning. How else might a word be encoded in the "storage bank"? Can you picture how "visual" encoding might work?

WILLIAM JAMES wrote, in 1893: "Suppose we try to recall a forgotten name. The state of our consciousness is peculiar. There is a gap therein; but no mere gap. It is a gap that is intensely active. A sort of wraith of the name is in it, beckoning us in a given direction, making us at moments tingle with the sense of our closeness and then letting us sink back without the longed-for term. If wrong names are proposed to us, this singularly definite gap acts immediately so as to negate them. They do not fit into its mould. And the gap of one word does not feel like the gap of another, all empty of content as both might seem necessarily to be when described as gaps" (p. 251).

The "tip of the tongue" (TOT) state involves a failure to recall a word of which one has knowledge. The evidence of knowledge is either an eventually successful recall or else an act of recognition that occurs, without additional training, when recall has failed. The class of cases defined by the conjunction of knowledge and a failure of recall is a large one. The TOT state, which James described, seems to be a small subclass in which recall is felt to be imminent.

For several months we watched for TOT states in ourselves. Unable to recall the name of the street on which a relative lives, one of us thought of *Congress* and *Corinth* and *Concord* and then looked up the address and learned that it was *Cornish*. The words that had come to mind have certain properties in common with the word that had been sought (the "target word"): all four begin with *Co;* all are two-syllable words; all put the primary stress on the first syllable. After this experience we began putting direct questions to ourselves when we fell into the TOT state, questions as to the number of syllables in the target word, its initial letter, etc.

Woodworth (1934), before us, made a record of data for naturally occurring TOT states and Wenzl (1932, 1936) did the same for German words. Their results are similar to those we obtained and consistent with the following preliminary characterization. When complete recall of a word is not presently possible but is felt to be imminent, one can often correctly recall the general type of the word; *generic* recall may succeed when particular recall fails. There seem to be two common varieties of generic recall. (a) Sometimes a part of the target word is recalled, a letter or two, a syllable, or affix. Partial recall is necessarily also *generic* since the class of words defined by the possession of any *part* of the target word will include words other than the target. (b) Sometimes the abstract form of the target is recalled, perhaps the fact that it was a two-syllable sequence with the primary stress on the first syllable. The whole word is represented in *abstract form recall* but not on the letter-by-letter level that constitutes its identity. The recall of an abstract form is also necessarily *generic,* since any such form defines a class of words extending beyond the target.

Wenzl and Woodworth had worked with small collections of data for naturally occurring TOT states. These data were, for the most part, provided by the investigators; were collected in an unsystematic fashion; and were analyzed in an impressionistic nonquantitative way. It seemed to us that such data left the facts of generic recall in doubt. An occasional correspondence between a retrieved word and a target word with respect to number of syllables, stress pattern or initial letter is, after all, to be expected by chance. Several months of "self-observation and asking-our-friends" yielded fewer than a dozen good cases and we realized that an improved method of data collection was essential.

We thought it might pay to "prospect" for TOT states by reading to S definitions of uncommon English words and asking him to supply the words. The procedure was given a preliminary test with nine Ss who were individually interviewed for 2 hrs each. In 57 instances an S was, in fact, "seized" by a TOT state. The signs of it were unmistakable; he would appear to be in mild torment, something like the brink of a sneeze, and if he found the word his relief was considerable. While searching for the target S told us all the words that came to his mind. He volunteered the information that some of them resembled the target in sound but not in meaning; others he was sure were similar in meaning but not in sound. The E intruded on S's agony with two questions: (a) How many syllables has the target word? (b) What is its first letter? Answers to the first question were correct in 47% of all cases and answers to the second question were correct in 51% of the cases. These outcomes encouraged us to believe that generic recall was real and to devise a group procedure that would further speed up the rate of data collection.

METHOD

Subjects

Fifty-six Harvard and Radcliffe undergraduates participated in one of three evening sessions; each session was 2 hrs long. The Ss were volunteers from a large General Education Course and were paid for their time.

Word List. The list consisted of 49 words which, according to the Thorndike-Lorge *Word Book* (1952), occur at least once per four million words but not so often as once per one million words. The level is suggested by these examples: *apse, nepotism, cloaca, ambergris,* and *sampan.* We thought the words used were likely to be in the passive or recognition vocabularies of our Ss but not in their active recall vocabularies. There were 6 words of 1 syllable; 19 of 2 syllables; 20 of 3 syllables; 4 of 4 syllables. For each word we used a definition from *The American College Dictionary* (Barnhart, 1948) edited so as to contain no words that closely resembled the one being defined.

Response Sheet. The response sheet was laid off in vertical columns headed as follows:

Intended word (+ One I was thinking of).
                    (− Not).
Number of syllables (1–5).
Initial letter.
Words of similar sound. (1. *Closest in sound)*
                           (2. *Middle   )*
                           (3. *Farthest in Sound)*
Words of similar meaning.
Word you had in mind if not intended word.

Procedure

We instructed Ss to the following effect.

In this experiment we are concerned with that state of mind in which a person is unable to think of a word that he is certain he knows, the state of mind in which a word seems to be on the tip of one's tongue. Our technique for precipitating such states is, in general, to read definitions of uncommon words and ask the subject to recall the word.

1. We will first read the definition of a low-frequency word.

2. If you should happen to know the word at once, or think you do, or, if you should simply not know it, then there is nothing further for you to do at the moment. Just wait.

3. If you are unable to think of the word but feel sure that you know it and that it is on the verge of coming back to you then you are in a TOT state and should begin at once to fill in the columns of the response sheet.

4. After reading each definition we will ask whether anyone is in the TOT state. Anyone who is in that state should raise his hand. The rest of us will then wait until those in the TOT state have written on the answer sheet all the information they are able to provide.

5. When everyone who has been in the TOT state has signalled us to proceed, we will read the target word. At this time, everyone is to write the word in the leftmost column of the response sheet. Those of

you who have known the word since first its definition was read are asked not to write it until this point. Those of you who simply did not know the word or who had thought of a different word will write now the word we read. For those of you who have been in the TOT state two eventualities are possible. The word read may strike you as definitely the word you have been seeking. In that case please write '+' after the word, as the instructions at the head of the column direct. The other possibility is that you will not be sure whether the word read is the one you have been seeking or, indeed, you may be sure that it is not. In this case you are asked to write the sign '−' after the word. Sometimes when the word read out is not the one you have been seeking your actual target may come to mind. In this case, in addition to the minus sign in the leftmost column, please write the actual target word in the rightmost column.

6. Now we come to the column entries themselves. The first two entries, the guess as to the number of syllables and the initial letter, are required. The remaining entries should be filled out if possible. When you are in a TOT state, words that are related to the target word do almost always come to mind. List them as they come, but separate words which you think resemble the target in sound from words which you think resemble the target in meaning.

7. When you have finished all your entries, but before you signal us to read the intended target word, look again at the words you have listed as 'Words of similar sound.' If possible, rank these, as the instructions at the head of the column direct, in terms of the degree of their seeming resemblance to the target. This must be done without knowledge of what the target actually is.

8. The search procedure of a person in the TOT state will sometimes serve to retrieve the missing word before he has finished filling in the columns and before we read out the word. When this happens please mark the place where it happens with the words "Got it" and *do not provide any more data.*

RESULTS

Classes of Data

There were 360 instances, across all words and all Ss, in which a TOT state was signalled. Of this total, 233 were positive TOTs. A positive TOT is one for which the target word is known and, consequently, one for which the data obtained can be scored as accurate or inaccurate. In those cases where the target was not the word intended but some other word which S finally recalled and wrote in the rightmost column his data were checked against that word, his effective target. A negative

TOT is one for which the S judged the word read out not to have been his target and, in addition, one in which S proved unable to recall his own functional target.

The data provided by S while he searched for the target word are of two kinds: explicit guesses as to the number of syllables in the target and the initial letter of the target; words that came to mind while he searched for the target. The words that came to mind were classified by S into 224 words similar in sound to the target (hereafter called "SS" words) and 95 words similar in meaning to the target (hereafter called "SM" words). The S's information about the number of syllables in, and the initial letter of the target may be inferred from correspondences between the target and his SS words as well as directly discovered from his explicit guesses. For his knowledge of the stress pattern of the target and of letters in the target, other than the initial letter, we must rely on the SS words alone since explicit guesses were not required.

To convey a sense of the SS and SM words we offer the following examples. When the target was *sampan* the SS words (not all of them real words) included: *Saipan, Siam, Cheyenne, sarong, sanching,* and *sympoon.* The SM words were: *barge, houseboat,* and *junk.* When the target was *caduceus* the SS words included: *Casadesus, Aeschelus, cephalus,* and *leucosis.* The SM words were: *fasces, Hippocrates, lictor,* and *snake.* The spelling in all cases is S's own.

We will, in this report, use the SM words to provide baseline data against which to evaluate the accuracy of the explicit guesses and of the SS words. The SM words are words produced under the spell of the positive TOT state but judged by S to resemble the target in meaning rather than sound. We are quite sure that the SM words are somewhat more like the target than would be a collection of words produced by Ss with no knowledge of the target. However, the SM words make a better comparative baseline than any other data we collected.

General Problems of Analysis

The data present problems of analysis that are not common in psychology. To begin with, the words of the list did not reliably precipitate TOT states. Of the original 49 words, all but *zither* succeeded at least once; the range was from one success to nine. The Ss made actual targets of 51 words not on the original list and all but five of these were pursued by one S only. Clearly none of the 100 words came even close to precipitating a TOT state in all 56 Ss. Furthermore, the Ss varied in their susceptibility to TOT states. There were nine who experienced none at all in a 2-hr period; the largest number experienced in such a period by one S was eight. In our data, then, the entries for one word will not usually involve the same Ss or even the same number of Ss as the entries for another word. The entries for one S need not involve the same words or even the same number of words as the entries for another S. Consequently for the tests we shall want to make there are no significance tests that we can be sure are appropriate.

In statistical theory our problem is called the "fragmentary data problem." The best thing to do with fragmentary data is to report them very fully and analyze them in several different ways. Our detailed knowledge of these data suggests that the problems are not serious for, while there is some variation in the pull of words and the susceptibility of Ss there is not much variation in the quality of the data. The character of the material recalled is much the same from word to word and S to S.

Number of Syllables

As the main item of evidence that S in a TOT state can recall with significant success the number of syllables in a target word he has not yet found we offer Table 12–1. The entries on the diagonal are instances in which guesses were correct. The order of the means of the explicit guesses is the same as the order of the actual numbers of syllables in the target words. The rank order correlation between the two is 1.0 and such a correlation is significant with a $p < .001$ (one-tailed) even when only five items are correlated. The modes of the guesses correspond exactly with the actual numbers of syllables, for the values one through three; for words of four and five syllables the modes continue to be three.

When all TOTs are combined, the contributions to the total effects of individual Ss and of individual words are unequal. We have made an analysis in which each word counts but once. This was accomplished by calculating the mean of the guesses made by all Ss for whom a particular word precipitated a TOT state and taking that mean as the score for that word. The new means calculated with all words equally weighted were, in order: 1.62; 2.30; 2.80; 3.33; and 3.50. These values are close to those of Table 12–1 and *rho* with the actual numbers of syllables continues to be 1.0.

We also made an analysis in which each S counts but once. This was done by calculating the mean of an S's guesses for all words of one syllable, the mean for all words of two syllables, etc. In comparing the means of guesses for words of different length one can only use those Ss who made at least one guess for each actual length to be compared. In the present data only words of two syllables and three syllables precipitated enough TOTs to yield a substantial number of such matched scores. There were 21 Ss who made guesses for both two-syllable and three-syllable words. The simplest way to evaluate the significance of the differences in these guesses is with the Sign Test. In only 6 of 21 matched scores was the mean guess for words of two syllables larger than the mean for words of three syllables. The difference is significant with a $p = .039$ (one-tailed). For actual words that were only one syllable apart in length, Ss were able to make a significant distinction in the correct direction when the words themselves could not be called to mind.

TABLE 12–1

ACTUAL NUMBERS OF SYLLABLES AND GUESSED NUMBERS
FOR ALL TOTs IN THE MAIN EXPERIMENT

| | | Guessed Numbers | | | | | No Guess | Mode | Mean |
		1	2	3	4	5			
Actual numbers	1	9	7	1	0	0	0	1	1.53
	2	2	55	22	2	1	5	2	2.33
	3	3	19	61	10	1	5	3	2.86
	4	0	2	12	6	2	3	3	3.36
	5	0	0	3	0	1	1	3	3.50

The 224 SS words and the 95 SM words provide supporting evidence. Words of similar sound (SS) had the same number of syllables as the target in 48% of all cases. This value is close to the 57% that were correct for explicit guesses in the main experiment and still closer to the 47% correct already reported for the pretest. The SM words provide a clear contrast; only 20% matched the number of syllables in the target. We conclude that S in a positive TOT state has a significant ability to recall correctly the number of syllables in the word he is trying to retrieve.

In Table 12–1 it can be seen that the modes of guesses exactly correspond with the actual numbers of syllables in target words for the values one through three. For still longer target words (four and five syllables) the means of guesses continue to rise but the modes stay at the value three. Words of more than three syllables are rare in English and the generic entry for such words may be the same as for words of three syllables; something like "three or more" may be used for all long words.

Initial Letter

Over all positive TOTs, the initial letter of the word S was seeking was correctly guessed 57% of the time. The pretest result was 51% correct. The results from the main experiment were analyzed with each word counting just once by entering a word's score as "correct" whenever the most common guess or the only guess was in fact correct; 62% of words were, by this reckoning, correctly guessed. The SS words had initial letters matching the initial letters of the target words in 49% of all cases. We do not know the chance level of success for this performance but with 26 letters and many words that began with uncommon letters the level must be low. Probably the results for the SM words are better than chance and yet the outcome for these words was only 8% matches.

We did an analysis of the SS and SM words, with each S counting just once. There were 26 Ss who had at least one such word. For each S we calculated the proportion of SS words matching the target in initial letter and the same proportion for SM words. For 21 Ss the proportions were not tied and in all but 3 cases the larger value was that of the SS words. The difference is significant by Sign Test with $p = .001$ (one- tailed).

The evidence for significantly accurate generic recall of initial letters is even stronger than for syllables. The absolute levels of success are similar but the chance baseline must be much lower for letters than for syllables because the possibilities are more numerous.

Syllabic Stress

We did not ask S to guess the stress pattern of the target word but the SS words provide relevant data. The test was limited to the syllabic location of the primary or heaviest stress for which *The American College Dictionary* was our authority. The number of SS words that could be used was limited by three considerations. (a) Words of one syllable had to be excluded because there was no possibility of variation. (b) Stress locations could only be matched if the SS word had the same number of syllables as the target, and so only such matching words could be used. (c) Invented words and foreign words could not be used because they do not appear in the dictionary. Only 49 SS words remained.

As it happened all of the target words involved (whatever their length) placed the primary stress on either the first or the second syllable. It was possible, therefore, to make a 2 × 2 table for the 49 pairs of target and SS words which would reveal the correspondences and

TABLE 12–2
SYLLABLES RECEIVING PRIMARY STRESS IN TARGET
WORDS AND SS WORDS

		Target words	
		1st syllable	2nd syllable
SS Words	1st syllable	25	6
	2nd syllable	6	12

noncorrespondences. As can be seen in Table 12–2 the SS words tended to stress the same syllable as the target words. The χ^2 for this table is 10.96 and that value is significant with $p < .001$. However, the data do not meet the independence requirement, so we cannot be sure that the matching tendency is significant. There were not enough data to permit any other analyses, and so we are left suspecting that S in a TOT state has knowledge of the stress pattern of the target, but we are not sure of it.

Letters in Various Positions

We did not require explicit guesses for letters in positions other than the first, but the SS words provide relevant data. The test was limited to the following positions: first, second, third, third-last, second-last and last. A target word must have at least six letters in order to provide data on the six positions; it might have any number of letters larger than six and still provide data for the six (relatively defined) positions. Accordingly we included the data for all target words having six or more letters.

Figure 12–1 displays the percentages of letters in each of six positions of SS words which matched the letters in the same positions of the corresponding targets. For comparison purposes these data are also provided for SM words. The SS curve is at all points above the SM curve; the two are closest together at the third-last position. The values for the last three positions of the SS curve quite closely match the values for the first three positions. The values for the last three positions of the SM curve, on the other hand, are well above the values for the first three positions. Consequently the *relative* superiority of the SS curve is greater in the first three positions.

The letter-position data were also analyzed in such a way as to count each target word just once, assigning each position in the target a single score representing the proportion of matches across all Ss for that position in that word. The order of the SS and SM points is preserved in this finer analysis. We did Sign Tests comparing the SS and SM values for each of the six positions. Figure 12–1 would suggest the SS values for the first three positions all exceeded the SM values with p's less than .01 (one-tailed). The SS values for the final two positions exceeded the SM values with p's less than .05 (one-tailed). The SS values for the third-last position were greater than the SM values but not significantly so.

The cause of the upswing in the final three positions of the SM curve may be some difference in the distribution of information in early and late positions of English words. Probably there is less variety in the later positions. In any case the fact that the SS curve lies above the SM

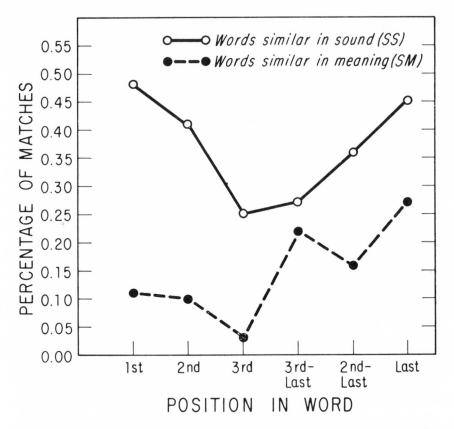

Figure 12–1. Percentages of letter matches between target words and SS words for six serial positions.

curve for the last three positions indicates that S in a TOT state has knowledge of the target in addition to his knowledge of English word structure.

Chunking of Suffixes

The request to S that he guess the initial letter of the target occasionally elicited a response of more than one letter; e.g., *ex* in the case of *extort* and *con* in the case of *convene*. This result suggested that some letter (or phoneme) sequences are stored as single entries having been "chunked" by long experience. We made only one test for chunking and that involved three-letter suffixes.

It did not often happen that an S produced an SS word that matched the target with respect to all of its three last letters. The question asked of the data was whether such three-letter matches occurred more often when the letters constituted an English suffix than when they did not. In order to determine which of the target words terminated in such a suffix, we entered *The American College Dictionary* with final trigrams. If there was an entry describing a suffix appropriate to the grammatical and semantic properties of the target we considered the trigram to be a suffix. There were 20 words that terminated in a suffix, including *fawning*, *unctuous*, and *philatelist*.

Of 93 SS words produced in response to a target terminating in a suffix, 30 matched the target in their final three letters. Of 130 SS words supplied in response to a target that did not terminate in a suffix only 5 matched the target in their final three letters. The data were also analyzed in a way that counts each S just once and uses only Ss who produced SS words in response to both kinds of target. A Sign Test was made of the difference between matches of suffixes and matches of endings that were not suffixes; the former were more common with $p = .059$ (one-tailed). A comparable Sign Test for the SM words was very far from significance. We conclude that suffix-chunking probably plays a role in generic recall.

Proximity to the Target and Quality of Information

There were three varieties of positive TOT states: (1) Cases in which S *recognized* the word read by E as the word he had been seeking; (2) Cases in which S *recalled* the intended word before it was read out; (3) Cases in which S *recalled* the word he had been seeking before E read the intended word and the recalled word was not the same as the word read. Since S in a TOT state of either type 2 or type 3 reached the target before the intended word was read and S in a TOT state of type 1 did not, the TOTs of the second and third types may be considered "nearer" the target than TOTs of the first type. We have no basis for ordering types 2 and 3 relative to one another. We predicted that Ss in the two kinds of TOT state that ended in recall (types 2 and 3) would produce more accurate information about the target than Ss in the TOT state that ended in recognition (type 1).

The prediction was tested on the explicit guesses of initial letters since these were the most complete and sensitive data. There were 138 guesses from Ss in a type 1 state and 58 of these, or 42%, were correct. There were 36 guesses from Ss in a type 2 state and, of these, 20, or 56%, were correct. There were 59 guesses from Ss in a type 3 state and of these 39, or 66%, were correct. We also analyzed the results in such a way as to count each word only once. The percentages correct were: for type 1, 50%; type 2, 62%; type 3, 63%. Finally, we performed an analysis counting each S just once but averaging together type 2 and type 3 results in order to bring a maximum number of Ss into the comparison. The combining action is justified since both type 2 and type 3 were states ending in recall. A Sign Test of the differences showed that guesses were more accurate in the states that ended in recall than in the states that ended in recognition; one-tailed $p < .01$. Supplementary analyses with SS and SM words confirmed these results. We conclude that when S is nearer his target his generic recall is more accurate than when he is farther from the target.

Special interest attaches to the results from type 2 TOTs. In the method of our experiment there is nothing to guarantee that when S said he recognized a word he had really done so. Perhaps when E read out a word, S could not help thinking that that was the word he had in mind. We ourselves do not believe anything of the sort happened. The single fact that most Ss claimed fewer than five positive TOTs in a 2-hr period argues against any such effect. Still it is reassuring to have the 36 type 2 cases in which S recalled the intended word *before* it was read. The fact that 56% of the guesses of initial letters made in type 2 states were correct is hard-core evidence of generic recall. It may be worth adding that 65% of the guesses of the number of syllables for type 2 cases were correct.

Judgments of the Proximity of SS Words

The several comparisons we have made of SS and SM words demonstrate that when recall is imminent S can distinguish among the words that come to mind those that resemble the target in form from those that do not resemble the target in form. There is a second kind of evidence which shows that S can tell when he is getting close (or "warm").

In 15 instances Ss rated two or more SS words for comparative similarity to the target. Our analysis contrasts those rated "most similar" (1) with those rated next most similar (2). Since there were very few words rated (3) we attempted no analysis of them. Similarity points were given for all the features of a word that have now been demonstrated to play a part in generic recall—with the single exception of stress. Stress had to be disregarded because some of the words were invented and their stress patterns were unknown.

The problem was to compare pairs of SS words, rated 1 and 2, for overall similarity to the target. We determined whether each member matched the target in number of syllables. If one did and the other did not, then a single similarity point was assigned the word that matched. For each word, we counted, beginning with the initial letter, the number of consecutive letters in common with the target. The word having the longer sequence that matched the target earned one similarity point. An exactly comparable procedure was followed for sequences starting from the final letter. In sum, each word in a pair could receive from zero to three similarity points.

We made Sign Tests comparing the total scores for words rated most like the target (1) and words rated next most like the target (2). This test was only slightly inappropriate since only two target words occurred twice in the set of 15 and only one S repeated in the set. Ten of 12 differences were in the predicted direction and the one-tailed $p = .019$. It is of some interest that similarity points awarded on the basis of letters in the middle of the words did not even go in the right direction. Figure 12–1 has already indicated that they also do not figure in Ss' judgments of the comparative similarity to the target of pairs of SS words. Our conclusion is that S at a given distance from the target can accurately judge which of two words that come to mind is more like the target and that he does so in terms of the features of words that appear in generic recall.

Conclusions

When complete recall of a word has not occurred but is felt to be imminent there is likely to be accurate generic recall. Generic recall of the *abstract form* variety is evidenced by S's knowledge of the number of syllables in the target and of the location of the primary stress. Generic recall of the *partial* variety is evidenced by S's knowledge of letters in the target word. This knowledge shows a bowed serial-position effect since it is better for the ends of a word than for the middle and somewhat better for beginning positions than for final positions. The accuracy of generic recall is greater when S is near the target (complete recall is imminent) than when S is far from the target. A person experiencing generic recall is able to judge the relative similarity to the target of words that occur to him and these judgments are based on the features of words that figure in partial and abstract form recall.

DISCUSSION

The facts of generic recall are relevant to theories of speech perception, reading, the understanding of sentences, and the organization of memory. We have not worked out all the implications. In this section we first attempt a model of the TOT process and then try to account for the existence of generic memory.

A Model of the Process

Let us suppose (with Katz and Fodor, 1963, and many others) that our long-term memory for words and definitions is organized into the functional equivalent of a dictionary. In real dictionaries, those that are books, entries are ordered alphabetically and bound in place. Such an arrangement is too simple and too inflexible to serve as a model for a mental dictionary. We will suppose that words are entered on keysort cards instead of pages and that the cards are punched for various features of the words entered. With real cards, paper ones, it is possible to retrieve from the total deck any subset punched for a common feature by putting a metal rod through the proper hole. We will suppose that there is in the mind some speedier equivalent of this retrieval technique.

The model will be described in terms of a single example. When the target word was *sextant*, Ss heard the definition: "A navigational instrument used in measuring angular distances, especially the altitude of sun, moon, and stars at sea." This definition precipitated a TOT state in 9 Ss of the total 56. The SM words included: *astrolabe, compass, dividers*, and *protractor*. The SS words included: *secant, sextet* and *sexton*.

The problem begins with a definition rather than a word and so S must enter his dictionary backwards, or in a way that would be backwards and quite impossible for the dictionary that is a book. It is not impossible with keysort cards, providing we suppose that the cards are punched for some set of semantic features. Perhaps these are the semantic "markers" that Katz and Fodor (1963) postulate in their account of the comprehension of sentences. We will imagine that it is somehow possible to extract from the definition a set of markers and that these are, in the present case: "navigation, instrument, having to do with geometry." Metal rods thrust into the holes for each of these features might fish up such a collection of entries as: *astrolabe, compass, dividers*, and *protractor*. This first retrieval, which is in response to the definition, must be semantically based and it will not therefore account for the appearance of such SS words as *sextet* and *sexton*.

There are four major kinds of outcome of the first retrieval and these outcomes correspond with the four main things that happen to Ss in the TOT experiment. We will assume that a definition of each word retrieved is entered on its card and that it is possible to check the input definition against those on the cards. The first possible outcome is that *sextant* is retrieved along with *compass* and *astrolabe* and the others and that the definitions are specific enough so that the one entered for *sextant* registers as matching the input and all the others as not-matching. This is the case of correct recall; S has found a word that matches the definition and it is the intended word. The second possibility is that *sextant* is not among the words retrieved and, in addition, the definitions entered for those retrieved are so imprecise that one of them (the definition for *compass*, for example) registers as matching the input. In this case S thinks he has found the target though he really has not. The third possibility is that *sextant* is not among the words retrieved, but the definitions entered for those retrieved are specific enough so that none of them will register a match with the input. In this case, S does not know the word and realizes the fact. The above three outcomes are the common ones and none of them represents a TOT state.

In the TOT case the first retrieval must include a card with the definition of *sextant* entered on it but with the word itself incompletely entered. The card might, for instance, have the following information about the word: two-syllables, initial s, final t. The entry would be a punchcard equivalent of S——T. Perhaps an incomplete entry of this sort is James's "singularly definite gap" and the basis for generic recall.

The S with a correct definition, matching the input, and an incomplete word entry will know that he knows the word, will feel that he almost has it, that it is on the tip of his tongue. If he is asked to guess the number of syllables and the initial letter he should, in the case we have imagined, be able to do so. He should also be able to produce SS words. The features that appear in the incomplete entry (two-syllables, initial s, and final t) can be used as the basis for a second retrieval. The subset of cards defined by the intersection of all three features would include cards for *secant* and *sextet*. If one feature were not used then *sexton* would be added to the set.

Which of the facts about the TOT state can now be accounted for? We know that Ss were able, when they had not recalled a target, to distinguish between words resembling the target in sound (SS words) and words resembling the target in meaning only (SM words). The basis for this distinction in the model would seem to be the distinction between the first and second retrievals. Membership in the first subset retrieved defines SM words and membership in the second subset defines SS words.

We know that when S had produced several SS words but had not recalled the target he could sometimes accurately rank-order the SS words for similarity to the target. The model offers an account of this ranking performance. If the incomplete entry for *sextant* includes three features of the word then SS words having only one or two of these features (e.g., *sexton*) should be judged less similar to the target than SS words having all three of them (e.g., *secant*).

When an SS word has all of the features of the incomplete entry (as do *secant* and *sextet* in our example) what prevents its being mistaken for the target? Why did not the S who produced *sextet* think that the word was "right"? Because of the definitions. The forms meet all the requirements of the incomplete entry but the definitions do not match.

The TOT state often ended in recognition; i.e., S failed to recall the word but when E read out *sextant* S recognized it as the word he had been seeking. The model accounts for this outcome as follows. Suppose that there is only the incomplete entry S——T in memory, plus the definition. The *E* now says (in effect) that there exists a word *sextant* which has the definition in question. The word *sextant* then satisfies all the data points available to *S;* it has the right number of syllables, the right initial letter, the right final letter, and it is said to have the right definition. The result is recognition.

The proposed account has some testable implications. Suppose that *E* were to read out, when recall failed, not the correct word *sextant* but an invented word like *sekrant* or *saktint* which satisfies the incomplete entry as well as does *sextant* itself. If *S* had nothing but the incomplete entry and *E*'s testimony to guide him then he should "recognize" the invented words just as he recognizes *sextant.*

The account we have given does not accord with intuition. Our intuitive notion of recognition is that the features which could not be recalled were actually in storage but less accessible than the features that were recalled. To stay with our example, intuition suggests that the features of *sextant* that could not be recalled, the letters between the first and the last, were entered on the card but were less "legible" than the recalled features. We might imagine them printed in small letters and faintly. When, however, the *E* reads out the word *sextant,* then *S* can make out the less legible parts of his entry and, since the total entry matches *E*'s word, *S* recognizes it. This sort of recognition should be "tighter" than the one described previously. *Sekrant* and *saktint* would be rejected.

We did not try the effect of invented words and we do not know how they would have been received but among the outcomes of the actual experiment there is one that strongly favors the faint-entry theory. Subjects in a TOT state, after all, sometimes recalled the target word without any prompting. The incomplete entry theory does not admit of such a possibility. If we suppose that the entry is not S——T but something more like Se*x tan*T (with the italicized lower-case letters representing the faint-entry section) we must still explain how it happens that the faintly entered, and at first inaccessible, middle letters are made accessible in the case of recall.

Perhaps it works something like this. The features that are first recalled operate as we have suggested, to retrieve a set of SS words. Whenever an SS word (such as *secant*) includes middle letters that are matched in the faintly entered section of the target then those faintly entered letters become accessible. The match brings out the missing parts the way heat brings out anything written in lemon juice. In other words, when *secant* is retrieved the target entry grows from Se*x tan*T to SE*x t*ANT. The retrieval of *sextet* brings out the remaining letters and S recalls the complete word—*sextant.*

It is now possible to explain the one as yet unexplained outcome of the TOT experiment. Subjects whose state ended in recall had, before they found the target, more correct information about it than did Ss whose state ended in recognition. More correct information means fewer features to be brought out by duplication in SS words and so should mean a greater likelihood that all essential features will be brought out in a short period of time.

All of the above assumes that each word is entered in memory just once, on a single card. There is another possibility. Suppose that there are entries for *sextant* on several different cards. They might all be incomplete, but at different points, or, some might be incomplete and one or more of them complete. The several cards would be punched for different semantic markers and perhaps for different associations so that the entry recovered would vary with the rule of retrieval. With this conception we do not require the notion of faint entry. The difference between features commonly recalled, such as the first and last letters, and features that are recalled with difficulty or perhaps only recognized, can be rendered in another way. The more accessible features are entered on more cards or else the cards on which they appear are punched for more markers; in effect, they are wired into a more extended associative net.

The Reason for Generic Recall

In adult minds words are stored in both visual and auditory terms and between the two there are complicated rules of translation. Generic recall involves letters (or phonemes), affixes, syllables, and stress location. In this section we will discuss only letters (legible forms) and will attempt to explain a single effect—the serial position effect in the recall of letters. It is not clear how far the explanation can be extended.

In brief overview this is the argument. The design of the English language is such that one word is usually distinguished from all others in a more-than-minimal way, i.e., by more than a single letter in a single position. It is consequently *possible* to recognize words when one has not stored the complete letter sequence. The evidence is that we do not store the complete sequence if we do not have to. We begin by attending chiefly to initial and final letters and storing these. The order of attention and of storage favors the ends of words because the ends carry more information than the middles. An incomplete entry will serve for recognition, but if words are to be produced (or recalled) they must be stored in full. For most words, then, it is eventually necessary to attend to the middle letters. Since end letters have been attended to from the first they should always be more clearly entered or more elaborately connected than middle letters. When recall is required, of words that are not very familiar to S, as it was in our experiment, the end letters should often be accessible when the middle are not.

In building pronounceable sequences the English language, like all other languages, utilizes only a small fraction of its combinatorial possibilities (Hockett, 1958). If a language used all possible sequences of phonemes (or letters) its words could be shorter, but they would be much more vulnerable to misconstruction. A change of any single letter would result in reception of a different word. As matters are actually arranged, most changes result in no word at all; for example: *textant, sixtant, sektant.* Our words are highly redundant and fairly indestructible.

Underwood (1963) has made a distinction for the learning of nonsense syllables between the "nominal" stimulus which is the syllable presented and the "functional" stimulus which is the set of characteristics of the syllable actually used to cue the response. Underwood reviews evidence showing that college students learning paired-associates do not learn any more of a stimulus trigram than they have to. If, for instance, each of a set of stimulus trigrams has a different initial letter, then Ss are not likely to learn letters other than the first, since they do not need them.

Feigenbaum (1963) has written a computer program (EPAM) which simulates the selective-attention aspect of verbal learning as well as many other aspects. "EPAM has a *noticing order for letters of syllables,* which prescribes at any moment a letter-scanning sequence for the matching process. Because it is observed that subjects generally consider end letters before middle letters, the noticing order is initialized as follows: first letter, third letter, second letter" (p. 304). We believe that the differential recall of letters in various positions, revealed in Figure 12–1, is to be explained by the operation in the perception of real words of a rule very much like Feigenbaum's.

Feigenbaum's EPAM is so written as to make it possible for the noticing rule to be changed by experience. If the middle position were consistently the position that differentiated syllables, the computer would learn to look there first. We suggest that the human tendency to look first at the beginning of a word, then at the end and finally the middle has "grown" in response to the distribution of information in words. Miller and Friedman (1957) asked English speakers to guess letters for various open positions in segments of English text that were 5, 7, or 11 characters long. The percentages of correct first guesses show a very clear serial position effect for segments of all three lengths. Success was lowest in the early positions, next lowest in the final positions, and at a maximum in the middle positions. Therefore, information was greatest at the start of a word, next greatest at the end, and least in the middle. Attention needs to be turned where information is, to the parts of the word that cannot be guessed. The Miller and Friedman segments did not necessarily break at word boundaries but their discovery that the middle positions of continuous text are more easily guessed than the ends applies to words.

Is there any evidence that speakers of English do attend first to the ends of English words? There is no evidence that the eye fixations of adult readers consistently favor particular parts of words (Woodworth and Schlosberg, 1954). However, it is not eye fixation that we have in mind. A considerable stretch of text can be taken from a single fixation point. We are suggesting that there is selection within this stretch, selection accomplished centrally; perhaps by a mechanism like Broadbent's (1958) "biased filter."

Bruner and O'Dowd (1958) studied word perception with tachistoscopic exposures too brief to permit more than one fixation. In each word presented there was a single reversal of two letters and the S knew this. His task was to identify the *actual* English word, responding as quickly as possible. When the *actual* word was AVIATION, Ss were presented with one of the following: VAIATION, AVITAION, AVIATINO. Identification of the actual word as AVIATION was best when S saw AVITAION, next best when he saw AVIATINO, and most difficult when he saw VAIATION. In general, reversal of the two initial letters made identification most difficult, reversal of the last two letters made it somewhat less difficult, reversal in the middle made least difficulty. This is what should happen if words are first scanned initially, then finally, then medially. But the scanning cannot be a matter of eye movements; it must be more central.

Selective attention to the ends of words should lead to the entry of these parts into the mental dictionary, in advance of the middle parts. However, we ordinarily need to know more than the ends of words. Underwood has pointed out (1963), in connection with paired-associate learning, that while partial knowledge may be enough for a stimulus syllable which need only be recognized it will not suffice for a response item which must be produced. The case is similar for natural language. In order to speak one must know all of a word. However, the words of the present study were low-frequency words, words likely to be in the passive or recognition vocabularies of the college-student Ss but not in their active vocabularies; stimulus items, in effect, rather than response items. If knowledge of the parts of new words begins at the ends and moves toward the middle we might expect a word like *numismatics*, which was on our list, to be still registered as NUM—— ICS. Reduced entries of this sort would in many contexts serve to retrieve the definition.

The argument is reinforced by a well-known effect in spelling. Jensen (1962) has analyzed thousands of spelling errors for words of 7, 9, or 11 letters made by children in the eighth and tenth grades and by junior college freshmen. A striking serial position effect appears in all his sets of data such that errors are most common in the middle of a word, next most common in the end, and least common at the start. These results are as they should be if the order of attention and entry of information is first, last, and then, middle. Jensen's results show us what happens when children are forced to produce words that are still on the recognition level. His results remind us of those bluebooks in which students who are uncertain of the spelling of a word write the first and last letters with great clarity and fill in the middle with indecipherable squiggles. That is what should happen when a word that can be only partially recalled must be produced in its entirety. End letters and a stretch of squiggles may, however, be quite adequate for recognition purposes. In the TOT experiment we have perhaps placed adult Ss in a situation comparable to that created for children by Jensen's spelling tests.

There are two points to clarify and the argument is finished. The Ss in our experiment were college students, and so in order to obtain words on the margin of knowledge we had to use words that are very infrequent in English as a whole. It is not our thought, however, that the TOT phenomenon occurs only with rare words. The absolute location of the margin of word knowledge is a function of S's age and education, and so with other Ss we would expect to obtain TOT states for words more frequent in English. Finally the need to produce (or recall) a word is not the only factor that is likely to encourage registration of its middle letters. The amount of detail needed to specify a word uniquely must increase with the total number of words known, the number from which any one is to be distinguished. Consequently the growth of vocabulary, as well as the need to recall, should have some power to force attention into the middle of a word.

REFERENCES

Barnhart, C. L. (Ed.) *The American college dictionary*. New York: Harper, 1948.

Broadbent, D. E. *Perception and communication*. New York: Macmillan, 1958.

Bruner, J. S., & O'Dowd, D. A note on the informativeness of words. *Language and Speech*, 1958, **1**, 98–101.

Feigenbaum, E. A. The simulation of verbal learning behavior. In E. A. Feigenbaum and J. Feldman (Eds.) *Computers and thought*. New York: McGraw-Hill, 1963. Pp. 297–309.

Hockett, C. F. *A course in modern linguistics*. New York: Macmillan, 1958.

James, W. *The principles of psychology*, Vol. I. New York: Holt, 1893.

Jensen, A. R. Spelling errors and the serial-position effect. *J. educ. Psychol.*, 1962, **53**, 105–109.

KATZ, J. J., & FODOR, J. A. The structure of a semantic theory. *Language*, 1963, 39, 170–210.

MILLER, G. A., & FRIEDMAN, ELIZABETH A. The reconstruction of mutilated English texts. *Inform. Control*, 1957, 1, 38–55.

THORNDIKE, E. L., & LORGE, I. *The teacher's word book of 30,000 words.* New York: Columbia University Press, 1952.

UNDERWOOD, B. J. Stimulus selection in verbal learning. In C. N. Cofer and B. S. Musgrave (Eds.) *Verbal behavior and learning: problems and processes.* New York: McGraw-Hill, 1963. Pp. 33–48.

WENZL, A. Empirische und theoretische Beiträge zur Erinnerungsarbeit bei erschwerter Wortfindung. *Arch. ges. Psychol.*, 1932, 85, 181–218.

WENZL, A. Empirische und theoretische Beiträge zur Erinnerungsarbeit bei erschwerter Wortfindung. *Arch. ges. Psychol.*, 1936, 97, 294–318.

WOODWORTH, R. S. *Psychology.* (3rd ed.). New York: Holt, 1934.

WOODWORTH, R. S., & SCHLOSBERG, H. *Experimental psychology.* (Rev. ed.). New York: Holt, 1954.

13.

Teaching Sign Language to a Chimpanzee

R. ALLEN GARDNER and
BEATRICE T. GARDNER

Children all over the world learn to speak. Does this universal acquisition of language reflect an inborn capacity, or is it based on learning? In either case, is it restricted to humans or can animals also acquire language? One way to approach these questions is to try to teach a language to an animal, which is precisely what the Gardners describe in the following article.

Would you say that Washoe, the chimpanzee described here, has acquired language? Before answering, reflect on what it means to "have a language."

Washoe had to be trained to use sign language. Does a human child spontaneously construct a language system, or does he similarly have to be trained?

THE EXTENT to which another species might be able to use human language is a classical problem in comparative psychology. One approach to this problem is to consider the nature of language, the processes of learning, the neural mechanisms of learning and of language, and the genetic basis of these mechanisms, and then, while recognizing certain gaps in what is known about these factors, to attempt to arrive at an answer by dint of careful scholarship (1). An alternative approach is to try to teach a form of human language to an animal. We chose the latter alternative and, in June 1966, began training an infant

Reprinted from *Science*, Vol. 165, pp. 664–72, 15 August 1969. Copyright 1969 by the American Association for the Advancement of Science. Reprinted by permission.

female chimpanzee, named Washoe, to use the gestural language of the deaf. Within the first 22 months of training it became evident that we had been correct in at least one major aspect of method, the use of a gestural language. Additional aspects of method have evolved in the course of the project. These and some implications of our early results can now be described in a way that may be useful in other studies of communicative behavior. Accordingly, in this article we discuss the considerations which led us to use the chimpanzee as a subject and American Sign Language (the language used by the deaf in North America) as a medium of communication; describe the general methods of training as they were initially conceived and as they developed in the course of the project; and summarize those results that could be reported with some degree of confidence by the end of the first phase of the project.

PRELIMINARY CONSIDERATIONS

The Chimpanzee as a Subject

Some discussion of the chimpanzee as an experimental subject is in order because this species is relatively uncommon in the psychological laboratory. Whether or not the chimpanzee is the most intelligent animal after man can be disputed; the gorilla, the orangutan, and even the dolphin have their loyal partisans in this debate. Nevertheless, it is generally conceded that chimpanzees are highly intelligent, and that members of this species might be intelligent enough for our purposes. Of equal or greater importance is their sociability and their capacity for forming strong attachments to human beings. We want to emphasize this trait of sociability; it seems highly likely that it is essential for the development of language in human beings, and it was a primary consideration in our choice of a chimpanzee as a subject.

Affectionate as chimpanzees are, they are still wild animals, and this is a serious disadvantage. Most psychologists are accustomed to working with animals that have been chosen, and sometimes bred, for docility and adaptability to laboratory procedures. The difficulties presented by the wild nature of an experimental animal must not be underestimated. Chimpanzees are also very strong animals; a full-grown specimen is likely to weigh more than 120 pounds (55 kilograms) and is estimated to be from three to five times as strong as a man, pound-for-pound. Coupled with the wildness, this great strength presents serious difficulties for a procedure that requires interaction at close quarters with a free-living animal. We have always had to reckon with the likelihood that at some point Washoe's physical maturity will make this procedure prohibitively dangerous.

A more serious disadvantage is that human speech sounds are unsuitable as a medium of communication for the chimpanzee. The vocal apparatus of the chimpanzee is very different from that of man (2). More important, the vocal behavior of the chimpanzee is very different from that of a man. Chimpanzees do make many different sounds, but generally vocalization occurs in situations of high excitement and tends to be specific to the exciting situations. Undisturbed, chimpanzees are usually silent. Thus, it is unlikely that a chimpanzee could be trained to make refined use of its vocalizations. Moreover, the intensive work of Hayes and Hayes (3) with the chimpanzee Viki indicates that a vocal language is not appropriate for this species. The Hayeses used modern, sophisticated, psychological methods and seem to have spared no effort to teach Viki to make speech sounds. Yet in 6 years Viki learned only four sounds that approximated English words (4).

Use of the hands, however, is a prominent feature of chimpanzee behavior; manipulatory mechanical problems are their forte. More to the point, even caged, laboratory chimpanzees develop begging and similar gestures spontaneously (5), while individuals that have had extensive contact with human beings have displayed an even wider variety of communicative gestures (6). In our choice of sign language we were influenced more by the behavioral evidence that this medium of communication was appropriate to the species than by anatomical evidence of structural similarity between the hands of chimpanzees and of men. The Hayeses point out that human tools and mechanical devices are constructed to fit the human hand, yet chimpanzees have little difficulty in using these devices with great skill. Nevertheless, they seem unable to adapt their vocalizations to approximate human speech.

Psychologists who work extensively with the instrumental conditioning of animals become sensitive to the need to use responses that are suited to the species they wish to study. Lever-pressing in rats is not an arbitrary response invented by Skinner to confound the mentalists; it is a type of response commonly made by rats when they are first placed in a Skinner box. The exquisite control of instrumental behavior by schedules of reward is achieved only if the original responses are well chosen. We chose a language based on gestures because we reasoned that gestures for the chimpanzee should be analogous to bar-pressing for rats, key-pecking for pigeons, and babbling for humans.

American Sign Language

Two systems of manual communication are used by the deaf. One system is the manual alphabet, or finger spelling, in which configurations of the hand correspond to letters of the alphabet. In this system the words of a spoken language, such as English, can be spelled out manually. The other system, sign language, consists of a set of manual configurations and gestures that correspond to particular words or concepts. Unlike finger spelling, which is the direct encoding of a spoken language, sign languages have their own rules of usage. Word-for-sign translation between a spoken language and a sign language yields results that are similar to those of word-for-word translation between two spoken languages: the translation is often passable, though awkward, but it can also be ambiguous or quite nonsensical. Also, there are national and regional variations in sign languages that are comparable to those of spoken languages.

We chose for this project the American Sign Language (ASL), which, with certain regional variations, is used by the deaf in North America. This particular sign language has recently been the subject of formal analysis (7). The ASL can be compared to pictograph writing in which some symbols are quite arbitrary and some are quite representational or iconic, but all are arbitrary to some degree. For example, in ASL the sign for "always" is made by holding the hand in a fist, index finger extended (the pointing hand), while rotating the arm at the elbow. This is clearly an arbitrary representation of the concept "always." The sign for "flower," however, is highly iconic; it is made by holding the fingers of one hand extended, all five fingertips touching (the tapered hand), and touching the fingertips first to one nostril then to the other, as if sniffing a flower. While this is an iconic sign for "flower," it is only one of a number of conventions by which the concept "flower" could be iconically represented; it is thus arbitrary to some degree. Undoubtedly, many of the signs of ASL that seem quite arbitrary today once had an iconic origin that was lost through years of stylized usage. Thus, the signs of ASL are neither uniformly arbitrary nor uniformly iconic; rather the degree of abstraction varies from sign to sign over a wide range. This would seem to be a useful property of ASL for our research.

The literate deaf typically use a combination of ASL and finger spelling; for purposes of this project we have avoided the use of finger spelling as much as possible. A great range of expression is possible within the limits of ASL. We soon found that a good way to practice signing among ourselves was to render familiar songs and poetry into signs; as far as we can judge, there is no message that cannot be rendered faithfully (apart from the usual problems of translation from one language to another). Technical terms and proper names are a problem when first introduced, but within any community of signers it is easy to agree on a convention for any commonly used term. For example, among ourselves we do not finger-spell the words *psychologist* and *psychology*, but render them as "think doctor" and "think science." Or, among users of ASL, "California" can be finger-spelled but is commonly rendered as "golden playland." (Incidentally, the sign for "gold" is made by plucking at the earlobe with thumb and forefinger, indicating an earring—another example of an iconic sign that is at the same time arbitrary and stylized.)

The fact that ASL is in current use by human beings is an additional advantage. The early linguistic environment of the deaf children of deaf parents is in some respects similar to the linguistic environment that we could provide for an experimental subject. This should permit some comparative evaluation of Washoe's eventual level of competence. For example, in discussing Washoe's early performance with deaf parents we have been told that many of her variants of standard signs are similar to the baby-talk variants commonly observed when human children sign.

Washoe

Having decided on a species and a medium of communication, our next concern was to obtain an experimental subject. It is altogether possible that there is some critical early age for the acquisition of this type of behavior. On the other hand, newborn chimpanzees tend to be quite helpless and vegetative. They are also considerably less hardy than older infants. Nevertheless, we reasoned that the dangers of starting too late were much greater than the dangers of starting too early, and we sought the youngest infant we could get. Newborn laboratory chimpanzees are very scarce, and we found that the youngest laboratory infant we could get would be about 2 years old at the time we planned to start the project. It seemed preferable to obtain a wild-caught infant. Wild-caught infants are usually at least 8 to 10 months old before they are available for research. This is because infants rarely reach the United States before they are 5 months old, and to this age must be added 1 or 2 months before final purchase and 2 or 3 months for quarantine and other medical services.

We named our chimpanzee Washoe for Washoe County, the home of the University of Nevada. Her exact age will never be known, but from her weight and dentition we estimated her age to be between 8 and 14 months at the end of June 1966, when she first arrived at our laboratory. (Her dentition has continued to agree with this initial estimate, but her weight has increased rather more than would be expected.) This is very young for a chimpanzee. The best available information indicates that infants are completely dependent until the age of 2 years and semidependent until the age of 4; the first signs of sexual maturity (for example, menstruation, sexual swelling) begin to appear at about 8 years, and full adult growth is reached between the ages of 12 and 16 (8). As for the complete lifespan, captive specimens have survived for well over 40 years. Washoe was indeed very young when she arrived; she did not have her first canines or molars, her hand-eye coordination was rudimentary, she had only begun to crawl about, and she slept a great deal. Apart from making friends with her and adapting her to the daily routine, we could accomplish little during the first few months.

Laboratory Conditions

At the outset we were quite sure that Washoe could learn to make various signs in order to obtain food, drink, and other things. For the project to be a success, we felt that something more must be developed. We wanted Washoe not only to ask for objects but to answer questions about them and also to ask us questions. We wanted to develop behavior that could be described as conversation. With this in mind, we attempted to provide Washoe with an environment that might be conducive to this sort of behavior. Confinement was to be minimal, about the same as that of human infants. Her human companions were to be friends and playmates as well as providers and protectors, and they were to introduce a great many games and activities that would be likely to result in maximum interaction with Washoe.

In practice, such an environment is readily achieved with a chimpanzee; bonds of warm affection have always been established between Washoe and her several human companions. We have enjoyed the interaction almost as much as Washoe has, within the limits of human endurance. A number of human companions have been enlisted to participate in the project and relieve each other at intervals, so that at least one person would be with Washoe during all her waking hours. At first we feared that such frequent changes would be disturbing, but Washoe seemed to adapt very well to this procedure. Apparently it is possible to provide an infant chimpanzee with affection on a shift basis.

All of Washoe's human companions have been required to master ASL and to use it extensively in her presence, in association with interesting activities and events and also in a general way, as one chatters at a human infant in the course of the day. The ASL has been used almost exclusively, although occasional finger spelling has been permitted. From time to time, of course, there are lapses into spoken English, as when medical personnel must examine Washoe. At one time, we considered an alternative procedure in which we would sign and speak English to Washoe simultaneously, thus giving her an additional source of informative cues. We rejected this procedure, reasoning that, if she should come to understand speech sooner or more easily than ASL, then she might not pay sufficient attention to our gestures. Another alternative, that of speaking English among ourselves and signing to Washoe, was also rejected. We reasoned that this would make it seem that big chimps talk and only little chimps sign, which might give signing an undesirable social status.

The environment we are describing is not a silent one. The human beings can vocalize in many ways, laughing and making sounds of pleasure and displeasure. Whistles and drums are sounded in a variety of imitation games, and hands are clapped for attention. The rule is that all meaningful sounds, whether vocalized or not, must be sounds that a chimpanzee can imitate.

TRAINING METHODS

Imitation

The imitativeness of apes is proverbial, and rightly so. Those who have worked closely with chimpanzees have frequently remarked on their readiness to engage in visually guided imitation. Consider the following typical comment of Yerkes (9): "Chim and Panzee would imitate many of my acts, but never have I heard them imitate a sound and rarely make a sound peculiarly their own in response to mine. As previously stated, their imitative tendency is as remarkable for its specialization and limitations as for its strength. It seems to be controlled chiefly by visual stimuli. Things which are seen tend to be imitated or reproduced. What is heard is not reproduced. Obviously an animal which lacks the tendency to reinstate auditory stimuli—in other words to imitate sounds—cannot reasonably be expected to talk. The human infant exhibits this tendency to a remarkable degree. So also does the parrot. If the imitative tendency of the parrot could be coupled with the quality of intelligence of the chimpanzee, the latter undoubtedly could speak."

In the course of their work with Viki, the Hayeses devised a game in which Viki would imitate various actions on hearing the command "Do this" (10). Once established, this was an effective means of training Viki to perform actions that could be visually guided. The same method should be admirably suited to training a chimpanzee to use sign language; accordingly we have directed much effort toward establishing a version of the "Do this" game with Washoe. Getting Washoe to imitate us was not difficult, for she did so quite spontaneously, but getting her to imitate on command has been another matter altogether. It was not until the 16th month of the project that we achieved any degree of control over Washoe's imitation of gestures. Eventually we got to a point where she would imitate a simple gesture, such as pulling at her ears, or a series of such gestures—first we make a gesture, then she imitates, then we make a second gesture, she imitates the second gesture, and so on—for the reward of being tickled.

Up to this writing, however, imitation of this sort has not been an important method for introducing new signs into Washoe's vocabulary.

As a method of prompting, we have been able to use imitation extensively to increase the frequency and refine the form of signs. Washoe sometimes fails to use a new sign in an appropriate situation, or uses another, incorrect sign. At such times we can make the correct sign to Washoe, repeating the performance until she makes the sign herself. (With more stable signs, more indirect forms of prompting can be used—for example, pointing at, or touching, Washoe's hand or a part of her body that should be involved in the sign; making the sign for "sign," which is equivalent to saying "Speak up"; or asking a question in signs, such as "What do you want?" or "What is it?") Again, with new signs, and often with old signs as well, Washoe can lapse into what we refer to as poor "diction." Of course, a great deal of slurring and a wide range of variants are permitted in ASL as in any spoken language. In any event, Washoe's diction has frequently been improved by the simple device of repeating, in exaggeratedly correct form, the sign she has just made, until she repeats it herself in more correct form. On the whole, she has responded quite well to prompting, but there are strict limits to its use with a wild animal—one that is probably quite spoiled, besides. Pressed too hard, Washoe can become completely diverted from her original object; she may ask for something entirely different, run away, go into a tantrum, or even bite her tutor.

Chimpanzees also imitate after some delay, and this delayed imitation can be quite elaborate (10). The following is a typical example of Washoe's delayed imitation. From the beginning of the project she was bathed regularly and according to a standard routine. Also, from her 2nd month with us, she always had dolls to play with. One day, during the 10th month of the project, she bathed one of her dolls in the way we usually bathed her. She filled her little bathtub with water, dunked the doll in the tub, then took it out and dried it with a towel. She has repeated the entire performance, or parts of it, many times since, sometimes also soaping the doll.

This is a type of imitation that may be very important in the acquisition of language by human children, and many of our procedures with Washoe were devised to capitalize on it. Routine activities—feeding, dressing, bathing, and so on—have been highly ritualized, with appropriate signs figuring prominently in the rituals. Many games have been invented which can be accompanied by appropriate signs. Objects and activities have been named as often as possible, especially when Washoe seemed to be paying particular attention to them. New objects and new examples of familiar objects, including pictures, have been continually brought to her attention, together with the appropriate signs. She likes to ride in automobiles, and a ride in an automobile, including the preparations for a ride, provides a wealth of sights that can be accompanied by signs. A good destination for a ride is a home or the university nursery school, both well stocked with props for language lessons.

The general principle should be clear: Washoe has been exposed to a wide variety of activities and objects, together with their appropriate signs, in the hope that she would come to associate the signs with their referents and later make the signs herself. We have reason to believe that she has come to understand a large vocabulary of signs. This was expected, since a number of chimpanzees have acquired extensive understanding vocabularies of spoken words, and there is evidence that even dogs can acquire a sizable understanding vocabulary of spoken words (11). The understanding vocabulary that Washoe has acquired, however, consists of signs that a chimpanzee can imitate.

Some of Washoe's signs seem to have been originally acquired by delayed imitation. A good example is the sign for "toothbrush." A part of the daily routine has been to brush her teeth after every meal. When this routine was first introduced Washoe generally resisted it. She gradually came to submit with less and less fuss, and after many months she would even help or sometimes brush her teeth herself. Usually, having finished her meal, Washoe would try to leave her high-chair; we would restrain her, signing "First, toothbrushing, then you can go." One day, in the 10th month of the project, Washoe was visiting the Gardner home and found her way into the bathroom. She climbed up on the counter, looked at our mug full of toothbrushes, and signed "toothbrush." At the time, we believed that Washoe understood this sign but we had not seen her use it. She had no reason to ask for the toothbrushes, because they were well within her reach, and it is most unlikely that she was asking to have her teeth brushed. This was our first observation, and one of the clearest examples, of behavior in which Washoe seemed to name an object or an event for no obvious motive other than communication.

Following this observation, the toothbrushing routine at mealtime was altered. First, imitative prompting was introduced. Then as the sign became more reliable, her rinsing-mug and toothbrush were displayed prominently until she made the sign. By the 14th month she was making the "toothbrush" sign at the end of meals with little or no prompting; in fact she has called for her toothbrush in a peremptory fashion when its appearance at the end of a meal was delayed. The "toothbrush" sign is not merely a response cued by the end of a meal; Washoe retained her ability to name toothbrushes when they were shown to her at other times.

The sign for "flower" may also have been acquired by delayed imitation. From her first summer with us, Washoe showed a great interest in flowers, and we took advantage of this by providing many flowers and pictures of flowers accompanied by the appropriate sign. Then one day in the 15th month she made the sign, spontaneously, while she and a companion were walking toward a flower garden. As in the case of "toothbrush," we believed that she understood the sign at this time, but we had made no attempt to elicit it from her except by making it ourselves in appropriate situations. Again, after the first observation, we proceeded to elicit this sign as often as possible by a variety of methods, most frequently by showing her a flower and giving it to her if she made the sign for it. Eventually the sign became very reliable and could be elicited by a variety of flowers and pictures of flowers.

It is difficult to decide which signs were acquired by the method of delayed imitation. The first appearance of these signs is likely to be sudden and unexpected; it is possible that some inadvertent movement of Washoe's has been interpreted as meaningful by one of her devoted companions. If the first observer were kept from reporting the observation and from making any direct attempts to elicit the sign again, then it might be possible to obtain independent verification. Quite understandably, we have been more interested in raising the frequency of new signs than in evaluating any particular method of training.

Babbling

Because the Hayeses were attempting to teach Viki to speak English, they were interested in babbling, and during the first year of their project they were encouraged by the number and variety of spontaneous vocalizations that Viki made. But, in time, Viki's spontaneous vocalizations decreased further and further to the point where the Hayeses felt that there was almost no vocal babbling from which to shape spoken language. In planning this project we expected a great deal of manual "babbling," but during the early months we observed very little behavior of this kind. In the course of the project, however, there has been a great increase in manual babbling. We have been particularly encouraged by the increase in movements that involve touching parts of the head and body, since these are important components of many signs. Also, more and more frequently, when Washoe has been unable to get something that she wants, she has burst into a flurry of random flourishes and arm-waving.

We have encouraged Washoe's babbling by our responsiveness; clapping, smiling, and repeating the gesture much as you might repeat "goo goo" to a human infant. If the babbled gesture has resembled a sign in ASL, we have made the correct form of the sign and have attempted to engage in some appropriate activity. The sign for "funny" was probably acquired in this way. It first appeared as a spontaneous babble that lent itself readily to a simple imitation game—first Washoe signed "funny," then we did, then she did, and so on. We would laugh and smile during the interchanges that she initiated, and initiate the game ourselves when something funny happened. Eventually Washoe came to use the "funny" sign spontaneously in roughly appropriate situations.

Closely related to babbling are some gestures that seem to have appeared independently of any deliberate training on our part, and that resemble signs so closely that we could incorporate them into Washoe's repertoire with little or no modification. Almost from the first she had a begging gesture—an extension of her open hand, palm up, toward one of us. She made this gesture in situations in which she wanted aid and in situations in which we were holding some object that she wanted. The ASL signs for "give me" and "come" are very similar to this, except that they involve a prominent beckoning movement. Gradually Washoe came to incorporate a beckoning wrist movement into her use of this sign. In Table 13–1 we refer to this sign as "come-gimme." As Washoe has come to use it, the sign is not simply a modification of the original begging gesture. For example, very commonly she reaches forward with one hand (palm up) while she gestures with the other hand (palm down) held near her head. (The result resembles a classic fencing posture.)

Another sign of this type is the sign for "hurry," which, so far, Washoe has always made by shaking her open hand vigorously at the wrist. This first appeared as an impatient flourish following some request that she had made in signs; for example, after making the "open" sign before a door. The correct ASL for "hurry" is very close, and we began to use it often, ourselves, in appropriate contexts. We believe that Washoe has come to use this sign in a meaningful way, because she has frequently used it when she, herself, is in a hurry—for example, when rushing to her nursery chair.

Instrumental Conditioning

It seems intuitively unreasonable that the acquisition of language by human beings could be strictly a matter of reiterated instrumental conditioning—that a child acquires language after the fashion of a rat that is conditioned, first, to press a lever for food in the presence of one stimulus, then to turn a wheel in the presence of another stimulus, and so on until a large repertoire of discriminated responses is acquired. Nevertheless, the so-called "trick vocabulary" of early childhood is probably acquired in this way, and this may be a critical stage

TABLE 13-1

Signs Used Reliably by Chimpanzee Washoe within Twenty-two Months of the Beginning of Training*

Signs	Description	Context
Come-gimme	Beckoning motion, with wrist or knuckles as pivot.	Sign made to persons or animals, also for objects out of reach. Often combined: "come tickle," "gimme sweet," etc.
More	Fingertips are brought together, usually overhead. (Correct ASL form: tips of the tapered hand touch repeatedly.)	When asking for continuation or repetition of activities such as swinging or tickling, for second helpings of food, etc. Also used to ask for repetition of some performance, such as a somersault.
Up	Arm extends upward, and index finger may also point up.	Wants a lift to reach objects such as grapes on vine, or leaves; or wants to be placed on someone's shoulder; or wants to leave potty-chair.
Sweet	Index or index and second fingers touch tip of wagging tongue. (Correct ASL form: index and second fingers extended side by side.)	For dessert; used spontaneously at end of meal. Also, when asking for candy.
Open	Flat hands are placed side by side, palms down, then drawn apart while rotated to palms up.	At door of house, room, car, refrigerator, or cupboard; on containers such as jars; and on faucets.
Tickle	The index finger of one hand is drawn across the back of the other hand. (Related to ASL "touch.")	For tickling or for chasing games.
Go	Opposite of "come-gimme."	While walking hand-in-hand or riding on someone's shoulders. Washoe usually indicates the direction desired.
Out	Curved hand grasps tapered hand; then tapered hand is withdrawn upward.	When passing through doorways; until recently, used for both "in" and "out." Also, when asking to be taken outdoors.
Hurry	Open hand is shaken at the wrist. (Correct ASL form: index and second fingers extended side by side.)	Often follows signs such as "come-gimme," "out," "open," and "go," particularly if there is a delay before Washoe is obeyed. Also, used while watching her meal being prepared.
Hear-listen	Index finger touches ear.	For loud or strange sounds: bells, car horns, sonic booms, etc. Also, for asking someone to hold a watch to her ear.

* The signs are listed in the order of their original appearance in her repertoire (see text for the criterion of reliability and for the method of assigning the date of original appearance).

TABLE 13-1 (continued)

Signs	Description	Context
Toothbrush	Index finger is used as brush, to rub front teeth.	When Washoe has finished her meal, or at other times when shown a toothbrush.
Drink	Thumb is extended from fisted hand and touches mouth.	For water, formula, soda pop, etc. For soda pop, often combined with "sweet."
Hurt	Extended index fingers are jabbed toward each other. Can be used to indicate location of pain.	To indicate cuts and bruises on herself or on others. Can be elicited by red stains on a person's skin or by tears in clothing.
Sorry	Fisted hand clasps and unclasps at shoulder. (Correct ASL form: fisted hand is rubbed over heart with circular motion.)	After biting someone, or when someone has been hurt in another way (not necessarily by Washoe). When told to apologize for mischief.
Funny	Tip of index finger presses nose, and Washoe snorts. (Correct ASL form: index and second fingers used; no snort.)	When soliciting interaction play, and during games. Occasionally, when being pursued after mischief.
Please	Open hand is drawn across chest. (Correct ASL form: finger tips used, and circular motion.)	When asking for objects and activities. Frequently combined: "Please go," "Out, please," "Please drink."
Food-eat	Several fingers of one hand are placed in mouth. (Correct ASL form: fingertips of tapered hand touch mouth repeatedly.)	During meals and preparation of meals.
Flower	Tip of index finger touches one or both nostrils. (Correct ASL form: tips of tapered hand touch first one nostril, then the other.)	For flowers.
Cover-blanket	Draws one hand toward self over the back of the other.	At bedtime or naptime, and, on cold days, when Washoe wants to be taken out.
Dog	Repeated slapping on thigh.	For dogs and for barking.
You	Index finger points at a person's chest.	Indicates successive turns in games. Also used in response to questions such as "Who tickle?" "Who brush?"
Napkin-bib	Fingertips wipe the mouth region.	For bib, for washcloth, and for Kleenex.
In	Opposite of "out."	Wants to go indoors, or wants someone to join her indoors.

TABLE 13-1 (continued)

Signs	Description	Context
Brush	The fisted hand rubs the back of the open hand several times. (Adapted from ASL "polish.")	For hairbrush, and when asking for brushing.
Hat	Palm pats top of head.	For hats and caps.
I-me	Index finger points at, or touches, chest	Indicates Washoe's turn, when she and a companion share food, drink, etc. Also used in phrases, such as "I drink," and in reply to questions such as "Who tickle?" (Washoe: "you"); "Who I tickle?" (Washoe: "Me.")
Shoes	The fisted hands are held side by side and strike down on shoes or floor. (Correct ASL form: the sides of the fisted hands strike against each other.)	For shoes and boots.
Smell	Palm is held before nose and moved slightly upward several times.	For scented objects: tobacco, perfume, sage, etc.
Pants	Palms of the flat hands are drawn up against the body toward waist.	For diapers, rubber pants, trousers.
Clothes	Fingertips brush down the chest.	For Washoe's jacket, nightgown, and shirts; also for our clothing.
Cat	Thumb and index finger grasp cheek hair near side of mouth and are drawn outward (representing cat's whiskers).	For cats.
Key	Palm of one hand is repeatedly touched with the index finger of the other. (Correct ASL form: crooked index finger is rotated against palm.)	Used for keys and locks and to ask us to unlock a door.
Baby	One forearm is placed in the crook of the other, as if cradling a baby.	For dolls, including animal dolls such as a toy horse and duck.
Clean	The open palm of one hand is passed over the open palm of the other.	Used when Washoe is washing, or being washed, or when a companion is washing hands or some other object. Also used for "soap."

in the acquisition of language by children. In any case, a minimal objective of this project was to teach Washoe as many signs as possible by whatever procedures we could enlist. Thus, we have not hesitated to use conventional procedures of instrumental conditioning.

Anyone who becomes familiar with young chimpanzees soon learns about their passion for being tickled. There is no doubt that tickling is the most effective reward that we have used with Washoe. In the early months, when we would pause in our tickling, Washoe would indicate that she wanted more tickling by taking our hands and placing them against her ribs or around her neck. The meaning of these gestures was unmistakable, but since we were not studying our human ability to interpret her chimpanzee gestures, we decided to shape an arbitrary response that she could use to ask for more tickling. We noted that, when being tickled, she tended to bring her arms together to cover the place being tickled. The result was a very crude approximation of the ASL sign for "more" (see Table 13–1). Thus, we would stop tickling and then pull Washoe's arms away from her body. When we released her arms and threatened to resume tickling, she tended to bring her hands together again. If she brought them back together, we would tickle her again. From time to time we would stop tickling and wait for her to put her hands together by herself. At first, any approximation to the "more" sign, however crude, was rewarded. Later, we required closer approximations and introduced imitative prompting. Soon, a very good version of the "more" sign could be obtained, but it was quite specific to the tickling situation.

In the 6th month of the project we were able to get "more" signs for a new game that consisted of pushing Washoe across the floor in a laundry basket. In this case we did not use the shaping procedure but, from the start, used imitative prompting to elicit the "more" sign. Soon after the "more" sign became spontaneous and reliable in the laundry-basket game, it began to appear as a request for more swinging (by the arms)—again, after first being elicited with imitative prompting. From this point on, Washoe transferred the "more" sign to all activities, including feeding. The transfer was usually spontaneous, occurring when there was some pause in a desired activity or when some object was removed. Often we ourselves were not sure that Washoe wanted "more" until she signed to us.

The sign for "open" had a similar history. When Washoe wanted to get through a door, she tended to hold up both hands and pound on the door with her palms or her knuckles. This is the beginning position for the "open" sign (see Table 13–1). By waiting for her to place her hands on the door and then lift them, and also by imitative prompting, we were able to shape a good approximation of the "open" sign, and would reward this by opening the door. Originally she was trained to make this sign for three particular doors that she used every day. Washoe transferred this sign to all doors; then to containers such as the refrigerator, cupboards, drawers, briefcases, boxes, and jars; and eventually—an invention of Washoe's—she used it to ask us to turn on water faucets.

In the case of "more" and "open" we followed the conventional laboratory procedure of waiting for Washoe to make some response that could be shaped into the sign we wished her to acquire. We soon found that this was not necessary; Washoe could acquire signs that were first elicited by our holding her hands, forming them into the desired configuration, and then putting them through the desired movement. Since this procedure of guidance is usually much more practical than waiting for a spontaneous approximation to occur at a favorable moment, we have used it much more frequently.

RESULTS

Vocabulary

In the early stages of the project we were able to keep fairly complete records of Washoe's daily signing behavior. But, as the amount of signing behavior and the number of signs to be monitored increased, our initial attempts to obtain exhaustive records became prohibitively cumbersome. During the 16th month we settled on the following procedure. When a new sign was introduced we waited until it had been reported by three different observers as having occurred in an appropriate context and spontaneously (that is, with no prompting other than a question such as "What is it?" or "What do you want?"). The sign was then added to a checklist in which its occurrence, form, context, and the kind of prompting required were recorded. Two such checklists were filled out each day, one for the first half of the day and one for the second half. For a criterion of acquisition we chose a reported frequency of at least one appropriate and spontaneous occurrence each day over a period of 15 consecutive days.

In Table 13–1 we have listed 30 signs that met this criterion by the end of the 22nd month of the project. In addition, we have listed four signs ("dog," "smell," "me," and "clean") that we judged to be stable, despite the fact that they had not met the stringent criterion before the end of the 22nd month. These additional signs had, nevertheless, been reported to occur appropriately and spontaneously on more than half of the days in a period of 30 consecutive days. An indication of the variety of signs that Washoe used in the course of a day is given by the following data: during the 22nd month of the study, 28 of the 34 signs listed were reported on at least 20 days, and the smallest number of different signs reported for a single day was 23, with a median of 29 (12).

The order in which these signs first appeared in Washoe's repertoire is also given in Table 13–1. We considered the first appearance to be the date on which three different observers reported appropriate and spontaneous occurrences. By this criterion, 4 new signs first appeared during the first 7 months, 9 new signs during the next 7 months, and 21 new signs during the next 7 months. We chose the 21st month rather than the 22nd month as the cutoff for this tabulation so that no signs would be included that do not appear in Table 13–1. Clearly, if Washoe's rate of acquisition continues to accelerate, we will have to assess her vocabulary on the basis of sampling procedures. We are now in the process of developing procedures that could be used to make periodic tests of Washoe's performance on samples of her repertoire. However, now that there is evidence that a chimpanzee can acquire a vocabulary of more than 30 signs, the exact number of signs in her current vocabulary is less significant than the order of magnitude—50, 100, 200 signs, or more—that might eventually be achieved.

Differentiation

In Table 13–1, column 1, we list English equivalents for each of Washoe's signs. It must be understood that this equivalence is only approximate, because equivalence between English and ASL, as between any two human languages, is only approximate, and because Washoe's usage does differ from that of standard ASL. To some extent her usage is indicated in the column labeled "Context" in Table 13–1, but the definition of any given sign must always depend upon her total vocabulary, and this has been continually changing. When she had very few signs for specific things, Washoe used the "more" sign for a wide class of requests. Our only restriction was that we discouraged the use of "more" for first requests. As she acquired signs for specific requests, her use of "more" declined until, at the time of this writing, she was using this sign mainly to ask for repetition of some action that she could not name, such as a somersault. Perhaps the best English equivalent would be "do it again." Still, it seemed preferable to list the English equivalent for the ASL sign rather than its current referent for Washoe, since further refinements in her usage may be achieved at a later date.

The differentiation of the signs for "flower" and "smell" provides a further illustration of usage depending upon size of vocabulary. As the "flower" sign became more frequent, we noted that it occurred in several inappropriate contexts that all seemed to include odors; for example, Washoe would make the "flower" sign when opening a tobacco pouch or when entering a kitchen filled with cooking odors. Taking our cue from this, we introduced the "smell" sign by passive shaping and imitative prompting. Gradually Washoe came to make the appropriate distinction between "flower" contexts and "smell" contexts in her signing, although "flower" (in the single-nostril form) (see Table 13–1) has continued to occur as a common error in "smell" contexts.

Transfer

In general, when introducing new signs we have used a very specific referent for the initial training—a particular door for "open," a particular hat for "hat." Early in the project we were concerned about the possibility that signs might become inseparable from their first referents. So far, however, there has been no problem of this kind: Washoe has always been able to transfer her signs spontaneously to new members of each class of referents. We have already described the transfer of "more" and "open." The sign for "flower" is a particularly good example of transfer, because flowers occur in so many varieties, indoors, outdoors, and in pictures, yet Washoe uses the same sign for all. It is fortunate that she has responded well to pictures of objects. In the case of "dog" and "cat" this has proved to be important because live dogs and cats can be too exciting, and we have had to use pictures to elicit most of the "dog" and "cat" signs. It is noteworthy that Washoe has transferred the "dog" sign to the sound of barking by an unseen dog.

The acquisition and transfer of the sign for "key" illustrates a further point. A great many cupboards and doors in Washoe's quarters have been kept secure by small padlocks that can all be opened by the same simple key. Because she was immature and awkward, Washoe had great difficulty in learning to use these keys and locks. Because we wanted her to improve her manual dexterity, we let her practice with these keys until she could open the locks quite easily (then we had to hide the keys). Washoe soon transferred this skill to all manner of locks and keys, including ignition keys. At about the same time, we taught her the sign for "key," using the original padlock keys as a referent. Washoe came to use this sign both to name keys that were presented to her and to ask for the keys to various locks when no key was in sight. She readily transferred the sign to all varieties of keys and locks.

Now, if an animal can transfer a skill learned with a certain key and lock to new types of key and lock, it should not be surprising that the same animal can learn to use an arbitrary response to name and ask for a certain key and then transfer that sign to new types of keys. Certainly, the relationship between the use of a key and the opening of locks is as arbitrary as the relationship between the sign for "key" and its many referents. Viewed in this way, the general phenomenon of transfer of training and the specifically linguistic phenomenon of labeling become very similar, and the problems that these phenomena pose for modern learning theory should require similar solutions. We do not mean to imply that the problem of labeling is less complex than has generally been supposed; rather, we are suggesting that the problem of transfer of training requires an equally sophisticated treatment.

Combinations

During the phase of the project covered by this article we made no deliberate attempts to elicit combinations or phrases, although we may have responded more readily to strings of two or more signs than to single signs. As far as we can judge, Washoe's early use of signs in strings was spontaneous. Almost as soon as she had eight or ten signs in her repertoire, she began to use them two and three at a time. As her repertoire increased, her tendency to produce strings of two or more signs also increased, to the point where this has become a common mode of signing for her. We, of course, usually signed to her in combinations, but if Washoe's use of combinations has been imitative, then it must be a generalized sort of imitation, since she has invented a number of combinations such as "gimme tickle" (before we had ever asked her to tickle us), and "open food drink" (for the refrigerator—we have always called it the "cold box").

Four signs—"please," "come-gimme," "hurry," and "more"—used with one or more other signs, account for the largest share of Washoe's early combinations. In general, these four signs have functioned as emphasizers, as in "please open hurry" and "gimme drink please."

Until recently, five additional signs—"go," "out," "in," "open," and "hear-listen"—accounted for most of the remaining combinations. Typical examples of combinations using these [five] are "go in" or "go out" (when at some distance from a door), "go sweet" (for being carried to a raspberry bush), "open flower" (to be let through the gate to a flower garden), "open key" (for a locked door), "listen eat" (at the sound of an alarm clock signaling mealtime), and "listen dog" (at the sound of barking by an unseen dog). All but the first and last of these six examples were inventions of Washoe's. Combinations of this type tend to amplify the meaning of the single signs used. Sometimes, however, the function of these five signs has been about the same as that of the emphasizers, as in "open out" (when standing in front of a door).

Toward the end of the period covered in this article we were able to introduce the pronouns "I-me" and "you," so that combinations that resemble short sentences have begun to appear.

CONCLUDING OBSERVATIONS

From time to time we have been asked questions such as, "Do you think that Washoe has language?" or "At what point will you be able to say that Washoe has language?" We find it very difficult to respond to these questions because they are altogether foreign to the spirit of our research. They imply a distinction between one class of communicative behavior that can be called language and another class that cannot. This in turn implies a well-established theory that could provide the distinction. If our objectives had required such a theory, we would certainly not have been able to begin this project as early as we did.

In the first phase of the project we were able to verify the hypothesis that sign language is an appropriate medium of two-way communication for the chimpanzee. Washoe's intellectual immaturity, the continuing acceleration of her progress, the fact that her signs do not remain specific to their original referents but are transferred spontaneously to new referents, and the emergence of rudimentary combinations all suggest that significantly more can be accomplished by Washoe during the subsequent phases of this project. As we proceed, the problems of these subsequent phases will be chiefly concerned with the technical business of measurement. We are now developing a procedure for testing Washoe's ability to name objects. In this procedure, an object or a picture of an object is placed in a box with a window. An observer, who does not know what is in the box, asks Washoe what she sees through the window. At present, this method is limited to items that fit in the box; a more ingenious method will have to be devised for other items. In particular, the ability to combine and recombine signs must be tested. Here, a great deal depends upon reaching a stage at which Washoe produces an extended series of signs in answer to questions. Our hope is that Washoe can be brought to the point where she describes events and situations to an observer who has no other source of information.

At an earlier time we would have been more cautious about suggesting that a chimpanzee might be able to produce extended utterances to communicate information. We believe now that it is the writers—who would predict just what it is that no chimpanzee will ever do—who must proceed with caution. Washoe's accomplishments will probably be exceeded by another chimpanzee, because it is unlikely that the conditions of training have been optimal in this first attempt. Theories of language that depend upon the identification of aspects of language that are exclusively human must remain tentative until a considerably larger body of intensive research with other species becomes available.

SUMMARY

We set ourselves the task of teaching an animal to use a form of human language. Highly intelligent and highly social, the chimpanzee is an obvious choice for such a study, yet it has not been possible to teach a member of this species more than a few spoken words. We reasoned that a spoken language, such as English, might be an inappropriate medium of communication for a chimpanzee. This led us to choose American Sign Language, the gestural system of communication used by the deaf in North America, for the project.

The youngest infant that we could obtain was a wild-born female, whom we named Washoe, and who was estimated to be between 8 and 14 months old when we began our program of training. The laboratory conditions, while not patterned after those of a human family (as in the studies of Kellogg and Kellogg and of Hayes and Hayes), involved a minimum of confinement and a maximum of social interaction with human companions. For all practical purposes, the only verbal communication was in ASL, and the chimpanzee was maximally exposed to the use of this language by human beings.

It was necessary to develop a rough-and-ready mixture of training methods. There was evidence that some of Washoe's early signs were acquired by delayed imitation of the signing behavior of her human companions, but very few, if any, of her early signs were introduced by immediate imitation. Manual babbling was directly fostered and did increase in the course of the project. A number of signs were introduced by shaping and instrumental conditioning. A particularly effective and convenient method of shaping consisted of holding Washoe's hands, forming them into a configuration, and putting them through the movements of a sign.

We have listed more than 30 signs that Washoe acquired and could use spontaneously and appropriately by the end of the 22nd month of the project. The signs acquired earliest were simple demands. Most of the later signs have been names for objects, which Washoe has used both as demands and as answers to questions. Washoe readily used noun signs to name pictures of objects as well as actual objects and has frequently called the attention of her companions to pictures and objects by naming them. Once acquired, the signs have not remained specific to the original referents but have been transferred spontaneously to a wide class of appropriate referents. At this writing, Washoe's rate of acquisition of new signs is still accelerating.

From the time she had eight or ten signs in her repertoire, Washoe began to use them in strings of two or more. During the period covered by this article we made no deliberate effort to elicit combinations other than by our own habitual use of strings of signs. Some of the combined forms that Washoe has used may have been imitative, but many have been inventions of her own. Only a small proportion of the possible combinations have, in fact, been observed. This is because most of Washoe's combinations include one of a limited group of signs that act as combiners. Among the signs that Washoe has recently acquired are the pronouns "I-me" and "you." When these occur in combinations the result resembles a short sentence. In terms of the eventual level of communication that a chimpanzee might be able to attain, the most promising results have been spontaneous naming, spontaneous transfer to new referents, and spontaneous combinations and recombinations of signs.

NOTES

1. See, for example, E. H. Lenneberg, *Biological Foundations of Language* (Wiley, New York, 1967).
2. A. L. Bryan, *Curr. Anthropol.* **4**, 297 (1963).
3. K. J. Hayes and C. Hayes, *Proc. Amer. Phil. Soc.* **95**, 105 (1951).
4. K. J. Hayes, personal communication. Dr. Hayes also informed us that Viki used a few additional sounds which, while not resembling English words, were used for specific requests.
5. R. M. Yerkes, *Chimpanzees* (Yale Univ. Press, New Haven, 1943).
6. K. J. Hayes and C. Hayes, in *The Non-Human Primates and Human Evolution*, J. A. Gavan, Ed. (Wayne Univ. Press, Detroit, 1955), p. 110; W. N. Kellogg and L. A. Kellogg, *The Ape and the Child* (Hafner, New York, 1967; originally published by McGraw-Hill, New York, 1933); W. N. Kellogg, *Science* **162**, 423 (1968).
7. W. C. Stokoe, D. Casterline, C. G. Croneberg, *A Dictionary of American Sign Language* (Gallaudet College Press, Washington, D.C., 1965); E. A. McCall, thesis, University of Iowa (1965).
8. J. Goodall, in *Primate Behavior*, I. DeVore, Ed. (Holt, Rinehart & Winston, New York, 1965), p. 425; A. J. Riopelle and C. M. Rogers, in *Behavior of Nonhuman Primates*, A. M. Schrier, H. F. Harlow, F. Stollnitz, Eds. (Academic Press, New York, 1965), p. 449.
9. R. M. Yerkes and B. W. Learned, *Chimpanzee Intelligence and Its Vocal Expression* (William & Wilkins, Baltimore, 1925), p. 53.
10. K. J. Hayes and C. Hayes, *J. Comp. Physiol. Psychol.* **45**, 450 (1952).
11. C. J. Warden and L. H. Warner, *Quart. Rev. Biol.* **3**, 1 (1928).
12. The development of Washoe's vocabulary of signs is being recorded on motion-picture film. At the time of this writing, 30 of the 34 signs listed in Table 13–1 are on film.
13. The research described in this article has been supported by National Institute of Mental Health grants MH-12154 and MH-34953 (Research Scientist Development Award to B. T. Gardner) and by National Science Foundation grant GB-7432. We acknowledge a great debt to the personnel of the Aeromedical Research Laboratory, Holloman Air Force Base, whose support and expert assistance effectively absorbed all of the many difficulties attendant upon the acquisition of a wild-caught chimpanzee. We are also grateful to Dr. Frances L. Fitz-Gerald of the Yerkes Regional Primate Research Center for detailed advice on the care of an infant chimpanzee. Drs. Emanual Berger of Reno, Nevada, and D. B. Olsen of the University of Nevada have served as medical consultants, and we are grateful to them for giving so generously of their time and medical skills. The faculty of the Sarah Hamilton Fleischmann School of Home Economics, University of Nevada, has generously allowed us to use the facilities of their experimental nursery school on weekends and holidays.

14.

The Creative Experience: An Interview with Noam Chomsky

STANLEY ROSNER and LAWRENCE E. ABT

Problem-solving may be considered an advanced stage of thinking, involving the ability to seek new solutions. Creativity, or creative thinking, goes one step further in that it involves a degree of problem-*finding* as well as inventive solutions that are both original and appropriate. Significant contributions in art, literature, or science usually demand superior intelligence. But even among those with the required intelligence, it is the rare person who can be truly creative. Researchers today are studying not only the creative process, but also the kinds of people who are creative, their personality, mental health, attitudes, even their birth order.

What follows is an interview with Noam Chomsky, whose significant contributions have essentially reoriented the modern study of linguistics. Does this interview reveal aspects of motivation, attitudes, or personality that you believe may be characteristic of the highly creative person? Does being creative necessarily mean that one must be nonconforming? To what degree do you think that significant discoveries or inventions are a matter of luck, of being in the right place at the right time? (Louis Pasteur once said, "Chance favors the prepared mind.")

Can you tell us something about your technique? Is it a matter of plugging away at a problem?

From *The Creative Experience*, edited by Stanley Rosner and Lawrence E. Abt. Copyright © 1970 by Stanley Rosner and Lawrence E. Abt. Reprinted by permission of Grossman Publishers.

No, I'm usually working on quite a number of different things at the same time, and I guess that during most of my adult life I've been spending quite a lot of time reading in areas where I'm not working at all. I seem to be able, without too much trouble, to work pretty intensively at my own scientific work at scattered intervals. Most of the reasonably defined problems have grown out of something accomplished or failed at in an early stage.

How does a new problem arise for you?

My work is pretty much an attempt to explain a variety of phenomena in which there is an enormous amount of data. In studying how one understands sentences, you can pile up data as high as the sky without any difficulty. But the data are pretty much uninterpreted, and the approach I've tried to take is to construct abstract theories that characterize the data in some well-defined fashion so that it is possible to see quite clearly where the theory you're constructing fails to account for the data or actually accounts for them.

In looking at my theories, I can see places where *ad hoc* elements have simply been put in to accommodate data or to make it aesthetically satisfying. While I'm reading about politics or anything else, some examples come to my mind that relate to the problems that I've been working on in linguistics, and I go and work on my problems in that latter area. Everything is going on at once in my mind, and I'm unaware of anything except the sudden appearance of possibly interesting ideas at some odd moment or the emergence of something that is relevant.

Would it be fair to say, then, that you have the problems you're working on in the back of your mind all the time?

All the time: yes, I dream about them. But I wouldn't call dreaming very different from really working.

Do you literally mean dreaming?

Yes, I mean it literally. Examples and problems are sort of floating through my mind very often at night. Sometimes, when I am sleeping fitfully, the problems that I've been working on are often passing through my mind.

Do they pass through your mind in a dream in the same form in which you were working on them?

Well, as far as I know, in exactly the same form. The dream life doesn't seem to have a different framework or to involve a different approach. So it's just a sort of slightly less concentrated and conscious version of the same thing as during the day.

How did you ever become interested in linguistics as a scientific field?

I think that my interest actually comes from two sources. In the first place, I sort of grew up with the study of language. As a child, I became interested because my father was working on a medieval Hebrew grammar, and I used to read his proofs when I was twelve or thirteen or so. So I knew something about historical linguistics from informal background, but I wasn't professionally interested in it at all. And then, when I got to college, I was much more interested in radical politics than anything else. I became involved with Zellig Harris in connection with left-wing Zionism (more accurately, radical alternatives to Zionism). He was the professor of linguistics at the University of Pennsylvania, and I had a lot of personal contact with him. I was really a kind of college dropout, having no interest in college at all because my interest in a particular subject was generally killed as soon as I took a course in it. And that includes psychology, incidentally.

I went to college with great enthusiasm, and I was interested in everything. But as soon as I took a course in some subject, that took care of that area. By the time I was a junior, I was perfectly willing to quit college and go to a kibbutz or something of that sort. Then I ran into Harris. He was the first person I'd met in college who was in any sense intellectually challenging, and we became very good friends afterward. He was perhaps twenty years older than I, and since I liked him and liked the things he was interested in, I took his courses, just to have something to do, and I got interested in the field and sort of put it into the center of my concerns. In retrospect, although it was really an independent influence upon me, it did tie in some way with my childhood.

What sort of work did your father do?

My father was a Hebrew teacher, and he did scholarly work on medieval Hebrew grammar, as I have said. He did a book on David Kimhi, a thirteenth-century Hebrew grammarian, and this was something I grew up with. At the time, it didn't seem to have any real contact with linguistics, but I now know that it really did in the sense that some of my own work later on was modeled on it, and quite consciously, on things that I had picked up totally informally from an acquaintance with general ideas in the history of linguistics.

Some of the reasons why some of my work was successful, I know, is because it grew out of a framework different from the accepted structural linguistics at the time. It was borrowed from some of the much older sources which at the time I didn't understand very well.

Do the sources you speak of grow out of, in part, the work of your father?

In part, definitely yes. The structural linguistics that I was studying grew out of the work of Leonard Bloomfield and others. It developed in part in parallel with radical behaviorism in psychology and was very similar to it, and in some ways equally trivial and beside the point, I think. That is, I think that the assumptions were just as debilitating, and the framework just as pointless. One of its characteristics is a sort of infantile obsession to worry about explanations. This is a point of view that was expressed quite explicitly by Martin Joos, for example. The work in structural linguistics, as I knew it, was concerned with collection and careful organization of data. This can be really deadening stuff, but it was really the tone of much of the field when I got into it. I was saved from this approach to some extent by the fact that I was acquainted with a different and more informal tradition which was concerned with explaining why a form has such and such a property and offering an historical explanation for it.

From the very beginning of my work I have tried to explain the characteristics of a given stage of the language by trying to understand what a person knows about his language, not by means of historical explanation which would be irrelevant, but rather by trying to attribute to him certain mental characteristics from which one could derive the facts—just as an historical linguist would seek to explain things by looking at the historical stages of its development. I was very early conscious of this different approach.

We assume that you mean that, in studying Hebrew, one would not be interested in studying a particular work and its various forms in terms of what a rabbi might say about it but rather a particular form is used because its author has certain psychological needs to express himself in a particular way.

Let me give you a more technical example which is closer to what I have in mind. If you take the Hebrew word *Malchay*, it seems to violate regular rules in that one would expect to have *kay* rather than *chay* after a closed syllable, as in the form *Malkee*. So why do we have *Malchay* and not *Malkay*, let's say? An historical linguist might argue, and I was aware of this when I was ten or twelve years old, that the underlying form at one stage of the language was *Malachim—Mala-keem* rather—and the *k* became *ch* after a vowel. At a later stage, the vowel was dropped so that you have a post-vocalic form appearing after a consonant, and that is why there is a violation of the apparent regularity that you don't have a *ch* after a consonant.

This is an historical explanation?

Yes, that's an historical explanation, but you know it's the kind of explanation that one can give for many phenomena. In the historical tradition in linguistics that I was loosely familiar with, this was typically the form of explanation offered. I have tried to ask comparable questions about how the speaker of the language organizes his knowledge so that the form is such and such or that the syntactical structure is such and such, and I think that this is the only innovation I've introduced into the field of linguistics.

Of course, most speakers of a language know nothing of what its history has been, but each, as a child, was faced with a mass of data that he has to make up some coherent theory about, and the theory has to be rich enough to enable him to carry out his normal creative use of language. It turns out, if the theories I have worked on are correct, that the theory of language the child develops has interesting formal similarities to some of the language's historical development. That is, they contain within them a kind of residue of historical evolution. What this really means, I think, is that at every stage of the language there's a very abstract theory that people who speak the language have that characterizes, through some process, the phonetic forms. What changes in historical evolution is sort of the tail end of this process, by and large. The common core of the language very rarely changes. After a long process of development, then, the language still may preserve more archaic features in its more abstract structure.

If you want a loose analogy, I ask you to think of Haeckel's theory of biological recapitulation. Suppose that it's true, for example, that in the ontogenetic development of an organism an early mutation will probably be lethal, whereas a mutation that affects a later stage of development may very well be viable. This is similar to phenomena that we encounter in the development of language. Of course you can't take the analogy literally. There are all sorts of reasons why it doesn't provide a perfect account of what occurs in language.

Has this approach led to an interest in why a particular individual, in the light of his particular history, speaks or uses a certain language?

That's an interesting question, but it's beyond the bounds of this kind of study. This is really an attempt to move into individual differences, and we don't have the tools, as yet, for this kind of inquiry. Perhaps this will some day change, but this is the present state of the field, I believe.

You mentioned earlier in our discussion that, in trying to construct a theory of something, you used abstraction and placed some reliance on intuition.

Yes, I always thought, from the beginning, that the whole scientific aura of linguistics and psychology was in part something of a fraud. And part of my belief came from the fact that under Harris' influence I became interested in school again and saw that things could be interesting. I started taking graduate courses in technical philosophy and mathematics and modern logic and began really studying some serious stuff. When you approach the behavioral sciences with this kind of background, you see right off that you've been totally missing the point. I mean it's a sort of mockery of science to use the framework of behaviorism with its narrow concept of theory and experimental design because nothing of this sort really goes on in serious science.

The work in linguistics was very similar. I mean that there was a lot of talk in the field about how scientific we were and how we were just like the physicists, and of course all that was missing was the intellectual content of what we were doing.

Is there some aspect of psychology that has been influential?

Yes. I've been very close, over the years, to people like George Miller who, I think, is moving in the right direction toward some conception of the cognitive processes that is far more abstract and deeply rooted than the behaviorist framework will tolerate, a conception that may offer some insight into some of these processes. Miller was one of the very few psychologists that I've had any acquaintance with, at least in this specific area, who was really able to see what is wrong with the behaviorist tradition and is really able to go on to the next stage.

I've found it very easy to work with him, and I've learned a lot from him, and I think he's learned a lot from me. We were able to work together very effectively. You are aware that there have been lots of changes in psycholinguistics in the past few years.

What about your book, Language and Mind?

This is based on a series of lectures that I gave at the University of California at Berkeley. They were addressed to a university-wide audience, and they were relatively non-technical. There was an attempt to draw together, in the first of three lectures, some historical developments in the study of language and mind. I really tried to show that there is a classical tradition that grows up in rationalist philosophy and psychology in the seventeenth century and continues with very interesting work to the mid-nineteenth century, when it is virtually replaced by a later "scientific" tradition. I put "scientific" in quotes because it was in another sense less scientific although it had more trappings of science than the earlier work in these fields. Of course, the newer research techniques increased enormously the available data as well as the reliability of data, but it seems to me that they entirely missed the point of, let's say, physics. That is, one should be interested in an intellectually satisfying deep explanatory theory, and this is more important than getting data accurate down to the tenth decimal place.

I tried to suggest that, by synthesizing these two traditions, one of which aimed at a basic understanding, and the other that is concerned with making sure that your data are reasonably correct and constitute a good sample, one can make scientific progress. One can begin to ask some of the old questions when using the refined methodology that did come out of this modern tradition, and you get some interesting answers. Well, you see, I'm convinced that language is species-specific as a biological attribute and that some of its deepest properties are really genetically determined. It's quite pointless to expect animals to speak or anything of that sort: It's just like expecting humans to fly. There is a sort of dogma to the effect that the human mentality is perfectly plastic and that humans can learn anything. I don't think this is true at all. I think human mentality is very narrowly constrained, and it can develop in certain directions and not in others; and one can see this, for example, by doing a careful analysis of cognitive processes, such as linguistic processes. That's roughly what my book's about.

So this approach has had quite an impact on the field generally?

That's not the question you should ask me, but my perception is that almost all of the young bright people in linguistics are vaguely acquainted with this area. There is plenty of conflict in this area, and my students think that I'm an old fuddy-duddy who doesn't understand a thing. I suspect that anyone looking in from the outside would have to say that most of the new work going on, whether you like it or not, is within this framework. In psychology, psycholinguistics still has a very heavy residue of the old verbal behavior formulation. Take a look at a journal, say the *Journal of Verbal Learning and Verbal Behavior.* About 90 percent of it is association studies: you know, the effect on changing the list position of items, and so on.

Are the findings of psychoanalysis relevant to your field?

Well, that's an interesting question. I've been searching to find some point of contact because I'm very much concerned with unconscious cognitive processes. It seems to me that the work we've done shows as conclusively as one can show with this kind of material that in these areas most of the processing of experience, at least with respect to language, is not only unconscious but is beyond the range of conscious processes. I mean that one cannot introspect into the way in which he interprets a sentence any more than he can introspect into the way he perceives physical objects or digests his food. As far as I have been able to determine, however, I'm not able to see anything in the Freudian tradition that tries to develop a notion of unconscious processes in the area of cognitive thinking. This seems to me a real gap.

But Freud does make a great deal out of the use of language, doesn't he?

Well, you see it's a very different kind of use. He's not talking about the unconscious cognitive processes, he's not talking about the thinking process; that is, how one makes an inference or how you understand what somebody says when he fashions a sentence, or how we perceive objects in the three dimensional world. This is a whole domain of questions that involve biological processes that are to an important extent species-specific. We want to know how these things are organized.

You'd be getting closer now to the questions Gestalt psychologists ask, wouldn't you?

In many ways. Except that I think the Gestalt psychologists are too peripheralistic in their concepts. Kohler, for example, tried to relate these considerations to field properties of the brain. I think that's too superficial: I mean that there's a much more abstract processing that goes on that probably has nothing to do with closure or any of these grossly physical properties of things. I've learned a lot from Gestalt psychology in the sense that it searches for integrative processes that aren't immediately evident in behavior. And also from other psychologists, like Lashley. Or, I should have learned from them. In fact, after I had learned independently just about everything Lashley had said, I discovered that he had done some very interesting work along just the lines that concerned me. Lashley was a professor at Harvard when I got there, and he had important things to say about language. I came as a graduate student and met all kinds of people, but I never even heard Lashley's name! About ten years later, Meyer Schapiro, the art historian at Columbia who knows everything about everything, told me that he couldn't understand why I didn't refer to Lashley because he had been saying many of the same things.

I discovered that Lashley had given a very sharp critique of what was going on at the time and had very interesting suggestions about the necessity for deeper integrative mechanisms not only for language but for coordinated motion and so on. There's been something of a Lashley revolution in the last few years. His papers have been reprinted and have influenced many in the field.

What we're interested in getting through to you is the birth of ideas. Is there some way we can separate this ongoing line of work you're involved in, or is it a kind of continuing process?

I just don't know. I know that the major work I've been doing for the past twenty years simply seems to be the obvious thing to do. For a long time I worked on it in near total isolation. Most of my work is published, but in fact I have a long, almost 1,000 page book, which I wrote when I was a graduate student at Harvard, that still isn't published.

In your present area?

Yes, and it has almost everything in it, in a general way, including the basic ideas. Lots of it is wrong. Nobody would read it at the time. A part of it was my doctoral dissertation which almost no one looked at at the time, that is the mid-fifties. I had been working along structural linguistic lines, following ideas of Harris, which were in some ways related to radical behaviorism. His idea was that there is no mental reality at all. The only thing you can do is develop analytic procedures which can be applied in a mechanical way, in principle programmed for a computer. You take a body of data, apply these analytic techniques, and the result is the grammar. This struck me initially as rather persuasive, and I worked for a long time trying to fill in the holes in the procedures that he had suggested, where they didn't work properly. For at least five years I worked very hard, and this was conventional linguistics. I knew more mathematics and logic than most people in the field at that time, and I was able to try more sophisticated techniques. But in spite of this it was a total fiasco, and gradually I began to work on this other approach. Because it didn't have any connection with the more conventional work, it aroused little interest. There were some exceptions. Particularly, I got a lot of encouragement and help from Morris Halle, who has been a close friend and colleague since we were graduate students.

However, I felt I was getting some place in explaining strange things about language and in finding regularities and principles that really worked. But this was totally out of the structure of the field at that time. Public lectures and articles that I submitted for publication met with the reaction that this work was not in linguistics. When my book went to a publisher in 1955, it got the same reaction. In 1953 I took a trip to Europe. I remember on the ship thinking about what I had been doing the previous five years and recognizing very clearly that one line of approach that I thoroughly believed is was an obvious failure. Another approach, which I was following because it intuitively seemed sort of right, though I didn't really believe in it, was working out. I then decided to abandon the first and commit myself entirely to the second.

Can you tell us what made the new approach seem "natural"?

When I first got into the field, I was really doing two things: I was learning the techniques and I was asking about the kinds of questions one might deal with using these techniques. The attempt to develop and apply these techniques led in a direction that grew quite fruitless. The other approach involved asking the most naive question about what happens when you as a person who speaks a language come across a sentence you've never heard before. It doesn't take a mathematician to know that the number of sentences that you come across and try to understand is astronomical. Obviously one must have in mind, somehow, a set of principles that are sufficiently rich to assign an interpretation to an arbitrary sentence that you've never encountered before. What would this principle be? Well you go ahead to search for it. For some reason it never occurred to me that this insight refuted all the work I had been doing. It was only after three or four years that it became obvious that I was really getting somewhere.

What do you mean that you were getting somewhere?

I was able to explain things about the language. For example, if you look at English, there are some funny curiosities. Take the formation of questions. When you form a question from "John will come tomorrow," the corresponding question is, "Will John come tomorrow?" On the other hand, when you form a question from "John reads a book" it is "Does John read a book?", not "Reads John a book?" On the other hand, you say, "Is John here?" not "Does John be here?" which would look like the analogue of "Does John read the book?" Now you can look at this as some crazy fact, but I was able to show that if you formulate certain fairly general principles, generative principles of language, then it had to be that way and exactly that way. In many areas it has been possible to show that we just know intuitively, as speakers of the language, the curious forms that sentences have because of some very general principles we have internalized and use quite unconsciously. This kind of example struck me as very exciting because it is more along the lines of what we know of science in general. We are interested not only in organizing data, and we get excited when we find an intuitively satisfying explanation.

What you have just said leads naturally, we think, into the questions of the roles of mood and the emotions in your work, which has been so largely abstract. Are you aware of the roles of your emotions and moods?

I know that some things get me very excited and other things are just dull. The exciting things are what one wants to follow. I can't describe them very well.

Do your ideas emerge when you are happy or unhappy?

I think it's probably the other way around. I'm so aware of the fact of having hit upon a train of thinking that seems to be getting somewhere that I get excited and so on, but I'm not aware of the opposite. I'm thinking of periods of my life when I've ranged very widely in mood but have not been different in productivity.

Does it ever happen that you find yourself up a blind alley?

Not too often. I've been kind of lucky in the sense that there have always been plenty of alleys that were open.

What do you do when you can't figure something out?

I turn to something else.

You don't bang your head against the wall?

Rarely, no.

You just stop for a while?

Yes, and I come back at a later time. There are still lots of things that I can't see any way to handle. Of course, you know that once I got graduate students—we have a very lively department with very bright kids—they provide all sorts of other ideas about the work. ·And also more blind alleys, too. There's a very real interplay here that I find very exciting.

Is Dr. Harris at M.I.T.?

No, he's at the University of Pennsylvania. In fact, we really lost intellectual contact in linguistics within a few years of our acquaintance, although we have stayed very close friends.

What about the place of visual images in your work? Are you dealing only with words, with images, or with auditory stimuli?

One part of what I was interested in for a number of years was really a kind of mathematics. It was the study of the formal properties of certain systems and rules, what kind of structures could be generated. The systems were suggested by language, but they were really considered in terms of themselves, and they were really part of the theory of abstract algebra or something of the sort. Working on these problems, I certainly used concrete models that involved visual imagery. I was interested in the formal properties of graphs and that sort of thing.

Your work appears very highly cerebral, and yet aren't you searching for meanings behind your thoughts?

As far as I am aware, it is "highly cerebral." Something that makes sense may be a very abstract principle that doesn't seem to have any direct connection with the data, and I have arrived at it through a complex series of processes. If it's surprising, it's exciting.

Something surprising is exciting?

If the principles themselves are implausible ones, in the sense that there is no a priori reason for language to be based on these principles rather than others, and if certain phenomena can be explained from the interplay of many such principles, it's exciting. There is a very intellectual relationship among the principles that one seeks.

What about the role of surprise in your work?

By searching the consequences of certain assumptions through a long process of inference, one is able to predict certain empirical results. If these results turn out to be correct, and if they do not directly reflect the assumptions upon which they are based, we have something that is surprising and exciting.

Surprising because it's not logical?

It's logical in the sense that there's a logical connection. It's very far from being self-evident. In fact, if you make slight modifications in the principles you thereby get overwhelming differences in the predictions which hopefully are false. In these cases you will discover things which yield satisfaction and really give the field life, as far as I'm concerned. If you didn't have such things, I wouldn't be interested in the field at this time.

Then your discovery of the relationships between your data and the generalizations of your principles is what's really creative for you?

Yes, that's right. That is *the* creative experience.

Are there aesthetic and affective reactions, too?

Yes, that's the whole business! It's the kind of experience I had when I was studying mathematics and logic really seriously and finally got to understand something: the same kind of excitement. Of course, I didn't discover it in that case, but in a sense you rediscover it when you finally grasp it, and it's that kind of experience that occasionally comes also from literature or music or something of the sort.

When you come upon a discovery like this, what about your techniques? Do you pursue it, do you get involved in it, is there a quality of urgency to get it down on paper, or do you just let it simmer?

This varies. For example, when I was a graduate student, I really worked out most of this stuff, although I wasn't communicating it to anyone, and I worked with a really incredible intensity. In looking back, I don't see how it was possible. In just a few months I wrote my book of close to 1,000 pages, and it had in it just about everything that I've done since, at least in a rough form.

There are some proofs over there. Do you just sit down at this typewriter, and the material all of a sudden comes out?

Yes, that's a different field, politics, and this is a 300 page book which is also the work of only a year or so really. But it's stuff that I've been thinking about for years. Ever since I was a child I've been thinking about the material in that book. For example, when I was a ten-year-old kid, I was very much interested in the Spanish Civil War, and I got to know about it through reading and friends. I remember writing an article for the school newspaper on the fall of Barcelona, for example. Since then I've been interested in the anarchist movement in Spain and other things, but I never dreamed of writing anything about it, but this book has a good bit of material on the anarchist revolution in Spain. It's a sort of distillation of things that I'd had on my mind for years and years, but had never bothered writing about.

Well, it sounds as if the pot's been boiling a long time and the soup's just getting ready to be served.

I guess so. Well, the linguistics thing was kind of like that, too, but it was over a shorter period. When I finally decided to write it down, it came very fast and freely. Most of the time I work directly at the typewriter. You know, I don't work it out and then write it up, but I sort of work it into the first draft. Even in my technical work I do that.

We have just one final question, we think. You spoke of the role of your father as a source of interest and stimulation. What about the role of your mother?

That would be more in the area of general concern about social issues, I suppose. As a matter of fact, one major part of my intellectual life has been politics. During my childhood, there was always plenty of discussion in my home about really interesting and important issues. I mean that my own linguistic work has always been a small part of my intellectual life. I have also been very much interested in philosophy and have read in it fairly extensively. For example, I have been quite interested recently in seventeenth and eighteenth century rationalist philosophy, in connection with issues that I've been thinking about in a vague way for a long time.

Have you published on this?

Yes, in 1966, a book called *Cartesian Linguistics*. It was a quite different departure.

What has your specific interest in philosophy been?

Well, it sort of converged upon a critique of empiricism.

Logical empiricism?

No, all empiricism. I got started with a critique of logical empiricism, but I really think that the whole empiricist tradition has some very fundamental flaws and these are responsible for the fact that it has had so little impact on the actual work in fields that have real intellectual content, as compared with its impact on weaker fields like psychology and linguistics or the social sciences. It seems to me that the empiricist framework has been debilitating in these fields because it tends to restrict theoretical and intellectual content, if taken very literally. That is a problem that interests me in intellectual history. That's why I'm so interested in the rationalist philosophy and its implications for biology and the human sciences.

Your interest, then, is the conditions of thinking?

Yes, and just what it means to be human. This involves some special kind of mind, a special type of biological development, special ways of dealing with interpersonal relations and intellectual structures, and so forth. I think the study of language fits in here.

There is one final question. You got into linguistics, and you weren't happy the way the field was at that time.

That is a little misleading. I wasn't aware of this until afterward. It took me several years to come to this realization.

There's something a little deceiving about this that we ought to go into. What is the place in your life of the need to prove something, to be competitive, which appears sort of hidden in what you've said.

It's not hidden at all! Well, for example, when I had come to believe that structural linguistics was on the wrong track, I began to work very hard in an attempt to provide a definitive disproof of the claims of people working in the field. My competitiveness was perfectly obvious and, although perhaps I shouldn't admit this, there was a sort of aggressive element in it that I am perfectly aware of.

PART IV

Emotions and Motivation

15.

On Emotions

WILLIAM JAMES

Most scientists agree that bodily changes (such as blushing, increased heart rate, quivering voice) are necessary characteristics of emotions. William James (whose turn-of-the-century views on psychology were presented in Selection 1) recognized the role of these bodily reactions in emotions, but argued against the common-sense notion that these bodily reactions are the *result* of an emotional experience (for instance, we are frightened and then perspire; we are angry and then our heart rate quickens). Instead, he said, the experience of an emotion is the *after-effect* of the bodily changes (for instance, we experience fear because we are perspiring; our heart rate quickens and *then* we experience anger). Note how effectively he argues this position in the following excerpt.

Subsequent research, having filled in our knowledge of how the nervous system works, has raised questions about James's notions of emotional experiences. We now know that electrical stimulation of appropriate areas of the brain, without any feedback from bodily activity, can produce strong emotional responses, such as rage. We also know that the patterns of physiological changes in different states of emotional arousal are not different enough to provide a basis for the many varieties of emotional experience. Yet there remains a legacy of concern about the physiological components of emotional states reflected in recent studies demonstrating that changed bodily states are essential in provoking emotional feelings. But, the studies show, these feelings also depend on a cognitive process by which a person labels or interprets the physiological changes. Your interpretation of

From *Psychology: Briefer Course* by William James. Reprinted with permission of Holt, Rinehart and Winston, Inc.

the sensations of physiological arousal (increased pulse rate, etc.) will be different when a sexually attractive person is walking by from when a huge dog is baring its teeth at you.

Try this (good actors do it all the time). Smile, hold it, start laughing to yourself quietly. Aren't you beginning to feel happier?

THE TROUBLE with the emotions in psychology is that they are regarded too much as absolutely individual things. So long as they are set down as so many eternal and sacred psychic entities, like the old immutable species in natural history, so long all that *can* be done with them is reverently to catalogue their separate characters, points, and effects. But if we regard them as products of more general causes (as 'species' are now regarded as products of heredity and variation), the mere distinguishing and cataloguing becomes of subsidiary importance. Having the goose which lays the golden eggs, the description of each egg already laid is a minor matter. I will devote the next few pages to setting forth one very general cause of our emotional feeling, limiting myself in the first instance to what may be called the *coarser* emotions.

The feeling, in the coarser emotions, results from the bodily expression. Our natural way of thinking about these coarser emotions is that the mental perception of some fact excites the mental affection called the emotion, and that this latter state of mind gives rise to the bodily expression. My theory, on the contrary, is that *the bodily changes follow directly the perception of the exciting fact, and that our feeling of the same changes as they occur* IS *the emotion.* Common-sense says, we lose our fortune, are sorry and weep; we meet a bear, are frightened and run; we are insulted by a rival, are angry and strike. The hypothesis here to be defended says that this order of sequence is incorrect, that the one mental state is not immediately induced by the other, that the bodily manifestations must first be interposed between, and that the more rational statement is that we feel sorry because we cry, angry because we strike, afraid because we tremble, and not that we cry, strike, or tremble because we are sorry, angry, or fearful, as the case may be. Without the bodily states following on the perception, the latter would be purely cognitive in form, pale, colorless, destitute of emotional warmth. We might then see the bear and judge it best to run, receive the insult and deem it right to strike, but we should not actually *feel* afraid or angry.

Stated in this crude way, the hypothesis is pretty sure to meet with immediate disbelief. And yet neither many nor far-fetched considerations are required to mitigate its paradoxical character, and possibly to produce conviction of its truth.

To begin with, *particular perceptions certainly do produce wide-spread bodily effects by a sort of immediate physical influence, antecedent to the arousal of an emotion or emotional idea.* In listening to poetry, drama, or heroic narrative we are often surprised at the cutaneous shiver which like a sudden wave flows over us, and at the heart-swelling and the lachrymal effusion that unexpectedly catch us at intervals. In hearing music the same is even more strikingly true. If we abruptly see a dark moving form in the woods, our heart stops beating, and we catch our breath instantly and before any articulate idea of danger can arise. If our friend goes near to the edge of a precipice, we get the well-known feeling of 'all-overishness,' and we shrink back, although we positively *know* him to be safe, and have no distinct imagination of his fall. The writer well remembers his astonishment, when a boy of seven or eight, at fainting when he saw a horse bled. The blood was in a bucket, with a stick in it, and, if memory does not deceive him, he stirred it round and saw it drip from the stick with no feeling save that of childish curiosity. Suddenly the world grew black before his eyes, his ears began to buzz, and he knew no more. He had never heard of the sight of blood producing faintness or sickness, and he had so little repugnance to it, and so little apprehension of any other sort of danger from it, that even at that tender age, as he well remembers, he could not help wondering how the mere physical presence of a pailful of crimson fluid could occasion in him such formidable bodily effects.

The best proof that the immediate cause of emotion is a physical effect on the nerves is furnished by *those pathological cases in which the emotion is objectless.* One of the chief merits, in fact, of the view which I propose seems to be that we can so easily formulate by its means pathological cases and normal cases under a common scheme. In every asylum we find examples of absolutely unmotived fear, anger, melancholy, or conceit; and others of an equally unmotived apathy which persists in spite of the best of outward reasons why it should give way. In the former cases we must suppose the nervous machinery to be so 'labile' in some one emotional direction that almost every stimulus (however inappropriate) causes it to upset in that way, and to engender the particular complex of feelings of which the psychic body of the emotion consists. Thus, to take one special instance, if inability to draw deep breath, fluttering of the heart, and that peculiar epigastric change felt as 'precordial anxiety,' with an irresistible tendency to take a somewhat crouching attitude and to sit still, and with perhaps other visceral processes not now known, all spontaneously occur together in a certain person, his feeling of their combination *is* the emotion of dread, and he is the victim of what is known as morbid fear. A friend who has had occasional attacks of this most distressing of all maladies tells me that in his case the whole drama seems to centre about the region of the heart and respiratory apparatus, that his main effort during the attacks is to get control of his inspirations and to slow his heart, and that the moment he attains to breathing deeply and to holding himself erect, the dread, *ipso facto,* seems to depart.

The emotion here is nothing but the feeling of a bodily state, and it has a purely bodily cause.

The next thing to be noticed is this, that *every one of the bodily changes, whatsoever it be, is* FELT, *acutely or obscurely, the moment it occurs.* If the reader has never paid attention to this matter, he will be both interested and astonished to learn how many different local bodily feelings he can detect in himself as characteristic of his various emotional moods. It would be perhaps too much to expect him to arrest the tide of any strong gust of passion for the sake of any such curious analysis as this; but he can observe more tranquil states, and that may be assumed here to be true of the greater which is shown to be true of the less. Our whole cubic capacity is sensibly alive; and each morsel of it contributes its pulsations of feeling, dim or sharp, pleasant, painful, or dubious, to that sense of personality that every one of us unfailingly carries with him. It is surprising what little items give accent to these complexes of sensibility. When worried by any slight trouble, one may find that the focus of one's bodily consciousness is the contraction, often quite inconsiderable, of the eyes and brows. When momentarily embarrassed, it is something in the pharynx that compels either a swallow, a clearing of the throat, or a slight cough; and so on for as many more instances as might be named. The various permutations of which these organic changes are susceptible make it abstractly possible that no shade of emotion should be without a bodily reverberation as unique, when taken in its totality, as is the mental mood itself. The immense number of parts modified is what makes it so difficult for us to reproduce in cold blood the total and integral expression of any one emotion. We may catch the trick with the voluntary muscles, but fail with the skin, glands, heart, and other viscera. Just as an artificially imitated sneeze lacks something of the reality, so the attempt to imitate grief or enthusiasm in the absence of its normal instigating cause is apt to be rather 'hollow.'

I now proceed to urge the vital point of my whole theory, which is this: *If we fancy some strong emotion, and then try to abstract from our consciousness of it all the feelings of its bodily symptoms, we find we have nothing left behind,* no 'mind-stuff' out of which the emotion can be constituted, and that a cold and neutral state of intellectual perception is all that remains. It is true that, although most people, when asked, say that their introspection verifies this statement, some persist in saying theirs does not. Many cannot be made to understand the question. When you beg them to imagine away every feeling of laughter and of tendency to laugh from their consciousness of the ludicrousness of an object, and then to tell you what the feeling of its ludicrousness would be like, whether it be anything more than the perception that the object belongs to the class 'funny,' they persist in replying that the thing proposed is a physical impossibility, and that they always *must* laugh if they see a funny object. Of course the task proposed is not the practical one of seeing a ludicrous object and annihilating one's tendency to laugh. It is the purely speculative one of subtracting certain elements of feeling from an emotional state supposed to exist in its fulness, and saying what the residual elements are. I cannot help thinking that all who rightly apprehend this problem will agree with the proposition above laid down. What kind of an emotion of fear would be left if the feeling neither of quickened heart-beats nor of shallow breathing, neither of trembling lips nor of weakened limbs, neither of goose-flesh nor of visceral stirrings, were present, it is quite impossible for me to think. Can one fancy the state of rage and picture no ebullition in the chest, no flushing of the face, no dilatation of the nostrils, no clenching of the teeth, no impulse to vigorous action, but in their stead limp muscles, calm breathing, and a placid face? The present writer, for one, certainly cannot. The rage is as completely evaporated as the sensation of its so-called manifestations, and the only thing that can possibly be supposed to take its place is some cold-blooded and dispassionate judicial sentence, confined entirely to the intellectual realm, to the effect that a certain person or persons merit chastisement for their sins. In like manner of grief: what would it be without its tears, its sobs, its suffocation of the heart, its pang in the breast-bone? A feelingless cognition that certain circumstances are deplorable, and nothing more. Every passion in turn tells the same story. A disembodied human emotion is a sheer nonentity. I do not say that it is a contradiction in the nature of things, or that pure spirits are necessarily condemned to cold intellectual lives; but I say that for *us* emotion dissociated from all bodily feeling is inconceivable. The more closely I scrutinize my states, the more persuaded I become that whatever 'coarse' affections and passions I have are in very truth constituted by, and made up of, those bodily changes which we ordinarily call their expression or consequence; and the more it seems to me that, if I were to become corporeally anaesthetic, I should be excluded from the life of the affections, harsh and tender alike, and drag out an existence of merely cognitive or intellectual form. Such an existence, although it seems to have been the ideal of ancient sages, is too apathetic to be keenly sought after by those born after the revival of the worship of sensibility, a few generations ago.

Let not this view be called materialistic. It is neither more nor less materialistic than any other view which says that our emotions are conditioned by nervous processes. No reader of this book is likely to rebel against such a saying so long as it is expressed in general terms; and if any one still finds materialism in the thesis now defended, that must be because of the special processes invoked. They are *sensational* processes, processes due to inward currents set up by physical happenings. Such processes have, it is true, always been regarded by the platonizers in psychology as having something peculiarly base about them. But our emotions must always be *inwardly* what they are, whatever be the physiological ground of their apparition. If they are deep, pure, worthy, spiritual facts on any conceivable theory of their physiological source, they remain no less deep, pure, spiritual, and worthy of regard on this present sensational theory. They carry their own inner measure of worth with them; and it is just as logical to use the present theory of the emotions for proving that sensational processes need not be vile and material, as to use their vileness and materiality as a proof that such a theory cannot be true.

This view explains the great variability of emotion. If such a theory is true, then each emotion is the resultant of a sum of elements, and each element is caused by a physiological process of a sort already well known. The elements are all organic changes, and each of them is the reflex effect of the exciting object. Definite questions now immediately arise—questions very different from those which were the only possible ones without this view. Those were questions of classification: "Which are the proper genera of emotion, and which the species under each?"—or of description: "By what expression is each emotion characterized?" The questions now are *causal:* "Just what changes does this object and what changes does that object excite?" and "How come they to excite these particular changes and not others?" We step from a superficial to a deep order of inquiry. Classification and description are the lowest stage of science. They sink into the background the moment questions of causation are formulated, and remain important only so far as they facilitate our answering these. Now the moment an emotion is causally accounted for, as the arousal by an object of a lot of reflex acts which are forthwith felt, *we immediately see why there is no limit to the number of possible different emotions which may exist, and why the emotions of different individuals may vary indefinitely,* both as to their constitution and as to the objects which call them forth. For there is nothing sacramental or eternally fixed in reflex action. Any sort of reflex effect is possible, and reflexes actually vary indefinitely, as we know.

In short, *any classification of the emotions is seen to be as true and as 'natural' as any other,* if it only serves some purpose; and such a question as "What is the 'real' or 'typical' expression of anger, or fear?" is seen to have no objective meaning at all. Instead of it we now have the question as to how any given 'expression' of anger or fear may have come to exist; and that is a real question of physiological mechanics on the one hand, and of history on the other, which (like all real questions) is in essence answerable, although the answer may be hard to find.

16.

The Heterosexual Affectional System in Monkeys

HARRY F. HARLOW

Harry Harlow was awarded the 1973 American Psychological Foundation Gold Medal Award for his work as a "creative scientist and dedicated investigator" who "enlarged the science of man through artful experimentation with monkeys." In studies extending over more than ten years, he has demonstrated the significant effects of early life experiences (mothering, peer contacts, and peer play) on subsequent social, affectional, and sexual relationships.

After reading this article, would you say that the need for affection is a drive independent of hunger? How about the need for peer contact?

Psychoanalytic (Freudian) theory stresses the focal role of sexuality in the development of interpersonal relationships. Does the research reported here support that emphasis? Which comes first, the inability to love and be intimate or the disturbance in sexuality?

THE INSPIRATION for this address came from observational data obtained from seven guinea pigs—two males and three females in a colony and two females brought in temporarily. Observations were provided by my ten-year-old daughter Pamela. These observations were made with love and endearment, and the behavior observed was endearment and love. Furthermore, these observations were made at a level of objectivity difficult for an adult to attain in this field.

Reprinted from *American Psychologist*, 1962, *17*, pp. 1–9. Copyright 1962 by the American Psychological Association. Reprinted by permission.

Male and female guinea pigs are very fond of each other. They stare blissfully into the limpid pink or ruby or midnight-blue pools of each other's eyes. They nuzzle and they cuddle and the end production is not characterized by rush or rape. After all, one does not have to hurry if there is no hurry to be had. This, Pamela has witnessed several times. A caged, virgin adult female was brought by a friend for mating. Twirp, Pamela's large, black, gentle male, was put into the cage with the new female. He purred, nuzzled her, brushed up against her, smelled and licked her, and gradually conquered the frightened animal. A half-hour later they were snuggled up next to each other, peaceful and content, and they lived in bliss for several weeks until another friend brought in her female and Twirp repeated his patient, gentle approach. Twirp has convinced me that some male guinea pigs, at least, are endowed with an innate sense of decency, and I am happy to say that this is the way most male monkeys behave. I presume that there are some men who have as deep a depth of dignity as guinea pigs.

The guest stands, unfortunately, ended peaceful coexistence in the colony. For many months the five adult guinea pigs had lived amiably in one large cage, with Twirp in command and the second male playing second fiddle. While Twirp was host to the visiting females, White Patch commanded the permanent harem. When Twirp was reintroduced to the colony cage, it took but ten seconds to discover that he would not be tolerated. White Patch bared his teeth and lunged at Twirp, and to save the males, a new cage was acquired.

This led to various divisions of the females and led Pamela to discover particular male guinea pigs like particular female guinea pigs, and they squeal piteously when separated, even when the female is so bulging with babies that she can offer the male nothing in terms of drive reduction. Particular female guinea pigs like particular male guinea pigs. Tastes seem fairly stable, for even after weeks of peaceful residence with the unfavored male, the female will still attempt to get to her favorite male, and after weeks of quiet residence with unfavored females, the male wil still try to get to his favorite female.

The females, like the males, defend their rights. In the happy one-cage days two females were separated from the group to care for their litters. White Thrush, in an advanced stage of pregnancy, lived alone with the males. When Chirp was returned to the colony cage after three weeks of maternal chores, both males approached enthusiastically, making friendly gestures. But Hell hath no fury like a female guinea pig spurned, and White Thrush would not tolerate infidelity. She hissed at Chirp, and lunged, and as Chirp fled from the cage, White Thrush pursued, teeth bared. The males also pursued, clucking and purring in anticipation. The males won, and White Thrush sulked the rest of the day. Guinea pigs apparently have a well-developed heterosexual affectional system.

Sex behavior in the guinea pig has been intensively investigated, and there are exhaustive studies on what has been called the sex drive, but I know of no previous mention of or allusion to the guinea pig's heterosexual affectional system. No doubt this stems from the paradigm which has been established for research in this area.

In a typical experiment a male guinea pig and a female guinea pig in estrus are taken from their individual cages, dropped into a barren chamber, and observed for 15 minutes. In such a situation there is a high probability that something is going to happen and that it will happen rapidly and repeatedly. The thing that happens will be reliable and valid, and all that one needs to do to score it is to count. It is my suggestion that from this time onward it be known as the "flesh count." Sometimes I wonder how men and women would behave if they were dropped naked into a barren chamber with full realization that they had only fifteen minutes to take advantage of the opportunities offered them. No doubt there would be individual differences, but we would obtain little information on the human heterosexual affectional system from such an experiment.

Sex is not an adventitious act. It is not here today and gone tomorrow. It starts with the cradle, and as a part of the human tragedy it wanes before the grave. We have traced and are tracing the development of the heterosexual affectional system in monkeys.

We believe that the heterosexual affectional system in the rhesus monkey, like all the other affectional systems, goes through a series of developmental stages—an infantile heterosexual stage, a preadolescent stage, and an adolescent and mature heterosexual stage. Although these stages are in considerable part overlapping and cannot be sharply differentiated in time, we would think of the infantile stage as lasting throughout the first year and being characterized by inadequate and often inappropriate sexual play and posturing. The preadolescent stage, beginning in the second year and ending in the third year in the female and the fourth year in the male, is characterized by adequate and appropriate sexual play and posturing, but incompleteness. The adolescent and adult stage is characterized by behaviors which are similar in form but give rise to productive outcomes which are also reproductive. . . .

Sexual invitation may be initiated by the female by a present pattern with buttocks oriented toward the male, tail elevated, and the female looking backward with a fear-grimace (not threat) pattern involving flattened ears and lip smacking. This pattern need not involve rape nor even rush on the part of the male. The male may also solicit either

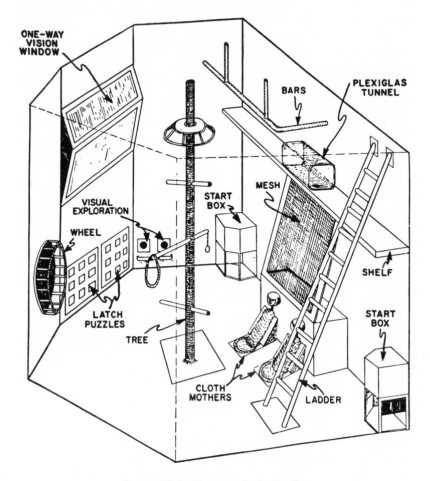

Figure 16–1. Playroom test situation.

grooming or more intimate favors. These patterns seldom elicit violent, uncontrolled, reflex behaviors. The male assume[s] the complex sex posture involving ankle clasp, dorsoventral mounting, and clasp of the female's buttocks. The partner demonstrates the complete female sexual pattern of elevating the buttocks, lowering the head, and looking backward. There have been millions of rhesus monkeys for millions of years, and there will be more in the future.

We have traced the development of the infantile heterosexual stage during the first year of life in two test situations using observational techniques. One is our playroom, illustrated in Figure 16–1, which consists of a room 8 ft. high with 36 feet of floor space. In this room are a platform, ladder, revolving wheel, and flying rings to encourage the infants' adaptation to a three-dimensional world, and there is an assortment of puzzles and toys for quieter activities. Two groups of four infants each, half of each group male and half female, have been observed in the playroom daily over many months. The second apparatus is shown in Figure 16–2. This is the playpen situation, and it consists of four large living cages and adjoining pens. Each living cage houses a mother and infant, and a three-inch by five-inch opening in the wall between cage and playpen units enables the infants to leave the home cage at any time but restrains the mothers. The playpen units are separated by wire-mesh panels which are removed one or two hours a day to allow the infants to interact in pairs the first 180 days and both in pairs and in groups of four during the next half-year of life. Again, we are referring to data gathered from two playpen setups, each housing four infants and their real or surrogate mothers. Insofar as the infantile heterosexual stage is concerned, it makes little or no difference from which situation we take our data.

The outstanding finding in both the playroom and playpen is that male and female infants show differences in sex behavior from the second month of life onward. The males show earlier and more frequent sex behavior than do females, and there are differences in the patterns displayed by the sexes. The males almost never assume the female sex-posture patterns, even in the earliest months. The females, on the other hand, sometimes display the male pattern of sex posturing, but this is infrequent after ten months of age. Predominantly, females

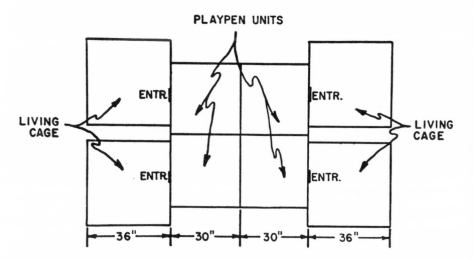

Figure 16–2. Playpen test situation.

show the female pattern and exceptional instances are to other females, not males. Frequency of sex behavior for both males and females increases progressively with age. There is no latency period—except when the monkeys are very tired.

The early infantile sexual behaviors are fragmentary, transient, and involve little more than passivity by the female and disoriented grasping and thrusting by the male. Thus, the male may thrust at the companion's head in a completely disoriented manner or laterally across the midline of the body. However, it is our opinion that these behaviors are more polymorphous than perverse.

Thus, as soon as the sexual responses can be observed and measured, male and female sexual behaviors differ in form. Furthermore, there are many other behaviors which differ between males and females as soon as they can be observed and measured. Figure 16–3 shows the development of threat responses by males and females in the playroom, and these differences are not only statistically significant, but they also have face validity. Analysis of this behavior shows that males threaten other males and females but that females are innately blessed with better manners; in particular, little girl monkeys do not threaten little boy monkeys.

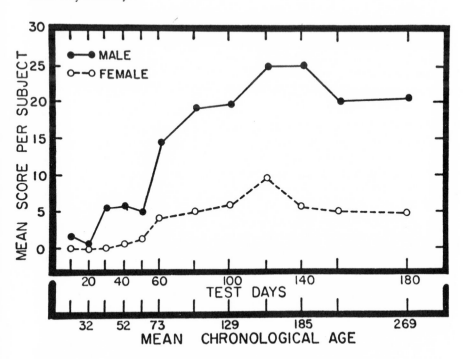

Figure 16–3. Frequency of threat responses by males and females in the playroom.

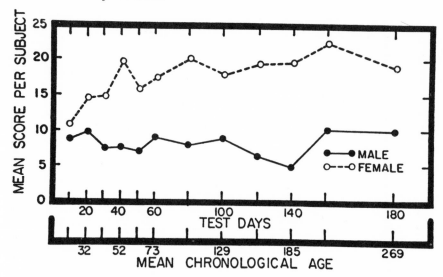

Figure 16–4. Frequency of withdrawal responses by males and females in the playroom.

The withdrawal pattern—retreat when confronted by another monkey—is graphed for the playroom in Figure 16–4, and the significance is obvious. Females evince a much higher incidence of passive responses, which are characterized by immobility with buttocks oriented toward the male and head averted, and a similar pattern, rigidity, in which the body is stiffened and fixed.

In all probability the withdrawal and passivity behavior of the female and the forceful behavior of the male gradually lead to the development of normal sex behaviors. The tendency for the female to orient away from the male and for the male to clasp and tussle at the female's buttocks predisposes the consorts to assume the proper positions. The development of the dorsally oriented male sex-behavior pattern as observed in the playroom situation is shown in Figure 16–5 and may be described as a composite yearning and learning curve.

Infant male and female monkeys show clear-cut differences in behavior of far greater social significance than neonatal and infantile sex responses. Grooming patterns, which are basic to macaque socialization, show late maturation, but as is seen in Figure 16–6, when they appear, they sharply differentiate the two sexes. Caressing is both a property and prerogative of the females. Basic to normal macaque socialization is the infant-infant or peer-peer affectional system, and this arises out of and is dependent upon the play patterns which we have described elsewhere and only mention here. As is shown in the solid lines of Figure 16–7, play behavior in the playroom is typically

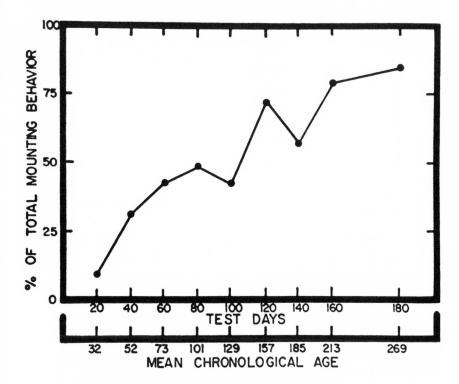

Figure 16–5. Percentage of all male mounts (immature and mature) in the playroom that shows dorsal orientation (mature pattern).

initiated by males, seldom by females. However, let us not belittle the female, for they also serve who only stand and wait. Contact play is far more frequent among the males than the females and is almost invariably initiated by the males. Playpen data graphed in Figure 16–8 show that real rough-and-tumble play is strictly for the boys.

I am convinced that these data have almost total generality to man. Several months ago I was present at a school picnic attended by 25 second-graders and their parents. While the parents sat and the girls stood around or skipped about hand in hand, 13 boys tackled and wrestled, chased and retreated. No little girl chased any little boy, but some little boys chased some little girls. Human beings have been here for two million years, and they'll probably be here two million more.

These secondary sex-behavior differences probably exist throughout the primate order, and, moreover, they are innately determined biological differences regardless of any cultural overlap. Because of their nature they tend automatically to produce sexual segregation during middle and later childhood, but fortunately this separation is neither

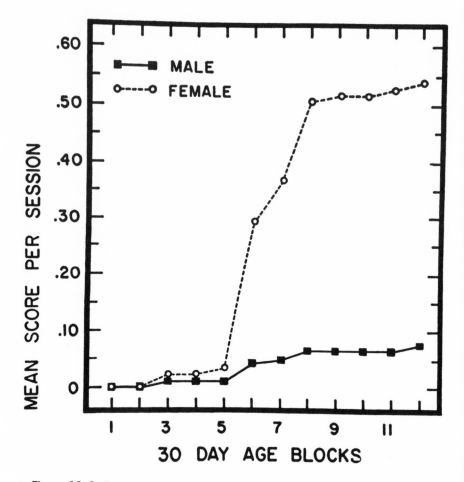

Figure 16–6. Frequency of grooming responses made by males and females in the playroom.

complete nor permanent. Behavioral differences may very well make it easy through cultural means to impose a sexual latency period in the human being from childhood to puberty. We emphasize the fact that the latency period is not a biological stage in which primary sex behavior is suppressed, but a cultural stage built upon secondary behavioral differences.

We believe that our data offer convincing evidence that sex behaviors differ in large part because of genetic factors. However, we claim no originality for the discovery of intersex behavioral differences. In 1759 Laurence Sterne in his book *Tristram Shandy* described male and female differences at the most critical period in Tristram Shandy's

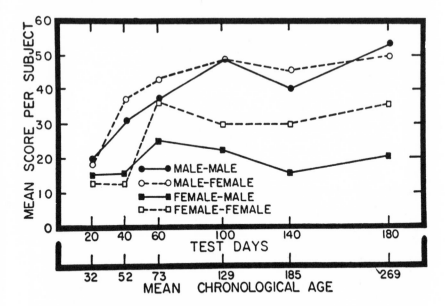

Figure 16–7. Frequency of play-initiations by males and females to monkeys of the same (male-male, female-female) and other sex (male-female, female-male). Observations are from the playroom.

development; indeed, it would not be possible to conceive of a more critical period.

"*Pray, my dear,* quoth my mother, *have you not forgot to wind up the clock?*———*Good G——! cried my father, making an exclamation, but taking care to moderate his voice at the same time———Did ever woman, since the creation of the world, interrupt a man with such a silly question?*"[1]

Men and women have differed in the past and they will differ in the future.

It is possible that the listener has been dismayed by the frequent reference to sex and the relatively infrequent reference to affection. Out of these infantile behavior patterns, both sexual and nonsexual, develop the affectional bonds and the social ordering that appear to be important or even essential to the full development of the heterosexual affectional system of macaques. Traumatic affectional errors, both transient and prolonged, may have devastating effects upon subsequent social and sexual behaviors.

[1] Sterne, Laurence. *The Life and Opinions of Tristram Shandy, Gentleman.* J. A. Work (ed.), New York: The Odyssey Press, 1940, p. 5.

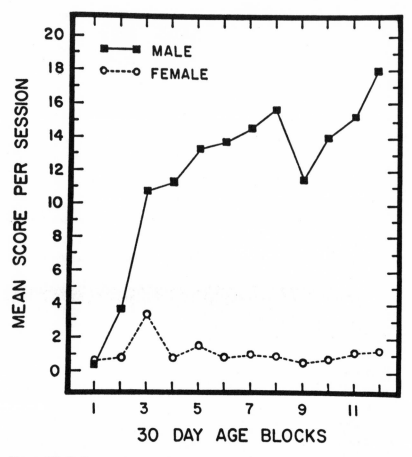

Figure 16–8. Frequency of occurrence of "rough-and-tumble" play for two males and two females in the playroom through the first year of life.

For some years we have been attempting to establish experimental neuroses in infant monkeys by having them live on unfriendly and inconsistent mother surrogates. One preparation was a rejecting mother that on schedule or demand separated her baby when a wire frame embedded in her spun-nylon covering was displaced violently upward and backward. The baby was disturbed, but as soon as the frame was returned to its resting position, the baby returned to cling to its surrogate mother as tightly as ever. Next we developed an air-blast mother with a series of nozzles down the entire center of her body which released compressed air under high pressure—an extremely noxious stimulus to monkeys. The blasted baby never even left the mother, but in its moments of agony and duress, clung more and more tightly to the unworthy mother. Where else can a baby get protection? Apparently our infant had never read Neal Miller's theory that avoidance gradients are precipitous and approach gradients gradual and tenuous, for love conquered all.

We next devised a shaking mother, which on schedule or demand shook her infant with unconscionable violence until its teeth chattered. The infant endured its tribulations by clinging more and more tightly. At the present time we believe we may be on the threshold of success through Jay Mowbray's creation of the porcupine mother, which extrudes brass spikes all over its ventral surface. Preliminary studies on two infants suggest that they are emotionally disturbed. Whether or not we eventually succeed, the fact remains that babies are reluctant to develop experimental neuroses, and at one time we even wondered if this were possible.

During the time that we were producing these evil mothers, we observed the monkeys which we had separated from their mothers at birth and raised under various mothered and nonmothered conditions. The first 47 baby monkeys were raised during the first year of life in wire cages so arranged that the infants could see and hear and call to other infants but not contact them. Now they are five to seven years old and sexually mature. As month after month and year after year have passed, these monkeys have appeared to be less and less normal. We have seen them sitting in their cages strangely mute, staring fixedly into space, relatively indifferent to people and other monkeys. Some clutch their heads in both hands and rock back and forth—the autistic behavior pattern that we have seen in babies raised on wire surrogates. Others, when approached or even left alone, go into violent frenzies of rage, grasping and tearing at their legs with such fury that they sometimes require medical care.

Eventually we realized that we had a laboratory full of neurotic monkeys. We had failed to produce neurotic monkeys by thoughtful planning and creative research, but we had succeeded in producing neurotic monkeys through misadventure. To err is human.

Because of housing pressures some of these monkeys and many of our surrogate-raised monkeys lived in pairs for several years while growing to sexual maturity, but we have seldom seen normal sex behavior, and we certainly have not had the validating criterion of newborn baby monkeys. Instead, these monkeys treat each other like brother and sister, proving that two can live in complete propinquity with perfect propriety as long as no one cares.

Their reason for being, as we saw it, was to produce babies for our researches, and so at this point we deliberately initiated a breeding program which was frighteningly unsuccessful. When the older, wire-cage-raised males were paired with the females at the peak of estrus, the introduction led only to fighting, so violent and vicious that separation was essential to survival. In no case was there any indication of normal sex behavior. Frequently the females were the aggressors; even the normal praying mantis waits until the sex act is completed.

Pairing such cloth-surrogate-raised monkeys as were sexually mature gave little better end results. Violent aggression was not the rule, and there was attempted sex behavior, but it was unreproductive since both the male and female behaviors were of the infantile type we have already described.

At this point we took the 17 oldest of our cage-raised animals, females showing consistent estrous cycles and males obviously mature, and engaged in an intensive re-education program, pairing the females with our most experienced, patient, and gentle males, and the males with our most eager, amiable, and successful breeding females. When the laboratory-bred females were smaller than the sophisticated males, the girls would back away and sit down facing the males, looking appealingly at these would-be consorts. Their hearts were in the right place, but nothing else was. When the females were larger than the males, we can only hope that they misunderstood the males' intentions, for after a brief period of courtship, they would attack and maul the ill-fated male. Females show no respect for a male they can dominate.

The training program for the males was equally unsatisfactory. They approached the females with a blind enthusiasm, but it was a misdirected enthusiasm. Frequently the males would grasp the females by the side of the body and thrust laterally, leaving them working at cross purposes with reality. Even the most persistent attempts by these females to set the boys straight came to naught. Finally, these females either stared at the males with complete contempt or attacked them in utter frustration. It became obvious that they, like their human counterpart, prefer mature men. We realized then that we had established, not a program of breeding, but a program of brooding.

We had in fact been warned. Our first seven laboratory-born babies were raised in individual cages while being trained on a learning test battery. William Mason planned to test their social behaviors subsequently, and great care had been taken to keep the babies socially isolated and to prevent any physical contacts. Neonatal baby monkeys require 24-hour-a-day care, and infant monkeys need ministrations beyond a 40-hour week. We had assigned the evening care to Kathy, a maternal bit of fluff who had worked for several years as a monkey tester while studying to become an elementary school teacher.

Checking on his wards one night near 10 P.M., Mason found Kathy sitting on the floor surrounded by seven baby monkeys, all eight of the primates playing happily together. Before the horrified scientist could express his outrage, Kathy had risen to her full height of five feet two. Already anticipating the carping criticisms which he was formulating, she shook her finger in his face and spoke with conviction: "Dr. Mason, I'm an education student and I know that it is improper and immoral to blight the social development of little children. I am right and you are wrong!"

Although we were angry with Kathy, we did think there was a certain humor in the situation and we did not worry about our monkeys. We simply transferred Kathy to an office job. Alas, she could not have been more right and we could not have been more wrong! We have already described the social-sexual life of these 7 monkeys and the next 40 to come.

Two years later we had more than theoretical reasons to be disturbed because Mason tested a group of these isolation-raised monkeys, then between 2.5 and 3.5 years of age, and found evidence of severe social abnormalities, which might be described as a sociopathic syndrome. He matched the laboratory-raised monkeys on the basis of weight and dentition patterns with monkeys that had been born and raised in the wild for the first 12 to 18 months, then captured and subjected to various kinds of housing and caging treatments for the next year or two. In the test situations the laboratory-raised monkeys, as compared with feral monkeys, showed infantile sexual behavior, absence of grooming, exaggerated aggression, and absence of affectional interaction as measured by cooperation.

We are now quite certain that this sociopathic syndrome does not stem from the fact that the baby monkeys were raised in the laboratory but from *how* they were raised in the laboratory. Our infants raised in the laboratory by real monkey mothers and permitted opportunity for the development of normal infant-infant affection demonstrate normal male and female sexual behavior when they enter the second year of life. Furthermore, our playroom and playpen studies show that infant monkeys raised on cloth mothers but given the opportunity to form normal infant-infant affectional patterns also develop normal sexual responses.

In a desperate attempt to assist a group of 18 three- to four-year-old cloth-surrogate-raised monkeys, half of them males and half females, we engaged in a group-psychotherapy program, placing these animals for two months on the monkey island in the Madison Zoo. Their summer vacation on the enchanted island was not without avail, and social grooming responses rapidly developed and were frequent in occurrence. After a few days of misunderstanding, patterns of social ordering developed, and a number of males and females developed friendship patterns. Unfortunately, sexual behavior was infrequent, and the behavior that was observed was completely inadequate—at least from our point of view. In desperation we finally introduced our most experienced, most patient, and most kindly breeding male, Smiley, and he rapidly established himself as king of the island and prepared to take full advantage of the wealth of opportunity which surrounded him. Fortunately, the traumatic experiences he encountered with unreceptive females have left no apparent permanent emotional scars, and now that he has been returned to our laboratory breeding colony, he is again making an important contribution to our research program. If normal sexual behavior occurred, no member of our observational team ever saw it, and had a female become pregnant, we would have believed in parthenogenesis.

But let us return to the monkeys that we left on the island and the older ones that we left in their cages. A year has passed, and the frustrations that both we and our monkeys experienced are in some small part nothing but a memory. We constructed larger and more comfortable breeding cages, and we designed a very large experimental breeding room 8 feet by 8 feet in size with appropriate platforms and a six-foot tree. Apparently we designed successful seraglios for I can report that not all love's labors have been lost. It does appear that the males are completely expendable unless they can be used in a program of artificial insemination. Certainly we can find no evidence that there is a destiny that shapes their ends unless some Skinnerite can help us with the shaping process. We have, however, had better success with some of the females, particularly the females raised on cloth surrogates.

Even so, one of the wire-cage-raised females is a mother and another is pregnant. Three cloth-surrogate females are mothers and four or five are expectant. We give all the credit to three breeding males. One, Smiley, does not take "no" for an answer. Smiley has a way with females. Patient, gentle, and persuasive, he has overcome more than one planned program of passive resistance. One female did not become pregnant until the fifth successive month of training. Month after month she has changed, and now she is mad about the boy. Male No. 342 behaves very much like Smiley. Even when females threaten him, he does not harm them. Given time, he has been able to overcome more than one reluctant dragon, and he is a master of the power of positive suggestion.

Breeding male No. 496 has helped us greatly, particularly with the younger, cloth-surrogate-raised females. His approach differs from that of Smiley and No. 342. His technique transcends seduction, and in contract bridge terms it may be described as an approach-forcing system.

Combining our human and male-monkey talents, we are winning

the good fight and imparting to naive and even resistant female monkeys the priceless gift of motherhood. Possibly it is a Pyrrhic victory. As every scientist knows, the solution of one scientific problem inevitably leads to another, and this is our fate. Month after month female monkeys that never knew a real mother, themselves become mothers—helpless, hopeless, heartless mothers devoid, or almost devoid, of any maternal feeling.

17.

The Achievement Motive

DAVID C. McCLELLAND

The study of motives is psychology's attempt to deal with the
question of why someone does something. Some motives, such as
hunger, thirst, and pain-avoidance, are potentially describable in
physiological terms, and are often referred to as drives. However,
other motives, often referred to as social motives, are
learned and reflect the impact of socialization. These motives
are especially interesting in the study of human behavior. They
are the motives involved when a soldier endures suffering and
hardships, a penitent fasts on a religious holiday, a musician
practices the guitar for six hours each day, or an author tries to
write a book.

In the following excerpt, McClelland first points out that a
motive is an inference based on some behavior and on the
conditions that seem to lead up to that behavior. He then
describes the development of a method for measuring differences
in one kind of social motive—the achievement motive (the
motive to excel, to succeed in competition, to meet challenges).

Can you conjure up some other way to measure the
achievement motive? Do you think it would correlate with
the measure described by McClelland?

Do you perceive any change in the strength of the achievement
motive over the past generation in young adult Americans? If
so, to what do you attribute this change?

Do you think the strength of the achievement motive is likely
to change much in an individual over the course of his lifetime?

Reprinted from pp. 36–46 of *The Achieving Society* by David C. McClelland (Van
Nostrand, 1961). Reprinted by permission.

(What happens when you suggest to a successful, retiring businessman that he can now "take it easy"?)

ASSESSING HUMAN MOTIVES

AT LEAST from the time of Plato and the Bhagavad-Gītā, Western philosophers have tended to see reason and desire as two distinctly different elements in the human mind. There would be little point here in giving a history of the various ways in which the "desiring" element has been conceived in the last 2,000 years, but suffice it to say that it always represented a kind of "motivational force" often opposed to but ultimately controllable by reason. At about the dawn of modern scientific psychology, in the middle of the nineteenth century, the relationship between these two psychic elements took on a very specific meaning largely under the influence of Darwin and the wide interest he and others aroused in the theory of evolution. Man was conceived as an animal engaged in a struggle for survival with nature. It was an obvious corollary to assume that because man struggled he had a desire or wish to survive. Biologists and psychologists were quick to point out how such a desire was mechanically controlled by the organism, since unmet physiological needs ordinarily triggered certain danger signals which would irritate or disturb the organism until the needs were satisfied.

The most obvious example is the hunger need. If the organism does not get food, it does not survive; therefore, it is equipped with danger signals (controlled perhaps by contractions of the empty stomach) which would be activated in the absence of food and so cause the organism to be active until it obtains food. The more or less "intelligent" activities of the organism, representing the old reasoning element in man, were conceived as originated and guided by the hunger drive, not in the teleological sense that the organism "knows" it needs food, but purely in the mechanical sense that hunger keeps the organism going until it manages to find some food substance which shuts off the danger signals. The most important theoretical advance made by psychologists who thought of human adaptation in these terms was the conceptual distinction they ultimately made between eating and hunger (the desire to eat). Common-sense psychology might suggest that the more a man eats, the more he wants to eat, in exactly the same sense that the more a man achieves, the more he must *want* to achieve. If, in fact, the two variables are so closely connected that desire to eat can be inferred without error from eating activity, then there is no need for the motive concept at all.

Since science is a parsimonious enterprise using as few concepts as it possibly can to explain what it tries to explain, it can get along without a variable which is always perfectly associated with another. But what behavioral scientists did at this juncture in history was to establish an *independent set of operations* for defining the strength of the hunger drive—independent that is, of the activity of eating. They defined the strength of the hunger drive in terms of the number of hours of food deprivation. They assumed that the longer an organism had been without food, the hungrier it would be, and they could then go about determining how different strengths of the hunger drive, as independently measured in this way, would influence various types of behavior, including even eating. They found, not too surprisingly, that when the strength of hunger was measured by hours of deprivation, it did not correlate at all perfectly with the tendency to eat. There were, and are, many disagreements, of course, as to the best method of measuring the hunger drive, but the only point of real significance here is that the way was opened to measure motivation independently of consummatory action. So psychologists have tended by and large to distinguish between motivation and action—between hunger and eating, and between the desire to achieve and actual achievement.

Nevertheless, much remained to be done. There was as yet no interest in the unique effects of particular drives. It is true that American psychologists studied not only the hunger drive, but also the thirst drive, the pain-avoidance drive, and other basic drives. Yet all these were conceived as functionally equivalent forces acting to energize human behavior until the organism managed to remove them by something it did. As might also be expected, there was no particular interest in individual differences in the strength of various motives. In fact the model of the hunger drive suggested that motive potentialities might be pretty much alike in all people and that their actual strength was primarily determined by changes in the external environment (e.g., lack of food). There was not much interest in the possibility that some particular person might have an especially strong hunger drive either because of biological endowment or because of some special learning experiences that had reinforced it. It remained for those more directly interested in human behavior and social motives to fill out the picture somewhat.

Many of them took their cue from Freud. Oddly enough he, too, had been strongly influenced by Darwin. He recognized the importance of survival needs like hunger, but concentrated his attention on the force that perpetuated the species—namely, sexual love. His general "model of motivation" remained not unlike the one adopted by the American psychologists of the functional school. A general motive force—the libido—drives man to invent through reason a variety of techniques or stratagems for diverting or satisfying it. But while the general model stayed the same, he made important empirical contributions that markedly influenced the direction research was to take.

For one thing he destroyed forever (except, perhaps, in the minds of economic theorists) the notion that motives are rational or can be rationally inferred from action. By concentrating his attention on notable irrationalities in behavior—slips of the tongue, forgetting of well-known facts, dreams, accidents, neurotic symptoms—he demonstrated over and over again that motives "are not what they seem." In fact they might be just the opposite. It could no longer be safely assumed that a man walks across the street because he wants to get to the other side. He might, in fact, want just the opposite—to enter a tavern on this side, a desire revealed indirectly by his exaggerated avoidance behavior. Since Freud, psychologists have accepted the fact that a simple act may be variously motivated. In the economic sphere, advertisers have long since taken advantage of Freud's findings in recognizing that a man doesn't buy a car just because he "needs" one in a rational sense, but because the possession of a particular kind of car may satisfy other motives—for power, prestige, or even sexual display. But how is one to know exactly what these other motives are? Here again, Freud provided us with an important clue in the method he himself used for discovering certain motives. He searched in dreams and free associations —in short, *in fantasy*—for clues to irrational motives. The limitation of his method was that it was always *ad hoc*. He proceeded, like the doctor he was, to analyze each symptom, for each person, or each dream as it came along, but did not provide scientists with measures of particular motives that would (1) enable different observers to agree what motives were operating with the degree of consensus necessary for science, (2) permit individuals to be compared as to the strength of a given motive, and (3) provide at least crude estimates of group levels or differences in human motives that would be of use to economists and other social theorists in dealing with the behavior of large groups of people.

MEASURING THE ACHIEVEMENT MOTIVE

The next step was to develop a method of measuring individual differences in human motivation firmly based on the methodology of experimental psychology and on the psychoanalytic insights of Freud and his followers. How this was accomplished might just as well be illustrated by reviewing briefly the history of the development of a measure of the achievement motive. The procedure, which has been described in full elsewhere (McClelland, *et al.*, 1953), may be briefly summarized as follows. First the achievement motive was aroused in a group of subjects to see what its effects on behavior might be. In this way we could

avoid the mistake of assuming *a priori* that the strength of the achievement motive may be inferred simply and directly from some particular
type of behavior. For example, actual achievement cannot be considered a safe index of the strength of the *need* to achieve any more
than eating can be considered a safe measure of the strength of the
hunger drive. In fact actual achievement is controlled by many more
forces than eating—desires for social approval, power, or knowledge—
to say nothing of ability factors, so that it is far less a reliable index of
the need to achieve than eating is of hunger.

Instead we need some more unique index of the presence of an
aroused desire for achievement. Ideally, of course, we might favor
something like a "psychic X-ray" that would permit us to observe
what was going on in a person's head in the same way that we can observe stomach contractions or nerve discharges in a hungry organism.
Lacking such a device, we can use the next best thing—a sample of a
person's spontaneous thoughts under minimum external restraints, in
short, of his waking fantasies and free associations, as already used by
Freud and many others to assess human motives. The question then
narrows down quite specifically to: What "unique" effects on fantasy
does an aroused state of achievement motivation have? If we can discover any, we can use these effects to infer the strength of "inner concerns" for achievement in subsequent studies.

Deciding how to arouse the achievement motive already involves to
a certain extent at least a rough definition of the motive being investigated. It is therefore important to report just how it was done. The
subjects initially were all male college students who were given a series
of tasks to perform that were introduced in the following way:

> The tests which you are taking directly indicate a person's general level
> of intelligence. These tests have been taken from a group of tests which
> were used to select people of high administrative capacity for positions in
> Washington during the past war. Thus, in addition to general intelli-
> gence, they bring out an individual's capacity to organize material, his
> ability to evaluate crucial situations quickly and accurately—in short, these
> tests demonstrate whether or not a person is suited to be a leader.
> (McClelland, Atkinson, Clark and Lowell, 1953, p. 105).

The important point about these instructions is that they stress the fact
that the individual is about to be evaluated in terms of standards of
excellence—intelligence and leadership capacity—which are ordinarily
of considerable importance to men in American culture. It is assumed
that such instructions will arouse in most of the people to whom the
tests were given a desire to do well, a desire to appear intelligent and
demonstrate some leadership capacity. It is, of course, unnecessary to
assume that these motives were conscious, or even present, in all of the
subjects tested. It is only necessary to assume that consciously or un-

consciously a motive to do well was aroused in more of the subjects to whom the instructions were given than in a comparable group of subjects to whom the tests and instructions were not given. Any differences in the subsequent fantasy behavior of the two groups might then be attributed to the difference in the level of arousal of the achievement motive in the two groups.

After the above tests had been completed, samples of the subjects' fantasies were collected by having them write brief five-minute stories suggested by pictures flashed on a screen for a few seconds. The pictures represented a variety of life situations centering particularly around work, because it was not known in advance exactly what associations would be most likely to be affected by arousing the achievement motive. In nontechnical language, the stories represented short samples of the things people are most likely to think about or imagine when they are in a state of heightened motivation having to do with achievement. It may be worth considering for a moment why fantasy as a type of behavior has many advantages over any other type of behavior for sensitively reflecting the effects of motivational arousal. In fantasy anything is at least symbolically possible—a person may rise to great heights, sink to great depths, kill his grandmother, or take off for the South Sea Islands on a pogo stick. Overt action, on the other hand, is much more constrained by limits set by reality or by the person's abilities. Furthermore, fantasy is more easily influenced than other kinds of behavior. Contrast it with problem-solving, for example. One might assume that how hard a person works would directly reflect the strength of his achievement motive. Yet how hard a person works is not easy to influence experimentally. Apparently most people develop a problem-solving "set" which is sufficient to keep them working at a more or less constant rate despite wide variations in feeling, such as those induced by extreme fatigue. In producing work, one motive can substitute for another so that even though the achievement motive may be weak in some people, their output may well be the same as somebody else's because of a stronger desire to please the experimenter.

This points to a third advantage of fantasy over any "overt" behavioral measure—namely, the way in which it gives clues as to *what motive* is aroused. Even if working behavior were more sensitive to experimental influences, one could not determine from the mere fact that a person was working harder what his motive was in working harder. It might be the achievement motive, or it might be the need for social approval, or the desire to get out of a situation as fast as possible and do something else. It is the fantasies of the person, his thoughts and associations, which give us his real "inner concerns" at the time he is working.

The next step was to compare the stories written by subjects whose achievement motives had presumably been aroused with those written by subjects under normal conditions. Certain differences immediately became apparent. The stories written under "aroused" conditions contained more references to "standards of excellence" and to doing well, or wanting to do well, with respect to the standards. A couple of actual stories will illustrate the point best. One of the pictures frequently used shows a boy sitting at a desk with a book open in front of him. Under normal conditions, it evokes a story like this one:

> A boy in a classroom who is daydreaming about something. He is recalling a previously experienced incident that struck his mind to be more appealing than being in the classroom. He is thinking about the experience and is now imagining himself in the situation. He hopes to be there. He will probably get called on by the instructor to recite and will be embarrassed.

Nothing in this story deals with achievement or with standards of excellence, but compare it with the following story:

> The boy is taking an hour written. He and the others are high-school students. The test is about two-thirds over and he is doing his best to think it through. He was supposed to study for the test and did so. But because it is factual, there were items he saw but did not learn. He knows he has studied the answers he can't remember and is trying to summon up the images and related ideas to remind him of them. He may remember one or two, but he will miss most of the items he can't remember. He will try hard until five minutes is left, then give up, go back over his paper, and be disgusted for reading but not learning the answers.

Obviously, here the boy is concerned about doing his best on the examination ("he is doing his best to think it through" and he is "disgusted for reading but not learning the answers"). Furthermore, there are a number of aspects of an achievement sequence specifically mentioned such as the fact that it is his fault that he is not doing well ("he saw but did not learn") and that he is trying out various ways of solving his problem ("trying to summon up the images and related ideas to remind him of them"). The fact that he is not successful in his achievement efforts is *not* taken to mean that the student who composed this story has a weaker achievement motive than someone who wrote a story in which problem-solving activities were successful. In fact, the precise advantage of the experimental method adopted is that it makes it unnecessary to make such decisions on "rational" grounds. One might make a case *a priori* for regarding images of success as more likely to be indicative of a strong and successful achievement drive than images of failure. One might also make a good *a priori* case for the exact opposite conclusion—that people who daydream about success are the very ones whose achievement motive is too weak to engage in actual attempts to do something in real life. To decide such a question on the grounds of what is most reasonable would be to fall into the error that plagued the psychology of economists and philosophers in the 19th century. The experimental approach makes *no* assumptions as to how the achievement motive is going to affect fantasy in advance: it simply takes whatever differences appear in fact between stories written under "aroused" and normal conditions so long as they make some kind of theoretical sense, and uses them as a means of detecting the presence of the achievement motive.

For example, it was thought in advance that arousal of the achievement motive might affect the outcome of the story, perhaps producing more successful or unsuccessful outcomes as compared with vague or indecisive ones. But in fact there were no differences in the frequency of various types of outcomes of the stories written under "aroused" conditions as compared with those written under normal conditions. So the outcome of the story, or of the achievement sequence in it, cannot be considered a sign of the presence of heightened achievement motivation, no matter how good an *a priori* case might be made for using it in this way. The point cannot be stressed too much. It was not logic that decided what aspects of fantasy would reflect achievement motivation. It was experimental fact. There is no need to list and define here the several different aspects of fantasy that did change under the influence of achievement arousal in college students, since they have been fully described elsewhere (McClelland *et al.*, 1953; Atkinson, 1958). It might be questioned though how general these effects would be. Perhaps an aroused achievement motive would influence the thoughts of Chinese, or Ancient Greeks, or Navaho Indians in quite different ways. Are the results obtained restricted to the male college population on which they were obtained? Ancient Greeks have not, of course, been tested, but Navahos have and their stories change in exactly the same ways under the influence of achievement arousal (McClelland *et al.*, 1953). So do those written by Brazilian students (Angelina, 1955), or high-school students in our culture from more unselected socioeconomic backgrounds. There may be cultural differences, but the data to date point to major similarities—inducing achievement motivation increases in all types of subjects thoughts of doing well with respect to some standard of good performance, of being blocked in the attempt to achieve, of trying various means of achieving, and of reacting with joy or sadness to the results of one's efforts.

The next step was to obtain a score for an individual by assuming that the more such thoughts he had under normal conditions, the stronger his motive to achieve must be, even in the absence of special instructions and experiences designed to arouse it. What the experiments had demonstrated was what channels people's thoughts turned to under achievement pressure. But suppose a person's thoughts run in those same channels without any external pressure. It seems reasonable to infer that he has a strong "inner concern" with achievement. Under normal testing conditions, the pictures used to elicit stories are sufficiently ambiguous to evoke a variety of ideas. If someone, however, in writing his stories consistently uses achievement-related ideas of the same kind as those elicited in everyone under achievement "pressure," then he would appear to be someone with a "bias," a "concern," or a "need" for achievement. So it was decided that a simple count of the number of such achievement-related ideas in stories written under normal testing conditions could be taken to represent the strength of a man's concern with achievement. The count has been called the score for *n* Achievement (abbreviation for "need for Achievement"), in order to have a technical term which points unmistakably to the fact that the measure was derived in a very particular way, and has an operational meaning quite distinct from estimates one might arrive at by inferring the strength of a person's achievement motive from his actual successful achievements, or from his frequent assertions that he is interested in getting ahead in the world. It remains only to say that the method just described for deriving the *n* Achievement measure can be applied to measuring *n* Affiliation, *n* Power (see Atkinson, 1958), and any other motive that an experimenter can demonstrate influences fantasy in regular and predictable ways.

REFERENCES

ANGELINA, A. L. *Un novo metodo para avaliar a motivacao humano* ("A new new method of evaluating human motivation"). Unpublished doctoral dissertation, Universidade de São Paolo, Brazil, 1955.

ATKINSON, J. W. (Ed.) *Motives in fantasy, action and society.* Princeton: Van Nostrand, 1958.

MCCLELLAND, D. C., ATKINSON, J. W., CLARKE, R. A., & LOWELL, E. L. *The achievement motive.* New York: Appleton-Century-Crofts, 1953.

18.

Yom Kippur, Air France, Dormitory Food, and the Eating Behavior of Obese and Normal Persons

RONALD GOLDMAN, MELVYN JAFFA, and STANLEY SCHACHTER

Medical reports indicate that at least 20 per cent of Americans are seriously overweight. Although there is still some question about genetic factors causing obesity, the fundamental cause, pure and simple, is overeating. But then, why do people overeat?

In a series of studies, the psychologist Stanley Schachter found that for normal-size individuals the impulse to eat is stimulated by the set of physiological cues resulting from food deprivation, whereas for obese persons the impulse to eat is triggered by external cues (taste, sight, passage of time).

The following article is another report from the professional literature in psychology. (We first came upon this style of reporting research results in Selection 12.) In this article, three tests are made of Schachter's hypothesis about external cues influencing eating in the obese, as contrasted with internal cues in normal-weight persons. Notice how the authors gradually build support for this conceptual scheme by testing its implications in a series of settings.

If it is indeed true that overweight people are stimulated to eat by external cues, how would you use this information in arranging a weight-reduction program?

If the obese person eats in response to external, rather than internal cues, then why does he ever *stop* eating as long as food is in front of him?

Reprinted from *Journal of Personality and Social Psychology*, 1968, *10*, pp. 117–23. Copyright 1968 by the American Psychological Association. Reprinted by permission.

THE RESULTS of recent studies[1] of the eating behavior of obese and normal subjects indicate that : (a) Physiological correlates of food deprivation such as gastric motility and hypoglycemia are directly related to eating and to the reported experience of hunger in normal-size subjects but unrelated in obese subjects (Schachter, Goldman, & Gordon, 1968; Stunkard & Koch, 1964); and (b) external or nonvisceral cues such as smell, taste, the sight of other people eating, the passage of time, etc., stimulate eating behavior in obese subjects to a greater extent than in normal subjects (Nisbett, 1968; Schachter & Gross, 1968). This paper will examine implications of these relationships in a variety of non-laboratory settings—specifically, religious fasting, tolerance of institutional food, and the effects of time-zone changes on eating behavior.

WHO FASTS ON YOM KIPPUR?

Evidence indicates that for obese subjects the impulse to eat is triggered by an external, food-relevant cue. In contrast, the impulse to eat for normal individuals appears to be stimulated by the set of physiological cues consequent on food deprivation. Assuming that blocking this impulse by doing without food is an irritating or painful state, it should follow that in circumstances where food-relevant external cues are sparse, or, where the individual can successfully distract himself from such external cues, the obese person should have a considerably easier time fasting or doing without food than should normal-size persons. The Schachter and Gross (1968) findings that the obese rarely eat breakfast or, on weekends, lunch can be construed as consistent with this expectation.

In order to test directly this expectation and some of its corollaries the relationship of overweight to fasting on Yom Kippur was studied. Yom Kippur, the Jewish Day of Atonement, is the most sacred of Jewish holy days and the only one for which fasting is commanded by Biblical Law. The traditional Jew begins his fast on the evening of Yom Kippur and does without food or water for 24 hours. Except when sleeping, he spends virtually all of his time in prayer in a synagogue, a physical environment notoriously barren of graven images, let alone food-related cues; a ritual conducted in Aramaic and Hebrew whose chief direct reference to food is passing mention of a scapegoat. Almost certainly informal conversations within the synagogue at this

[1] These studies were supported by National Science Foundation Grant GS732. Our thanks are due to Sidney Morgenbesser and Stanley Engelstein for advice about Yom Kippur.

time must to some degree be concerned with the fast; but the ritual proper and the physical surroundings are virtually devoid of food-relevant cues.

Among contemporary Jews, observance of Yom Kippur ranges from those who meticulously adhere to every detail described to those who are only vaguely aware that there is such a day. Between these extremes lies every variation of token or partial observance—people who will spend only an hour or two in synagogue, Jews who do without regular meals but sneak half a sandwich and a sip of celery tonic, and so on.

Given this characterization of Yom Kippur, if these speculations about obesity and fasting are correct, it should follow among Jews for whom the day has any meaning that (a) Fat Jews will be more likely to fast than normally built Jews; (b) the difficulty of fasting will, for obese Jews, depend upon the abundance of food-related cues in their immediate environment, while for normal Jews these two variables will be unrelated. Thus it should be anticipated that fat, fasting Jews who spend a great deal of time in synagogue will suffer less from fasting than fat, fasting Jews who spend little time in synagogue and there will be no such relationship for normal, fasting Jews. Plausibly, there will be far fewer food-related cues in the synagogue than on the street or at home. The likelihood, therefore, that the impulse to eat will be triggered is greater out of synagogue than in. For normal Jews, this distinction is of less importance. In or out of synagogue, stomach pangs are still stomach pangs.

In order to test these expectations, a few days after Yom Kippur, 1965, a questionnaire was administered to all of the students in several classes in introductory social science and psychology at the City University of New York and at New York University. The questionnaire was anonymous and designed to learn from Jewish respondents their sex, height, and weight, whether or not they had fasted on Yom Kippur, how unpleasant they had found the fast, and a variety of other information relevant to how religious they were and their experiences during Yom Kippur.

Since these hypotheses are irrelevant to Jews who are totally irreligious and only dimly aware of the holiday and its proscriptions, our sample for analysis is limited to those Jews who gave some indication of being religious. The criterion is simple and derives from answers to the question, "Approximately how many times have you been to synagogue in the last year?" Any Jew who had been to synagogue at least once during the past year, for some reason other than a wedding or a bar mitzvah, was considered a religious Jew. Of a total of 748 questionnaires, 456 were from Jewish respondents (247 men, 209 women). Of these, 296

TABLE 18–1
OBESITY AND FASTING ON YOM KIPPUR

	Obese Jews	Normal Jews
Fasters	49	163
Non-fasters	10	74

Note.—$\chi^2 = 4.74$, $p < .05$.

respondents (160 men, 136 women) are, by this criterion, religious Jews.[2]

The basic data on obesity and fasting are presented in Table 18–1. Whether or not a subject fasted was determined by his answer to the question, "Did you attempt to fast last Wednesday for the Yom Kippur holiday?" Anyone who answered "Yes" is classified as a faster. The Metropolitan Life Insurance Company (1959) norms for height and weight were used to calculate weight deviations. Subjects were classified as obese if their weight deviations fell among the top 20% of all subjects of their own sex, a cutoff point used in the three studies described in this paper. In this sample, any male who was 15.4% overweight or more is classified as obese. For females, a 20% cutoff point includes girls who, from their answers to the questions about weight and height, are as little as 4.8% overweight. Despite the fact that one would hardly consider a woman, truly of this slight weight deviation, as obese, we have, for consistency's sake, employed the 20% cutoff point for both males and females in all of the studies described in this paper. Not wishing to debate the pros and cons of this procedure we note simply that in the two studies in this paper involving females, employing a higher cutoff point for females tends to strengthen the main effects.

The data in Table 18–1 are clearly consistent with expectations. Among fat religious Jews 83.1% fasted on Yom Kippur. In comparison, 68.8% of normal Jews fasted. Obesity does play a part in determining who fasts on Yom Kippur.[3]

[2] Included in this group of religious Jews are 25 respondents who had not been to synagogue during the past year but who had fasted on Yom Kippur. In puzzling over just how to classify such respondents, it seemed to us that undertaking the Yom Kippur fast was, at least, as good an indication of religiousness as attending synagogue once or twice during the year. These non-synagogue-going fasters are, then, classified as religious. It should be noted, however, that the main effects of the study (and the statistical levels of confidence involved) remain much the same whether or not this subgroup is treated as religious.

[3] There is a tendency for obese respondents to be slightly more religious than normal subjects, that is, to attend synagogue slightly more during the year. Though this is a nonsignificant difference, it is troubling, for obviously the more religious are more likely to fast. In order to check on this alternative interpretation, the proportion of fasters among obese and normal respondents of various degrees of religiosity (as measured by the amount of synagogue going) was compared. At every point of comparison from slightly religious (one or two visits to synagogue) to extremely religious (20 or more visits), the obese are more likely to fast.

Let us examine next the impact of those factors presumed to differentially affect the difficulty of fasting for normal and obese subjects. In keeping with our general scheme, we have assumed that the presence or absence of food-relevant cues directly affects the ease with which an obese person fasts and has less impact on a normal person. If one accepts our characterization of the synagogue on Yom Kippur as devoid of food-related cues, it should be anticipated that for obese fasters answers to the question "For how many hours did you attend religious services this Yom Kippur?" will be negatively related to ratings of fasting unpleasantness as measured by a scale headed, "Insofar as you did fast this Yom Kippur, how unpleasant an experience was it?" The more hours in synagogue, the less exposure to food-relevant cues and the less unpleasant should fasting be for the externally controlled obese person. For the normal faster, attuned to his viscera, there should be little relationship.

The data are consistent with these expectations. For the obese, the correlation between hours in synagogue and unpleasantness is $-.50$. For normals, the correlation is only $-.18$. Testing the difference between these correlations, $z = 2.19$, which is significant at the .03 level. For the obese the more time in synagogue the less of an ordeal is fasting; for normals, hours in synagogue has little to do with the difficulty of the fast.

WHO EATS DORMITORY FOOD?

The taste or quality of food can be considered an external determinant of eating behavior. As such, food quality should have more of an effect on obese than on nonobese eaters. In an experiment designed to test this hypothesis Nisbett (1968) found that when the available food was generally rated as good, obese subjects ate more than did normals, who ate more than did skinny subjects. When the food was considered bad, this trend tended to reverse with skinny subjects eating more than either normal or obese subjects. Generalizing from these findings, it seems reasonable to assume that taste will not only have an effect on how much fat, as compared with normal, subjects eat, but on where they eat. It seems a plausible guess that the obese will be more drawn to good restaurants and more repelled by bad ones than will normal subjects.

At Columbia, students have the option of eating in the university dining halls or in any of the swarm of more or less exotic restaurants and delicatessens that surround this metropolitan campus. It is probably small surprise to the reader to learn that typical campus opinion of dormitory food is unfavorable. Student-conducted surveys document widespread dissatisfaction with the university dining halls, enumerating complaints about cold food, poor service, stale desserts, etc., etc. (University Dormitory Council, 1964).

If an undergraduate elects to eat in a dormitory dining hall, he may if he chooses join a prepay food plan at the beginning of the school year. For $500 he purchases a meal contract which entitles him to a weekly meal ticket worth $16.25 with which he can pay for food at the university dining hall or snack bar. Anytime after November 1, the student may cancel his food contract by paying a penalty of $15, and the remainder of his money is refunded. If general campus opinion of dormitory food is at all realistically based, those for whom taste or food quality is most important should be most likely to discontinue their food contracts. Obese students should be more likely to drop out of the food plan than normal students.

TABLE 18–2
RELATIONSHIP OF OBESITY TO RENEWING MEAL CONTRACTS

	Obese	Normal
Dropped meal contract	32	100
Renewed meal contract	5	49

Note.—$\chi^2 = 5.40$, $p < .05$.

The sample for this study is the entire body of freshmen entering Columbia in 1965 who signed up for the food plan on first entering the college. There were 698 students in this freshman class, 211 of whom signed food contracts. This sample is limited to freshmen first because they constitute the bulk of meal-plan subscribers and second because the noncommuters among them are required to live in dormitories during their entire first academic year. Thus, their decision to leave the plan could not be affected by moving out of the dormitories as it could for upperclassmen. All freshmen fraternity pledges (five obese and 16 normal students) are also eliminated from the sample, for pledges automatically, and without penalty, switch to eating at their fraternity houses when they pledge.

Weight deviations were computed from records in the Dean of Students' office using the Metropolitan Life Insurance Company (1959) norms.[4] As in the other studies in this report, the top 20% of the weight-deviation distribution is classified as obese. For this sample, this includes all students who were 11.3% overweight or more.

The basic data are presented in Table 18–2, where it can be seen that

---

[4] For 25 of the 211 freshmen who signed food contracts, the existing records were incomplete or unavailable so that it was impossible to determine weight deviation. Table 18–2 includes the 186 cases for whom the data are complete.

expectancies are confirmed. Some 86.5% of fat freshmen let their contracts expire as compared with the 67.1% of normal students who
dropped out of the meal plan. Obesity does, to some extent, predict
who chooses to subsist on institutional food.

ADJUSTING TO TIME ZONE CHANGES

There are occasions when there is a market discrepancy or opposition between external cues relevant to eating and the internal, physiological correlates of food deprivation or satiation, for example, being
served a gorgeous dessert after consumption of a mammoth meal or
confronted with some nauseating, rudely prepared concoction after a
period of starvation. Our line of thought leads to the expectation that
the obese will be relatively more affected by the external cue than will
the normal subject, that is, he will eat more of the dessert and less of
the mess. Studies by Hashim and Van Itallie (1965) and Nisbett (1968)
do, in good part, support these expectations.

A more subtle instance of this opposition of cues is represented by
the Schachter and Gross (1968) study in which, by means of doctored
clocks, subjects were manipulated into believing that the time was later
or earlier than the true time. If we assume that the intensity of gastric
motility, etc., is a function of true time (i.e., hours since last meal),
then this clock manipulation can create circumstances in which external and internal cues are, to some degree, in opposition. For example,
a subject may be under the clock-produced impression that it is after
his usual dinner time while in actuality it is before this time. In such
circumstances, Schachter and Gross found that the manipulated external cue almost entirely determined how much obese subjects ate and
did not similarly affect normal subjects.

Long-distance East-West travel creates a state which is, in a way, a
real life analogue of this time-manipulation experiment. Given time-
zone changes, the traveler, biologically more than ready to eat, may arrive at his destination at a local time still hours away from routine eating times and from the barrage of food-related external cues invariably
synchronized with culturally routinized meal times. A jet flight leaving
Paris at 12:00 noon requires 8 hours to reach New York, where on
arrival the local time is 2:00 P.M. If the passenger has eaten an early
lunch on the plane and no dinner, he is, on arrival, physiologically
more than ready for a full meal but still 4 or 5 hours away from local
dinner hours. Whatever mode he chooses of coping with his situation,
eating a full meal on arrival, snacking, or putting off a meal until local
dinner time, his situation is for a time an uncomfortable one, characterized by a marked discrepancy between his physiological state and
locally acceptable eating hours and he must, in short order, adjust to

an entirely new eating schedule. A prediction is by no means unequivocal, but from the variety of facts already presented it seems an
intuitively sound guess that the obese will have an easier time in this
situation than will normal travelers.

Thanks to the good offices of the Medical Department of Air France
we have had access to data which to some extent permit evaluation of
this hypothesis. Concerned with medical and psychological effects of
time-zone changes, Air France studied a sample of flight crew members
assigned to transatlantic routes (Lavernhe, Lafontaine, & Laplane,
1965). The subjects of this inquiry were 194 male and 42 female personnel regularly flying the Paris–New York and Paris-Montreal routes. On
the East to West journey these flights are scheduled to leave Paris
roughly around noon, French time, fly for approximately 8 hours, and
land in North America sometime in the early afternoon, Eastern time.
Flight crew members eat lunch shortly after takeoff and, being occupied with landing preparations and servicing passenger needs, are
not served another meal during the flight. They land in North America
some 7 hours after their last meal at a time that is generally past the
local lunch hour and well before local dinner time.

The Air France study was *not* directly concerned with reports of
hunger or eating behavior, but the investigators systematically noted
all individuals who volunteered that they "suffered from the discor-
dance between their physiological state and meal time in America."[5]
This coding appears to apply chiefly to fliers who complain about the
fact that they either do without food or make do with a snack until
local dinner time.

The basic data are presented in Figure 18–1, which plots the proportion of complainers at each quintile of the weight-deviation distribution of this group of flying personnel. Because of the stringent physical
requirements involved in air crew selection there are, of course, relatively few really obese people in this sample. Despite this fact, it is evident that there is a consistent relation between the extent of weight
deviation and the likelihood of spontaneously mentioning difficulties in
adjusting to the discrepancy between physiological state and local meal
times. The more overweight the French flier, the less likely he is to be
troubled by this discrepancy. The linear nature of the relationship is
consistent with the results of Nisbett's (1966) experiment. Comparing
groups of extremely skinny, fat, and normal subjects, Nisbett demonstrated that the impact of the external cue, taste, on eating behavior
was a direct function of the degree of overweight.

Testing the significance of the differences in these data by the pro-

---

[5] J. Lavernhe and E. Lafontaine, personal communication, 1966.

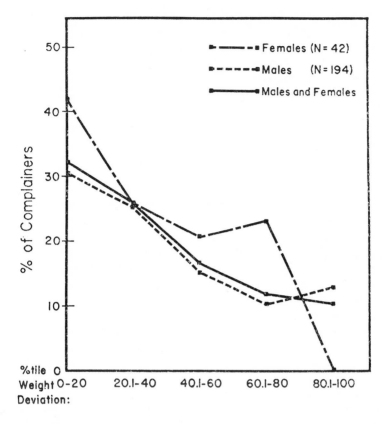

Range of Weight Deviation:
Males (−20.7% to −9.2%) (−9.1% to −3.4%) (−3.1% to +1.7%)
      (+1.9% to +9.0%) (+9.8% to +29.2%)
Females (−21.5% to −12.5%) (−10.7% to 7.5%) (−6.9% to −4.1%)
      (−3.8% to +0.5%) (+0.6% to +11.4%)

Figure 18–1. The relationship of weight deviation to complaining about the effects of time-zone changes on eating.

cedure employed in the two previous studies, we find $\chi^2 = 2.93$ ($p <$ .10) for the heaviest quintile of French fliers compared with the remainder of the sample. If we compare all of those flying personnel who are overweight (.1% to 29.9% overweight) with all of those who are not overweight (0% to 21.5% underweight) the data distribute as in Table 18–3, where it can be seen that 11.9% of the overweight complain as compared with 25.2% of the nonoverweight ($\chi^2 = 6.52$, $p < .02$). Apparently fatter, flying Frenchmen are less likely to be troubled by the effects of time changes on eating.

TABLE 18–3
RELATIONSHIP OF WEIGHT DEVIATION TO COMPLAINING ABOUT
THE EFFECTS OF TIME-ZONE CHANGES ON EATING BEHAVIOR

	Subjects who are:	
Subjects who:	Overweight	Not overweight
Complain	12	34
Don't complain	89	101

Note—$\chi^2 = 6.52$, $p < .02$.

DISCUSSION

From these three studies we know the following facts: (*a*) Fat Jews are more likely to fast on Yom Kippur than normal Jews; (*b*) for fat, fasting Jews there is an inverse relationship between the "unpleasantness" of fasting and the number of hours spent in synagogue on Yom Kippur. There is no such relationship for normally built Jews who fast; (*c*) fat freshmen are more likely to drop university meal plan contracts than are normal freshmen; (*d*) fatter French fliers are less likely to be troubled by the effects of time-zone changes on eating routine than are thinner French fliers.

We have chosen to interpret these facts in terms of a conceptual scheme involving assumptions about the relationship between weight deviation and the relative potency of external and internal stimulants to eating. These three studies were designed to test specific implications of this schema in appropriate field settings. As with any field research, alternative explanations of these findings are legion and, within the context of any specific study, impossible to overrule. Except for the most obvious alternatives, we have chosen to avoid the tedium of listing and feebly feuding with more or less plausible alternative interpretations—a procedure whose chief virtue would be the demonstration that we are aware of our interpretive problems even if we can do nothing about them.

There is, however, one alternative interpretation cogent not only to the present studies but to some of the findings in our various laboratory experiments. Two of these field studies, Yom Kippur and Air France, are concerned with some aspect of fasting behavior and the ease with which the obese can do without food[6]—a finding deriving from and related to the laboratory demonstration that manipulated food deprivation has no effect on the eating of the obese. Rather than the interpretation we have elected, which rests on the assumption that the obese do not label the physiological correlates of food deprivation as

[6] Other investigators who have noted this phenomenon in various contexts are Brown and Pulsifer (1965) and Duncan, Jinson, Fraser, and Christori (1962).

hunger, one could suggest that the obese are, after all, overweight, that they have large stores of body fat and, within the time limits of these studies, that they actually do not experience such states as gastric motility and hypoglycemia. Though a plausible hypothesis, the available evidence suggests that for gastric motility, at least, the hypothesis is not correct. The Stunkard and Koch (1964) study of gastric contractions and self-reports of hunger was in essence conducted under fasting conditions. Subjects ate their regular dinners, ate no breakfast, and at 9:00 A.M. came to the laboratory where, having swallowed a gastric balloon, they remained for 4 hours. During this period the extent of gastric motility was much the same for obese and normal subjects. The obese simply did not coordinate the statement, "I feel hungry" with periods of gastric motility while normal subjects did.[7]

One final point in defense of our general schema. It is the case that nonobvious derivations do plausibly follow from this formulation of the interrelationships of external and internal determinants of eating behavior. For example, the negative correlation between hours in synagogue and the unpleasantness of fasting for the obese and the lack of such correlation for normal subjects must follow from this set of ideas and we can conceive of no alternative conceptualization of this entire body of data which would lead to this prediction. In any case, whatever the eventual interpretation of the three studies, if one permutes these facts, the implications are unassailable: fasting, fat, French freshmen fly farther for fine food.

REFERENCES

BROWN, J. D., & PULSIFER, D. H. Outpatient starvation in normal and obese subjects. *Aerospace Medicine,* March 1965, 267–269.

DUNCAN, G., JINSON, W., FRASER, R., & CHRISTORI, F. Correction and control of intractable obesity. *Journal of the American Medical Association,* 1962, 181, 309–312.

HASHIM, S. A., & VAN ITALLIE, T. B. Studies on normal and obese subjects with a monitored food dispensing device. *Annals of the New York Academy of Sciences,* 1965, 131, 654–661.

[7] One final datum from our own studies also suggests that this alternative interpretation is incorrect. If it is correct that the intensity of the physiological correlates of food deprivation is, within time limits, less for the obese than for normal subjects it should follow that, under any conditions, obese subjects will find it easier to fast. The data on the relation of hours in synagogue to self-ratings of fasting difficulty in the Yom Kippur study indicate, however, that this is not the case. Obese subjects who spend most of the day in synagogue (8 or more hours) do suffer considerably less from fasting than do normal subjects who spend the same amount of time in synagogue. However, among those who spend little time in synagogue (2 hours or less), the obese report more difficulty with the fast than do normals. It would appear that the obese have an easier time doing without food than do normals in the absence of external, food-relevant cues but a more difficult time in the presence of such cues.

LAVERNHE, J., LAFONTAINE, E., & LAPLANE, R. An investigation on the subjective effects of time changes on flying staff in civil aviation. Air France Medical Department paper delivered before the Aerospace Medical Association, April, 1965. (Mimeo)

METROPOLITAN LIFE INSURANCE COMPANY. New weight standards for men and women. *Statistical Bulletin*, 1959, **40**, 1–4.

NISBETT, R. E. Taste, deprivation, and weight determinants of eating behavior. *Journal of Personality and Social Psychology*, 1968, **10**, 107–116.

SCHACHTER, S., GOLDMAN, R., & GORDON, A. The effects of fear, food deprivation, and obesity on eating. *Journal of Personality and Social Psychology*, 1968, **10**, 91–97.

SCHACHTER, S., & GROSS, L. Manipulated time and eating behavior. *Journal of Personality and Social Psychology*, 1968, **10**, 98–106.

STUNKARD, A., & KOCH, C. The interpretation of gastric motility: I. Apparent bias in the report of hunger by obese persons. *Archives of General Psychiatry*, 1964, **11**, 74–82.

UNIVERSITY DORMITORY COUNCIL. Report on food services at Columbia University. *Columbia Spectator*, March 9, 1964, p. 1.

PART V

Perception and Levels of Awareness

19.

The Split Brain

MAYA PINES

Among the most interesting results to come out of the neuro-
psychological laboratories in the past ten years are those developed
by R. W. Sperry and his collaborators. These investigators studied
the effects of surgically severing the connective tissue (the corpus
callosum) between the left and right hemispheres in the brain
of human subjects. The operation, referred to as hemispheral com-
missurotomy, was performed mostly on epileptics in an attempt to
reduce the severity of their seizures. But post-operative study
of these patients, described in the following chapter from a book
by a talented science writer, provided striking data on the different
functions of the two hemispheres and the dramatic effects of
their separation on perceptual and language abilities.

LINKED TOGETHER like Siamese twins right down the middle of our
brains, two very different persons inhabit our heads. One of them is
verbal, analytical, dominant. The other is artistic but mute, and still
almost totally mysterious.

These are the left and right hemispheres of our brains, the twin shells
that cover the central brain stem. In normal people, they are connected
by millions of nerve fibers which form a thick cable called the corpus
callosum. If this cable is cut, as must be done in certain cases of
severe epilepsy, a curious set of circumstances occurs. The left side of
the brain—the speaking half—no longer knows what the right side is do-

ing, yet it insists on finding excuses for whatever the mute half has done, and still operates under the illusion that they are one person.

As a result of these extraordinary findings of the past decade, brain scientists have begun to wonder whether our normal feeling of being just one person is also an illusion, even though our brains remain whole. Are the two halves of our brains integrated into a single soul? Is one hemisphere always dominant over the other? Or do the two persons in our brains take turns at directing our activities and thoughts?

Theologians are not alone in watching this research with fascination —and some misgivings. It has aroused the interest of many others who are concerned with human identity. As they soon realize, all roads lead to Dr. Roger Sperry, a California Institute of Technology professor of psychobiology who has the gift of making—or provoking—important discoveries.

Sperry was already famous before he began studying people and animals whose brains had been split in two. In a series of elegant experiments, he had shown that there exists a very precise chemical coding system in the brain that allows specific nerve cells—for example, those concerned with vision—to find their way through a tangle of other nerve fibers, even when obstacles are placed in their path, and somehow connect with the appropriate cells so as to reach specific terminals in the visual cortex. Next he began to study visual perception and memory. He wanted to find out what happened when an animal learned certain discriminations that involved the visual cortex—when it learned, for instance, to push a panel marked with a circle rather than a square. Where in its brain was that knowledge stored?

He put the question to a young graduate student, suggesting that he investigate how cats that have learned a new skill with only one eye and one hemisphere transfer this information to the other eye. The young student, Ronald Myers (now chief of the Laboratory of Perinatal Physiology at the National Institute of Neurological Diseases and Stroke), worked with this idea for the next six years. First he developed a method of cutting through the cats' optic chiasm (the point at which the optic nerves meet and cross) so as to sever the nerve fibers that normally cross from left eye to right hemisphere and vice versa, sparing only those that connect with the same side of the brain. Despite the surgery, the cats saw quite well. Myers then placed a patch over one of their eyes and trained the one-eyed creatures to distinguish between a circle and a square, knowing that the information they acquired would go to only one hemisphere. When he switched their eye patches to cover their trained eyes, however, the cats performed just as well as before. Their memory of this skill was intact. This meant either that the knowledge was stored in the central brain stem, well below the twin hemispheres, or that the knowledge acquired by one hemisphere had somehow been transmitted to the other.

"Obviously the corpus callosum was the next thing to test," recalls Dr. Myers. "But from the available evidence, cutting it would have no effect. If the surgery is properly done, the animals are up the next day and you see nothing." By all outward appearances, a split-brain cat or monkey is perfectly normal: it can run, eat, mate, solve problems as if nothing had happened to it. When surgeons first split the brain of a human being in the 1930's (to remove a tumor deep in the brain), they did so with much trepidation, expecting a terrible change in their patient, a total deterioration of his psyche. To their amazement, they saw no change at all. The corpus callosum seemed to serve no purpose, despite its large size (it is about 3½ inches long and a quarter of an inch thick in humans). "What is the function of the corpus callosum?" professors would ask their students in the 1940's; as no one knew, they replied facetiously, "It transmits epileptic seizures from one hemisphere to the other." As recently as 1951, Karl Lashley saw only one other use for it: "To keep the hemispheres from sagging."

Nevertheless, Myers proceeded with the next step in the research plan. After cutting through the cats' optic chiasm, he split their corpus callosum as well, separating their left and right hemispheres. Then he trained them as before, with one eye covered. When he removed the cover from this eye and placed it over the other eye, however, there was a dramatic change: the cats reacted as if they had never seen the patterns before. They took just as long to learn the difference between a circle and a square with the second eye as they had with the first. Myers was elated, and the question was finally settled: it was the corpus callosum that transmitted memories and learning from one hemisphere to the other. The thick cable of fibers stood revealed as the sole means of communication between the two halves of the cerebral cortex. Without it cats could be trained quite separately with each eye. When Myers tried teaching some split-brain cats to select the circle with their left eye and the square with their right, he found that they learned this without the slightest evidence of conflict. They would act in opposite ways, according to which eye was open—as if they had two entirely separate brains.

In animals, a split brain may prove relatively unimportant. After all, both hemispheres are enclosed in a single head, attached to a single body, and normally exposed to identical experiences. Furthermore, the left and right halves of their brains do exactly the same job. But this is not the case for human beings.

Alone among the mammals, man has developed different uses for each half of his brain. This asymmetry, which we all recognize when

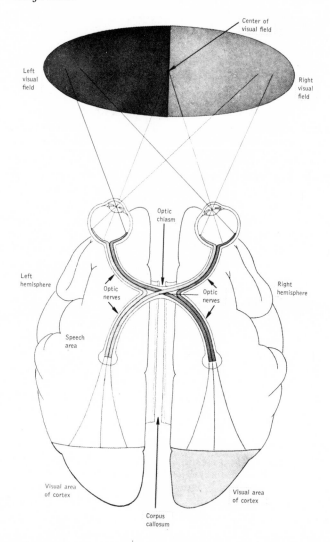

Figure 19–1. Visual input to the bisected brain. From "The Split Brain in Man" by Michael S. Gazzaniga. Copyright © 1967 by Scientific American, Inc. All rights reserved.

we say whether we're right- or left-handed, is the glorious mechanism through which man is enabled to speak. It is what separates us from the apes. There are various theories about how it developed and whether it is present right from birth, but it is quite clear that by the time a child reaches the age of ten, one hemisphere—usually the left—has taken over the task of language.

For simpler operations, such as receiving sensations from one's hand or ordering movements to one's foot, the human brain remains generally symmetrical. The nerve impulses that carry messages from one side of the body travel up the spinal column and cross over into the opposite side of the brain, there to form a sort of mirror image of the parts they represent. The nerve connections involved are set at birth in an incredibly precise fashion that allows the brain to know instantly where certain sensations come from and where to aim specific instructions.

When tasks become more complex, however, this mirrorlike representation is abandoned. Then the association areas of the brain come into play and each one develops in its own way, according to experience. Since we have only one mouth (unlike the dolphin, which has separate phonation mechanisms on the right and left sides of its body), there is no need for right and left speech centers in the brain. On the contrary, these might conflict with each other and compete for control of the speech mechanisms. In most people, therefore, the speech centers are limited to one side of the brain, usually the left, though about 15 percent of left-handed people have speech on both sides.

Even among the left-handed, the left hemisphere generally controls speech. This near monopoly of the left hemisphere was recognized in the early eighteenth century, when surgeons examined the brains of people who had lost the power of speech and found severe damage on the left side. Why this should be so preordained is not clear. The left hemisphere tends to become dominant in other ways as well. For example, it controls the right hand, which does most of man's skilled work with tools.

Around the age of one, notes psychologist Jerome Bruner, babies suddenly master what he calls "the two-handed obstacle box," a simple puzzle developed by Harvard's Center for Cognitive Studies to study how babies learn the value of two-handedness. The baby will push and hold a transparent cover with one hand, for the first time, while the other hand reaches inside the box for a toy, even though nobody has taught him this skill. To Bruner this seems extraordinary, for it shows that the baby has learned to distinguish between two kinds of grip—the power, or "holding," grip, which stabilizes an object, usually with the left hand, and the precision, or "operating," grip, which does the work, usually with the right. Monkeys and apes also develop a precision grip, says Bruner, but only in man, with his asymmetry, does the power grip migrate to the left hand while the precision grip migrates to the right. This is the beginning of a long road leading to the distinctively human use of tools and toolmaking.

If the left hemisphere does all this, why do we need a right hemisphere? Experiments with split-brain cats and monkeys could not shed much light on the differing specialties of man's two hemispheres. The study of the two personalities in our brain did not really begin until 1961, when Sperry became interested in a forty-eight-year-old veteran whose head had been hit by bomb fragments during World War II.

A few years after his injury, W. J. had begun to have epileptic fits; these became so frequent and so severe that nothing could control them. He would fall down, unconscious and foaming at the mouth, often hurting himself as he fell. For more than five years, doctors at Los Angeles' White Memorial Medical Center tried every conceivable remedy, without success. Finally Drs. Philip Vogel and Joseph Bogen cut through his corpus callosum, and the seizures stopped, as if by magic. There was a rocky period of recovery, during which W. J., a man of above-average intelligence, could not speak, but within a month he announced that he felt better than he had in years. He appeared unchanged in personality. He seemed perfectly normal.

Meanwhile, Sperry had interested a graduate student, Michael Gazzaniga, in performing a series of tests on W. J., together with him and Dr. Bogen. Gazzaniga soon discovered some extremely odd things about his subject. To begin with, W. J. could carry out verbal commands ("Raise your hand," or "Bend your knee") only with the right side of his body. He could not respond with his left side. Evidently the right hemisphere, which controls the left limbs, did not understand that kind of language. When W. J. was blindfolded, he couldn't even tell what part of his body was touched if it happened to be on the left side.

In fact, as the tests proceeded, it became increasingly difficult to think of W. J. as a single person. His left hand kept doing things his right hand deplored, if it was aware of them at all. Sometimes he would try to pull his pants down with one hand, while pulling them up with the other. Once he threatened his wife with his left hand while his right hand tried to come to his wife's rescue and bring the belligerent hand under control. Gazzaniga, now a professor of psychology at New York University, recalls that he was playing horseshoes with W. J. in the patient's back yard when W. J. picked up an ax with his left hand. Alarmed, Gazzaniga discreetly left the scene. "It was entirely likely that the more aggressive right hemisphere might be in control," he explains. And since he couldn't communicate with it, he didn't want to be the victim in a test case of "which half-brain does society punish or execute."

Only the left half-brain could speak. The right one remained forever mute, unable to do any tasks that required judgment or interpretation based on language. Of course, it was also unable to read. This meant that whenever he was faced with a page of printed matter, W. J. could read only the words on the right half of his visual field, which projected to his left hemisphere. His right hemisphere seemed blind.

Reading thus became very difficult and tiring for him. He also found it impossible to write any words with his left hand, although he had been able to do so with a little effort before his operation. (He was thoroughly right-handed.)

Indeed, from the early tests on W. J. it appeared at first that his right hemisphere was nearly imbecilic. But then came the day when W. J., with a pencil in his left hand, was shown the outline of a Greek cross. Swiftly and surely, he copied it, drawing the entire figure with one continuous line. When he was asked to copy the same cross with his clever right hand, however, he could not do it. He drew a few lines in a disconnected way, as if he could see only one small part of the cross at a time, and was unable to finish the pattern. With six separate strokes, he had made only half of the cross. Urged to do more, he added a few lines but then stopped before completing it and said he was done. It was clearly not a lack of motor control, but a defect in conception—in striking contrast with the quick grasp of his nonverbal half.

Since then, a tantalizing picture of the brain's mute hemisphere has begun to emerge. Far from being stupid, the right half-brain is merely speechless and illiterate. It actually perceives, feels, and thinks in ways all its own, which in some cases may prove superior. The only problem is to communicate with it nonverbally, as if it were an exceedingly intelligent animal.

There are some revealing movies of the first split-brain patients to be studied in Sperry's lab. (By now, eighteen patients have been tested there.) One sequence shows a twelve-year-old boy seated before a screen with his eyes fixed on a point in the center of it. When pictures of various objects are flashed to the right or left of this point, each picture is seen only by the opposite hemisphere. A picture is flashed in the boy's left visual field, which is controlled by his right half-brain, and the boy says he saw nothing. (That, of course, is the left hemisphere speaking.) But at the same time his left hand (controlled by his right hemisphere) searches behind the screen, rejecting a wide variety of objects, until it finally finds, by touch, what it is looking for: a pair of scissors, to match the scissors that the right hemisphere saw on the screen.

In other frames, W. J. is seen trying to arrange some colored blocks according to a diagram. He has no trouble at all doing this construction test with his left hand. But when his right hand tries, it gets hopelessly mixed up. Impatiently, his left hand shoots forward to help him, but the experimenter pushes it back. The right hand continues turning the blocks this way and that, achieving nothing. Again the left hand tries to come to the rescue, only to be pushed back. Peeved, W. J. sits on that hand to keep it quiet. But he still can't do the block design with his right hand. When he is told he can try it with both hands, however, the situation grows even worse: the two hands seem to fight for control, with the right hand tearing down whatever the left hand has built.

In spatial abilities, the right hemisphere is clearly tops. It also recognizes faces better than the dominant left, as was shown recently with the aid of some very curious split faces developed by two of Dr. Sperry's colleagues, Drs. Colwyn Trevarthen and Jerre Levy. They cut several pictures of faces in two, then stuck some unlikely combinations together—the left side of an old man with the right side of a young woman, for instance—and flashed each composite picture briefly on a screen. The spilt-brain patients who were used as subjects for this experiment kept their eyes fixed on a red dot in the center of the composite, so that the half-face in their left visual field could be projected only to their right hemisphere, and vice versa. After each composite picture had appeared on the screen, the patients were shown a choice of faces and asked to "point to the face you saw." Whether they used their right or left hand, they always pointed to the face matching the half that had been flashed on the left side of the screen, the half that had projected to the right side of their brain. This indicates that recognizing faces is a special ability for which the right hemisphere is dominant, the researchers believe. The left hemisphere never had a chance to select its candidate, since the right hemisphere always made the choice first. (Even in a split-brain patient, the right hemisphere can still control some movements of the right hand, as well as the left.) When, instead of pointing, the patients were asked to *tell* what they had seen, however, they made the opposite choice and described the half-face on the right, since that was the only thing their verbal side had seen. But they replied strangely, as if in a dream, explaining that they were confused. Sometimes they said, vaguely, that they didn't quite remember. However, they never once complained that there had been anything strange about the picture itself.

In general, the right hemisphere seems better at grasping the total picture, the Gestalt, of a scene. And this talent cannot be limited to people whose brains have been split. It must be a form of specialization in all people, resulting from a division of labor much like that which gave language to the left hemisphere.

How many other special skills or talents are the province of the right hemisphere? Nobody knows. But many of man's more poetic or imaginative aspects may stem from there. A few years ago the Russian psychologist A. R. Luria described a composer who became speechless after a stroke, yet went on to compose better music than ever before. He could no longer *write* the notes, but he could play and remember them. Other people who lost the use of their right hemisphere remained able to speak, but could no longer remember melodies. So musical talent, too, appears to be located in the right hemisphere.

Nor is the right hemisphere totally wordless, after all. With the exception of W. J., who had had more damage to his brain before his operation, the patients examined in Sperry's lab have usually proved able to understand simple nouns and a few elemental verbs with their right hemisphere. Some could even add up to ten, as long as this was expressed nonverbally.

There is thus a lot of brainpower in the mute, inarticulate hemisphere. Coupled with this comes a full complement of emotions. One part of the movie made in Sperry's lab shows a young woman beginning to smile in an embarrassed way as the picture of a nude is flashed in her left visual field. When she is asked what was on the screen, however, the young woman replies that she saw nothing. Again the nude is flashed on the left side of the screen. This time the young woman blushes. A slow grin spreads across her face, and she even hides her face in embarrassment. But when asked what she saw, she again insists that there was nothing there. Pressed to explain why she was laughing, all she can say is, "Oh, that funny machine!"

Just as the right hemisphere can make the whole face laugh (though the left hemisphere does not know why), it can make it express displeasure, even after the corpus callosum has been cut. "This is evidenced in frowning, wincing, negative head-shaking, and the like, in test situations where the minor hemisphere hears the major making stupid verbal mistakes—in other words, where the correct answer is known only to the minor hemisphere," notes Sperry. "The minor hemisphere seems in such situations to be definitely annoyed by the erroneous vocal response of its better half." At such times, though, the verbal half-brain would be unable to tell why the face to which it is attached frowned or winced, or why the head shook.

All these abilities point to the presence, in the right hemisphere, of "a second, separate, conscious system that is definitely human in nature," as Sperry puts it. Nevertheless, the dominant hemisphere clearly does not trust its twin, at least in split-brain patients, and generally prefers to ignore it, if not put it down. The left hemisphere will usually deny that the left hand can do anything like retrieving, out of a grab bag, some object previously felt by that hand. When asked to do this for the first time, Sperry's subjects generally complain that they cannot "work with that hand," that the hand is "numb," or that they "just can't feel anything" or "can't do anything with it." If the left hand then proceeds to do the job correctly, and this is pointed out to the patient, the speaking half will reply, "Well, I was just guessing," or, "Well, I must have done it unconsciously." It never even acknowledges the existence of its twin.

Much mystery surrounds the behavior of the two half-brains in normal people. Nobody knows whether these twin halves also ignore each other, actively inhibit each other, co-operate, compete, or take turns at the controls. Sperry believes that they mostly co-operate, because of the 200 million fibers connecting them. But there are other opinions.

The best clues come from children and adults who have had terrible accidents. If a child's left hemisphere is destroyed by a head injury or tumor before he is five or maybe even ten years old, he can learn to speak again—sometimes after a year of silence. His right half-brain will slowly take over the job. Not so for adults, who regain some speech after a stroke only if they have enough uninjured tissue remaining near the injury, on the left side. They cannot use their right half-brain for speaking. If a young child is injured in the right hemisphere, however, he will also experience difficulty with speech, though an adult would not.

"The young child has speech and language on both sides of his head," Gazzaniga believes. "He is, to some extent, a split brain, whose hemispheres tend to develop independently and duplicate each other." At birth, the corpus callosum is only partly developed. It isn't until a child is about two years old that the link between his two hemispheres becomes really functional, so that everything experienced by one side is instantly available to the other. At that point, duplication of learning becomes less frequent, and true specialization begins.

By the age of ten, dominance for speech—and probably for other skills as well—is fixed. Tasks of synthesis, spatial perception, and music apparently go to the right side. The left side gets all the sequential, verbal, analytical, computerlike activities. And, strangely, "excellence in one tends to interfere with top-level performance in the other," Sperry notes. To avoid bottlenecks, eventually most of the traffic flows in one direction, while few opportunities arise for the other hemisphere to develop its own skills. The "traffic cop" in this case may well be the corpus callosum. The speech learned by the right hemisphere in early childhood is thus functionally suppressed. In time, it may be lost or perhaps erased.

In California, recently, two young psychologists have been studying how normal people use or suppress their hemispheres. When you write a letter, for instance, does the left side of your brain show more electrical activity than the right? By pasting electrodes on the scalps of volunteers, Drs. Robert Ornstein and David Galin of the Langley Porter Neuropsychiatric Institute in San Francisco have found that this is indeed the case, at least in right-handed people. The left side of their brains produced the characteristic fast waves of attention or activity, while the right side relaxed with slow, high-amplitude waves, including the alpha rhythm. When the volunteers were asked simply to *think* about writing a letter, thus eliminating the effect of muscle movements, the pattern was exactly the same. Their right half-brain again relaxed, idle, and their left half showed fast waves. A similar pattern appeared when they read a column of print, did mental arithmetic, made up a list of verbs beginning with the letter "R," and completed sentences. But exactly the reverse happened when they tried to reproduce designs with four-colored blocks, remember musical tones, or draw with an Etch-a-Sketch: this time, the left side of the brain had more alpha rhythms, as if it were turned off, while the right side showed fast waves.

"Our opinion is that in most ordinary activities, we simply alternate between cognitive modes, rather than integrating them," declare Orstein and Galin. "These modes complement each other but do not readily substitute for each other." Thus, when people are asked to describe a spiral staircase, they may begin by using words, but soon switch to hand gestures.

Ideally we should be able to turn on the appropriate hemisphere and turn off the other, whenever the task requires it. But in fact we cannot always do so. "Most people are dominated by one mode or the other," observes Dr. Orstein. "They either have difficulty in dealing with crafts and body movements, or difficulty with language." Culture apparently has a lot to do with this. Children from poor black neighborhoods generally learn to use their right hemisphere far more than their left—and later do badly on verbal tasks. Other children, who have learned to verbalize everything, find this approach a hindrance when it comes to copying a tennis serve or learning a dance step. Analyzing these movements verbally just slows them down and interferes with direct learning through the right hemisphere.

"We don't have the flexibility we could have," says Ornstein. "We are under the illusion of having more control than we really do." Early in life, it seems, we become shaped either as a "left-hemisphere type," who functions in a largely verbal world, or as a "right-hemisphere type," who relies more on nonverbal means of expression. These are two basically different approaches to the world.

So fundamental are these differences that they influence even the direction in which our eyes turn when we think. This was discovered by Dr. Merle Day, of the VA hospital in Downey, Illinois, but I learned it from Dr. Ernest Hilgard, of Stanford University, while talking to him about his work on hypnosis. Dr. Hilgard suddenly stared at me, leaning close to my eyes, and said, "Count the number of letters in Minnesota." I did so, avoiding his gaze to concentrate better. "You looked to the right," announced Dr. Hilgard when I finished. This meant that my left hemisphere was more easily activated than my right, he explained. Since electrical stimulation in the right side of the brain makes both eyes veer to the left, and vice versa, looking to the right while thinking showed that the left hemisphere was preferred. However, it also meant that I was not very hypnotizable, since various experiments have shown the right hemisphere to be more amenable to hypnosis. People who look to the left tend to prefer non-verbal tasks, to favor their right hemisphere, and to be easily hypnotized. An unusually large proportion of those who look to the right, as I did, turn out to be scientists, researchers, writers, or others who spend much of their time at analytical tasks.

When the habit of always using the same side of the brain becomes too pronounced, it can narrow one's personality, Drs. Ornstein and Galin believe. The two researchers are currently working on a test that may enable them to tell which half-brain a person chronically favors, and whether this habit interferes with the ability to shift dominance to the other side when necessary. They plan to try it out on people who are really specialized, such as Ralph Nader (a left-hemisphere type who has no hobbies of any kind) and right-hemisphere potters, dancers, and sculptors ("preferably people who have trouble with language"). They expect to find significant differences between the two groups. This should give them a tool with which to guide children or adults to new aspects of themselves, to open them to a full range of experiences.

Eventually, they hope, people will learn to activate the left or right hemisphere voluntarily. This has already been tried in their lab. With electrodes on their scalp to record changes in their brains' electrical activity, and earphones to inform them instantly of how they are doing, half a dozen volunteers have attempted to increase the asymmetry between their two half-brains. So far the results appear promising: nearly all of the volunteers have managed to activate one hemisphere more than the other, through feedback. They have produced as much asymmetry in this way as when actually concentrating on mental arithmetic or drawing. One subject produced even more asymmetry through bio-feedback than through a change of tasks.

Some training of this kind may prove particularly useful for children who suffer from what is generally called dyslexia, or specific learning disabilities—a variety of subtle perceptual difficulties that interfere with reading, writing, or spelling. About 10 percent of the nation's children cannot process the information received from their eyes or ears with sufficient accuracy. Despite normal vision and hearing, and normal or even superior intelligence, they may confuse left and right or up and down, or give other evidence of poor co-ordination. Their symptoms have baffled doctors for years. At a National Academy of Sciences conference in 1969, Dr. Sperry suggested that their problem may be "an overly strong, or extensive, perhaps bilateral, development of the verbal, major-hemisphere type of organization that tends to interfere with an adequate development of spatial gnosis [knowledge] in the minor hemisphere." If there is verbal development on both sides of the brain, the right hemisphere's special skills cannot fully emerge. At the same time, the verbal, analytic skills may suffer from what Gazzaniga calls a problem in decision-making—"Like a husband and wife trying to decide what to have for breakfast; one of them's got to take the lead." If these children don't have a well-established decision system, and then receive two different interpretations of the world, they may be confused or slowed down. Through practice, they might learn to rely on one hemisphere more than the other, thus straightening out their lines of command.

All these attempts at making better use of the hemispheres' specialties pale before the urgency of aiding people who have lost one half of their brain through a stroke. The most pathetic of these patients are those who strain to speak, write, express themselves, but cannot, because the left side of their brain has been damaged by a blocked blood vessel. With only their right hemisphere available, they are speechless. Yet there is some preliminary evidence that they may be trained to communicate again, in a rudimentary way.

Surely the right hemisphere of a human being is cleverer than the whole brain of a chimpanzee, Gazzaniga reasoned. And if chimpanzees can be taught to converse through sign language or plastic symbols, as they appear to have been recently (see [Selection 13]), why couldn't stroke victims learn to communicate as well?

Fired up with enthusiasm after a visit to Santa Barbara, where Dr. David Premack had taught a chimp to communicate by means of plastic symbols, Gazzaniga suggested to a graduate student, Andrea Velletri Glass, that she start reading up on aphasia (the inability to speak) and prepare for a great project. For the next two years, Ms. Glass worked with a series of speechless patients at NYU's Institute of Rehabilitation Medicine, half an hour a day, five days a week. Her first patient was an eighty-four-year-old woman who could neither speak nor understand speech, but who could see that Ms. Glass was young and smiling at her. She responded, smiling feebly back. Ms. Glass then showed her some kitchen objects: two identical pots, for instance, and a spoon. She indicated that she wanted the woman to pick out the two objects that were alike, and she repeated the procedure with two forks and a knife, and two bananas and an orange. Her patient understood very rapidly. (With chimpanzees, teaching the concepts "same" and "different" is a long and tedious business.) Then came the first "word"—a green, doughnut-shaped cutout that Ms. Glass had made out of construction paper. Laying out the two identical pots on a table, she placed the cutout between them. With her mobile, expressive face, she urged her patient to do the same. It did not take the old woman long to figure out that she should insert the cutout between all objects that were the same. She did so, with her good left hand. Her reward: a big smile and expressions of joy on Ms. Glass's face. Next she learned the word "different"—a hexagon made of orange paper. Within two months, she had a vocabulary of some twelve symbols that she could pick out and place in the appropriate order to make simple statements, such as "Andrea pours water." She knew nouns, negatives, and a question mark, but verbs were extremely difficult.

"We've had twelve patients so far," says Gazzaniga, "and it works! That is, it works if they are still bright-eyed. If they are emotionally flat, if they don't want your smile, why should they arrange those shapes to please you?"

Dr. Premack's chimpanzees have learned much more language than these patients, but only after highly intensive lessons (several hours a day) for two years, rather than short lessons for two months. This raises the possibility that the stroke victims, too, could develop a working vocabulary with which to express their basic needs and feelings. Unfortunately, Ms. Glass had to stop her lessons after a short time as each patient was dismissed from the hospital and sent to a nursing home in another part of the country. The eighty-four-year-old woman, for instance, went off to Florida, and Ms. Glass herself is now moving to Pittsburgh. But eventually she hopes to expand this kind of program to incorporate the whole nursing staff in a hospital, the family, and, if necessary, the nursing homes where her patients will live. "Half an hour a day is all right for experimental purposes," she says, "but to really help the patients, they should be encouraged to use the system twelve hours a day." The symbols could then be made of Velcro, which sticks to a Velcro board at any angle, and the word each symbol represents could be printed on it for the benefit of all the literate people who wish to communicate with the patient.

It is not yet clear how far these patients could progress, given enough time. In part this depends on whether their memory is still good—some of them were approaching senility at the time of their strokes. But the research team was surprised to find how much most of the patients could do with their left hands: they could pick out printed words from nonsense syllables, and even spell some simple words when given cut-out letters to handle. This was far more than these global aphasics had been given credit for, and the team found it highly encouraging.

We can experience many things outside of the normal language system, as do young children before they learn to speak. Gazzaniga recently tested two patients at the Cornell Medical School who were being examined for brain tumors. They were about to undergo angiograms—X-rays of their brain's blood vessels, made visible with a special dye. While a needle was in place in their left carotid artery, in the neck, to prepare them for the injection of dye, small doses of Amytal (an anesthetic) were injected into their left hemisphere, putting it briefly to sleep—a method used in many studies of brain function. The purpose was to show exactly which side their speech center was on.

"It's a very dramatic procedure," reports Gazzaniga. "The patient lies on a table, with both hands held in the air. Twenty seconds after the drug goes in, his right hand sinks down—he's completely paralyzed on the right side, though the other side of his brain remains awake, for a minute and a half. This is our testing time. We put an object, say a cigarette, in his left hand. He feels it. His right hemisphere, which controls that hand, is wide-awake. We remove the cigarette. Then the effects of the Amytal wear off and the left hemisphere wakes up. We ask the patient how he feels. 'Fine,' he replies. 'What did I put in your hand?' I ask. 'I don't know,' says the patient. 'Are you sure?' 'Yes,' he says. Then we show him a series of objects—a pencil, a pad of paper, a comb, a cigarette—and ask him, 'Which one was it?' In spite of everything he has said, his left hand immediately points to the cigarette."

This shows that the memory trace, or engram, of the cigarette was encoded in his right hemisphere, and that it could be expressed nonverbally, but that the verbal side of his brain did not have access to it.

"It's a psychiatrist's dream," Gazzaniga says. "Something that's there, in the patient's brain, and that influences his behavior, but that he can't get at!" It may explain why memories formed in earliest childhood are inaccessible, he notes. The memories may be sharp and clear. They may control future behavior. But since they were formed before the child learned to speak, they cannot be recalled through the language system, not even through what the Russian psychologist Lev Vygotsky called "inner speech," speech for oneself, or thought.

Vygotsky believed that thought is born through words. Without words, he said, quoting a Russian poet, "My thought, unembodied, returns to the realm of shadows." Our earliest memories, too, dwell in a realm of shadows. And yet, something was experienced, and something of its flavor remains to haunt us through the rest of our lives.

Perhaps the right hemisphere's functions are too shrouded in shadows to be called thought. According to the Australian physiologist Sir John Eccles, a Nobel Prize winner, the right hemisphere cannot truly think. He makes a clear distinction between mere "consciousness," which we share with animals, and the world of language, thought, and culture, which is man-made. Animals can be conditioned, but they cannot create a culture, he claims. Primates leave no constructions, no art, nothing that can live beyond their own time, despite a brain almost as large as man's. In his opinion, everything that is truly human derives from the left hemisphere, where the speech center is, and where interactions between brain and mind occur. When the right hemisphere of a woman whose brain has been split sees something that makes her smile or blush, it's not correct to say she can't *report* why she smiled—she doesn't *know* why she smiled. Only the left hemisphere can have true thoughts or true knowledge, through language.

"Could the right half of the brain appreciate Chaplin's silent movies?" Eccles was asked at a meeting of the Society for Neuro-science recently. "How would you know?" he shot back, to much laughter in the audience. Both the report of such appreciation and our understanding of it would require the left hemisphere.

Nevertheless, the evidence increasingly favors a generous view of the right half-brain, whose role may be far more important than we know today.

When Einstein was asked how he arrived at some of his most original ideas, he explained that he rarely thought in words at all. "A thought comes, and I may try to express it in words afterwards," he said. His concepts first appeared through "physical entities"—certain signs and more or less clear images that he could reproduce and combine. These elements were "of visual and some of muscular type," he added. "Conventional words or other signs have to be sought for laboriously only in a secondary stage, when the mentioned associative play is sufficiently established and can be reproduced at will." This held true only for his creative work in physics; in other activities, he had no trouble with words. He liked to compose limericks, and his letters were both fluent and pithy. Apparently he could make exceptionally good use of both sides of his brain. However, his love of music and his reliance on nonverbal concepts seem to indicate a preference for his right hemisphere.

For centuries we have concentrated largely on the verbal side of our brains: the side that produces things we know how to analyze and measure. Our mute half-brain remains uncharted. We know almost nothing about how the right hemisphere thinks, or how it might be educated—and we have just begun to discover how much it contributes to the complex, creative acts of man.

20.

ESP and Credibility in Science

R. A. McCONNELL

Along with the growing interest in meditation, yoga, the mystical, and the occult in the last decade, there has been increasing interest in extrasensory perception (ESP). Although the reasons for this trend are in themselves worth speculating on, our present focus is on perception. More specifically, our focus is directed on the possibility of perceiving something that is beyond the reach of the presently known human sense organs (that is, extrasensory). Most psychologists view ESP with considerable skepticism and believe that the positive findings can be accounted for by inadequate experimental design, misinterpreted statistics, or outright trickery. Nonetheless, at least two past presidents of the American Psychological Association have suggested that the various ESP phenomena (telepathy, clairvoyance, and precognition) are worthy of further investigation.

The following article is a lecture given by a scientist to an introductory psychology class defending ESP studies and criticizing psychologists for their alleged prejudgment of the research results. Lest you find his arguments too convincing, you might want to consider why, if indeed there is perception that is extrasensory, the black-jack tables at gambling casinos don't go broke.

IN DISCUSSING extrasensory perception (ESP) before psychology students, it is not uncommon to stress the credulity of the public. Perhaps, instead, we ought to examine the credibility of scientists—including those on both sides of the controversy.

Reprinted from *American Psychologist*, 1969, *24*, pp. 531–38. Copyright 1969 by the American Psychological Association. Reprinted by permission.

In ESP research whom shall we trust? One can rather easily imagine experimental precautions to keep participating subjects from cheating. But how do we know whether the experimenter is deliberately deceiving us? And in a world where people believe all kinds of nonsense, how can we be sure that the experimenter is not deceiving himself?

Let us suppose that 10 experimenters independently get the same result. Can we accept it? Ten is not a large number. There are about 150,000 names in *American Men of Science*. We may reasonably assume that at least 10,000 of these hold beliefs about the nature of reality that the majority of scientists would regard as wholly without foundation. Thus, on a subject like ESP, where there are no recognized authorities, why should we accept the word of 10 experimenters—or, for that matter, a thousand? Are we not, all of us, creatures of our culture? Is there any way we can be sure that a scientist in any field is as rational as he pretends to be?

Questions concerning the credibility of scientists are rarely asked in our classrooms. I have wondered why. Perhaps it makes us uncomfortable to consider the possibility of incompetence, dishonesty, or mental illness among professional people. Whatever the reason, this is forbidden territory for study.

Once in a long while, these embarrassing ideas do come to the surface. Someone, a little bolder or a little more eccentric than the rest of us, may write an article that slips by the editorial censor. When that happens, we have a chance to learn what people really think.

When I accepted this invitation to talk to you, I was told I could give you an advance reading assignment. I asked that you read an eight-page article on ESP by G. R. Price (1955) that appeared in *Science* together with several letters to the editor (Soal; Rhine; Meehl & Scriven; Bridgman; Price; Rhine, 1956) written in reply to Price. These papers are currently available as part of the Bobbs-Merrill reprint series that is widely used for teaching psychology, and they have thus acquired a quasi-official status as source documents to which the very young may be exposed.

I also suggested that you read an analysis of Price's article (McConnell, 1955) that appeared in the *Journal of Parapsychology* and that was not included in the Bobbs-Merrill series. I hope that most of you have had a chance to study these references, which I shall now discuss briefly.

Price, a chemist by profession, presented a well-supported argument showing that existing experimental evidence constitutes conclusive proof of ESP if one accepts the good faith and sanity of the experimenters. But he went on to say that all of the otherwise convincing evidence for ESP can be easily explained away if one assumes that experimenters, working in collaboration with their witnesses, have intentionally faked their results.

Perhaps the most interesting thing about this unsubstantiated suggestion of fraud is that it was published on the first page of the most influential scientific journal in the United States. I will not say whether Price intended what he wrote as a joke. That is a riddle that I leave to you to answer. The important question is not whether Price took himself seriously, but whether you and I ought to do so.

I believe, as apparently does Price, that all kinds of fraud, even by highly placed scientists, are possible and that it is conceivable that there might be collaboration between two scientists in perpetuating a scientific hoax. Nevertheless, I think that those who accept Price's argument fail to understand two important things about science as a social enterprise.

First, they fail to realize that the way to tell whether a number of scientists are collaborating in a hoax is to consider the intricate web of public and private motivation, belief, and retribution that determines the behavior of professional people in our culture. Price suggested that scientists, university teachers, medical doctors, and intellectually prominent persons who have assisted in the investigation of ESP may have engaged in conscious collusive fraud. Price answered the question of how one might get such people to become willing accomplices by saying: "In recruiting, I would appeal not to desire for fame or material gain but to the noblest motives, arguing that much good to humanity could result from a small deception designed to strengthen religious belief." An experienced lawyer or even a politician would laugh at this explanation of a supposed conspiracy among well-educated and fully engaged members of our society, but evidently quite a few scientists find it plausible.

Second, those scientists who take Price seriously do not understand scientific method. Price suggested that the way to establish the scientific truth of ESP is to carry out a fraudproof experiment. In his words: "What is needed is one completely convincing experiment." He described in specific detail how this might be done by using prominent scientists and stage magicians as witnesses, backed up by motion pictures of the entire proceedings, plus photomicrographs of welded seals, and so on. This is nonsense because it assumes that scientific proof is of the same nature as legal proof. On the contrary, the acceptance of a scientific principle does not, and never can, depend upon the honesty of individual scientists.

I wish I had time to pursue with you the subtle psychological question of the nature of scientific proof and of how the method of science deals with individual experimenter error as well as mass irrationality. Those of you who are especially interested may wish to read a book by T. S. Kuhn (1962) titled *The Structure of Scientific Revolutions*. Here today, I can only say that in my opinion, wittily or unwittingly, Price's article is a hoax about hoaxes and about the nature of science.

If you were to ask: "What does it signify that Price successfully placed his article in our most important journal of science?" I would answer as follows: There is a facade of respectability and belief that covers all of the activities of society and makes it possible for men to work together and for society to exist. Most people—including those who are well educated—are unaware of this false front and lose their equilibrium when they are forced by circumstances to penetrate behind it. On the other hand, those of you who are intellectually alienated from our culture understand quite well that this pretense exists. I hope that some day you will also understand why it is necessary and that it is not the contrivance of a group of evil men but reflects what existential philosophers refer to as "the human condition."

This curtain of propriety and convention exists in science also, where it allows us to believe that all is well with our knowledge system. ESP or any other revolutionary discovery may seem to threaten science. From time to time, when such a challenge is offered, the stagehands nervously fumble, the curtain slips, and we see a little of the normally concealed machinery. We get a glimpse of underlying reality, a glimpse of the ignorance and fear that govern the inner affairs of the mind of man. Such was the case when *Science* published Price's critique of ESP. That is why his article is important.

EVIDENCE AND BELIEF

Then, what about ESP? If laboratory scientists lack sophistication about human nature and even about the methodology of science, how do we decide for ourselves whether ESP is real or imaginary, true or false?

Before we try to answer so difficult a question, let us go back to the beginning. I shall give you an operational definition of ESP that you may find a bit confusing. Then I shall describe a test for ESP that I hope will make the matter clear to you.

The definition goes this way: "Extrasensory perception is a response to an unknown event not presented to any known sense." I shall not try to explain it. Instead, let me describe the test.

I have brought with me a deck of ESP cards. These cards have five different kinds of symbols printed on them: a circle, a square, a plus, a star, and wavy lines. Altogether, there are 25 cards, 5 of each kind.

Suppose I shuffle these cards, hide them, and ask you to guess them. By the theory of chance probability, the number you would most often get right is five. Sometimes you would get four or six or seven. Only once in a long while would you get 15 right out of 25. In fact, if you got more than 10 right very often, you would begin to suspect that it was not just good luck. It might even be ESP.

Of course, you could not be sure. It might be luck—or it might be something else. If you look closely at the backs of these cards, sometimes you can see the symbol showing through. Perhaps in this way you recognized some of the cards when I shuffled them. Or again, every time I asked whether you were ready for your next guess, perhaps I gave you a hint without knowing it. Perhaps, unconsciously, I raised the tone of my voice just a little when I came to each star—because I think of stars as being "higher" than the other symbols, or for some other trivial reason.

You can see that there are many subtle ways for information to leak through by sight or by sound. No serious scientist would try to conduct an ESP experiment in this fashion. My only purpose in showing you these cards is to let you know how some of the early tests for ESP were done at Duke University 35 years ago. I regard these cards as a museum piece, although they are a lot of fun and can be used in preliminary testing.

The experiments that are carried out today are often so complex that one cannot evaluate them without advanced training in statistics, physics, and psychology. For this reason, and because the field is too large to describe in one lecture, I have prepared a list of reading materials. Some of these are intended to show the scope of the subject (Heywood, 1964; Langdon-Davies, 1961; McConnell, 1966; Murphy & Dale, 1961); others are experimental reports (Anderson & McConnell, 1961; McConnell & Forwald, 1967a, 1967b, 1968; McConnell, Snowdon, & Powell, 1955; Sinclair, 1962; Soal & Bateman, 1954).

You will notice that I have listed only my own journal articles. For this I offer my apology along with the following explanation. In any frontier field of science there are experimental hazards. If someone questions the soundness of what I recommend to you as evidence, I can probably do a better job of explaining if I have chosen research with which I am most familiar. I also want to convey the idea that there has been a large amount of work done in this field. If you study my papers and cannot find anything wrong with them, you ought to remember that there have been perhaps a hundred other investigators who have found substantial evidence for ESP under controlled experimental conditions.

ESP is a controversial idea in psychology. Nevertheless, the psychologists whom I know personally agree with me on many things. I am sure we agree on what constitutes good quality experimental laboratory research. We also agree that there is a sizable body of high-grade evidence for ESP in the literature.

In 1947 I visited Duke University in North Carolina where a man by the name of Rhine was doing experiments on ESP. I wanted to get acquainted with Rhine and with the people who were working under him. Even more important, I wanted to talk to those faculty members who rejected Rhine's work. I rented a dormitory room, and during four weeks I interviewed everyone I could, beginning with the President of the University and working down to assistant professors in various departments. I shall not have time to describe that adventure, but I will tell you what I was told by one professor of psychology in a private interview.

He said that he was familiar with the experimental literature of ESP and that, in his opinion, if it were anything else *but* ESP, one-tenth of the published evidence would already have established the phenomenon. He also explained that he would not accept ESP himself because, as he put it, he found "a world without ESP a more comfortable place in which to live."

That trip to Duke University was part of a larger investigation that made me decide to leave engineering electronics, in which I had acquired some experience, and to devote my life to the investigation of ESP and related effects.

That was 20 years ago. What has happened in this field since then? Among other things, there has been time to publish 20 more volumes of the *Journal of Parapsychology*. That comes to about 4,000 pages of research. There have been several thousand additional pages in the *Journal of the American Society for Psychical Research* and in the English and Continental journals. You might think that the argument would be settled by now.

Only recently, a brilliant young psychologist, who is here on your campus, gave a lecture on ESP in which he said "I tend to believe the evidence is as good as it is for many of our other psychological phenomena." He also said that "Psychologists will not be interested in ESP until there is a repeatable experiment."

Where my psychologist friends and I disagree, is that I believe that the available evidence for ESP is sufficient to establish its reality beyond all reasonable doubt. My psychologist friends think that the evidence is not yet conclusive. I do not regard this difference of opinion as very important. I am happy to allow anyone the privilege of doubt.

How else does the position of professional psychologists whom I know differ from my own? Perhaps the main difference—the really important difference—lies in our interpretation of the history and methodology of science—in what today we call the philosophy of science.

For one thing, my friends seem to believe that the only good evidence for ESP must come from controlled experimentation in a laboratory. My own belief is that all available evidence must be weighed, taking into account its source and the conditions under which it was gathered.

Perhaps it will clarify the problem if I say that there are only two important kinds of scientific evidence in this world: our own evidence and someone else's. Since most of us are not in a position to gather evidence of ESP, my remarks apply especially to other people's evidence.

The first thing to remember is that, no matter how reputable the scientific journal, someone else's evidence is always suspect. And if the matter is important, we ought to be *aggressively* skeptical about it.

Whether we are listening to a tale of a ghost in a haunted house or reading the tightly edited *Journal of Experimental Psychology*, we have to concern ourselves with two questions: what is the content of the report and what are the competence and motivation of the observer?

What I am suggesting is that our attitude toward *all* supposedly scientific reports must be that of the psychologist in receiving an introspective account from a human subject in a laboratory experiment—for it must be remembered that, as far as the reader is concerned, a journal article by a distant scientist is in some ways even less dependable than what psychologists, often condescendingly, refer to as a "verbal report."

From a study of the history of science, I have come to two conclusions in this connection: (*a*) the evidence presented in scientific journals by professional scientists for all kinds of ordinary phenomena is not as good as commonly supposed, and (*b*) on a controversial subject where the professionals do not agree, the evidence of the layman may have considerable scientific value. As corollaries, I suggest that the textbooks of science are often wrong and that contrary popular opinion is sometimes right. Let us examine these ideas.

STOREHOUSES OF KNOWLEDGE?

Textbooks are the storehouses of man's knowledge. They are presumed to contain all of the things we know to be true. If you are becoming a scientist, you will spend at least 18 years studying from books. It would be not entirely unfair to call most of this training a "brainwashing" process. Nearly everything you learn as factual reality must be accepted upon the word of some recognized authority and not upon your own firsthand experience. It should be a matter of concern to you whether you have been told the truth for those 18 years. Just how bad are the textbooks we use? Let me take an example from the field of geology.

Did you know that until the year 1800 the highest scientific authorities thought that there was no such thing as a meteorite? After all, there are no stones in the sky; so stones cannot fall out of the sky. Only a superstitious person would believe in meteorites.

Many of you are familiar with the work of Lavoisier. He was the founder of modern chemistry. He discovered that burning is the combining of oxygen with other things, and he helped to show that the formula for water is H_2O. He was one of the great scientists of all time.

In 1772 Lavoisier signed a report to the French Academy of Science in which he said he had examined a stone that was believed to have fallen from the sky in a great blaze of light. Lavoisier said in his report that this was just an ordinary stone that had been struck by lightning and had melted partly into glass while lying on the ground.

Eventually, of course, the leaders of science decided that meteorites do come from outer space, and they revised the textbooks accordingly. But in doing so, they forgot to mention that there had ever been any argument about the matter. So here we are, living in the space age, without realizing how hard it is to discover the truth about even a simple thing like meteorites, which can be seen as meteors in the sky on any clear night, and which have been found upon the surface of the earth since the dawn of history.

Even worse, as students, we have no way of estimating how many arguments are still going on in science and how many mistakes—truly serious mistakes—there are in the textbooks from which we study. It is my guess that we can safely believe nearly all of what is said in the physics and chemistry books. But we ought to believe only half of the ideas in the biological sciences—although I am not sure which half. And we should accept as final very little in the social sciences, which try to explain why groups of people behave as they do.

Our subject today is extrasensory perception, which belongs in psychology, one of the biological sciences. ESP is something about which the "authorities" are in error. Most psychology textbooks omit the subject entirely as unworthy of serious attention. But these books are mistaken, because ESP is a real psychological phenomenon.

Of course, I am only giving you my individual opinion about ESP. I do not want you to base your belief upon what I tell you. When you have studied advanced psychology and statistics, and when you come to realize that your professors cannot be expected to teach you everything you wish to know, then I hope you will go to the scientific journals and study the experiments that have been done and decide for yourself.

MENTAL RADIO

I have already discussed the credibility of experts and the errors we find in science textbooks. I would like to turn next to the other half of my thesis, namely, that evidence from a layman may sometimes have scientific value.

Figure 20–1

Most of you are familiar with the name Upton Sinclair, who was a socialist reformer and a writer active in the first half of the twentieth century. He died in 1968 at the age of 90. In his time he wrote nearly 90 books. One of the best known of these, published in 1906, was called *The Jungle*. It told about the cruel and unsanitary conditions in the processing of beef in the Chicago stock yards. As a result of that book, laws were passed, and today the situation is much improved. In a very real sense, all of us are indebted to this man.

Sinclair discovered that his wife had an unusual amount of what was then known as "psychic ability." (That was before the beginning of the ESP controversy.) After three years of serious experimentation, he wrote a book about it: *Mental Radio* (1962, orig. publ. 1930).

In his experiments, Sinclair, or someone else, would draw a secret picture and ask Mrs. Sinclair to draw another picture to match it. Some of the pairs of pictures are presented in the following examples.[1] The one on the left is always the original picture, and the one on the right is what Mrs. Sinclair got by ESP.

Sometimes the pictures were made as far apart as 40 miles. At other times the target picture was held by Mrs. Sinclair in her hand—without looking, of course—while she concentrated before drawing her matching picture. The degree of success did not seem to depend upon distance.

Let us examine some of the pictures. In Figure 20–1 we see an almost perfect ESP response. It is a knight's helmet. Notice that for every important line in the left-hand picture there is a corresponding line on the right.

Compare that with Figure 20–2. Here, the response on the right is not quite the same as the target on the left, but the idea is the same.

[1] Illustrations from *Mental Radio* by Upton Sinclair are reproduced by permission of the Estate of Upton Sinclair.

Figure 20–2

The next slide is Figure 20–3. Sinclair drew a football as a target. Mrs. Sinclair made the drawing on the right, but she thought it was "a baby calf with a belly band." Why did her ESP make this mistake? We cannot be sure, but we think it had something to do with the fact that in her childhood she had known a queer old man who raised calves as parlor pets and dressed them in embroidered belly bands.

Figure 20–3

Figure 20–4 is another instance of the right shape with a wrong interpretation. Upton Sinclair drew a volcano, and Mrs. Sinclair drew what she called a black beetle. The beetle is upside down. If you turn the example over, you can more easily recognize its antennae and legs.

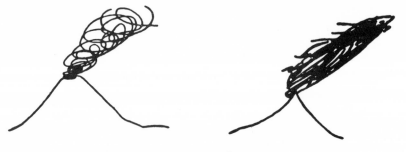

Figure 20–4

In Figure 20–5 Sinclair drew a fish hook, which turned into two flowers.

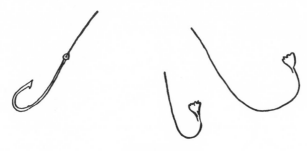

Figure 20–5

Figure 20–6 shows a fragmentary response. Sinclair drew a balloon. The response on the right is what his wife received by "mental radio." She was not sure what it was, so she wrote beside the picture: "Shines in sunlight, must be metal, a scythe hanging among vines or strings."

Figure 20–6

In Figure 20–7 on the left is a swastika. Mrs. Sinclair drew the response on the right. She did not know what it meant, but she wrote beside it, "These things somehow belong together, but won't get to-

Figure 20–7

gether." You can see some of her words which were accidentally included when the printer made the book. Here is the beginning of "These" and "belong" and "but won't" and "together."

Figure 20–8 is a pair of drawings in which a stick man became a skull and crossbones.

Figure 20–8

Notice that in Figure 20–9, Mrs. Sinclair left out some of the stars and added a moon instead.

Figure 20–9

In Figure 20–10 Sinclair drew an umbrella. His wife responded with this curious picture, which she described in writing beside it as follows:

Figure 20–10

"I feel that it is a snake crawling out of something—vivid feeling of snake, but it looks like a cat's tail." I might mention that she had a special fear of snakes, having grown up on a plantation in a Mississippi swamp.

The last example is the American flag and a response to it that could hardly be called a chance coincidence (Figure 20–11).

Figure 20–11

You have seen a selection of 11 pictures out of a total of 290 trials made by Mrs. Sinclair. Perhaps 4 of the 11 would be called direct target hits. The rest are partial hits. Out of the 290 tries, 23% were rated by Upton Sinclair as hits, 53% were partial hits, and 24% were failures.

Of course, before you can be sure that these pictures were made by ESP, many questions must be answered. Because Upton Sinclair and his wife were laymen, you will have to pay particular attention to their competence and motivation. On the other hand, one important feature of Sinclair's book is that you do not have to be a scientist to understand it. Even though you may not have studied statistics and psychology, you can read the book yourself and make up your mind as to its value on the basis of common sense. When you do, I think you will arrive at the same conclusion that many scientists have reached by entirely different kinds of experiments. I think you will decide that extrasensory perception is a reality regardless of the skepticism of the psychological profession.

A MATTER OF INTEREST

I have been told by my friends that psychologists will not be interested in ESP until someone discovers a repeatable experiment. Upton Sinclair repeated his experiments over a period of three years. In London, a mathematician by the name of Soal (Soal & Bateman, 1954) repeated certain card-guessing experiments again and again over a period of six years using two subjects and many different witnesses. What do psychologists mean by a repeatable experiment?

Evidently, they mean an experiment that is "repeatable by prescription." They want a standard experimental procedure that can be described on paper by which any qualified person—or at least some qualified persons—can guarantee to produce ESP upon demand. I must confess that we have not yet reached that stage in ESP research. And, until we do, I can sympathize with my skeptical friends. I can see why they, as busy individuals with other interests, are unwilling to reach a firm position about the reality of ESP.

What I cannot understand is why they say: "Psychologists will not be *interested* in ESP until there is a repeatable experiment."

It is a statement of fact the psychologists are *not* interested in ESP. Recently, I had occasion to examine a number of psychology textbooks. Only one of them mentioned ESP—that book, by Hilgard and Atkinson (1967). After reading the four pages which these authors devote to ESP, I have only two minor critical observations to offer.

The first is that the authors have given too much space to finding fault with unimportant papers. They go back 25 years to a journal article in which they accuse an ESP experimenter of overanalyzing his data. I am sure that comparable examples of weak statistical method could be found in any one of the quantitative journals of the APA—and we would not need to go back a generation in time to do it.

My second comment is that Hilgard and Atkinson may have tended to damage their own scholarly reputations by recommending as a "scholarly review" a book by C. E. M. Hansel (1966) titled *ESP: A Scientific Evaluation*. This book has been reviewed by S. S. Stevens of Harvard, who regards ESP as a Rabelaisian joke and who gave Hansel his unqualified approval. If you like amusing book reviews, I suggest that you read Stevens (1967). I regret that I do not have time here today to document for you the basis of my unfavorable opinion of Hansel's book.

I have wandered over many facets of ESP. I shall now summarize what I think are the most important ideas. Since the scientific study of ESP was begun by the London Society for Psychical Research in 1882, there have been hundreds and perhaps thousands of experiments done with a care typical of the journals of the APA. Many psychologists of high repute admit that the evidence is as good as that for other phenomena that are accepted by their profession.

Surprising though it may seem, most of this research on ESP has been done by people who were not psychologists. From this fact and from the usual psychology textbook treatment of the subject as well as from private discussion, we know that psychologists are *not* interested in ESP. This raises a question—a very mysterious question that I invite you to try to answer: Why are psychologists not interested in ESP?*

REFERENCES

ANDERSON, M. L., & McCONNELL, R. A. Fantasy testing for ESP in a fourth and fifth grade class. *Journal of Psychology*, 1961, **52**, 491–503.

CLARK, K. E., et al. The scientific and professional aims of psychology. *American Psychologist*, 1967, **22**, 49–76.

HANSEL, C. E. M. *ESP: A scientific evaluation.* New York: Scribner's, 1966.

HEYWOOD, R. *ESP: A personal memoir.* New York: Dutton, 1964.

HILGARD, E. R., & ATKINSON, R. C. *Introduction to psychology.* New York: Harcourt, Brace & World, 1967.

KUHN, T. S. *The structure of scientific revolutions* (Vol. II, No. 2, of the *International Encyclopedia of Unified Science*). Chicago: University of Chicago Press, 1962.

LANGDON-DAVIES, J. *On the nature of man.* New York: New American Library Corporation, 1961.

LINDER, R. Light one candle. *American Psychologist*, 1967, **22**, 804–805.

McCONNELL, R. A. Price in *Science. Journal of Parapsychology*, 1955, **19**, 258–261.

McCONNELL, R. A. ESP research at three levels of method. *Journal of Parapsychology*, 1966, **30**, 195–207.

McCONNELL, R. A. The ESP scholar. *Contemporary Psychology*, 1968, **13**, 41. (a)

McCONNELL, R. A. The structure of scientific revolutions: An epitome. *Journal of the American Society for Psychical Research*, 1968, **62**, 321–327. (b)

McCONNELL, R. A., & FORWALD, H. Psychokinetic placement: I. A re-examination of the Forwald-Durham experiment. *Journal of Parapsychology*, 1967, **31**, 51–69. (a)

McCONNELL, R. A., & FORWALD, H. Psychokinetic placement: II. A factorial study of successful and unsuccessful series. *Journal of Parapsychology*, 1967, **31**, 198–213. (b)

McCONNELL, R. A., & FORWALD, H. Psychokinetic placement: III: Cube-releasing devices. *Journal of Parapsychology*, 1968, **32**, 9–38.

McCONNELL, R. A., SNOWDON, R. J., & POWELL, K. F. Wishing with dice. *Journal of Experimental Psychology*, 1955, **50**, 269–275.

MURPHY, G., & DALE, L. A. *Challenge of psychical research.* New York: Harper, 1961.

PRICE, G. R. Science and the supernatural. *Science*, 1955, **122**, 359–367.

SINCLAIR, U. *Mental radio.* Springfield, Ill.: Charles C. Thomas, 1962.

SOAL, S. G., & BATEMAN, F. *Modern experiments in telepathy.* London: Faber & Faber, 1954.

SOAL, S. G.; RHINE, J. B.; MEEHL, P. E.; & SCRIVEN, M.; BRIDGMAN, P. W.; PRICE, G. R.; RHINE, J. B. (Letters to the editor in rejoinder to G. R. Price.) *Science*, 1956, **123**, 9–19.

STEVENS, S. S. The market for miracles. *Contemporary Psychology*, 1967, **12**, 1–3.

---

* Those who wish to answer this question might start their odyssey by visiting Clark *et al.* (1967) and Linder (1967).

21.

Clinical and Psychological Effects of Marihuana in Man

ANDREW T. WEIL, NORMAN E. ZINBERG, and JUDITH M. NELSEN

There are many drugs that can produce perceptual and other psychological effects. Some of these drugs are especially conducive to changed levels of perceptual awareness. The most dramatic perceptual alterations occur with drugs such as LSD, mescaline, and psilocybin, which are referred to as "hallucinogens" by those who choose to emphasize that one effect of the drug is to produce hallucinations and as "psychedelics" by those who wish to emphasize the mind-expanding effects.

Marihuana is a hallucinogen of considerably less potency than the others. (Indeed, the hallucinogenic effect of marihuana, when taken in low to moderate dosages, is so reduced that many researchers prefer not to classify it as a hallucinogenic drug at all.) Nevertheless, marihuana, which is second only to alcohol as the drug of choice by young people today, does produce changes in levels of perceptual awareness, together with a mildly euphoric, relaxed state. However, despite the widespread use and the variety of controversial statements that have been made by "informed sources" about the effects of marihuana, there have been remarkably few well-controlled studies of either the short- or long-term effects. The study reprinted here is perhaps the first to investigate systematically and with appropriate controls the physiological, attentional, and psychomotor effects of marihuana in experienced and inexperienced users.[*]

[*] These investigators report on the social and personality similarities and differences in their group of subjects in another article; see: Norman E. Zinberg and Andrew T. Weil, "A Comparison of Marihuana Users and Nonusers," *Nature,* 1970, *226,* 119–23.

Reprinted from *Science,* Vol. 162, pp. 1234–42, 13 December 1968. Copyright 1968 by the American Association for the Advancement of Science. Reprinted by permission.

Based on your reading of this article and discussions you have
had with friends, how much of the "perceptual enhancement"
accompanying marihuana smoking do you think is a function of the
smoker's expectation of what the drug will do to him?

In the spring of 1968 we conducted a series of pilot experiments on
acute marihuana intoxication in human subjects. The study was not
undertaken to prove or disprove popularly held convictions about
marihuana as an intoxicant, to compare it with other drugs, or to introduce our own opinions. Our concern was simply to collect some long
overdue pharmacological data. In this article we describe the primitive
state of knowledge of the drug, the research problems encountered in
designing a replicable study, and the results of our investigations.

Marihuana is a crude preparation of flowering tops, leaves, seeds,
and stems of female plants of Indian hemp *Cannabis sativa* L.; it is
usually smoked. The intoxicating constituents of hemp are found in
the sticky resin exuded by the tops of the plants, particularly the
females. Male plants produce some resin but are grown mainly for
hemp fiber, not for marihuana. The resin itself, when prepared for
smoking or eating, is known as "hashish." Various *Cannabis* preparations are used as intoxicants throughout the world; their potency varies
directly with the amount of resin present (1). Samples of American
marihuana differ greatly in pharmacological activity, depending on
their compositions (tops contain most resin; stems, seeds, and lower
leaves least) and on the conditions under which the plants were grown.
In addition, different varieties of *Cannabis* probably produce resins
with different proportions of constituents (2). Botanists feel that only
one species of hemp exists, but work on the phytochemistry of the
varieties of this species is incomplete (3). Chronic users claim that
samples of marihuana differ in quality of effects as well as in potency;
that some types cause a preponderance of physical symptoms, and that
other types tend to cause greater distortions of perception or of
thought.

Pharmacological studies of *Cannabis* indicate that the tetrahydro-
cannabinol fraction of the resin is the active portion. In 1965,
Mechoulam and Gaoni (4) reported the first total synthesis of (−) Δ^1-
trans-tetrahydrocannabinol (THC), which they called "the psychoto-
mimetically active constituent of hashish (marihuana)." Synthetic THC
is now available for research in very limited supply.

In the United States, the use of *Cannabis* extracts as therapeutics
goes back to the 19th century, but it was not until the 1920's that use
of marihuana as an intoxicant by migrant Mexican laborers, urban

Negroes, and certain Bohemian groups caused public concern (3). Despite increasingly severe legal penalties imposed during the 1930's, use of marihuana continued in these relatively small populations without great public uproar or apparent changes in numbers or types of users until the last few years. The fact that almost none of the studies devoted to the physiological and psychological effects of *Cannabis* in man [were] based on controlled laboratory experimentation escaped general notice. But with the explosion of use in the 1960's, at first on college campuses followed by a spread downward to secondary schools and upward to a portion of the established middle class, controversy over the dangers of marihuana generated a desire for more objective information about the drug.

Of the three known studies on human subjects performed by Americans, the first (see 5) was done in the Canal Zone with 34 soldiers; the consequences reported were hunger and hyperphagia, loss of inhibitions, increased pulse rate with unchanged blood pressure, a tendency to sleep, and unchanged performance of psychological and neurological tests. Doses and type of marihuana were not specified.

The second study, known as the 1944 LaGuardia Report (6), noted that 72 prisoners, 48 of whom were previous *Cannabis* users, showed minimum physiological responses, but suffered impaired intellectual functioning and decreased body steadiness, especially well demonstrated by nonusers after high doses. Basic personality structures remained unchanged as subjects reported feelings of relaxation, disinhibition, and self-confidence. In that study, the drug was administered orally as an extract. No controls were described, and doses and quality of marihuana were unspecified.

Williams *et al.* in 1946 (7) studied a small number of prisoners who were chronic users; they were chiefly interested in effects of long-term smoking on psychological functioning. They found an initial exhilaration and euphoria which gave way after a few days of smoking to indifference and lassitude that somewhat impaired performance requiring concentration and manual dexterity. Again, no controls were provided.

Predictably, these studies, each deficient in design for obtaining reliable physiological and psychological data, contributed no dramatic or conclusive results. The 1967 President's Commission on Law Enforcement and the Administration of Justice described the present state of knowledge by concluding (3): "No careful and detailed analysis of the American experience [with marihuana] seems to have been attempted. Basic research has been almost nonexistent." Since then, no other studies with marihuana itself have been reported, but in 1967 Isbell (8) administered synthetic THC to chronic users. At doses of 120 μg/kg orally or 50 μg/kg by smoking, subjects reported this drug to be similar to marihuana. At higher doses (300 to 400 μg/kg orally or 200 to 250 μg/kg by smoking), psychotomimetic effects occurred in most subjects. This synthetic has not yet been compared with marihuana in nonusers or given to any subjects along with marihuana in double-blind fashion.

Investigations outside the United States have been scientifically deficient, and for the most part have been limited to anecdotal and sociological approaches (9–12). So far as we know, our study is the first attempt to investigate marihuana in a formal double-blind experiment with the appropriate controls. It is also the first attempt to collect basic clinical and psychological information on the drug by observing its effects on marihuana-naive human subjects in a neutral laboratory setting.

RESEARCH PROBLEMS

That valid basic research on marihuana is almost nonexistent is not entirely accounted for by legislation which restricts even legitimate laboratory investigations or by public reaction sometimes verging on hysteria. A number of obstacles are intrinsic to the study of this drug. We now present a detailed description of our specific experimental approach, but must comment separately on six general problems confronting the investigator who contemplates marihuana research.

1. Concerning the route of administration, many pharmacologists dismiss the possibility of giving marihuana by smoking because, they say, the dose cannot be standardized (13). We consider it not only possible, but important to administer the drug to humans by smoking rather than by the oral route for the following reasons. (i) Smoking is the way nearly all Americans use marihuana. (ii) It is possible to have subjects smoke marihuana cigarettes in such a way that drug dosage is reasonably uniform for all subjects. (iii) Standardization of dose is not assured by giving the drug orally because little is known about gastrointestinal absorption of the highly water-insoluble cannabinols in man. (iv) There is considerable indirect evidence from users that the quality of the intoxication is different when marihuana or preparations of it are ingested rather than smoked. In particular, ingestion seems to cause more powerful effects, more "LSD-like" effects, longer-lasting effects, and more hangovers (12, 14). Further, marihuana smokers are accustomed to a very rapid onset of action due to efficient absorption through the lungs, whereas the latency for onset of effects may be 45 or 60 minutes after ingestion. (v) There is reported evidence from experiments with rats and mice that the pharmacological activities of

natural hashish (not subjected to combustion) and hashish sublimate (the combustion products) are different (*14*).

2. Until quite recently, it was extremely difficult to estimate the relative potencies of different samples of marihuana by the techniques of analytical chemistry. For this study, we were able to have the marihuana samples assayed spectrophotometrically (*15*) for THC content. However, since THC has not been established as the sole determinant of marihuana's activity, we still feel it is important to have chronic users sample and rate marihuana used in research. Therefore, we assayed our material by this method as well.

3. One of the major deficiencies in previous studies has been the absence of negative control or placebo treatments, which we consider essential to the design of this kind of investigation. Because marihuana smoke has a distinctive odor and taste, it is difficult to find an effective placebo for use with chronic users. The problem is much less difficult with nonusers. Our solution to this dilemma was the use of portions of male hemp stalks (*16*), devoid of THC, in the placebo cigarettes.

4. In view of the primitive state of knowledge about marihuana, it is difficult to predict which psychological tests will be sensitive to the effects of the drug. The tests we chose were selected because, in addition to being likely to demonstrate effects, they have been used to evaluate many other psychoactive drugs. Of the various physiological parameters available, we chose to measure (i) heart rate, because previous studies have consistently reported increases in heart rate after administration of marihuana (for example, *5*); (ii) respiratory rate, because it is an easily measured vital sign, and depression has been reported (*11, 17*); (iii) pupil size, because folklore on effects of marihuana consistently includes reports of pupillary dilatation, although objective experimental evidence of an effect of the drug on pupils has not been sought; (iv) conjunctival appearance, because both marihuana smokers and eaters are said to develop red eyes (*11*); and (v) blood sugar, because hypoglycemia has been invoked as a cause of the hunger and hyperphagia commonly reported by marihuana users, but animal and human evidence of this effect is contradictory (*6, 10, 11*). [The LaGuardia Report, quoted by Jaffe in Goodman and Gilman (*18*) described hyperglycemia as an effect of acute intoxication.] We did not measure blood pressure because previous studies have failed to demonstrate any consistent effect on blood pressure in man, and we were unwilling to subject our volunteers to a nonessential annoyance.

5. It is necessary to control set and setting. "Set" refers to the subject's psychological expectations of what a drug will do to him in relation to his general personality structure. The total environment in which the drug is taken is the setting. All indications are that the form of marihuana intoxication is particularly dependent on the interaction

of drug, set, and setting. Because of recent increases in the extent of use and in attention given this use by the mass media, it is difficult to find subjects with a neutral set toward marihuana. Our method of selecting subjects (described below), at the least, enabled us to identify the subjects' attitudes. Unfortunately, too many researchers have succumbed to the temptation to have subjects take drugs in "psychedelic" environments or have influenced the response to the drug by asking questions that disturb the setting. Even a question as simple as, "How do you feel?" contains an element of suggestion that alters the drug-set-setting interaction. We took great pains to keep our laboratory setting neutral by strict adherence to an experimental timetable and to a prearranged set of conventions governing interactions between subjects and experimenters.

6. Medical, social, ethical, and legal concerns about the welfare of subjects are a major problem in a project of this kind. Is it ethical to introduce people to marihuana? When can subjects safely be sent home from the laboratory? What kind of follow-up care, if any, should be given? These are only a few specific questions with which the investigator must wrestle. Examples of some of the precautions we took are as follows. (i) All subjects were volunteers. All were given psychiatric screening interviews and were clearly informed that they might be asked to smoke marihuana. All nonusers tested were persons who had reported that they had been planning to try marihuana. (ii) All subjects were driven home by an experimenter; they agreed not to engage in unusual activity or operate machinery until the next morning and to report any unusual, delayed effects. (iii) All subjects agreed to report for follow-up interviews 6 months after the experiment. Among other things, the check at 6 months should answer the question whether participation in the experiment encouraged further drug use. (iv) All subjects were protected from possible legal repercussions of their participation in these experiments by specific agreements with the Federal Bureau of Narcotics, the Office of the Attorney General of Massachusetts, and the Massachusetts Bureau of Drug Abuse and Drug Control (19).

SUBJECTS

The central group of subjects consisted of nine healthy, male volunteers, 21 to 26 years of age, all of whom smoked tobacco cigarettes regularly but had never tried marihuana previously. Eight chronic users of marihuana also participated, both to "assay" the quality of marihuana received from the Federal Bureau of Narcotics and to enable the experimenters to standardize the protocol, using subjects familiar with their responses to the drug. The age range for users was also 21 to 26 years. They all smoked marihuana regularly, most of them every day or every other day.

The nine "naive" subjects were selected after a careful screening process. An initial pool of prospective subjects was obtained by placing advertisements in the student newspapers of a number of universities in the Boston area. These advertisements sought "male volunteers at least 21 years old, for psychological experiments." After nonsmokers were eliminated from this pool, the remaining volunteers were interviewed individually by a psychiatrist who determined their histories of use of alcohol and other intoxicants as well as their general personality types. In addition to serving as a potential screening technique to eliminate volunteers with evidence of psychosis, or of serious mental or personality disorder, these interviews served as the basis for the psychiatrist's prediction of the type of response an individual subject might have after smoking marihuana. (It should be noted that no marihuana-naive volunteer had to be disqualified on psychiatric grounds.) Only after a prospective subject passed the interview was he informed that the "psychological experiment" for which he had volunteered was a marihuana study. If he consented to participate, he was asked to sign a release, informing him that he would be "expected to smoke cigarettes containing marihuana or an inert substance." He was also required to agree to a number of conditions, among them that he would "during the course of the experiment take no psychoactive drugs, including alcohol, other than those drugs administered in the course of the experiment."

It proved extremely difficult to find marihuana-naive persons in the student population of Boston, and nearly 2 months of interviewing were required to obtain nine men. All those interviewed who had already tried marihuana volunteered this information quite freely and were delighted to discuss their use of drugs with the psychiatrist. Nearly all persons encountered who had not tried marihuana admitted this somewhat apologetically. Several said they had been meaning to try the drug but had not got around to it. A few said they had no access to it. Only one person cited the current laws as his reason for not having experimented with marihuana. It seemed clear in the interviews that many of these persons were actually afraid of how they might react to marihuana; they therefore welcomed a chance to smoke it under medical supervision. Only one person (an Indian exchange student) who passed the screening interview refused to participate after learning the nature of the experiment.

The eight heavy users of marihuana were obtained with much less difficulty. They were interviewed in the same manner as the other subjects and were instructed not to smoke any marihuana on the day of their appointment in the laboratory.

Subjects were questioned during screening interviews and at the conclusion of the experiments to determine their knowledge of marihuana effects. None of the nine naive subjects had ever watched anyone smoke marihuana or observed anyone high on marihuana. Most of them knew of the effects of the drug only through reports in the popular press. Two subjects had friends who used marihuana frequently; one of these (No. 4) announced his intention to "prove" in the experiments that marihuana really did not do anything; the other (No. 3) was extremely eager to get high because "everyone I know is always talking about it very positively."

SETTING

Greatest effort was made to create a neutral setting. That is, subjects were made comfortable and secure in a pleasant suite of laboratories and offices, but the experimental staff carefully avoided encouraging any person to have an enjoyable experience. Subjects were never asked how they felt, and no subject was permitted to discuss the experiment with the staff until he had completed all four sessions. Verbal interactions between staff and subjects were minimum and formal. At the end of each session, subjects were asked to complete a brief form asking whether they thought they had smoked marihuana that night; if so, whether a high dose or a low dose; and how confident they were of their answers. The experimenters completed similar forms on each subject.

MARIHUANA

Marihuana used in these experiments was of Mexican origin, supplied by the Federal Bureau of Narcotics (20). It consisted of finely chopped leaves of *Cannabis,* largely free of seeds and stems. An initial batch, which was judged to be of low potency by the experimenters on the basis of the doses needed to produce symptoms of intoxication in the chronic users, was subsequently found to contain only 0.3 percent of THC by weight. A second batch, assayed at 0.9 percent THC, was rated by the chronic users to be "good, average" marihuana, neither exceptionally strong nor exceptionally weak compared to their usual supplies. Users consistently reported symptoms of intoxication after smoking about 0.5 gram of the material with a variation of only a few puffs from subject to subject. This second batch of marihuana was used in the experiments described below; the low dose was 0.5 gram, and the high dose was 2.0 grams.

All marihuana was administered in the form of cigarettes of standard size made with a hand-operated rolling machine. In any given experimental session, each person was required to smoke two cigarettes in succession (Table 21-1).

TABLE 21-1
COMPOSITION OF THE DOSE*

Dose	Marihuana in each cigarette (g)	Total dose marihuana (2 cigarettes) (g)	Approximate dose THC
Placebo	—	—	
Low	0.25	0.5	4.5 mg
High	1.0	2.0	18 mg

* The placebo cigarette consisted of placebo material, tobacco filler, and mint leaves for masking flavor. The low dose was made up of marihuana, tobacco filler, and mint leaves. The high dose consisted of marihuana and mint leaves.

Placebo material consisted of the chopped outer covering of mature stalks of male hemp plants; it contained no THC. All cigarettes had a tiny plug of tobacco at one end and a plug of paper at the other end so that the contents were not visible. The length to which each cigarette was to be smoked was indicated by an ink line. Marihuana and placebos were administered to the naive subjects in double-blind fashion. Scented aerosols were sprayed in the laboratory before smoking, to mask the odor of marihuana. The protocol during an experimental session was as follows. The sessions began at approximately 5:30 P.M.

Time	Procedure
0:00	Physiological measurements; blood sample drawn
0:05	Psychological test battery No. 1 (base line)
0:35	Verbal sample No. 1
0:40	Cigarette smoking
1:00	Rest period
1:15	Physiological measurements; blood sample drawn
1:20	Psychological test battery No. 2
1:50	Verbal sample No. 2
1:55	Rest period (supper)
2:30	Physiological measurements
2:35	Psychological test battery No. 3
3:05	End of testing

EXPERIMENTAL SESSIONS

Chronic users were tested only on high doses of marihuana with no practice sessions. Each naive subject was required to come to four sessions, spaced about a week apart. The first was always a practice session, in which the subject learned the proper smoking technique and during which he became thoroughly acquainted with the tests and the protocol. In the practice session, each subject completed the entire protocol, smoking two hand-rolled tobacco cigarettes. He was instructed to take a long puff, to inhale deeply, and to maintain inspiration for 20 seconds, as timed by an experimenter with a stopwatch. Subjects were allowed 8 to 12 minutes to smoke each of the two cigarettes. One purpose of this practice smoking was to identify and eliminate individuals who were not tolerant to high doses of nicotine, thus reducing the effect of nicotine on the variables measured during subsequent drug sessions (21). A surprising number (five) of volunteers who had described themselves in screening interviews as heavy cigarette smokers, "inhaling" up to two packs of cigarettes a day, developed acute nicotine reactions when they smoked two tobacco cigarettes by the required method. Occurrence of such a reaction disqualified a subject from participation in the experiments.

In subsequent sessions when cigarettes contained either drug or placebo, all smoking was similarly supervised by an experimenter with a stopwatch. Subjects were not permitted to smoke tobacco cigarettes while the experiment was in progress. They were assigned to one of the three treatment groups listed in Table 21–2.

TABLE 21–2
ORDER OF TREATMENT

	Drug Session		
Group	1	2	3
I	High	Placebo	Low
II	Low	High	Placebo
III	Placebo	Low	High

PHYSIOLOGICAL AND PSYCHOLOGICAL MEASURES

The physiological parameters measured were heart rate, respiratory rate, pupil size, blood glucose level, and conjunctival vascular state. Pupil size was measured with a millimeter rule under constant illumination with eyes focused on an object at constant distance. Conjunctival appearance was rated by an experienced experimenter for dilation of blood vessels on a 0 to 4 scale with ratings of 3 and 4 indicating "significant" vasodilatation. Blood samples were collected for immediate determinations of serum glucose and for the serum to be frozen and stored for possible future biochemical studies. Subjects were asked not to eat and not to imbibe a beverage containing sugar or caffeine during the 4 hours preceding a session. They were given supper after the second blood sample was drawn.

The psychological test battery consisted of (i) the Continuous Performance Test (CPT)—5 minutes; (ii) the Digit Symbol Substitution Test (DSST)—90 seconds; (iii) CPT with strobe light distraction—5 minutes; (iv) self-rating bipolar mood scale—3 minutes; and (v) pursuit rotor—10 minutes.

The Continuous Performance Test was designed to measure a subject's capacity for sustained attention (22). The subject was placed in a darkened room and directed to watch a small screen upon which six letters of the alphabet were flashed rapidly and in random order. The subject was instructed to press a button whenever a specified critical letter appeared. The number of letters presented, correct responses, and errors of commission and omission were counted over the 5-minute period. The test was also done with a strobe light flickering at 50 cycles per second. Normal subjects make no or nearly no errors on this test either with or without strobe distraction; but sleep deprivation, organic brain disease, and certain drugs like chlorpromazine adversely affect performance. Presence or absence of previous exposure to the task has no effect on performance.

The Digit Symbol Substitution Test is a simple test of cognitive function (see Figure 21–1). A subject's score was the number of correct answers in a 90-second period. As in the case of the CPT, practice should have little or no effect on performance.

The self-rating bipolar mood scale used in these experiments was one developed by Smith and Beecher (23) to evaluate subjective effects of morphine. By allowing subjects to rate themselves within a given category of moods, on an arbitrary scale from $+3$ to -3, it minimizes suggestion and is thus more neutral than the checklist often employed in drug testing.

The pursuit rotor measures muscular coordination and attention. The subject's task was to keep a stylus in contact with a small spot on a moving turntable. In these experiments, subjects were given ten 30-second trials in each battery. The score for each trial was total time in contact with the spot. There is a marked practice effect on this test, but naive subjects were brought to high levels of performance during their practice session, so that the changes due to practice were reduced during the actual drug sessions. In addition, since there was a different order of treatments for each of the three groups of naive subjects, any session-to-session practice effects were minimized in the statistical analysis of the pooled data.

At the end of the psychological test battery, a verbal sample was collected from each subject. The subject was left alone in a room with a tape recorder and instructions to describe "an interesting or dramatic experience" in his life until he was stopped. After exactly 5 minutes he was interrupted and asked how long he had been in the recording room. In this way, an estimate of the subject's ability to judge time was also obtained.

RESULTS

1. Safety of Marihuana in Human Volunteers

In view of the apprehension expressed by many persons over the safety of administering marihuana to research subjects, we wish to emphasize that no adverse marihuana reaction occurred in any of our subjects. In fact the five acute nicotine reactions mentioned earlier were far more spectacular than any effects produced by marihuana.

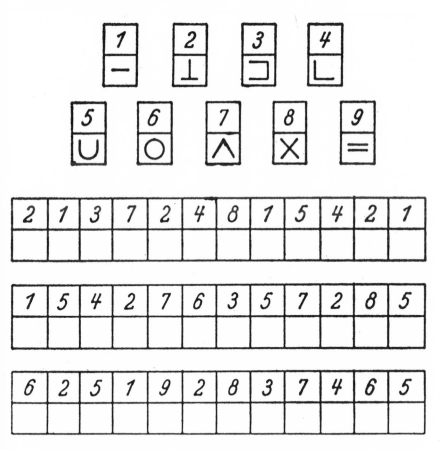

Figure 21–1. This is a sample of the Digit Symbol Substitution Test as used in these studies. On a signal from the examiner the subject was required to fill as many of the empty spaces as possible with the appropriate symbols. The code was always available to the subject during the 90-second administration of the test. [This figure appeared originally in **Psychopharmacologia** 5, 164 (1964).]

In these experiments, observable effects of marihuana were maximum 15 minutes after smoking. They were diminished between 30 minutes and 1 hour, and they were largely dissipated 3 hours after the end of smoking. No delayed or persistent effects beyond 3 hours were observed or reported.

2. Intoxicating Properties of Marihuana in a Neutral Setting

With the high dose of marihuana (2.0 grams), all chronic users became "high" (24) by their own accounts and in the judgment of experimenters who had observed many persons under the influence of marihuana. The effect was consistent even though prior to the session some of these subjects expressed anxiety about smoking marihuana and submitting to tests in a laboratory.

On the other hand, only one of the nine naive subjects (No. 3) had a definite "marihuana reaction" on the same high dose. He became markedly euphoric and laughed continuously during his first battery of tests after taking the drug. Interestingly, he was the one subject who had expressed his desire to get high.

3. Comparison of Naive and Chronic User Subjects

Throughout the experiments it was apparent that the two groups of subjects reacted differently to identical doses of marihuana. We must caution, however, that our study was designed to allow rigorous statistical analysis of data from the naive group—it was not designed to permit formal comparison between chronic users and naive subjects. The conditions of the experiment were not the same for both groups: the chronic users were tested with the drug on their first visit to the laboratory with no practice and were informed that they were to receive high doses of marihuana. Therefore, differences between the chronic and naive groups reported below—although statistically valid—must be regarded as trends to be confirmed or rejected by additional experiments.

4. Recognition of Marihuana Versus Placebo

All nine naive subjects reported that they had not been able to identify the taste or smell of marihuana in the experimental cigarettes. A few subjects remarked that they noticed differences in the taste of the three sets of cigarettes but could not interpret the differences. Most subjects found the pure marihuana cigarettes (high dose) more mild than the low doses or placebo cigarettes, both of which contained tobacco.

The subjects' guesses of the contents of cigarettes for their three sessions are presented in Table 21–3. It is noteworthy that one of the two subjects who called the high dose a placebo was the subject (No. 4) who had told us he wanted to prove that marihuana really did nothing.

TABLE 21–3
SUBJECTS' APPRAISAL OF THE DOSE

Actual Dose	Guessed Dose			Fraction Correct
	Placebo	Low	High	
Placebo	8	1		8/9
Low	3	6		6/9
High	2	6	1	1/9

There were three outstanding findings: (i) most subjects receiving marihuana in either high or low dose recognized that they were getting a drug; (ii) most subjects receiving placebos recognized that they were receiving placebos; (ii) most subjects called their high dose a low dose, but none called his low dose a high dose, emphasizing the unimpressiveness of their subjective reactions.

5. Effect of Marihuana on Heart Rate

The mean changes in heart rate from base-line rates before smoking the drug to rates at 15 and 90 minutes after smoking marihuana and placebo (Table 21–4) were tested for significance at the .05 level by an analysis of variance; Tukey's method was applied for all possible comparisons (Table 21–5). In the naive subjects, marihuana in low dose or high dose was followed by increased heart rate 15 minutes after smoking, but the effect was not demonstrated to be dose-dependent. The high dose caused a statistically greater increase in the heart rates of chronic users than in those of the naive subjects 15 minutes after smoking.

Two of the chronic users had unusually low resting pulse rates (56 and 42), but deletion of these two subjects (No. 11 and No. 15) still gave a significant difference in mean pulse rise of chronic users compared to naives. Because the conditions of the sessions and experimental design were not identical for the two groups, we prefer to report this difference as a trend that must be confirmed by further studies.

6. Effect of Marihuana on Respiratory Rate

In the naive group, there was no change in respiratory rate before and after smoking marihuana. Chronic users showed a small but statistically significant increase in respiratory rate after smoking, but we do not regard the change as clinically significant.

7. Effect of Marihuana on Pupil Size

There was no change in pupil size before and after smoking marihuana in either group.

TABLE 21–4
Change in Heart Rate (Beat/Min) After Smoking the Best Material*

Subject	15 Minutes			90 Minutes		
	Placebo	Low	High	Placebo	Low	High
Naive subjects						
1	+16	+20	+16	+20	− 6	− 4
2	+12	+24	+12	− 6	+ 4	− 8
3	+ 8	+ 8	+26	− 4	+ 4	+ 8
4	+20	+ 8			+20	− 4
5	+ 8	+ 4	− 8		+22	− 8
6	+10	+20	+28	−20	− 4	− 4
7	+ 4	+28	+24	+12	+ 8	+18
8	− 8	+20	+24	− 3	+ 8	−24
9		+20	+24	+ 8	+12	
Mean	+7.8	+16.9	+16.2	+0.8	+7.6	−2.9
S.E.	2.8	2.7	4.2	3.8	3.2	3.8
Chronic subjects						
10		+32			+ 4	
11		+36			+36	
12		+20			+12	
13		+ 8			+ 4	
14		+32			+12	
15		+54			+22	
16		+24				
17		+60				
Mean		+33.2			+15.0	
S.E.		6.0			5.0	

* Results are recorded as a change from the base line 15 minutes and 90 minutes after the smoking session.

TABLE 21–5
Significance of Differences (at the .05 level) in Heart Rate*

Comparison	15 Minutes	90 Minutes
Low dose versus placebo	Significant	Significant
High dose versus placebo	Significant	Not significant
Low dose versus high dose	Not significant	Significant
Chronic users versus high dose	Significant	Significant

* Results of Tukey's test for all possible comparisons.

TABLE 21–6
Significance of Differences (at the .05 level) for the Digit Symbol Substitution Test*

Comparison	15 Minutes	90 Minutes
Low dose versus placebo	Significant	Significant
High dose versus placebo	Significant	Significant
Low dose versus high dose	Significant	Not significant
Chronic users versus high dose	Significant	Significant

* Results of Tukey's test for all possible comparisons.

TABLE 21–7
DIGIT SYMBOL SUBSTITUTION TEST*

	15 Minutes			90 Minutes		
Subject	Placebo	Low	High	Placebo	Low	High
			Naive subjects			
1	− 3	−	+ 5	− 7	+ 4	+ 8
2	+10	−8	−17	− 1	−15	− 5
3	− 3	+6	− 7	−10	+ 2	− 1
4	+ 3	−4	− 3		− 7	
5	+ 4	+1	− 7	+ 6		− 8
6	− 3	−1	− 9	+ 3	− 5	−12
7	+ 2	−4	− 6	+ 3	− 5	− 4
8	− 1	+3	+ 1	+ 4	+ 4	− 3
9	− 1	−4	− 3	+ 6	− 1	−10
Mean	+ 0.9	−1.2	− 5.1	+ 0.4	− 2.6	− 3.9
S.E.	1.4	1.4	2.1	1.9	2.0	2.0
			Chronic users			
10			− 4			−16
11			+ 1			+ 6
12			+11			+18
13			+ 3			+ 4
14			− 2			− 3
15			− 6			+ 8
16			− 4			
17			+ 3			
Mean			+ 0.25			+ 2.8
S.E.			1.9			4.7

* Change in scores from base line (number correct) 15 and 90 minutes after the smoking session.

8. Effect of Marihuana on Conjunctival Appearance

Significant reddening of conjunctivae due to dilatation of blood vessels occurred in one of nine subjects receiving placebo, three of nine receiving the low dose of marihuana, and eight of nine receiving the high dose. It occurred in all eight of the chronic users receiving the high dose and was rated as more prominent in them. The effect was more pronounced 15 minutes after the smoking period than 90 minutes after it.

9. Effect of Marihuana on Blood Sugar

There was no significant change in blood sugar levels after smoking marihuana in either group.

10. Effect of Marihuana on the Continuous Performance Test

Performance on the CPT and on the CPT with strobe distraction was unaffected by marihuana for both groups of subjects.

11. Effect of Marihuana on the Digit Symbol Substitution Test

The significance of the differences in mean changes of scores at the .05 level was determined by an analysis of variance by means of Tukey's method for all possible comparisons. Results of these tests are summarized in Tables 21–6 and 21–7.

The results indicate that : (i) Decrements in performance of naive subjects following low and high doses of marihuana were significant at 15 and 90 minutes after smoking. (ii) The decrement following marihuana was greater after high dose than after low dose at 15 minutes after taking the drug, giving preliminary evidence of a dose-response relationship. (iii) Chronic users started with good base-line performance and improved slightly on the DSST after smoking 2.0 grams of marihuana, whereas performance of the naive subjects was grossly impaired. Experience with the DSST suggests that absence of impairment in chronic users cannot be accounted for solely by a practice effect. Still, because of the different procedures employed, we prefer to report this difference as a trend.

12. Effect of Marihuana on Pursuit Rotor Performance

This result is presented in Table 21–8. Again applying Tukey's method in an analysis of variance, we tested differences in mean changes in scores (Table 21–9). Decrements in performance of naive subjects after both low and high doses of marihuana were significant at 15 and 90 minutes. This effect on performance followed a dose-response relation on testing batteries conducted at both 15 minutes and 90 minutes after the drug was smoked.

All chronic users started from good baselines and improved on the

TABLE 21–8
PURSUIT ROTOR (NAIVE SUBJECTS). CHANGES IN SCORES
(AVERAGES OF TEN TRIALS) FROM BASE LINE (SECONDS).

Subject	15 Minutes			90 Minutes		
	Placebo	Low	High	Placebo	Low	High
1	+1.20	−1.04	−4.01	+1.87	−1.54	−6.54
2	+0.89	−1.43	−0.12	+0.52	+0.44	−0.68
3	+0.50	−0.60	−6.56	+0.84	−0.96	−4.34
4	+0.18	−0.11	+0.11	+0.06	+1.95	−1.37
5	+3.20	+0.39	+0.13	+2.64	+3.33	+0.34
6	+3.45	−0.32	−3.46	+2.93	+0.22	−2.26
7	+0.81	+0.48	−0.79	+0.63	+0.16	−0.52
8	+1.75	−0.39	−0.92	+2.13	+0.40	+1.02
9	+3.90	−1.94	−2.60	+3.11	−0.97	−3.09
Mean	+1.8	−0.6	−2.0	+1.6	+0.3	−1.9
S.E.	0.5	0.3	0.8	0.4	0.5	0.8

TABLE 21–9
SIGNIFICANCE OF DIFFERENCES (AT THE .05 LEVEL) FOR THE PURSUIT ROTOR.
RESULTS OF TUKEY'S TEST FOR ALL POSSIBLE COMPARISONS,
15 AND 90 MINUTES AFTER THE SMOKING SESSION.

Comparison	15 Minutes	90 Minutes
Low dose versus placebo	Significant	Significant
High dose versus placebo	Significant	Significant
Low dose versus high dose	Significant	Significant

pursuit rotor after smoking marihuana. These data are not presented, however, because it is probable that the improvement was largely a practice effect.

13. Effect of Marihuana on Time Estimation

Before smoking, all nine naive subjects estimated the 5-minute verbal sample to be 5 ± 2 minutes. After placebo, no subject changed his guess. After the low dose, three subjects raised their estimates to 10 ± 2 minutes, and after the high dose, four raised their estimates.

14. Subjective Effects of Marihuana

When questioned at the end of their participation in the experiment, persons who had never taken marihuana previously reported minimum subjective effects after smoking the drug, or, more precisely, few effects like those commonly reported by chronic users. Nonusers reported little euphoria, no distortion of visual or auditory perception, and no confusion. However, several subjects mentioned that "things seemed to take longer." Below are examples of comments by naive subjects after high doses.

Subject 1: "It was stronger than the previous time (low dose) but I really didn't think it could be marihuana. Things seemed to go slower."

Subject 2: "I think I realize why they took our watches. There was a sense of the past disappearing as happens when you're driving too long without sleeping. With a start you wake up to realize you were asleep for an instant; you discover yourself driving along the road. It was the same tonight with eating a sandwich. I'd look down to discover I'd just swallowed a bite but I hadn't noticed it at the time."

Subject 6: "I felt a combination of being almost-drunk and tired, with occasional fits of silliness—not my normal reaction to smoking tobacco."

Subject 8: "I felt faint briefly, but the dizziness went away, and I felt normal or slightly tired. I can't believe I had a high dose of marihuana."

Subject 9: "Time seemed very drawn out. I would keep forgetting what I was doing, especially on the continuous performance test, but somehow every time an "X" (the critical letter) came up, I found myself pushing the button."

After smoking their high dose, chronic users were asked to rate them-selves on a scale of 1 to 10, 10 representing "the highest you've ever been." All subjects placed themselves between 7 and 10, most at 8 or 9. Many of these subjects expressed anxiety at the start of their first battery of tests after smoking the drug when they were feeling very high. Then they expressed surprise during and after the tests when they judged (correctly) that their performance was as good as or better than it had been before taking the drug.

The effect of marihuana on the self-rating mood scale, the effect of marihuana on a 5-minute verbal sample, and the correlation of per-sonality type with subjective effects of marihuana will be reported separately.

DISCUSSION

Several results from this study raise important questions about the ac-tion of marihuana and suggest directions for future research. Our find-ing that subjects who were naive to marihuana did not become subjectively "high" after a high dose of marihuana in a neutral setting is interesting when contrasted with the response of regular users who consistently reported and exhibited highs. It agrees with the reports of chronic users that many, if not most, people do not become high on their first exposure to marihuana even if they smoke it correctly. This puz-zling phenomenon can be discussed from either a physiological or psy-chosocial point of view. Neither interpretation is entirely satisfactory. The physiological hypothesis suggests that getting high on marihuana occurs only after some sort of pharmacological sensitization takes place. The psychosocial interpretation is that repeated exposure to marihuana reduces psychological inhibition, as part of, or as the result of a learning process.

Indirect evidence makes the psychological hypothesis attractive. Anxiety about drug use in this country is sufficiently great to make worthy of careful consideration the possibility of an unconscious psy-chological inhibition or block on the part of naive drug takers. The subjective responses of our subjects indicate that they had im-agined a marihuana effect to be much more profoundly disorganizing than what they experienced. For example, subject No. 4, who started with a bias against the possibility of becoming high on marihuana, was able to control subjectively the effect of the drug and report that he had received a placebo when he had actually gotten a high dose. As anxiety about the drug is lessened with experience, the block may de-crease, and the subject may permit himself to notice the drug's effects.

It is well known that marihuana users, introducing friends to the drug, do actually "teach" them to notice subtle effects of the drug on consciousness (25). The apparently enormous influence of set and setting on the form of the marihuana response is consistent with this hypothesis, as is the testimony of users that, as use becomes more frequent, the amount of drug required to produce intoxication decreases—a unique example of "reverse tolerance." (Regular use of many intoxicants is accompanied by the need for increasing doses to achieve the same effects.)

On the other hand, the suggestion arising from this study that users and nonusers react differently to the drug, not only subjectively but also physiologically, increases the plausibility of the pharmacological-sensitization hypothesis. Of course, reverse tolerance could equally well be a manifestation of this sensitization.

It would be useful to confirm the suggested differences between users and nonusers and then to test in a systematic manner the hypothetical explanations of the phenomenon. One possible approach would be to continue to administer high doses of marihuana to the naive subjects according to the protocol described. If subjects begin reporting high responses to the drug only after several exposures, in the absence of psychedelic settings, suggestions, or manipulations of mood, then the likelihood that marihuana induces a true physiological sensitization or that experience reduces psychological inhibitions, permitting real drug effects to appear, would be increased. If subjects fail to become high, we could conclude that learning to respond to marihuana requires some sort of teaching or suggestion.

An investigation of the literature of countries where anxieties over drug use are less prominent would be useful. If this difference between responses of users and nonusers is a uniquely American phenomenon, a psychological explanation would be indicated, although it would not account for greater effects with smaller doses after the initial, anxiety-reducing stage.

One impetus for reporting the finding of differences between chronic and naive subjects on some of the tests, despite the fact that the experimental designs were not the same, is that this finding agrees with the statements of many users. They say that the effects of marihuana are easily suppressed—much more so than those of alcohol. Our observation, that the chronic users after smoking marihuana performed on some tests as well as or better than they did before taking the drug, reinforced the argument advanced by chronic users that maintaining effective levels of performance for many tasks—driving, for example (26)—is much easier under the influence of marihuana than under that of other psychoactive drugs. Certainly the surprise that the chronic users expressed when they found they were performing more effectively on the CPT, DSST, and pursuit rotor tests than they thought they would is remarkable. It is quite the opposite of the false sense of improvement subjects have under some psychoactive drugs that actually impair performance.

What might be the basis of this suppressibility? Possibly, the actions of marihuana are confined to higher cortical functions without any general stimulatory or depressive effect on lower brain centers. The relative absence of neurological—as opposed to psychiatric—symptoms in marihuana intoxication suggests this possibility (7).

Our failure to detect any changes in blood sugar levels of subjects after they had smoked marihuana forces us to look elsewhere for an explanation of the hunger and hyperphagia commonly reported by users. A first step would be careful interviewing of users to determine whether they really become hungry after smoking marihuana or whether they simply find eating more pleasurable. Possibly, the basis of this effect is also central rather than due to some peripheral physiological change.

Lack of any change in pupil size of subjects after they had smoked marihuana is an enlightening finding especially because so many users and law enforcement agents firmly believe that marihuana dilates pupils. (Since users generally observe each other in dim surroundings, it is not surprising that they see large pupils.) This negative finding emphasizes the need for data from carefully controlled investigations rather than from casual observation or anecdotal reports in the evaluation of marihuana. It also agrees with the findings of others that synthetic THC does not alter pupil size (8, 27).

Finally, we would like to comment on the fact that marihuana appears to be a relatively mild intoxicant in our studies. If these results seem to differ from those of earlier experiments, it must be remembered that other experimenters have given marihuana orally, have given doses much higher than those commonly smoked by users, have administered potent synthetics, and have not strictly controlled the laboratory setting. As noted in our introduction, more powerful effects are often reported by users who ingest preparations of marihuana. This may mean that some active constituents which enter the body when the drug is ingested are destroyed by combustion, a suggestion that must be investigated in man. Another priority consideration is the extent to which synthetic THC reproduces marihuana intoxication—a problem that must be resolved before marihuana research proceeds with THC instead of the natural resin of the whole plant.

The set, both of subjects and experimenters, and the setting must be recognized as critical variables in studies of marihuana. Drug, set, and setting interact to shape the form of a marihuana reaction. The researcher who sets out with prior conviction that hemp is psychotomimetic or a "mild hallucinogen" is likely to confirm his conviction experimentally (10), but he would probably confirm the opposite hypothesis if his bias were in the opposite direction. Precautions to insure neutrality of set and setting, including use of a double-blind procedure as an absolute minimum, are vitally important if the object of investigation is to measure real marihuana-induced responses.

CONCLUSIONS

1. It is feasible and safe to study the effects of marihuana on human volunteers who smoke it in a laboratory.

2. In a neutral setting persons who are naive to marihuana do not have strong subjective experiences after smoking low or high doses of the drug, and the effects they do report are not the same as those described by regular users of marihuana who take the drug in the same neutral setting.

3. Marihuana-naive persons do demonstrate impaired performance on simple intellectual and psychomotor tests after smoking marihuana; the impairment is dose-related in some cases.

4. Regular users of marihuana do get high after smoking marihuana in a neutral setting but do not show the same degree of impairment of performance on the tests as do naive subjects. In some cases, their performance even appears to improve slightly after smoking marihuana.

5. Marihuana increases heart rate moderately.

6. No change in respiratory rate follows administration of marihuana by inhalation.

7. No change in pupil size occurs in short term exposure to marihuana.

8. Marihuana administration causes dilatation of conjunctival blood vessels.

9. Marihuana treatment produces no change in blood sugar levels.

10. In a neutral setting the physiological and psychological effects of a single, inhaled dose of marihuana appear to reach maximum intensity within one-half hour of inhalation, to be diminished after 1 hour, and to be completely dissipated by 3 hours.

NOTES

1. R. J. Bouquet, *Bull. Narcotics* 2, 14 (1950).
2. F. Korte and H. Sieper, in *Hashish: Its Chemistry and Pharmacology*, G. E. W. Wolstenholme and J. Knight, Eds. (Little, Brown, Boston, 1965), pp. 15–30.
3. Task Force on Narcotics and Drug Abuse, the President's Commission on Law Enforcement and the Administration of Justice, *Task Force Report: Narcotics and Drug Abuse* (1967), p. 14.
4. R. Mechoulam, and Y. Gaoni, *J. Amer. Chem. Soc.* 67, 3273 (1965).
5. J. F. Siler, W. L. Sheep, L. B. Bates, G. F. Clark, G. W. Cook, W. A. Smith, *Mil. Surg.* (November 1933), pp. 269–280.

6. Mayor's Committee on Marihuana, *The Marihuana Problem in the City of New York,* 1944.
7. E. G. Williams, C. K. Himmelsbach, A. Winkler, D. C. Ruble, B. J. Lloyd, *Public Health Rep.* **61,** 1059 (1946).
8. H. Isbell, *Psychopharmacologia* **11,** 184 (1967).
9. I. C. Chopra and R. N. Chopra, *Bull. Narcotics* **9,** 4 (1957).
10. F. Ames, *J. Ment. Sci.* **104,** 972 (1958).
11. C. J. Miras, in *Hashish: Its Chemistry and Pharmacology,* G. E. W. Wolstenholme and J. Knight, Eds. (Little, Brown, Boston, 1965), pp. 37–47.
12. J. M. Watt, in *Hashish: Its Chemistry and Pharmacology,* G. E. W. Wolstenholme and J. Knight, Eds. (Little, Brown, Boston, 1965), pp. 54–66.
13. AMA Council on Mental Health, *J. Amer. Med. Ass.* **204,** 1181 (1968).
14. G. Joachimoglu, in *Hashish: Its Chemistry and Pharmacology,* G. E. W. Wolstenholme and J. Knight, Eds. (Little, Brown, Boston, 1965), pp. 2–10.
15. We thank M. Lerner and A. Bober of the U.S. Customs Laboratory, Baltimore, for performing this assay.
16. We thank R. H. Pace and E. H. Hall of the Peter J. Schweitzer Division of the Kimberly-Clark Corp. for supplying placebo material.
17. S. Garattini, in *Hashish: Its Chemistry and Pharmacology,* G. E. W. Wolstenholme and J. Knight, Eds. (Little, Brown, Boston, 1965), pp. 70–78.
18. J. H. Jaffee, in *The Pharmacological Basis of Therapeutics,* L. S. Goodman and A. Gilman, Eds. (Macmillan, New York, ed. 3, 1965), pp. 299–301.
19. We thank E. L. Richardson, Attorney General of the Commonwealth of Massachusetts, for permitting these experiments to proceed and N. L. Chayet for legal assistance. We do not consider it appropriate to describe here the opposition we encountered from governmental agents and agencies and from university bureaucracies.
20. We thank D. Miller and M. Seifer of the Federal Bureau of Narcotics (now part of the Bureau of Narcotics and Dangerous Drugs, under the Department of Justice) for help in obtaining marihuana for this research.
21. The doses of tobacco in placebo and low-dose cigarettes were too small to cause physiological changes in subjects who qualified in the practice session.
22. K. E. Rosvold, A. F. Mirsky, I. Sarason, E. D. Bransome, L. H. Beck, *J. Consult. Psychol.* **20,** 343 (1956); A. F. Mirsky and P. V. Cardon, *Electroencephalogr. Clin. Neurophysiol.* **14,** 1 (1962); C. Kornetsky and G. Bain, *Psychopharmacologia* **8,** 277 (1965).
23. G. M. Smith and H. K. Beecher, *J. Pharmacol.* **126,** 50 (1959).
24. We will attempt to define the complex nature of a marihuana high in a subsequent paper discussing the speech samples and interviews.
25. H. S. Becker, *Outsiders: Studies in the Sociology of Deviance* (Macmillan, New York, 1963), chap. 3.
26. Although the motor skills measured by the pursuit rotor are represented in driving ability, they are only components of that ability. The influence of marihuana on driving skill remains an open question of high medico-legal priority.
27. L. E. Hollister, R. K. Richards, H. K. Gillespie, in preparation.

28. Sponsored and supported by Boston University's division of psychiatry, in part through PHS grants MH12568, MH06795-06, MH7753-06, and MH33319, and the Boston University Medical Center. The authors thank Dr. P. H. Knapp and Dr. C. Kornetsky of the Boston University School of Medicine, Department of Psychiatry and Pharmacology, for consistent support and excellent advice, and J. Finkelstein of . . . New York City for his support at a crucial time.

PART VI

Personality: Theories and Assessment

22.

An Introduction to Psychoanalysis

SIGMUND FREUD

Freud's controversial theories have for many years been influential in the study of personality. At first Freud's theories met with opposition from other scientists and physicians who were reluctant to accept either his premise that man is not in full control of his mental life or the significant role he gave to sexual impulses in the development of personality. Although these concerns still account for some of the dissident reactions to his theories, today other criticisms are more often heard: that the theories have less validity in today's age of anxiety and alienation than in the Victorian age of repression; that the theories are not set forth as scientifically testable propositions; and that the theories focus on instinctual drives but ignore cognitive or intellectual aspects of the personality. Despite all this, few scholars would deny that Freud was an original thinker and an eloquent writer.

In 1915, when Freud was convinced that he was unable to get an unprejudiced hearing in academic and medical circles, he was invited to present a series of lectures to medical students in Vienna. He assumed no previous knowledge of psychoanalytic theory on the part of the students; indeed he assumed that their prior training would have already made them skeptical of what he had to say. Therefore, in these lectures, he was as convincing, yet as clear and conversational, as he could be. The following excerpt is the first of these lectures.

Would a Freudian say he was being defensive?

I ᴅᴏ not know what knowledge any of you may already have of psycho-analysis, either from reading or from hearsay. But having regard to the title of my lectures—Introductory Lectures on Psycho-Analysis—I am bound to proceed as though you knew nothing of the subject and needed instruction, even in its first elements.

One thing, at least, I may pre-suppose that you know—namely, that psycho-analysis is a method of medical treatment for those suffering from nervous disorders; and I can give you at once an illustration of the way in which psycho-analytic procedure differs from, and often even reverses, what is customary in other branches of medicine. Usually, when we introduce a patient to a new form of treatment we minimize its difficulties and give him confident assurances of its success. This is, in my opinion, perfectly justifiable, for we thereby increase the probability of success. But when we undertake to treat a neurotic psycho-analytically we proceed otherwise. We explain to him the difficulties of the method, its long duration, the trials and sacrifices which will be required of him; and, as to the result, we tell him that we can make no definite promises, that success depends upon his endeavours, upon his understanding, his adaptability and his perseverance. We have, of course, good reasons, into which you will perhaps gain some insight later on, for adopting this apparently perverse attitude.

Now forgive me if I begin by treating you in the same way as I do my neurotic patients, for I shall positively advise you against coming to hear me a second time. And with this intention I shall explain to you how of necessity you can obtain from me only an incomplete knowledge of psycho-analysis and also what difficulties stand in the way of your forming an independent judgment on the subject. For I shall show you how the whole trend of your training and your accustomed modes of thought must inevitably have made you hostile to psycho-analysis, and also how much you would have to overcome in your own minds in order to master this instinctive opposition. I naturally cannot foretell what degree of understanding of psycho-analysis you may gain from my lectures, but I can at least assure you that by attending them you will not have learnt how to conduct a psycho-analytic investigation, nor how to carry out a psycho-analytic treatment. And further, if any one of you should feel dissatisfied with a merely cursory acquaintance with psycho-analysis and should wish to form a permanent connection with it, I shall not merely discourage him, but I shall actually warn him against it. For as things are at the present time, not only would the choice of such a career put an end to all chances of academic success, but, upon taking up work as a practitioner, such a man would find himself in a community which misunderstood his aims and intentions, regarded him with suspicion and hostility, and let loose upon him all the latent evil impulses harboured within it. Perhaps you can infer from the accompaniments of the war now raging in Europe what a countless host that is to reckon with.

However, there are always some people to whom the possibility of a new addition to knowledge will prove an attraction strong enough to survive all such inconveniences. If there are any such among you who will appear at my second lecture in spite of my words of warning they will be welcome. But all of you have a right to know what these inherent difficulties of psycho-analysis are to which I have alluded.

First of all, there is the problem of the teaching and exposition of the subject. In your medical studies you have been accustomed to use your eyes. You see the anatomical specimen, the precipitate of the chemical reaction, the contraction of the muscle as the result of the stimulation of its nerves. Later you come into contact with the patients; you learn the symptoms of disease by the evidence of your senses; the results of pathological processes can be demonstrated to you, and in many cases even the exciting cause of them in an isolated form. On the surgical side you are witnesses of the measures by which the patient is helped, and are permitted to attempt them yourselves. Even in psychiatry, demonstration of patients, of their altered expression, speech and behaviour, yields a series of observations which leave a deep impression on your minds. Thus a teacher of medicine acts for the most part as an exponent and guide, leading you as it were through a museum, while you gain in this way a direct relationship to what is displayed to you and believe yourselves to have been convinced by your own experience of the existence of the new facts.

But in psycho-analysis, unfortunately, all this is different. In psycho-analytic treatment nothing happens but an exchange of words between the patient and the physician. The patient talks, tells of his past experiences and present impressions, complains, and expresses his wishes and his emotions. The physician listens, attempts to direct the patient's thought-processes, reminds him, forces his attention in certain directions, gives him explanations and observes the reactions of understanding or denial thus evoked. The patient's unenlightened relatives —people of a kind to be impressed only by something visible and tangible, preferably by the sort of 'action' that may be seen at a cinema—never omit to express their doubts of how "mere talk can possibly cure anybody." Their reasoning is of course as illogical as it is inconsistent. For they are the same people who are always convinced that the sufferings of neurotics are purely "in their own imagination." Words and magic were in the beginning one and the same thing, and even to-day words retain much of their magical power. By words one of us can give to another the greatest happiness or bring about utter despair; by words the teacher imparts his knowledge to the student; by words the orator sweeps his audience with him and determines its judgements and decisions. Words call forth emotions and are universally the means by which we influence our fellow-creatures. Therefore let us not despise the use of words in psycho-therapy and let us be content if we may overhear the words which pass between the analyst and the patient.

But even that is impossible. The dialogue which constitutes the analysis will admit of no audience; the process cannot be demonstrated. One could, of course, exhibit a neurasthenic or hysterical patient to students at a psychiatric lecture. He would relate his case and his symptoms, but nothing more. He will make the communications necessary to the analysis only under the conditions of a special affective relationship to the physician; in the presence of a single person to whom he was indifferent he would become mute. For these communications relate to all his most private thoughts and feelings, all that which as a socially independent person he must hide from others, all that which, being foreign to his own conception of himself, he tries to conceal even from himself.

It is impossible, therefore, for you to be actually present during a psycho-analytic treatment; you can only be told about it, and can learn psycho-analysis, in the strictest sense of the word, only by hearsay. This tuition at second hand, so to say, puts you in a very unusual and difficult position as regards forming your own judgement on the subject, which will therefore largely depend on the reliance you can place on your informant.

Now imagine for a moment that you were present at a lecture in history instead of in psychiatry, and that the lecturer was dealing with the life and conquests of Alexander the Great. What reason would you have to believe what he told you? The situation would appear at first sight even more unsatisfactory than in the case of psycho-analysis, for the professor of history had no more part in Alexander's campaigns than you yourselves; the psycho-analyst at least informs you of matters in which he himself has played a part. But then we come to the question of what evidence there is to support the historian. He can refer you to the accounts of early writers who were either contemporaries or who lived not long after the events in question, such as Diodorus, Plutarch, Arrian, and others; he can lay before you reproductions of the preserved coins and statues of the king, and pass round a photograph of the mosaic at Pompeii representing the battle at Issus. Yet, strictly speaking, all these documents only prove that the existence of Alexander and the reality of his deeds were already believed in by former generations of men, and your criticism might begin anew at this point. And then you would find that not everything reported of Alexander is worthy of belief or sufficiently authenticated in detail, but I can hardly suppose that you would leave the lecture-room in doubt altogether as to the reality of Alexander the

Great. Your conclusions would be principally determined by two considerations: first, that the lecturer could have no conceivable motive for attempting to persuade you of something which he did not himself believe to be true, and secondly, that all the available authorities agree more or less in their accounts of the facts. In questioning the accuracy of the early writers you would apply these tests again, the possible motives of the authors and the agreement to be found between them. The result of such tests would certainly be convincing in the case of Alexander, probably less so in regard to figures like Moses and Nimrod. Later on you will perceive clearly enough what doubts can be raised against the credibility of an exponent of psycho-analysis.

Now you will have a right to ask the question: If no objective evidence for psycho-analysis exists and no possibility of demonstrating the process, how is it possible to study it at all or to convince oneself of its truth? The study of it is indeed not an easy matter, nor are there many people who have thoroughly learned it; still, there is, of course, some way of learning it. Psycho-analysis is learnt first of all on oneself, through the study of one's own personality. This is not exactly what is meant by introspection, but it may be so described for want of a better word. There is a whole series of very common and well-known mental phenomena which can be taken as material for self-analysis when one has acquired some knowledge of the method. In this way one may obtain the required conviction of the reality of the processes which psycho-analysis describes, and of the truth of its conceptions, although progress on these lines is not without its limitations. One gets much further by submitting oneself to analysis by a skilled analyst, undergoing the working of the analysis in one's own person and using the opportunity to observe the finer details of the technique which the analyst employs. This, eminently the best way, is of course only practicable for individuals and cannot be used in a class of students.

The second difficulty you will find in connection with psycho-analysis is not, on the other hand, inherent in it, but is one for which I must hold you yourselves responsible, at least in so far as your medical studies have influenced you. Your training will have induced in you an attitude of mind very far removed from the psycho-analytical one. You have been trained to establish the functions and disturbances of the organism on an anatomical basis, to explain them in terms of chemistry and physics, and to regard them from a biological point of view; but no part of your interest has ever been directed to the mental aspects of life, in which, after all, the development of the marvellously complicated organism culminates. For this reason a psychological attitude of mind is still foreign to you, and you are accustomed to regard it with suspicion, to deny it a scientific status, and to leave it to the general public, poets, mystics, and philosophers. Now this limitation in you is undoubtedly detrimental to your medical efficiency; for on meeting a patient it is the mental aspects with which one first comes into contact, as in most human relationships, and I am afraid you will pay the penalty of having to yield a part of the curative influence at which you aim to the quacks, mystics, and faith-healers whom you despise.

I quite acknowledge that there is an excuse for this defect in your previous training. There is no auxiliary philosophical science that might be of service to you in your profession. Neither speculative philosophy nor descriptive psychology, nor even the so-called experimental psychology which is studied in connection with the physiology of the sense-organs, as they are taught in the schools, can tell you anything useful of the relations existing between mind and body, or can give you a key to comprehension of a possible disorder of the mental functions. It is true that the psychiatric branch of medicine occupies itself with describing the different forms of recognizable mental disturbances and grouping them in clinical pictures, but in their best moments psychiatrists themselves are doubtful whether their purely descriptive formulations deserve to be called science. The origin, mechanism, and interrelation of the symptoms which make up these clinical pictures are undiscovered: either they cannot be correlated with any demonstrable changes in the brain, or only with such changes as in no way explain them. These mental disturbances are open to therapeutic influence only when they can be identified as secondary effects of some organic disease.

This is the lacuna which psycho-analysis is striving to fill. It hopes to provide psychiatry with the missing psychological foundation, to discover the common ground on which a correlation of bodily and mental disorder becomes comprehensible. To this end it must dissociate itself from every foreign preconception, whether anatomical, chemical, or physiological, and must work throughout with conceptions of a purely psychological order, and for this very reason I fear that it will appear strange to you at first.

For the next difficulty I shall not hold you, your training or your mental attitude, responsible. There are two tenets of psycho-analysis which offend the whole world and excite its resentment; the one conflicts with intellectual, the other with moral and aesthetic prejudices. Let us not underestimate these prejudices; they are powerful things, residues of valuable, even necessary, stages in human evolution. They are maintained by emotional forces, and the fight against them is a hard one.

The first of these displeasing propositions of psycho-analysis is this: that mental processes are essentially unconscious, and that those which are conscious are merely isolated acts and parts of the whole psychic entity. Now I must ask you to remember that, on the contrary, we are accustomed to identify the mental with the conscious. Consciousness appears to us as positively the characteristic that defines mental life, and we regard psychology as the study of the content of consciousness. This even appears so evident that any contradiction of it seems obvious nonsense to us, and yet it is impossible for psycho-analysis to avoid this contradiction, or to accept the identity between the conscious and the psychic. The psycho-analytical definition of the mind is that it comprises processes of the nature of feeling, thinking, and wishing, and it maintains that there are such things as unconscious thinking and unconscious wishing. But in doing so psycho-analysis has forfeited at the outset the sympathy of the sober and scientifically minded, and incurred the suspicion of being a fantastic cult occupied with dark and unfathomable mysteries.[1] You yourselves must find it difficult to understand why I should stigmatize an abstract proposition, such as "The psychic is the conscious," as a prejudice; nor can you guess yet what evolutionary process could have led to the denial of the unconscious, if it does indeed exist, nor what advantage could have been achieved by this denial. It seems like an empty wrangle over words to argue whether mental life is to be regarded as co-extensive with consciousness or whether it may be said to stretch beyond this limit, and yet I can assure you that the acceptance of unconscious mental processes represents a decisive step towards a new orientation in the world and in science.

As little can you suspect how close is the connection between this first bold step on the part of psycho-analysis and the second to which I am now coming. For this next proposition, which we put forward as one of the discoveries of psycho-analysis, consists in the assertion that impulses, which can only be described as sexual in both the narrower and the wider sense, play a peculiarly large part, never before sufficiently appreciated, in the causation of nervous and mental disorders. Nay, more, that these sexual impulses have contributed invaluably to the highest cultural, artistic, and social achievements of the human mind.

In my opinion, it is the aversion from this conclusion of psychoanalytic investigation that is the most significant source of the opposition it has encountered. Are you curious to know how we ourselves account for this? We believe that civilization has been built up, under the pressure of the struggle for existence, by sacrifices in gratification of the primitive impulses, and that it is to a great extent for ever being re-created, as each individual, successively joining the community, repeats the sacrifice of his instinctive pleasures for the common good. The sexual are amongst the most important of the instinctive forces thus utilized: they are in this way sublimated, that is to say, their energy is

---

[1] [Literally: "that wishes to build in the dark and fish in murky waters."—TR.]

turned aside from its sexual goal and diverted towards other ends, no longer sexual and socially more valuable. But the structure thus built up is insecure, for the sexual impulses are with difficulty controlled; in each individual who takes up his part in the work of civilization there is a danger that a rebellion of the sexual impulses may occur, against this diversion of their energy. Society can conceive of no more powerful menace to its culture than would arise from the liberation of the sexual impulses and a return of them to their original goal. Therefore society dislikes this sensitive place in its development being touched upon; that the power of the sexual instinct should be recognized, and the significance of the individual's sexual life revealed, is very far from its interests; with a view to discipline it has rather taken the course of diverting attention away from this whole field. For this reason, the revelations of psycho-analysis are not tolerated by it, and it would greatly prefer to brand them as aesthetically offensive, morally reprehensible, or dangerous. But since such objections are not valid arguments against conclusions which claim to represent the objective results of scientific investigation, the opposition must be translated into intellectual terms before it can be expressed. It is a characteristic of human nature to be inclined to regard anything which is disagreeable as untrue, and then without much difficulty to find arguments against it. So society pronounces the unacceptable to be untrue, disputes the results of psycho-analysis with logical and concrete arguments, arising, however, in affective sources, and clings to them with all the strength of prejudice against every attempt at refutation.

But we, on the other hand, claim to have yielded to no tendency in propounding this objectionable theory. Our intention has been solely to give recognition to the facts as we found them in the course of painstaking researches. And we now claim the right to reject unconditionally any such introduction of practical considerations into the field of scientific investigation, even before we have determined whether the apprehension which attempts to force these considerations upon us is justified or not.

These, now, are some of the difficulties which confront you at the outset when you begin to take an interest in psycho-analysis. It is probably more than enough for a beginning. If you can overcome their discouraging effect, we will proceed further.

23.

Humanism in Personology

SALVATORE R. MADDI and PAUL T. COSTA

Personality is the relatively consistent, yet flexible, pattern of behaviors, attitudes, and values that is characteristic of a particular individual. Personality psychology is the study of these characteristics—how they vary among individuals, to what degree they are consistent within the individual, and to what degree they are common among individuals. More recently, some theorists, like the authors of the following article, have shown a preference for the term "personology," feeling that it is more appropriate for the directions they chose to follow in their study of human lives. This approach emphasizes individuality, uniqueness, identity, inner man, self-awareness, inner experience, the goals and meaning of life, and, in general, all those aspects of the personality that are distinctly and uniquely human.

Maddi and Costa in the following excerpt from their book explain how they view this humanistic approach to the study of personality, and contrast this "third force" with the other two prominent approaches to personality psychology, the psychodynamic (essentially psychoanalytic) and the behavioristic approaches. Based on your reading of this material, what comments do you think they would make about the community Skinner proposes in *Walden Two* (see Selection 10)? Can you see any ways in which Skinner's conception of freedom and responsibility is basically humanistic?

Reprinted from Salvatore R. Maddi and Paul T. Costa, *Humanism in Personology* (Chicago: Aldine-Atherton, Inc. 1972); copyright 1972 © by Salvatore R. Maddi and Paul T. Costa. Reprinted by permission of the authors and Aldine Publishing Company.

THESE DAYS in psychology one hears all sorts of talk—favorable and critical, open and clandestine, rational and emotional—about a gathering third force, a humanistic surging that will set the field straight, once and for all. Abraham Maslow (1962) was responsible for the phrase, "the third force." The other two psychological forces, classical Freudianism and positivistic behaviorism, have dominated psychology for most of its recent history.

NONHUMANISM AND HUMANISM

Logical positivism and extreme behaviorism, with their emphases on observable responses rather than thoughts and feelings, external pressures rather than internal promptings, and only those concepts that can be clearly formulated no matter how trivial the result, can easily be considered nonhumanistic. Actually, under the influence of positivistic behaviorism, psychology became defined as "the science of behavior" rather than "the science of the mind, or psyche," and lower animals became more popular as subjects for study than humans. Under the sway of positivistic behaviorism, the human is hardly regarded as special, much less unique.

Why classical Freudianism may be regarded as nonhumanistic is not as easily understood. After all, man is the only important subject for study in psychoanalysis, and thought and feelings certainly receive much more attention than mere observable responses. It is not, however, the topics or data of psychoanalysis that adherents to the third force find objectionable. Rather, third-force followers reject what they see as an attempt in Freudianism to manipulate and denigrate people, to deal with them in nonhuman ways. The problem with classical Freudianism is the nature of its explanations of human behavior, not its subject matter *per se*.

Freudian explanations of human behavior emanate from certain assumptions[1] that betray a pessimistic attitude. For example, Freudianism assumes that man's inheritance is a set of selfish and animalistic instincts, and that a conflict between the individual and society is inevitable, since society is concerned with the common good. The only way to deal with such a conflict is to compromise by defending not only against direct expression but even against full awareness of the instinctual drives. Because society is the stronger of the two forces, the compromise must take the form of the individual subordinating his instinctual gratification to social acceptability. As a functioning adult, the individual inhibits sexual and aggressive impulses, defends against

[1] See Maddi, 1968.

embarrassing awareness of these impulses, and even suppresses memories of what he may have thought or done as a child. Since conflict between the individual and society is inevitable, it is assumed that unconscious motivation and defensiveness are ubiquitous, and that man can never truly know himself. One implication of this is that pride in oneself and one's accomplishments, and trust in the veracity of one's experience and mentation, must always be to some degree a failure of humility. These assumptions about human behavior hardly convince third-force adherents that classical Freudianism conceives of man's thoughts, feelings, and actions as valuable *per se*. The aim of psychoanalysis seems to be to strip man of a sense of dignity, and convince him that he stands no higher than the other animals. For psychoanalysts to insist that they accept and love man, despite his weakness and follies, does not help much.

Humanism, as espoused by third-force adherents, leads to a psychology that is not only centered on the human being but sets a positive value on those of his capabilities and aspirations that seem to distinguish him from lower animals and make him the master of his own fate. Choice, will-power, conceptual thought, imagination, introspection, self-criticism, aspirations for the future, and creativity are important topics in humanism, for they refer to capabilities and interests that seem unique to man as a species. If these qualities are not, strictly speaking, unique to man, they are so highly developed in him that the humanistic position has a strong appeal for everyone, including psychologists.

Modern existentialism also contains an important message for third-force adherents, for only man is endowed with the ability to reflect on his own actions and question the meaning and value of his own existence. Suicide, as a negative conclusion to such questioning, seems to be a uniquely human phenomenon. Indeed, when one reviews the characteristics of man that seem so apparently to distinguish him from other species, it is difficult to understand why the humanistic position has so many opponents in contemporary psychology.

Humanism is not only concerned with the characteristics setting man apart from other living things. Also important are the characteristics that set each man apart from other men. Individuality—the thoughts, fantasies, strivings, worries, triumphs, and tragedies that sum up to one particular person's existence and no one else's—is always a central topic in humanistic positions. Indeed, it is common for humanistic psychologists to assert that one cannot really understand behavior by studying separate parts of it in isolation. Complete understanding requires putting all the parts together and employing a knowledge of the characteristics of wholes. The same person who learns slowly in the classroom and is unable to direct his attention effectively under scrutiny may well be able to produce a masterpiece in the solitude of his own home. To take any part of this person's behavior in isolation from another—indeed, in isolation from many, many others, such as the intensity and content of his interpersonal relationships or the nurturance and directedness of his parents' actions toward him—would be to fail in understanding what was going on.

Many humanists assert that complete understanding is not even merely a matter of putting all the parts of behavior together so that they make a whole. A whole is not necessarily just the sum of its parts—it can and usually does have new properties of its own. So, in our example, the person's inability to function in groups having an evaluative connotation may actually enhance, rather than detract from, his ability to create in isolation. In order to appreciate this, one would have to think of that person's creative functioning as an unique and unpredictable outcome of the interaction of the experiences and activities that comprise his life.

Finally, the focus on the experiences of the individual in humanistic doctrines more or less requires that originality or creativity will be an important topic for study. This requirement is virtually by definition, for the only way to be an individual is to be original. You must do the originating, for if you merely borrow from someone else you will not have become an individual.

It should be apparent in all this that humanism takes a very optimistic, laudatory view of man. In the history of philosophical thought, humanism has always made a hero of man, and the contemporary third force in psychology is certainly no exception.

HUMANISM IN PERSONOLOGY

If humanism were to have any thrust at all in psychology, it would certainly not be surprising to find the impact in personology, the field that concerns itself directly with man's most human characteristics, including what gives a person his unique manner and appearance, dictates his own particular influence on his world, and governs his own reactions to external pressures. When pursuing such concerns of personology, one almost inevitably compares the approaches to and solutions of life's problems by different persons, and in the process it is natural to ask such questions as how relatively adequate is a person's personality and how effective is his life style. Indeed, so natural are such questions that it is a rare theory of personality which does not contain some definition of mental health and illness, however worded, however explicit. The point to be recognized is that personology, by virtue of its subject matter, is heavily concerned with evaluations of man in his psychological endeavors. Humanism, as a stance, is a positive evaluation, an article of faith in man's capabilities that stands in contrast to those conceptualizations that are negative or neutral.

If it seems peculiar to assert that personology is by its nature an evaluative enterprise, some thought should be given to the evolution of psychology out of philosophy. In philosophy, the analogous field to personality is character, and the study of character would have little purpose if it did not concern ethics. The philosopher's distinction between virtue and vice is quite likely analogous to the psychologist's distinction between mental health and illness. With these points in mind, it does not seem surprising that so many personologists should have started out as clergymen, or the sons of clergymen. To be sure, there are important differences in the purposes and uses of evaluations made in personology and in philosophy, but all that is important here is to recognize that it is appropriate that humanism and other evaluative stances regarding man should find a place in personology.

Indeed, if personology is by its nature an evaluative enterprise, it would bespeak ineffectiveness not to make one's evaluations explicit. Asserting that one is not evaluating, that one is not being as arbitrary as philosophers, while one considers such topics as marital relations, intimate versus contractual relationships, the translation of fantasy into action, aggressiveness and competition as well as cooperation, work productiveness and efficiency, and so forth, is a dangerous kind of denial. The only way that personologists will get to do their inherently evaluative task well is to confront that task explicitly and discuss openly the merits and limitations of various evaluative positions. The three theorists to be considered in this book all agree with this proposition.

> I'm sorry that psychology has officially cut itself off from philosophy because this means no more than giving up good philosophies for bad ones. Every man living has a philosophy, an uncriticized, uncorrectable, unimprovable, unconscious one. If you want to improve it, and make it more realistic, more useful, and more fruitful, you have to be conscious of it, and *work* with it, criticize it, improve it. This most people (including most psychologists) don't do. (Maslow, 1956, p. 5)

Likewise, in an essay first published in 1954 dealing with "personalistic philosophy," Allport argued that the psychological analysis of human personality must come to terms with philosophy:

> Having made this pious disclaimer, let us hasten to admit that whether he knows it or not, every psychologist gravitates towards an ontological position. Like a satellite he slips into the orbit of positivism, naturalism, idealism, personalism. One of these, or some other explicit philosophy

exerts a pull upon his own silent presuppositions, even though he may remain ignorant of the affinity that exists. It is shortsighted of him to deny the dependence—or to refuse to articulate, as best he can, his own thinking about human nature with that brand of philosophy with which it is most closely allied. (Allport, 1960, p. 17)

REFERENCES

ALLPORT, G. W. Open system and personality theory. *Journal of Abnormal and Social Psychology,* 1960, **61**, 301–10.

MADDI, S. R. *Personality Theories: A Comparative Analysis.* Homewood, Ill.: Dorsey Press, 1968.

MASLOW, A. H. *Toward a Psychology of Being.* Princeton: D. Van Nostrand Company, 1962.

MASLOW, A. H. *Eupsychian Management: A Journal.* Homewood, Ill.: Richard D. Irwin, 1965.

24

Sex-Role Identity

A role is a pattern of responses that is expected of a person in a particular social context. We all play many roles—a father scolding his child, an avid basketball fan booing the referee, a buddy drinking it up in the local tavern—but one of the most pervasive roles we play is the sex-role, the behavior expected of us because of our gender.

The following two articles should be considered in juxtaposition. They represent two perspectives on the question of sex-role behavior.

Kagan describes the development of sex-role identity, how a child learns to be male or female in our society. Weisstein expresses dissatisfaction with what she sees as the sexist norms of our culture and resentment at what she feels are fallacious arguments in support of current sex-role expectancies. Read both articles and then consider these questions:

How much of the sex-role is innate?

Are the current male and female patterns due to systematic inculcation of these norms by parents and society, or are they due to biological roots? In short, how much is socialization and how much is hormones?

All kinds of social roles change over time. Will the sex-role, as described by Kagan, be obsolete in ten years?

24a.

Check One: __Male __Female

JEROME KAGAN

EVERY PERSON wants to know how good, how talented and how masculine or feminine he or she is. Of the many attributes that go into the concept of self, sex-role identity is one of the most important.

It may seem odd that anyone should be unsure of his sex-role identity. A five-foot, 11-inch, 18-year-old human with X and Y chromosomes, testes, penis and body hair is, by definition, a male. It would seem that all such men should regard themselves as equally masculine. But the human mind, in its perversity, does not completely trust anatomical characteristics and insists upon including psychological factors in the final judgment. Man is as foolish as the cowardly lion who had to be reassured of his courage by the Wizard of Oz.

A sex-role identity is a person's belief about how well his biological and psychological characteristics correspond to his or her concept of the ideal male or female. The definition of the ideal—the sex-role standard—is influenced by the values of his particular culture. A Kyoto girl is taught that gentleness is the most important feminine quality; a Los Angeles girl learns that physical beauty is an essential quality.

A person is said to have a strong or firm sex-role identity when his subjective judgment of himself comes up to the standards of the ideal. If there are major discrepancies between the ideal and a person's view of himself, he has a weak or fragile sex-role identity.

To get at the dynamic significance of a person's sex-role identity, we must confront four questions: (1) How does a person initially learn sex-role standards? (2) Just what is the content of the standards? (3) Are some sex-role standards generalized across cultures? (4) What are the implications of a firm sex-role identity and a fragile one?

A child learns sex-role standards the way he learns many other concepts. He learns that an object that is round, made of rubber, and bounces is called a ball. He learns more about the definition of a ball by watching how it is used, by listening to people talk about it, and by playing with one himself. By the age of two he has learned that certain objects are called boys and men; others, girls and women. He learns the definition by noting what they do, how they look, and what they wear, and by listening and watching as others discuss the sexes. The categorization of human beings into the two sexes, usually in place by two and a half years, is one of the earliest conceptual classifications a child makes.

Sex roles are defined not only by physical attributes and behavior, but also by opinions, feelings and motives. Most American girls regard an attractive face, a hairless body, a small frame and moderate-sized breasts as ideal physical characteristics. American boys regard height, large muscles, and facial and body hair as ideal.

Some psychological traits that differentiate males from females are changing in American life. Aggression is one of the primary sex-typed behaviors. The traditional sex-role standard inhibits aggression in females, but licenses and encourages it in boys and men. It is difficult to find a psychological study of Americans that fails to note more aggressive behavior among males than among females.

Young children agree that males are more dangerous and punishing than females. This view also persists at a symbolic level: Six-year-olds believe that a tiger is a masculine animal, and that a rabbit is feminine. In one experiment, pairs of pictures were shown to young children. On the first run, the child selected from each pair the picture that was most like his father. The second time, the child selected the picture that was more like his mother. In the third run, he picked the one more like himself. Boys and girls alike classified the father as darker, larger, more dangerous and more angular than the mother. The boys classified themselves as darker, larger, more dangerous and more angular than the girls.

These perceptions are not limited to our culture. Charles Osgood of the University of Illinois showed similar pairs of abstract designs or pictures to adults from four different language groups: American, Japanese, Navajo and Mexican-Spanish. He asked each adult to indicate which picture of the pair best fitted the concept of man and which fitted the concept of woman. As the children had done, the adults from all four cultures classified men as large, angular and dark and women as small, round and light.

Dependency, passivity and conformity are also part of the traditional sex-role standard. Females in America and in most European countries are permitted these qualities; boys and men are pressured to *inhibit* them. Thus men experience greater conflict over being passive; females experience greater conflict over being aggressive.

These differences over aggressive and dependent behavior are reflected in a person's action, and in a reluctance to perceive these qualities in others. As part of an extensive personality assessment, 71 typical, middle-class American adults watched while some pictures depicting aggression and some depicting dependency were flashed onto a screen at great speed. Each person was asked to describe each picture after it was flashed seven times. The women had greater difficulty than the men in recognizing the aggressive scenes; the men had greater difficulty in recognizing the dependency scenes.

Sex-role standards dictate that the female must feel needed and desired by a man. She must believe that she can arouse a male sexually, experience deep emotion and heal the psychological wounds of those she loves. The standards for males also stress the ability to arouse and to gratify a love object, but they also include a desire to be independent in action and to dominate others and to be able to control the expression of strong emotions, especially fear and helplessness.

The American male traditionally has been driven to prove that he was strong and powerful; the female to prove that she was capable of forming a deeply emotional relationship that brought satisfaction and growth to the partner—sweetheart or child.

These values are reflected in the behavior of young children from diverse cultures. John and Beatrice Whiting of Harvard University observed children from six cultures and found that the boys were more aggressive and dominant than the girls. The girls were more likely than boys to offer help and support to other children.

In one study, my colleagues and I observed two-year-old boys and girls in a large living room. The girls were more likely than boys to stay in close physical contact with their mothers during the first five minutes. Then a set of toys was brought into the room and the children were allowed to play for a half hour. Most children left their mothers immediately and began to play. However, after 15 or 20 minutes many became bored and restless. The girls tended to drift back to their mothers, while the boys preferred to wander around the room. Michael Lewis of Educational Testing Services has reported similar differences in children only one year old. Linda Shapiro of Harvard has studied pairs of two-year-olds (two boys or two girls) in a natural setting and found the girls more trusting, more cooperative, more nurturing and less fearful of each other than the boys.

It is interesting to note that the rhesus monkey and the baboon, who are not taught sex-role standards, display behavioral differences that resemble those observed in young children. Harry Harlow and his colleagues at the University of Wisconsin have found that threatening gestures and rough-and-tumble contact play are more frequent among young male than among young female monkeys, whereas passivity in stress is more frequent among the females.

Some of the differences between males and females seem to stretch across cultures and species, suggesting that sex-role standards are neither arbitrary nor completely determined by the social groups. Each culture, in its wisdom, seems to promote those behaviors and values that are biologically easiest to establish in each of the two sexes.

The individual's sex-role identity, as noted, is his opinion of his maleness or femaleness, not a summary of his physical attributes. In one study, Edward Bennett and Larry Cohen of Tufts University asked American adults to select from a list of adjectives those that best described their personalities. The women described themselves as weak, fearful, capable of warmth and desirous of friendly and harmonious relationships with others. The men described themselves as competent, intelligent and motivated by power and personal accomplishment.

Sex-role identity differences among children arise from three sources:

First, a family-reared child is predisposed to assume that he or she is more like his or her parent of the same sex than like any other adult, and is inclined to imitate that parent. If a father is bold and athletic, his son is more likely to believe he possesses these masculine attributes than is a boy whose father is not athletic.

Second, the child is vulnerable to the special definition of sex roles shared by his peer group. A boy who is clumsy on the playing field is more likely to question his sex-role identity if he lives in a neighborhood devoted to athletics than he is if he lives in a community that values intellectual prowess.

Third, sex-role identity depends heavily on the quality of sexual interaction in adolescence. The sex-role identity has two important six-year periods of growth: one prior to puberty when acquisition of peer valued sex-role characteristics is primary, and one during adolescence, when success in heterosexual encounters is crucial. If the adolescent is unable to establish successful heterosexual relationships, he will begin to question his sex-role identity. To the adult, the potential for attracting the affection of another and entering into a satisfactory sexual union is the essence of the sex-role standard.

Let us consider the implications of a firm sex-role identity and a fragile one. Each of us tries all the time to match his traits to his notion of the ideal sex role. This is but one facet of the human desire to gain as much information about the self as possible. When one feels close to his ideal standard, his spirits are buoyed. He is confident he can come even closer, and he makes the attempt. If he feels he is far from his standard, he may turn away from it and accept the role of a feminine man (or a masculine woman). Acceptance of a culturally inappropriate role reduces the terrible anxiety that comes from recognizing in one's self a serious deviation from an ideal that cannot be obtained. The only possible defense is to redefine the ideal in attainable terms.

The continuing attempt to match one's attributes to the sex-role ideal allows men to display a more intense involvement than women in difficult intellectual problems. Males are supposed to be more competent in science and mathematics; as academic excellence is necessary for vocational success, it, therefore, is an essential component of a man's sex-role identity.

Adolescent girls view intellectual striving as a form of aggressive behavior because it involves competition with a peer. Since many females believe they should not be overly competitive, they inhibit intense intellectual striving. A visit to college dining halls often reveals males arguing so intensely that the air crackles with hostility. Intense debate in the female dining hall is less frequent because it threatens the girl's sex-role identity. Men seem to be better able to argue about an issue because they do not always take an attack on an opinion as an attack on the person.

Although intense intellectual striving is more characteristic of adult men than it is of women, this is not the case among young children. In the primary grades, girls outperform boys in all areas. The ratio of boys to girls with reading problems ranges as high as six to one. One reason for this difference is that the average American six- or seven-year-old boy sees school as a feminine place. On entering school he meets female teachers who monitor painting, coloring and singing, and put a premium on obedience, suppression of aggression and restlessness. These values are clearly more appropriate for girls than for boys. Studies of children affirm that they see school as feminine and seven-year-old boys naturally resist the complete submission it demands. If this is true, a community with a large proportion of male teachers should have a smaller proportion of boys with serious reading retardation. Some American communities, such as Akron, Ohio, are testing the hypothesis.

Depression and anxiety affect the sexes differently. Women are likely to suffer psychological stress when it is suggested that they are not attractive, loving or emotional. Some women experience serious depression after giving birth because they do not feel strong love for the infant and they question their femininity. Men become anxious at suggestions that they are impotent or not competent, successful or dominant. Depression is likely to follow a man's career failure.

The sex-role standards of a society are not static, and changes in the standards that surround sexuality and dependence are just becoming evident. The American woman has begun to assume a more active role in sexual behavior; her mother and grandmother assumed passive postures. This reach for independence has extensive social implications. Some college-educated women feel that dependence, especially on men, is an undesirable feminine trait. They want to prove that they can function as competently and autonomously as men and this pushes them to develop academic and career skills.

Why? The intense effort spent on getting into and staying in college has persuaded the young woman that she should use her hard-won intellectual skills in a job. And technology has made it less necessary for a woman to do routine housework and forced her to look outside the home for proof of her usefulness.

Most human beings seek the joy of accomplishment. A man tries to gratify this need in his job and he has something concrete with which to prove his effectiveness—an invention, a manuscript, a salary check. Woman once met her need to be useful by believing that her sweetheart, husband or children required her wisdom, skill and personal affection. Instant dinners, permissive sexual mores, and freedom for children have undermined this role. It is too early to predict the effect of this female unrest. It should lead to a more egalitarian relation between the sexes. It could make each partner so reluctant to submerge his individual autonomy and admit his need for the other that each walks a lonely and emotionally insulated path. Let us hope it does not.

Psychology Constructs the Female, or The Fantasy Life of the Male Psychologist (with Some Attention to the Fantasies of His Friends, the Male Biologist and the Male Anthropologist)

NAOMI WEISSTEIN

IT IS an implicit assumption that the area of psychology which concerns itself with personality has the onerous but necessary task of describing the limits of human possibility. Thus when we are about to consider the liberation of women, we naturally look to psychology to tell us what "true" liberation would mean: what would give women the freedom to fulfill their own intrinsic natures. Psychologists have set about describing the true natures of women with a certainty and a sense of their own infallibility rarely found in the secular world. Bruno Bettelheim, of the University of Chicago, tells us (1965) that "We must start with the realization that, as much as women want to be good scientists or engineers, they want first and foremost to be womanly companions of men and to be mothers." Erik Erikson of Harvard University (1964), upon noting that young women often ask whether they can "have an identity before they know whom they will marry, and for whom they will make a home," explains somewhat elegiacally that "Much of a young woman's identity is already defined in her kind of attractiveness and in the selectivity of her search for the man (or men) by whom she wishes to be sought." Mature womanly fulfillment, for Erikson, rests on the fact that a woman's "somatic design harbors an 'inner space' destined to bear the offspring of chosen men, and with it, a biological, psychological, and ethical commitment to take care of human infancy"! Some psychiatrists even see the acceptance of woman's role by women as a solution to societal problems. "Woman is nurturance," writes Joseph Rheingold (1964), a psychiatrist at Harvard Medical School, "anatomy decrees the life of a woman . . . when women grow up without dread of their biological functions and without subversion by feminist doctrine, and therefore enter upon motherhood with a sense of fulfillment and altruistic sentiment, we shall attain the goal of a good life and a secure world in which to live it." (p. 714)

These views from men who are assumed to be experts reflect, in a surprisingly transparent way, the cultural consensus. They not only assert that a woman is defined by her ability to attract men, they see no alternative definitions. They think that the definition of a woman in terms of a man is the way it should be; and they back it up with psychosexual incantation and biological ritual curses. A woman has an identity if she is attractive enough to obtain a man, and thus, a home; for this will allow her to set about her life's task of "joyful altruism and nurturance."

Business certainly does not disagree. If views such as Bettelheim's and Erikson's do indeed have something to do with real liberation for women, then seldom in human history has so much money and effort been spent on helping a group of people realize their true potential. Clothing, cosmetics, home furnishings, are multi-million dollar businesses: if you don't like investing in firms that make weaponry and flaming gasoline, then there's a lot of cash in "inner space." Sheet and pillowcase manufacturers are concerned to fill this inner space:

> Mother, for a while this morning, I thought I wasn't cut out for married life. Hank was late for work and forgot his apricot juice and walked out without kissing me, and when I was all alone I started crying. But then the postman came with the sheets and towels you sent, that look like big bandana handkerchiefs, and you know what I thought? That those big red and blue handerchiefs are for girls like me to dry their tears on so they can get busy and do what a housewife has to do. Throw open the windows and start getting the house ready, and the dinner, maybe clean the silver and put new geraniums in the box. *Everything to be ready for him when he walks through that door.* (Fieldcrest 1966; emphasis added.)

Of course, it is not only the sheet and pillowcase manufacturers, the cosmetics industry, the home furnishings salesmen who profit from and make use of the cultural definitions of man and woman. The example above is blatantly and overtly pitched to a particular kind of sexist stereotype: the child nymph. But almost all aspects of the media are normative, that is, they have to do with the ways in which beautiful people, or just folks, or ordinary Americans, should live their lives. They define the possible; and the possibilities are usually in terms of what is male and what is female. Men and women alike are waiting for Hank, the Silva Thins man, to walk back through that door.

It is an interesting but limited exercise to show that psychologists and psychiatrists embrace these sexist norms of our culture, that they do not see beyond the most superficial and stultifying media conceptions of female nature, and that their ideas of female nature serve industry and commerce so well. Just because it's good for business doesn't mean it's wrong. What I will show is that it *is wrong;* that there isn't the tiniest shred of evidence that these fantasies of servitude and childish dependence have anything to do with women's true potential; that the idea of the nature of human possibility which rests on the accidents of individual development of genitalia, on what is possible today because of what happened yesterday, on the fundamentalist myth of sex organ causality, has strangled and deflected psychology so that it is relatively useless in describing, explaining or predicting humans and their behavior.

It then goes without saying that present psychology is less than worthless in contributing to a vision which could truly liberate—men as well as women.

The central argument of my paper, then, is this. Psychology has nothing to say about what women are really like, what they need and what they want, essentially because psychology does not know. I want to stress that this failure is not limited to women; rather, the kind of psychology which has addressed itself to how people act and who they are has failed to understand, in the first place, why people act the way they do, and certainly failed to understand what might make them act differently.

The kind of psychology which has addressed itself to these questions divides into two professional areas: academic personality research, and clinical psychology and psychiatry. The basic reason for failure is the same in both these areas: the central assumption for most psychologists of human personality has been that human behavior rests on an individual and inner dynamic, perhaps fixed in infancy, perhaps fixed by genitalia, perhaps simply arranged in a rather immovable cognitive network. But this assumption is rapidly losing ground as personality psychologists fail again and again to get consistency in the assumed personalities of their subjects (Block, 1968). Meanwhile, the evidence is collecting that what a person does and who she believes herself to be, will in general be a function of what people around her expect her to be, and what the overall situation in which she is acting implies that she is. Compared to the influence of the social context within which a person lives, his or her history and "traits," as well as biological makeup, may simply be random variations, "noise" superimposed on the true signal which can predict behavior. . . .

THE SOCIAL CONTEXT

Even when psychological theory is constructed so that it may be tested, and rigorous standards of evidence are used, it has become increasingly clear that in order to understand why people do what they do, and certainly in order to change what people do, psychologists must turn away from the theory of the causal nature of the inner dynamic and look to the social context within which individuals live.

Before examining the relevance of this approach for the question of women, let me first sketch the groundwork for this assertion.

In the first place, it is clear (Block, 1968) that personality tests never yield consistent predictions; a rigid authoritarian on one measure will be an unauthoritarian on the next. But the reason for this inconsistency is only now becoming clear, and it seems overwhelmingly to have much more to do with the social situation in which the subject finds him/herself than with the subject him/herself.

In a series of brilliant experiments, Rosenthal and his co-workers (Rosenthal and Jacobson, 1968; Rosenthal, 1966) have shown that if one group of experimenters has one hypothesis about what they expect to find, and another group of experimenters has the opposite hypothesis, both groups will obtain results in accord with their hypotheses. The results obtained are not due to mishandling of data by biased experimenters; rather, somehow, the bias of the experimenter creates a changed environment in which subjects actually act differently. For instance, in one experiment, subjects were to assign numbers to pictures of men's faces, with high numbers representing the subject's judgment that the man in the picture was a successful person, and low numbers representing the subject's judgment that the man in the picture was an unsuccessful person. Prior to running the subjects, one group of experimenters was told that the subjects tended to rate the faces high; another group of experimenters was told that the subjects tended to rate the faces low. Each group of experimenters was instructed to follow precisely the same procedure: they were required to read to subjects a set of instructions, and to *say nothing else.* For the 375 subjects run, the results showed clearly that those subjects who performed the task with experimenters who expected high ratings gave high ratings, and those subjects who performed the task with experimenters who expected low ratings gave low ratings. How did this happen? The experimenters all used the same words; it was something in their conduct which made one group of subjects do one thing, and another group of subjects do another thing.*

The concreteness of the changed conditions produced by expectation is a fact, a reality: even with animal subjects, in two separate studies (Rosenthal & Fode, 1960; Rosenthal & Lawson, 1961), those experimenters who were told that rats learning mazes had been especially bred for brightness obtained better learning from their rats than did experimenters believing their rats to have been bred for dullness. In a very recent study, Rosenthal and Jacobson (1968) extended their analysis to the natural classroom situation. Here, they tested a group of students and reported to the teachers that some among the students tested "showed great promise." Actually, the students so named had been selected on a random basis. Some time later, the experimenters retested the group of students: those students whose teachers had been told that they were "promising" showed real and dramatic increments in their IQs as compared to the rest of the students. Something in the conduct of the teachers towards those who the teachers believed to be the "bright" students, made those students brighter.

Thus, even in carefully controlled experiments, and with no outward or conscious difference in behavior, the hypotheses we start with will influence enormously the behavior of another organism. These studies are extremely important when assessing the validity of psychological studies of women. Since it is beyond doubt that most of us start with notions as to the nature of men and women, the validity of a number of observations of sex differences is questionable, even when these observations have been made under carefully controlled conditions. Second, and more important, the Rosenthal experiments point quite clearly to the influence of social expectation. In some extremely important ways, people are what you expect them to be, or at least they behave as you expect them to behave. Thus, if women, according to Bettelheim, want first and foremost to be good wives and mothers, it is extremely likely that this is what Bruno Bettelheim, and the rest of society, want them to be.

There is another series of brilliant social psychological experiments which point to the overwhelming effect of social context. These are the obedience experiments of Stanley Milgram (1965) in which subjects are asked to obey the orders of unknown experimenters, orders which carry with them the distinct possibility that the subject is killing somebody.

In Milgram's experiments, a subject is told that he/she is administering a learning experiment, and that he/she is to deal out shocks each

---

* I am indebted to Jesse Lemisch for his valuable suggestions in the interpretation of these studies.

time the other "subject" (in reality, a confederate of the experimenter) answers incorrectly. The equipment appears to provide graduated shocks ranging upwards from 15 volts through 450 volts; for each of four consecutive voltages there are verbal descriptions such as "mild shock," "danger, severe shock," and, finally, for the 435 and 450 volt switches, a red XXX marked over the switches. Each time the stooge answers incorrectly, the subject is supposesd to increase the voltage. As the voltage increases, the stooge begins to cry in pain; he/she demands that the experiment stop; finally, he/she refuses to answer at all. When he/she stops responding, the experimenter instructs the subject to continue increasing the voltage; for each shock administered the stooge shrieks in agony. Under these conditions, about 62½% of the subjects administered shocks that they believed to be possibly lethal.

No tested individual differences between subjects predicted how many would continue to obey, and which would break off the experiment. When forty psychiatrists predicted how many of a group of 100 subjects would go on to give the lethal shock, their predictions were orders of magnitude below the actual percentages; most expected only one-tenth of one per cent of the subjects to obey to the end.

But even though *psychiatrists* have no idea how people will behave in this situation, and even though individual differences do not predict which subjects will obey and which will not, it is easy to predict when subjects will be obedient and when they will be defiant. All the experimenter has to do is change the social situation. In a variant of Milgram's experiment, two stooges were present in addition to the "victim"; these worked along with the subject in administering electric shocks. When these two stooges refused to go on with the experiment, only ten per cent of the subjects continued to the maximum voltage. This is critical for personality theory. It says that behavior is predicted from the social situation, not from the individual history.

Finally, an ingenious experiment by Schachter and Singer (1962) showed that subjects injected with adrenalin, which produces a state of physiological arousal in all but minor respects identical to that which occurs when subjects are extremely afraid, became euphoric when they were in a room with a stooge who was acting euphoric, and became extremely angry when they were placed in a room with a stooge who was acting extremely angry.

To summarize: If subjects under quite innocuous and noncoercive social conditions can be made to kill other subjects and under other types of social conditions will positively refuse to do so; if subjects can react to a state of physiological fear by becoming euphoric because there is somebody else around who is euphoric or angry because there is somebody else around who is angry; if students become intelligent because teachers expect them to be intelligent, and rats run mazes better because experimenters are told the rats are bright, then it is obvious that a study of human behavior requires, first and foremost, a study of the social contexts within which people move, the expectations as to how they will behave, and the authority which tells them who they are and what they are supposed to do.

BIOLOGICALLY BASED THEORIES

Biologists also have at times assumed they could describe the limits of human potential from their observations not of human, but of animal behavior. Here, as in psychology, there has been no end of theorizing about the sexes, again with a sense of absolute certainty surprising in "science." These theories fall into two major categories.

One category of theory argues that since females and males differ in their sex hormones, and sex hormones enter the brain (Hamburg & Lunde in Maccoby, 1966), there must be innate behavioral differences. But the only thing this argument tells us is that there are differences in physiological state. The problem is whether these differences are at all relevant to behavior.

Consider, for example, differences in levels of the sex hormone testosterone. A man who calls himself Tiger* has recently argued (1970) that the greater quantities of testosterone found in human males as compared with human females (of a certain age group) determines innate differences in aggressiveness, competitiveness, dominance, ability to hunt, ability to hold public office, and so forth. But Tiger demonstrates in this argument the same manly and courageous refusal to be intimidated by evidence which we have already seen in our consideration of the clinical and psychiatric tradition. The evidence does not support his argument, and in most cases, directly contradicts it. Testosterone level does not seem to be related to hunting ability, dominance, or aggression, or competitiveness. As Storch has pointed out (1970), all normal *male mammals* in the reproductive age group produce much greater quantities of testosterone than females; yet many of these males are neither hunters nor are they aggressive (e.g. rabbits). And, among some hunting mammals, such as the large cats, it turns out that more hunting is done by the female than the male. And there exist primate species where the female is clearly more aggressive, competitive, and dominant than the male (Mitchell, 1969; and see below). Thus, for some species, being female, and therefore, having less testosterone than the male of that species means hunting more, or being more aggressive, or being more dominant. Nor does having *more* tes-

---

* Schwarz-Belkin (1914) claims that the name was originally Mouse, but this may be a reference to an earlier L. Tiger (putative).

tosterone preclude behavior commonly thought of as "female": there exist primate species where females do not touch infants except to feed them; the males care for the infants at all times (Mitchell, 1969; see fuller discussion below). So it is not clear what testosterone or any other sex-hormonal difference means for differences in nature, or sex-role behavior.

In other words, one can observe identical types of behavior which have been associated with sex (e.g. "mothering") in males and females, despite known differences in physiological state, i.e. sex hormones, genitalia, etc. What about the converse to this? That is, can one obtain differences in behavior given a single physiological state? The answer is overwhelmingly yes, not only as regards non-sex-specific hormones (as in the Schachter and Singer 1962 experiment cited above), but also as regards gender itself. Studies of hermaphrodites with the same diagnosis (the genetic, gonadal, hormonal sex, the internal reproductive organs, and the ambiguous appearances of the external genitalia were identical) have shown that one will consider oneself male or female depending simply on whether one was defined and raised as male or female (Money, 1970; Hampton & Hampton, 1961):

> There is no more convincing evidence of the power of social interaction on gender-identity differentiation than in the case of congenital hermaphrodites who are of the same diagnosis and similar degree of hermaphroditism but are differently assigned and with a different postnatal medical and life history. (Money, 1970, p. 743).

Thus, for example, if out of two individuals diagnosed as having the adrenogenital syndrome of female hermaphroditism, one is raised as a girl and one as a boy, each will act and identify her/himself accordingly. The one raised as a girl will consider herself a girl; the one raised as a boy will consider himself a boy; and each will conduct her/himself successfully in accord with that self-definition.

So, identical behavior occurs given different physiological states; and different behavior occurs given an identical physiological starting point. So it is not clear that differences in sex hormones are at all relevant to behavior.

The other category of theory based on biology, a reductionist theory, goes like this. Sex-role behavior in some primate species is described, and it is concluded that this is the "natural" behavior for humans. Putting aside the not insignificant problem of observer bias (for instance, Harlow, 1962, of the University of Wisconsin, after observing differences between male and female rhesus monkeys, quotes Lawrence Sterne to the effect that women are silly and trivial, and concludes that "men and women have differed in the past and they will differ in the future"), there are a number of problems with this approach.

The most general and serious problem is that there are no grounds to assume that anything primates do is necessary, natural, or desirable in humans, for the simple reason that humans are not non-humans. For instance, it is found that male chimpanzees placed alone with infants will not "mother" them. Jumping from hard data to ideological speculation, researchers conclude from this information that *human* females are necessary for the safe growth of human infants. It would be reasonable to conclude, following this logic, that it is quite useless to teach human infants to speak, since it has been tried with chimpanzees and it does not work.

One strategy that has been used is to extrapolate from primate behavior to "innate" human preference by noticing certain trends in primate behavior as one moves phylogenetically closer to humans. But there are great difficulties with this approach. When behaviors from lower primates are directly opposite to those of higher primates, or to those one expects of humans, they can be dismissed on evolutionary grounds—higher primates and/or humans grew out of that kid stuff. On the other hand, if the behavior of higher primates is counter to the behavior considered natural for humans, while the behavior of some lower primate is considered the natural one for humans, the higher primate behavior can be dismissed also, on the grounds that it has diverged from an older, prototypical pattern. So either way, one can select those behaviors one wants to prove as innate for humans. In addition, one does not know whether the sex-role behavior exhibited is dependent on the phylogenetic rank, or on the environmental conditions (both physical and social) under which different species live.

Is there then any value at all in primate observations as they relate to human females and males? There is a value but it is limited: its function can be no more than to show some extant examples of diverse sex-role behavior. It must be stressed, however, that this is an extremely limited function. The extant behavior does not begin to suggest all the possibilities, either for non-human primates or for humans. Bearing these caveats in mind, it is nonetheless interesting that if one inspects the limited set of observations of existing non-human primate sex-role behaviors, one finds, in fact, a much larger range of sex-role behavior than is commonly believed to exist. "Biology" appears to limit very little; the fact that a female gives birth does not mean, even in non-humans, that she necessarily cares for the infant (in marmosets, for instance, the male carries the infant at all times except when the infant is feeding [Mitchell, 1969]); "natural" female and male behavior varies all the way from females who are much more aggressive and competitive than males (e.g. Tamarins, see Mitchell, 1969) and male "mothers" (e.g. Titi monkeys, night monkeys, and marmosets; see

Mitchell, 1969)* to submissive and passive females and male antag-
onists (e.g. rhesus monkeys).

But even for the limited function that primate arguments serve, the
evidence has been misused. Invariably, those primates have been
cited which exhibit exactly the kind of behavior that the proponents of
the biological fixedness of human female behavior wish were true for
humans. Thus, baboons and rhesus monkeys are generally cited: males
in these groups exhibit some of the most irritable and aggressive behavior found in primates, and if one wishes to argue that females are
naturally passive and submissive, these groups provide vivid examples.
There are abundant counter examples, such as those mentioned above
(Mitchell, 1969); in fact, in general, a counter example can be found for
every sex-role behavior cited, including, as mentioned in the case of
marmosets, male "mothers."

But the presence of counter examples has not stopped florid and
overarching theories of the natural or biological basis of male privilege
from proliferating. For instance, there have been a number of theories
dealing with the innate incapacity in human males for monogamy.
Here, as in most of this type of theorizing, baboons are a favorite example, probably because of their fantasy value: the family unit of the
hamadryas baboon, for instance, consists of a highly constant pattern
of one male and a number of females and their young. And again, the
counter examples, such as the invariably monogamous gibbon, are
ignored.

An extreme example of this maiming and selective truncation of the
evidence in the service of a plea for the maintenance of male privilege
is a recent book, *Men in Groups* (1969) by Tiger (see above, especially
footnote). The central claim of this book is that females are incapable
of "bonding" as in "male bonding." What is "male bonding"? Its surface definition is simple: ". . . a particular relationship between two
or more males such that they react differently to members of their
bonding units as compared to individuals outside of it" (pp. 19-20). If
one deletes the word male, the definition, on its face, would seem to include all organisms that have any kind of social organization. But this
is not what Tiger means. For instance, Tiger asserts that females are incapable of bonding; and this alleged incapacity indicates to Tiger that
females should be restricted from public life. Why is bonding an exclusively male behavior? Because, says Tiger, it is seen in male primates.
All male primates? No, very few male primates. Tiger cites two examples where male bonding is seen: rhesus monkeys and baboons. Surprise, surprise. But not even all baboons: as mentioned above, the

---

* All these are lower-order primates, which makes their behavior with reference
to humans unnatural, or more natural; take your choice.

hamadryas social organization consists of one-male units; so does that of the Gelada baboon (Mitchell, 1969). And the great apes do not go in for male bonding much either. The "male bond" is hardly a serious contribution to scholarship; one reviewer for *Science* has observed that the book ". . . shows basically more resemblance to a partisan political tract than to a work of objective social science," with male bonding being ". . . some kind of behavioral phlogiston" (Fried, 1969, p. 884).

In short, primate arguments have generally misused the evidence; primate studies themselves have, in any case, only the very limited function of describing some possible sex-role behavior; and at present, primate observations have been sufficiently limited so that even the range of possible sex-role behavior for non-human primates is not known. This range is not known since there is only minimal observation of what happens to behavior if the physical or social environment is changed. In one study (Itani, 1963), different troops of Japanese macaques were observed. Here, there appeared to be cultural differences: males in 3 out of the 18 troops observed differed in their amount of aggressiveness and infant-caring behavior. There could be no possibility of differential evolution here; the differences seemed largely transmitted by infant socialization. Thus, the very limited evidence points to some plasticity in the sex-role behavior of non-human primates; if we can figure out experiments which massively change the social organization of primate groups, it is possible that we might observe great changes in behavior. At present, however, we must conclude that given a constant physical environment, non-human primates do not change their social conditions by themselves very much and thus the "innateness" and fixedness of their behavior is simply not known. Thus, even if there were some way, which there isn't, to settle on the behavior of a particular primate species as being the "natural" way for humans, we would not know whether or not this were simply some function of the present social organization of that species. And finally, once again it must be stressed that even if non-human primate behavior turned out to be relatively fixed, this would say little about our behavior. More immediate and relevant evidence, e.g. the evidence from social psychology, points to the enormous plasticity in human behavior, not only from one culture to the next, but from one experimental group to the next. One of the most salient features of human social organization is its variety; there are a number of cultures where there is at least a rough equality between men and women (Mead, 1949). In summary, primate arguments can tell us very little about our "innate" sex-role behavior; if they tell us anything at all, they tell us that there is no one biologically "natural" female or male behavior, and that sex-role behavior in non-human primates is much more varied than has previously been thought.

CONCLUSION

In brief, the uselessness of present psychology (and biology) with regard to women is simply a special case of the general conclusion: one must understand the social conditions under which humans live if one is going to attempt to explain their behavior. And, to understand the social conditions under which women live, one must understand the social expectations about women.

How are women characterized in our culture, and in psychology? They are inconsistent, emotionally unstable, lacking in a strong conscience or superego, weaker, "nuturant" rather than productive, "intuitive" rather than intelligent, and, if they are at all "normal," suited to the home and the family. In short, the list adds up to a typical minority group stereotype of inferiority (Hacker, 1951): if they know their place, which is in the home, they are really quite lovable, happy, childlike, loving creatures. In a review of the intellectual differences between little boys and little girls, Eleanor Maccoby (1966) has shown that there are no intellectual differences until about high school, or, if there are, girls are slightly ahead of boys. At high school, girls begin to do worse on a few intellectual tasks, such as arithmetic reasoning, and beyond high school, the achievement of women now measured in terms of productivity and accomplishment drops off even more rapidly. There are a number of other, non-intellectual tests which show sex differences; I choose the intellectual differences since it is seen clearly that women start becoming inferior. It is no use to talk about women being different but equal; all of the tests I can think of have a "good" outcome and a "bad" outcome. Women usually end up at the "bad" outcome. In light of social expectations about women, what is surprising is that little girls don't get the message that they are supposed to be stupid until high school; and what is even more remarkable is that some women resist this message even after high school, college, and graduate school.

My paper began with remarks on the task of the discovery of the limits of human potential. Psychologists must realize that it is they who are limiting discovery of human potential. . . . They assume that people move in a context-free ether, with only their innate dispositions and their individual traits determining what they will do. Until psychologists begin to respect evidence, and until they begin looking at the social context within which people move, psychology will have nothing of substance to offer in this task of discovery. I don't know what immutable differences exist between men and women apart from differences in their genitals; perhaps there are some other unchangeable differences; probably there are a number of irrelevant differences. But it is clear that until social expectations for men and women are equal, until we provide equal respect for both men and women, our answers to this question will simply reflect our prejudices.

REFERENCES

ASTIN, A. W., "The functional autonomy of psychotherapy." *American Psychologist*, 1961, **16**, 75–78.

BARRON, F. & LEARY, T., "Changes in psychoneurotic patients with and without psychotherapy." *J. Consulting Psychology*, 1955, **19**, 239–245.

BETTELHEIM, B., "The Commitment required of a woman entering a scientific profession in present day American society." *Woman and the Scientific Professions*, The MIT symposium on American Women in Science and Engineering, 1965.

BLECK, J., "Some reasons for the apparent inconsistency of personality." *Psychological Bulletin*, 1968, **70**, 210–212.

BREGIN, A. E., "The effects of psychotherapy: negative results revisited." *Journal of Consulting Psychology*, 1963, **10**, 244–250.

CARTWRIGHT, R. D. & VOGEL, J. L., "A comparison of changes in psychoneurotic patients during matched periods of therapy and no-therapy." *Journal of Consulting Psychology*, 1960, **24**, 121–127.

ERIKSON, E., "Inner and outer space: reflections on womanhood." *Daedalus*, 1964, **93**, 582–606.

EYSENCK, H. J., "The effects of psychotherapy: an evaluation." *Journal of Consulting Psychology*, 1952, **16**, 319–324.

FIELDCREST—Advertisement in the *New Yorker*, 1965.

FREUD, S., *The Sexual Enlightenment of Children*, Collier Books Edition, 1963.

FRIED, M. H., "Mankind excluding women," review of Tiger's *Men in Groups*. *Science*, 1969, **165**, 883–884.

GOLDSTEIN, A. P. & DEAN, S. J., *The investigation of Psychotherapy: Commentaries and Readings*. John Wiley & Sons, New York: 1966.

HACKER, H. M., "Women as a minority group," *Social Forces*, 1951, **30**, 60–69.

HAMBURG, D. A. & LUNDE, D. T., "Sex hormones in the development of sex differences in human behavior." In Maccoby, ed., *The Development of Sex Differences*, pp. 1–24, Stanford University Press, 1966.

HAMPTON, J. L. & HAMPTON, J. C., "The ontogenesis of sexual behavior in man." In Young, W. C., ed., *Sex and Internal Secretions*, pp. 1401–1432, 1966.

HARLOW, H. F., "The heterosexual affectional system in monkeys." *The American Psychologist*, 1962, **17**, 1–9.

HOOKER, E., "Male homosexuality in the Rorschach." *Journal of Projective Techniques*, 1957, **21**, 18–31.

ITANI, J., "Paternal care in the wild Japanese monkeys, *Macaca fuscata*." In C. H. Southwick (ed.), *Primate Social Behavior*, Princeton: Van Nostrand, 1963.

LITTLE, K. B. & SCHNEIDMAN, E. S., "Congruences among interpretations of psychological and anamestic data. *Psychological Monographs*, 1959, **73**, 1–42.

MACCOBY, ELEANOR E., "Sex differences in intellectual functioning." In Maccoby, ed., *The development of sex differences*, 25–55. Stanford University Press: 1966.

MASTERS, W. H. & JOHNSON, V. E., *Human Sexual Response,* Little Brown: Boston, 1966.

MEAD, M., *Male and Female: A Study of the Sexes in a Changing World,* William Morrow: New York, 1949.

MILGRAM, S., "Some conditions of obedience and disobedience to authority." *Human Relations,* 1965a, **18**, 57–76.

MILGRAM, S., "Liberating effects of group pressures." *Journal of Personality and Social Psychology,* 1965b, **1**, 127–134.

MITCHELL, G. D., "Paternalistic behavior in primates." *Psychological Bulletin,* 1969, **71**, 399–417.

MONEY, J., "Sexual dimorphism and homosexual gender identity," *Psychological Bulletin,* 1970, **6**, pp. 425–440.

POWERS, E. & WITMER, H., *An Experiment in the Prevention of Delinquency,* New York: Columbia University Press, 1951.

RHEINGOLD, J., *The Fear of Being a Woman,* Grune & Stratton: New York, 1964.

ROSENTHAL, R., "On the social psychology of the psychological experiment: the experimenter's hypothesis as unintended determinant of experimental results." *American Scientist,* 1963, **51**, 268–283.

ROSENTHAL, R., *Experimenter Effects in Behavioral Research,* New York: Appleton-Century-Crofts, 1966.

ROSENTHAL, R. & JACOBSON, L., *Pygmalion in the Classroom: Teacher Expectation and Pupil's Intellectual Development,* New York: Holt, Rinehart & Winston, 1968.

ROSENTHAL, R. & LAWSON, R., "A longitudinal study of the effects of experimenter bias on the operant learning of laboratory rats." Unpublished manuscript, Harvard University, 1961.

ROSENTHAL, R. & PODE, K. L., "The effect of experimenter bias on the performance of the albino rat." Unpublished manuscript, Harvard University, 1960.

ROTTER, J. B., "Psychotherapy." *Annual Review of Psychology,* 1960, **11**, 381–414.

SCHACHTER, S. & SINGER, J. E., "Cognitive, social and physiological determinants of emotional state," *Psychological Review,* 1962, **63**, 379–399.

SCHWARTZ-BELKIN, "Les Fleurs du Mal" in *Festschrift für Gordon Piltdown,* New York, Ponzi Press, 1914.

STORCH, M., "Reply to Tiger." Unpublished manuscript, 1970.

TIGER, L., *Men in Groups,* New York: Random House, 1969.

TIGER, L., "Male dominance? Yes. A sexist plot? No," *New York Times Magazine,* Section N, Oct. 25, 1970.

TRUAX, C. B., "Effective ingredients in psychotherapy: an approach to unraveling the patient-therapist interaction," *Journal of Counseling Psychology,* 1963, **10**, 256–263.

25.

A Critique of the Interview

E. LOWELL KELLY

An interview is simply a goal-directed conversation. Although it is probably the most widely used technique for personality assessment, a number of significant sources of error are built into the process—errors that derive from the interviewer (the influence of his needs and prejudgments) and from the interviewee (his anxiety, his attempt to show himself up well or poorly as the case may be, his efforts to out-guess the interviewer). Together these sources of error considerably detract from the validity of the interview as a personality assessment procedure.

The following article was a speech to a group of medical educators, who characteristically use the interview to get at personality factors in selecting applicants for admission to medical schools. In view of the questionable validity of interviews, Kelly suggests that perhaps the greatest value of the interview in such cases is that it makes the interviewer feel better!

Hypothesize this situation: You are to select a wife or husband, using either the very best possible computerized matching or a two-hour face-to-face interview. Which procedure would you follow? Which would more likely yield a sustained relationship?

MY OWN work with the interview as a selection technique extends back to a study of its value in the selection of pilots in the civilian pilot training program just before World War II and to its use in the selection of pilots in the Navy Air Arm. After the war, I was concerned with evaluating the interview in the selection of candidates for training in the

Reprinted from *Journal of Medical Education,* 1957 (Part 2), 32, pp. 78–84. Copyright 1957 by Association of American Medical Colleges. Reprinted by permission.

doctoral program in clinical psychology in the Veterans Administration. During the last few years, I have had some contact with the interview's use in the selection of medical school candidates.

In all of these instances we have tried to create an experimental situation in which we could ascertain, "Does the interview work as well as it seems to?" Everybody thinks it works, but does it? In each of these instances where we have put the interview to a test and collected data in a fashion whereby we could determine whether it added anything to the accuracy of the prediction of performance without benefit of the interview, we have had to come up with the conclusion that it was not worth the cost. All evidence suggests that it gives a great deal of satisfaction to the persons who use it; they usually feel good about it, but we have not been able to demonstrate in any of these investigations the utility of the interview. And, in view of its cost in terms of professional time, our findings raise serious doubt whether it can be defended as an economical procedure.

RESEARCH ON THE VALIDITY OF THE INTERVIEW

Our findings are not surprising in view of the entire story of the published findings with respect to the validity of the selection interview. In reviewing some of this research, I am going to quote quite extensively from a paper I prepared for an audience a couple of years ago under the title of "An Evaluation of the Interview as a Selective Technique," originally presented to a conference on testing problems arranged by the Educational Testing Service.[1]

Now, what is this evidence about the interview? Here I am going to hit only the highlights. A number of years ago Scott and Hollingworth,[2] in independent pioneer investigations, reported surprisingly low interjudge agreements between interviewers regarding sales ability of prospective salesmen. Since that time many comparable studies have been conducted and practically all of the research findings point to similarly-low interjudge agreement and, where criteria are available, to very low validities. Some of the more recent findings are those growing out of our own project at the University of Michigan. I will review them very briefly.

In our work on the selection of clinical psychologists, we used two interviews. The first was an hour long, conducted by a staff member who had previously made judgment of the candidate on the basis of

[1] *Proceedings of the 1953 Invitational Conference on Testing Problems.* Princeton, New Jersey: Educational Testing Service, 1953.

[2] Scott, W. D. "Selection of Employees by Means of Quantitative Determinations," *Annals of Amer. Academy of Polit. and Soc. Sci.* 65, 1916.

Hollingworth, H. L. *Vocational Psychology and Character Analysis.* New York: Appleton, 1929.

the credential file, which contains letters exchanged between the University and the student, references, and so on. The second interview was a two-hour one conducted by a different staff member with the same candidate. The second interviewer had previously made an intensive study of the credential file, studied all the scores on the objective and projective tests, read the candidate's autobiography, looked at the biographical inventory, and tried to integrate all of this information. These interviews were carried out by trained, professional persons who were permitted to structure the interviews in the manner they believed most useful for the task at hand. The validity of interviewer judgments made before and corrected after the interview was estimated against a dozen different criteria obtained four years later.

The results were such as to force us to conclude that neither the short interview, made with relatively little information, or the long one, made with lots of previous information, contributed to our assessment program. Actually, the increase in validity was just infinitesimal. At least the validity of these interviews was not negative as was true in a recent study reported by Thayer,[3] who attempted to predict the subsequent field success of missionaries to whom a body of psychological tests had been administered some 20 years earlier. In this study an admittedly fallible criterion, i.e., success as a missionary, was predicted by a correlation of .53 with the psychological test battery, but the ratings made by the secretary of a missionary selection board on the basis of an interview, references, and other papers actually showed a negative correlation with later success in the field.

Perhaps the most cogent evidence for doubting the validity of a conventional selection interview appeared in a recent article by Holt and Luborsky[4] which reports on a research project on the selection of psychiatrists. In contrast with our own Michigan assessment program, this Menninger Project relied most heavily on judgment based on the selection interview and a battery of individually administered psychological tests. Each applicant was independently interviewed by three psychiatrists, each of whom made a prediction regarding the candidate's probable success in psychiatric training at the Menninger School of Psychiatry.

I would like to call your attention to the fact that in many ways this was almost an ideal situation for testing the validity of an interview. First, it should be noted that the interviews were conducted by staff psychiatrists presumably expert in the art of interviewing. Secondly, and this is very important, the predictions made were with respect to

[3] Thayer, C. R. "The Relationship of Certain Psychological Test Scores to Subsequent Ratings of Missionary Field Success," *Univ. Pittsburgh Bull.*, 1952, p. 48.
[4] Holt, R. R. and Luborsky, L. "Research in the Selection of Psychiatrists: a Second Interim Report," *Bull. Menninger Clinic* 16, 1952, pp. 125–35.

performance in a local situation—their own training program, the program with which the interviewers were thoroughly familiar. Finally, although Holt and Luborsky don't provide evidence on the point, many of these interviewers were actually a part of the team that evaluated the success of these individuals two or three years later in the program. This would have resulted in raising the correlations if there had been some overlap.

In spite of these seemingly optimal conditions, the validity of these interviewer judgments are shockingly low, the median being .06 for 14 interviewers. Only one of these 14 presumably expert interviewers had a validity large enough to achieve statistical significance at the 1 per cent level.

I might also mention that at one point in our work on selecting pilots we had three interviewers working on interviewing prospective pilots. Our eventual evaluation of them as interviewers showed just about as many of them with negative validities as with plus validities. The average validity was right around zero. We didn't have a single interviewer who in this study did better than chance. We had hoped that maybe we would find some who had significantly high positive correlation, and then we could figure out ways of selecting selection interviewers, perhaps by having other interviewers select them!

Evidence of this kind does not prove that the interview is valueless as a technique of personnel selection. There may be some situations in which some interviewers are able to use the technique and arrive at judgments with high predictive validity. If so, it seems most unfortunate that they have not been reported in the literature. On the contrary, all evidence available suggests that the technique is apt to have sufficiently low validity, even under optimal conditions, to make doubtful its general utility as a selection device.

Now, this leads to what I have called a very interesting paradox. We are forced to conclude that the most widely and confidently used technique of personnel selection is one for which there is surprisingly little evidence of validity. This curious situation appears to have its parallel in the clinical field in the current popularity of projective techniques, largely unvalidated for predictive purposes. There is also an analogy in the field of education where widespread use of essay examinations continues, although they have in many studies been shown to have very serious deficiencies.

I am very curious about what it is that these techniques have in common. In all three instances, the choice of technique is obviously based on factors other than evidence of validity. Now, I don't pretend to know what these factors are, but I have a hunch as to what is going on. Note that in each of these three instances, the technique is chosen and used by professional persons confronted with the necessity of making decisions about people—decisions which are significant in the organization of which they are a part or to the persons about which they are made. One cannot take lightly such responsibilities as deciding whether it is A or B that is hired for a particular job, C or D that goes to a mental hospital, E or F that gets into medical school. Ideally such decisions should be made on the basis of tested techniques with high predictive validity.

Unfortunately, as we know, such techniques don't exist. The best of our tools lead to but fallible predictions of later criterion behavior in all of these domains. They enable us to guess right much more often than wrong, but they are still subject to many errors of prediction.

In the case of psychometric tests, we go about calculating the correlation, and so we have a reasonably precise estimate of our accuracy and of the magnitude of our errors. In the impersonal situation of a selection program based on psychometric procedures, we seem to be able to tolerate the truth of our fallibility, knowing at least that we are not making as many errors as we would make if we didn't use these things. Now, in many situations, many persons do not appear to be able to accept the inevitability of errors in decisions and in predictions, especially about important decisions. Such persons go about idealistically searching for an instrument with more sensitivity to human behavior and personality. Noting evidences of such sensitivity in the writings of poets, dramatists, and philosophers, they conclude that the best instrument for the task is another human being, perhaps themselves. They then proceed to try out some newly developed instrument, or an old one that they have heard of someone else using; they interview a few people and interpret their handwriting or read their essays or read their *Draw-a-Picture Test* or something else—and lo and behold, the instrument seemed to work and work well.

Since the instrument, that is the human being, and the technique worked so well why shouldn't it be used for some practical purpose such as in a selection situation? And so the interviewer and projectionist and the proponent of the essay test go to work. In each case the technique is apt to be employed by a person already pretty well convinced of the validity or the correctness of the decision that he is making. Under the circumstances it is not surprising that the user of the technique rarely finds occasion to submit himself and the technique to a true validity check. Instead, as a result of each decision made, a decision which just doesn't dare be wrong, he becomes more and more convinced of the validity of the technique and of himself. If someone else insists on investigating the validity of the technique he can find all sorts of good reasons why the results of the study aren't to be taken seriously. The most common is the criterion isn't any good, or "I am not surprised that you didn't find that bunch of interviewers so good; they aren't very well trained." But the implication is always, "If I hadn't been too busy, if you would have checked on me you would have found that my validity is good."

Once having committed oneself to the position that a human being is the most essential part of the assessment process, it follows that the choice of specific techniques to be used is likely to be one that enhances the role of the human being who uses it. What are the conditions that lead to an enhancement of the feeling of the importance of the user on the part of the user? It should be one that provides for maximum flexibility, that is, he can adapt it to every situation. There should be nothing cut and dried about it. He can be the judge as to how the interview should go. It should be one that requires the extensive use of good judgment, his good judgment. Furthermore, it should be one that provides a maximum of information to be integrated by the human mind. The more information you get the better judgment you make. This is just horse sense, isn't it? Anybody knows that to be true. The interview, especially the unstructured interview, rates high in each of these respects, and hence I suggest that it serves admirably to reduce the threat of anxiety which otherwise would be present in persons who accept the responsibility for making judgments about decisions important in the lives of other people. I really think that when we place in the hands of a person the responsibility for making judgments like this, we have to give him the right to use whatever technique of anxiety-reduction that he finds convenient. Whether it has any validity or not, as long as we insist on his making judgments for which we don't have any better means of making good judgments, then we ought to let him believe in anything he wants and people can get the wildest ideas as to what they should believe in. . . .

IMPLICATIONS OF THE RESEARCH RESULTS

What I have tried to do is look at the selection interview and ask why it is that the validity research turns out as it does. Information, whether obtained in an interview, from an autobiography, or from a transcript, is useful only if one knows its relevance to the criterion or criteria one is attempting to predict. If such knowledge is not available, there is a real risk that the information will be used in a manner that will reduce the accuracy of the predictions that are made. As an example—and an illustration of how one can make inferences about the implicit "theory" or hypothesis used by interviewers or members of an admissions committee—let me refer briefly to certain of the findings from a current study. In the study we are doing at the University of Michigan we find the best single predictor of general medical achievement (as measured by over-all grades and *National Board Examination* scores) to be premedical college grades. We also find, curiously enough, that the number of premedical credit hours in inorganic chemistry and in biology submitted by the applicant is negatively correlated with medical school grades. This is not surprising, I think. The weak student, who feels himself weak, or whose adviser feels the student is weak, is very apt to take additional courses in chemistry or biology. Medical educators may not like it, but at least some misguided advisers recommend this. At any rate, we find a significantly negative correlation between the number of hours in such courses and our criterion of medical achievement.

It so happens that in this study we also have the ratings assigned each applicant by the five members of the admissions committee; thus, we are able to relate the ratings of these judges not only to the criterion but also to all of the other predictor variables. Although this involves a great deal of computation we are fortunate in having available an electronic computer. All we have to do is digest the results afterwards! We were particularly interested to discover that one of the five judges doesn't allow his judgment to be influenced at all by the amount of chemistry or biology on an applicant's record. His ratings, although not as predictive as premedical grades alone, are the best of the ratings for the several members of the admissions committee. The other four members of the medical admissions committee, it turns out, all make the mistake of allowing themselves to be favorably influenced by the number of hours of chemistry or biology in the transcript; they rate such people as better risks, which in turn reduces the validity of their prediction.

In closing I am going to stick my neck out and predict with a very high level of confidence that the selection interview will continue to be a widely used and highly respected technique. No amount of evidence, negative evidence, regarding its validity seems likely to change the situation. I predict that the popularity of the interview will decrease only when and to the degree that more valid techniques and devices are developed to do the practical jobs of selection in our complex society. These must be done by somebody and in some way.

26.

MMPI: Professional Use by Professional People

STARKE R. HATHAWAY

Second only to the interview, the personality questionnaire or self-report inventory is the most commonly used technique for the assessment of personality. The MMPI (Minnesota Multiphasic Personality Inventory) is perhaps the most widely used and, in certain respects, the most carefully constructed of these questionnaires. The MMPI consists of 550 statements, covering a wide range of topics from general interests to psychiatric symptomatology, to which the test-taker indicates his agreement or disagreement. The clinically significant items of the various scales that comprise the MMPI were derived empirically by comparing the responses of a large number of psychiatrically disturbed patients with the responses of people who could be reasonably assumed to be mentally "normal." These scales were then checked out with a second group of disturbed patients, and items that did not continue to discriminate between patients and "normals" were deleted from the scales (a process known as "cross-validation"). The end-result of these procedures was a series of scales that provide an objective assessment of some of the major personality characteristics associated with psychological maladjustment.

Several years ago the MMPI and tests like it came under considerable fire from social critics, the public, and even from congressional committees. They all felt that the tests asked improper questions, represented an invasion of privacy and, when asked of job applicants, violated their Fifth Amendment rights. Starke Hathaway is one of the originators of the MMPI. Here is his response to these criticisms, in the course of which he

Reprinted from *American Psychologist*, 1964, *19*, pp. 204–10. Copyright 1964 by the American Psychological Association. Reprinted by permission.

describes the rationale for the test. Are you satisfied with his answers?

THIS LONG letter was prompted by a courteous inquiry that I received. The inquiry referred to the use of the MMPI as an aid in the selection of policemen from among applicants. It was pointed out that there are laws against inquiry about religious affiliation and the specific issue was the presence in the MMPI of items relating to religion.

LETTER TO MR. R.

First I would like to express my appreciation of your reasonably expressed inquiry about the MMPI as possibly offensive in the statements that relate to religious activities and which might provide personal information on which discriminatory acts might be based. Because of sporadic public antagonism to psychological testing, and in view of our mutual concern for our civil liberties, I am going to answer you at considerable length and with unusual care. I shall send copies of this answer to the Psychological Corporation and to others who may be concerned. Let me assure you at the outset that I believe I am proceeding from a considered position rather than from a defensive attitude that could lead me to irrationally protect the MMPI, other such tests, or psychologists in general. I believe that I would be among the first to criticize some of the uses to which tests are put, and some of those who use them improperly. I must also immediately make it clear that I am antagonistic to ignorant attacks upon tests. Tests are not offensive elements; the offensive elements, if any, come with the misuse of tests. To attack tests is, to a certain extent, comparable to an attack upon knives. Both good and bad use of knives occurs because they are sharp instruments. To eliminate knives would, of course, have a limiting effect upon the occurrence of certain hostile acts, but it would also greatly limit the activities of surgeons. I simply discriminate between the instrument and the objectives and applications of the persons who wield it. I am calling attention to the difference between a switchblade knife, which is good for nothing but attack, and a scalpel knife, good for healing purposes but which can also be used as a weapon. I hope that no one will think that any test was devised in the same spirit that switchblade knives were devised. It is absurd if someone holds the belief that psychologists malignantly developed instruments such as the MMPI for use against the welfare of man, including of course man's personal liberties and rights. But if the MMPI and such tests have origins analogous to the scalpel, and are really perversely used to man's disadvantage, we are properly concerned. Let me turn to a history of the MMPI items about which you have inquired.

I should begin with an account of the origin of the MMPI itself. I believe I am competent to do this and I hope you will see that its origins were motivated toward virtue as I have suggested above. In about 1937, J. C. McKinley, then head of the Department of Neuropsychiatry of the Medical School at the University of Minnesota, supported me in a venture which grew out of a current problem in our psychopathic hospital. The problem lay in the fact that insulin therapy as a treatment method for certain forms of mental disease had just become a widespread method of treatment. Different clinics were finding highly varied values. Some reported the treatment to be exceedingly effective; others said it was ineffective. The treatment was somewhat dangerous to patients, and it was exceedingly expensive in terms of hospitalization and nursing care. McKinley happened to be one of the neuropsychiatrists of the time who felt that more careful investigation should be undertaken before such treatments were applied, and in particular before we used them on our patients.

It occurred to us that the difficulty in evaluation of insulin treatment lay largely in the fact that there was no good way to be assured that the patients treated by this method in one clinic were like those treated in another clinic. This was due to the fact that the estimations of the nature of a person's mental illness and of its severity were based upon professional judgment, and could vary with the training background of the particular psychiatrist as well as with his personal experiences. Obviously, if the patients treated at one center were not like those treated at another center, the outcome of treatment might be different. At that time there was no psychological test available that would have helped to remove the diagnostic decisions on the patients in two clinics from the personal biases of the local staffs. There was no way that our hospital staff could select a group of patients for the new treatment who would be surely comparable in diagnosis and severity of illness to those from some other setting. It became an obvious possibility that one might devise a personality test which, like intelligence tests, would somewhat stabilize the identification of the illness and provide an estimate of its severity. Toward this problem the MMPI research was initiated.

I have established that decisions about the kind and severity of mental illness depend upon the psychological examinations of the psychiatrists and other professional persons. The items upon which the judgments are based constitute the symptoms of mental maladjustment or illness. Such symptoms have for many, many years been listed in the textbooks of psychiatry and clinical psychology that treat with mental disorder. These symptoms are verbal statements from or about the patient. The simplest and most obvious form of these symptoms are statements that confess feelings of unhappiness, depression, and the like. The statements may also be less personal, as in complaints about one's lot in life and about the inability to find employment or the mistreatment by others.

In summary, the symptoms of mental illness and unhappiness are represented in verbal complaints or statements that relate to personal feelings or personal experiences or reactions to job and home. It should be immediately apparent that unlike most physical illnesses, these verbally presented complaints or symptoms usually do not permit direct observation by others. If a patient reports a painful nodule or abdominal pain, the reported pain can usually be observed by some physical or nonverbal means that lends credence to the complaint. Many symptoms of mental illness are contrastingly difficult to observe by nonverbal means. It is almost impossible to establish that the person presenting the symptom is actually suffering from a distortion of his psychologically healthy mental state by some psychological complex. There is much arbitrariness even in the statement, "I am unhappy." Frequently no physical observation can be brought to bear upon the statement. The complainant may look unhappy and may even add that he is suicidal, yet friends and the examiner can agree that he is, "just asking for sympathy, is no worse off than the average." There is no way of solidly deciding what the words really mean. This point is crucial to what I am writing. If it is not clear at this point, reference books on semantics should be consulted. S. I. Hayakawa would be a good source.

I know of no method which will permit us to absolutely assess unhappiness or mental illness, either as to kind or severity, unless we start from inescapable symptoms that are verbally expressed and subject to the vagaries in the personal connotations of words and phrases. In initiating the research upon what was to produce the MMPI, we collected as many as we could find of the symptomatic statements recognized by authorities as indicative of unhappiness and mental illness. There were hundreds of these statements. We had at one time well over a thousand of them. Every one of these symptomatic statements had already been written into the literature or had been used as a practical bit of clinical evidence in the attempt to understand patients. I repeat this because I want to thoroughly emphasize that every item in the MMPI came from assumed relationships to the assessment of human beings for better diagnosis and treatment of possible mental illness.

Now with all this preamble I am prepared to discuss the particular items that you have highlighted in your letter. It happens that, among the many items collected and finally selected to make up the MMPI, there were at least 19 relating to religion in one way or another (see Table 26–1).

TABLE 26–1

	Male		Female	
	True	No Answer	True	No Answer
I am very religious (more than most people).	8	9	11	9
Religion gives me no worry.	83	4	70	4
I go to church almost every week.	42	3	52	4
I pray several times every week.	50	3	83	2
I read in the Bible several times a week.	21	5	30	3
I feel sure that there is only one true religion.	49	8	51	11
I have no patience with people who believe there is only one true religion.	56	4	47	10
I believe there is a God.	92	5	96	2
I believe there is a devil and a hell in afterlife.	63	14	67	14
I believe in a life hereafter.	76	12	87	7
I believe in the second coming of Christ.	57	18	68	12
Christ performed miracles such as changing water into wine.	69	16	77	15
The only miracles I know of are simply tricks that people play on one another.	37	10	27	14
A minister can cure disease by praying and putting his hand on your head.	4	10	5	11
Everything is turning out just like the prophets of the Bible said it would.	52	29	54	32
My soul sometimes leaves my body.	8	18	5	12
I am a special agent of God.	14	13	16	21
I have had some very unusual religious experiences.	20	5	13	2
I have been inspired to a program of life based on duty which I have since carefully followed.	42	14	50	15

I have listed these items to remind you again of the ones you cited, and I have added others that may further illustrate what I am saying. Now you have asked why we included these statements on religion among the possible symptoms of psychological maladjustment. Why should these items still appear in the MMPI?

In the first instance, the subject matter evidenced in the symptoms of depressed or otherwise mentally disturbed persons often largely centers in religion. There is a well-recognized pattern of psychological distortion to which we apply the term religiosity. When we use the word "religiosity," we indicate a symptomatic pattern wherein the process of an intercurrent psychological maladjustment is evidenced by extremes of religious expression that are out of the usual context for even the deeply religious person. A bishop friend of mine once illustrated the problem he sometimes had in this connection by his account of a parishioner who had routinely given a tithe as his offering toward support of the church, but who, within a few weeks, had increased the amount he gave until it was necessary for him to embezzle money for his weekly offering. Surely, my friend said, there is more here than ordinary devotion; there is something which should be considered from another frame of reference. In this anecdote there is an element of the symptomatic pattern, religiosity. But, as is true of nearly every other aspect of human personality to which the MMPI refers, no one item will ordinarily establish this distortion of the ordinarily meaningful position of religion. And no one item can be used to detect the problem as it occurs in various persons. Two persons rarely express even their usual religious feelings in identical ways.

It never occurred to us in selecting these items for the MMPI that we were asking anything relative to the particular religion of our patients. It obviously did not occur to us that there were other than the Christian orientation wherein religiosity might be observed. Because of this oversight on our part, several of our MMPI symptoms that we assumed were indicative of religiosity happen to be obviously related to the Christian religion, although we find that most persons simply translate to their own orientation if it is different. I should hasten to add that although these symptoms were hoped to be specific to persons who suffer from religiosity, they have not all turned out that way. Not every aspect of religion is at times a symptom of mental illness. Certainly it is obvious that there is nothing symptomatic in admitting to one's personal acceptance or rejection of several of the items. The point at which a group of items becomes consistent in suggesting symptoms is subtle to distinguish. As my bishop friend's story illustrated, it is not unusual that one contributes to religious work even though there exists a doubtful extreme. As I will show below, all these items are endorsed or rejected by some ordinary, normal people. If any of the items have value toward clinical assessment, the value comes in combination with other items which probably will not seem to relate to religion.

The MMPI, which started out so small and inconspicuously, has become a world-known and -used instrument. We did not expect this outcome. If I were to select new items, I would again include items that related to religiosity. I would this time, of course, try to avoid the implication that the religiosity occurred only among adherents to the Christian faith. I am obviously unhappy about the limited applicability of these items, but I am, in the same sense, unhappy about other items in the MMPI. A considerable number of the items have been challenged by other groups from other standpoints. By this I mean only to remind those concerned about these religiosity items that there are frankly stated items on sex, there are items on body functions, there are items on certain occupations; in fact, there are items on most every aspect of psychological life that can be symptomatic of maladjustment and unhappiness. If the psychologist cannot use these personal items to aid in the assessment of people, he suffers as did the Victorian physician who had to examine his female patients by feeling the pulse in the delicate hand thrust from behind a screen. I shall come back to this point later, but it is obvious that if we were making a new MMPI, we would again be faced either with being offensive to subgroupings of people by personal items they object to or, if we did not include personal items and were inoffensive, we would have lost the aim of the instrument.

One may protest that the MMPI is intended for the patient, the mentally ill person, not applicants to schools, high-school children, or to those being considered for jobs. I cannot give a general defense of every such use, but this is a time when preventive health is being emphasized. We urge everyone to get chest X rays and to take immunizing shots. We are now beginning to advocate general surveys with such psychological instruments as the MMPI. The basic justification is the same. We hope to identify potential mental breakdown or delinquency in the school child before he must be dragged before us by desperate parents or by other authority. We hope to hire police, who are given great power over us, with assurance that those we put on the rolls should have good personal qualities for the job. This is not merely to protect us, this also is preventive mental health, since modern job stability can trap unwary workers into placements that leave them increasingly unhappy and otherwise maladjusted. If the personality of an applicant is not appropriate to the job, neither employer nor applicant should go ahead. We have always recognized the employer's use of this principle in his right to personal interview with applicants. Since the items and responses are on record, the MMPI and such devices could be considered to be a more fair method of estimation than the personal interview, and, when they are machine scored, they make possible much greater protection from arbitrary personal judgments and the open ended questions that are standard for personal interviews.

It seems to me that the MMPI examination can be rather comparable to the physical examination for selection of persons. One would not wish to hire a person with a bad heart when the job required behavior that was dangerous to him. I think it would be equally bad to hire a person as a policeman whose psychological traits were inappropriate and then expect him to do dangerous things or shoot to kill as a policeman is expected to do. There is, from physical and psychological examinations, a protection to the person being hired as well as to those hiring him. This is not meant as an argument for the use of the MMPI in every placement that requires special skills or special personality traits. I am arguing a general point.

I would next like to take up MMPI items to bring out a new line of evidence which, I am sorry to say, is not familiar to some psychologists, but which is of importance in giving you an answer to your questions. Turn again to the above items, particularly to the "True" response frequencies. We will look at implications about the people taking the MMPI as we interpret the True frequencies of response for these items.

Before we do so, we should consider the source of the frequency figures. The males and females who provided these standard data, which are the basis for all MMPI standards, were persons who came to the University Hospitals bringing patients or who were around the hospitals at the time when we were collecting data. Only those were tested who were not under a doctor's care and who could be reasonably assumed to be normal in mind and body. These persons, whom we call the normal adult cross-section group, came from all over Minnesota, from every socioeconomic and educational level; there is reason to believe that they are a proper representation of the rank and file people of Minnesota. It is probably well known that, in the main, Minnesota population was drawn from North European stock, is largely Christian in background, and has a rather small number in the several minority groups. Certainly, it can hardly be said that this population is unduly weighted with extremists in the direction of over-emphasis upon religion or in atheism or in other belief characteristics. Probably one would expect this population to be rather more religious than the average for all the states. Finally, the majority of the persons who provided these basic norms were married persons and most were parents. Data given in the table can be found in the fundamental book on the MMPI, *An MMPI Handbook* by Dahlstrom and Welsh (1960).

But now consider the items. Let us assume, as is often naively assumed, that when one answers an item one tells the truth about oneself. Of course, there is no requirement that those who take the MMPI should tell the truth, and this is a very important point. Also, I have tried to establish that truth is a very complicated semantic concept. But let us assume for the moment that people do tell the truth as they see it. Take the item, "I go to church almost every week." According to the data given, 42% of the men and 52% of the women go to church almost every week. Now these data are representative of the whole state. I am sure that ministers of the state would be gratified if all these people were reporting accurately. Parenthetically, I suppose that "church" was read as "synagogue" or "temple" without much trouble. But I do not know what percentage of people are actually estimated to go to some church almost every week. At any rate I cannot conceive that 42% of the men of the state of Minnesota are in church nearly every week even if 52% of the women are. I even cannot conceive that half of the men in Minnesota and 83% of the women actually pray several times a week. I might imagine that 21% of the men and 30% of the women would read in the Bible several times a week. This would represent about one-fifth of all the men and about one-third of all the women. My real impression is that people simply do not know that much about the Bible. However, take the next item. Here it says that one feels sure there is only one true religion. To this about half of the men and half of the women answered True. Perhaps these might be considered bigoted, but what of the ones who have obviously answered false? There seems to be a great deal of religious tolerance here; about half of the persons of Minnesota do not even express a belief that there is only one true religion.

It is true that a high percentage say they believe there is a God. This seems to be a noncommittal item, since most people are aware that God has many meanings. The item which follows it, however, which permits denying or accepting a belief in a devil and hell in afterlife, is quite interesting. Twenty-three percent of men and 19% of women reject this belief. By contrast, a life hereafter is denied by 24% of men and by 13% of women. The second coming of Christ is expected by only 57% of men and 68% of women if we accept what these figures seem to say. Again, with reversal, Christ as a miracle worker is doubted by 31% of men and by 23% of women. Stated more directly, 37% of men and 27% of women come straight out and say that miracles were not performed. The item apparently includes Old and New Testament sources among others. On down in the list, one finds that only 14% of men and 16% of women believe themselves to be special agents of God.

I think I have gone over enough of these items to provide a suggestion of what I am going to next point out. But I would like to add two more MMPI items in sharper illustration of the point. These two additional items have nothing obvious to do with religion. The first of them is, "I almost never dream," and the second is, "I dream frequently." One of the first things we found in the early studies of MMPI items was that the same person frequently answered True to both these items. When asked about the seeming contradiction, such a person would respond, among other possibilities, by saying to the first item that surely he had very few dreams. But, coming to the next item, he changed his viewpoint to say that he dreamed frequently as compared to some of the people he knew. This shift of emphasis led us to recognize that, in addition to the general semantic problem developed above, when people respond to items, they also do not usually respond with the connotations we expect. Apparently even if the people are telling a truth of some kind, one would need an interview with them to know what they really intend to report by answering True or False. I suppose this is similar to the problem of the oath of allegiance over which some people are so concerned. One may state that he is loyal to the United States, for example, yet really mean that he is deeply convinced that its government should be overthrown and that, with great loyalty to his country, he believes revolution to be the only salvation for the country. However much we might object to it, this belief would permit a person to swear to his loyalty in complete honesty. I think most everyone is aware of this problem about oaths, and it is a routine one with MMPI item responses.

In summary of all this, if one wished to persecute those who by their answers to these items seemed inconsistent with some religious or atheistic pattern of beliefs, there would be an embarrassingly large number of ordinary people in Minnesota who would be open to suspicion both ways. In reality, the responses made to these items have many variations in truth and meaning. And it would betray considerable ignorance of the practical psychology of communication if any absolute reliance were placed on responses.

As a final but most significant point relative to these items, I should point out that administration of the MMPI requires that those who are taking the test be clearly informed that they may omit any item they do not wish to answer for whatever purpose. I have never seen any studies that have drawn conclusions from the omission of particular items by a particular person. We found that items among these that are being considered were unusually frequently omitted. You may notice this in the No Answer columns. One-third of all the respondents failed to answer the item relative to the Bible and the prophets, for example. This is a basic fact about the MMPI and such tests, and I cannot see why this freedom will not permit to each person the latitude to preserve his privacy if he is afraid. Still again I would add that, in many settings, possibly nearly every setting, where the MMPI is used in group administration, those who take it are permitted to refuse the whole test. I admit that this might seem prejudicial, and I suspect that if anyone chooses to protect himself, he will do it by omitting items rather than by not taking the test at all. Is refusal to take the test any different from refusing to subject oneself to an employment or admission interview by a skilled interviewer? I think that some people who have been writing about the dangers of testing must have an almost magical belief in tests. Sometimes, when I feel so at a loss in attempting to help someone with a psychological problem, I wish that personality tests were really that subtle and powerful.

Groups of items called scales, formed into patterns called profiles, are the useful product of tests like the MMPI. I note that in your inquiry you show an awareness that the MMPI is usually scored by computers. The scales that are used for most interpretation include 10 "clinical" scales. These are the ones that carry most of the information. Several other scales indicate whether the subject understood and followed the directions. No one of these main scales has less than 30 items in it and most of them have many more than 30. The scores from the machine come back not only anonymously indicating the number of items answered in a way that counts on the scale, but the scores are usually already transformed into what we call T or standard scores. These T scores are still more remote from the particular items that make up a scale. The graphic array of T scores for the scales are finally printed into the profile.

In this connection, there is a very pretty possibility offered by the development of computer scoring. If we wish to take advantage of the presumed advantages of the use of tests, yet be assured that particular item responses shall not be considered, then we only need to be assured that those using the test do not score it, must send it straightway to the computer center, and, in the end, receive back only the profiles which are all that should be used in any case. The original test may be destroyed.

The scales of the profile were not arbitrarily set up. The MMPI is an experimentally derived instrument. If an item counts on a scale, I want to make it very clear that that item counts, not because some clinician or somebody thought that the item was significant for measuring something about human personality, but it counts because in the final analysis well-diagnosed groups of maladjusted, sometimes mentally ill persons answered the item with an average frequency differing from the average frequency of the normative group that I have used for the above illustrative data. This is an exceedingly significant point and is probably least often understood by those who have not had psychometric training. No one read or composed these items to decide what it meant if one of them were answered True or False. The meanings of the items came from the fact that persons with a certain kind of difficulty answered in an average way different from the "normal" standard. For example, the item "I go to church almost every week" is counted on a scale for estimating the amount of depression. We did not just decide that going to church was related to depression. We had the response frequencies from men who complained that they were depressed. They answered True with a frequency of only 20%. You will note that the normals answered True with a frequency of 42%—22% more often. Now this difference also turned up for women who were depressed. We adopted a False response to this item as a count on the depression scale of the MMPI.

We do not even now know why depressed people say they go to church less often. Note that you are not depressed if you say False to this one item. Actually, 55% of the normals answered False. Use of the item for an MMPI scale depended on the fact that even more of the depressed persons answered False and so if you say False you have added one item more in common with depressed people than with the normals despite the fact that more than half the normals answered as you did.

Even psychologists very familiar with the MMPI cannot tell to which scale or scales an item belongs without looking it up. People often ask for a copy of a test so they can cite their objections to items they think objectionable, and they assume that the meaning of the item is obvious and that they can tell how it is interpreted. I am often asked what specified items mean. I do not know because the scoring of the scales has become so abstracted that I have no contact with items.

One more point along this line. Only 6 of the above 19 items are counted on one of the regular scales that are mostly used for personality evaluation. Four more are used on a measure that is only interpreted in estimation of the ability of the subject to follow directions and to read well enough. In fact, about 200 of the whole set of items did not end up on any one of the regularly used scales. But, of course, many of these 200 other items occur on one or another of the many experimental MMPI scales that have been published.

We cannot change or leave out any items or we lose an invaluable heritage of research in mental health. To change even a comma in an item may change its meaning. I would change the words of some items, omit some, and add new ones if I could. A new test should be devised, but its cost would be on the order of a $100,000 and we are not at this time advanced enough so that the new one would be enough better to compensate for the loss of the research and diagnostic value of the present MMPI even in view of its manifest weaknesses.

The subject of professional training brings me to my next line of response. It is appropriate that the public should be aware of the uses of such tests as the MMPI, but I have repeatedly pointed out that it is far more important that the public should be aware of the persons who are using the test and of the uses to which it is put. In this context, the distributor of the MMPI, the Psychological Corporation of New York City, accepts and practices the ethical principles for test distributors that have been promulgated by the American Psychological Association. These rules prohibit the sale of tests to untrained or incompetent persons. Use or possession of the MMPI by others is prohibited but, since this carries no present penalty, the distributor is helpless except for his control of the supply. Tests, as I have said above, are not like switchblade knives, designed to be used against people; they offer potential contributions to happiness. And I cannot believe that a properly accredited clinical psychologist or psychiatrist or physician who may use the MMPI would under any circumstances use it to the disadvantage of the persons being tested. If he does so, he is subject to the intraprofessional ethical-practice controls that are explicit and carry sanctions against those of us who transgress. The MMPI provides data which, like certain medical data, are considered by many to be helpful in guidance and analysis and understanding of people. Of course, in the making of this point, I am aware that there is no absolute meaning to what is ethical. What one group may think should be done about a certain medical-examination disclosure may be considered by another group to be against the patient's interest. I cannot do more than extend this ubiquitous ethical dilemma to the use of the personality test.

The essential point is that such tests should not be used except in professional circles by professional people and that the data it provides should be held confidential and be protected within the lawful practice of ethics. When these requirements are not met, there is reason for complaint. I hope I have made it clear that it is also my conviction that the MMPI will hurt no one, adult or child, in the taking of it. Without defending all uses of it, I surely defend it, and instruments like it, when they are in proper hands and for proper purposes. Monachesi and I have tested 15,000 ninth-grade school children with the MMPI. This took us into public schools all over the state, even into some parochial schools. In all of this testing, we had no difficulties with children, parents, or teachers except for a few courteous inquiries. We are now publishing what we hope will be significant data from this work, data bearing on delinquency and school dropout. We believe that this work demonstrates that properly administered, properly explained, and properly protected tests are acceptable to the public.

At the beginning of this statement I warned that I was going to make it quite long because I felt deeply on the matter. I hope I have not sounded as though I were merely being defensive, protecting us from those who would burn tests and who for good reasons are exceedingly sensitive about psychological testing. I am apologetic if I have sounded too much like the professional scientist and have seemed to talk down to the issue or to be too minutely explicit. I have not meant to insult by being unduly simple, but I have felt that I had to expand adequately on the points. As for psychologists who are those most widely applying such tests, I am aware that the public will look with increasing seriousness upon those who are entrusted with problems of mental health and the assessment of human actions.

I will end with a repetition of my feeling that, while it is desirable for the public to require ethical practices of those using tests, the public may be reassured that the psychologists, physicians, and others who use these new tests will be even more alert to apply the intra-professional controls that are a requisite to professional responsibility. But I must emphasize that it is not to public advantage to so limit these professional judgments that we fail to progress in mental-health research and applications from lack of freedom to use the best instruments we have and to develop better ones.

REFERENCE

DAHLSTROM, W. G., & WELSH, G. S. *An MMPI handbook: A guide to use in clinical practice and research.* Minneapolis: Univer. Minnesota Press, 1960.

PART VII

Behavior Disorders and Psychotherapy

27.

The Invisible Sickness

ELTON B. McNEIL

The essential data used in the study of abnormal psychology are human lives—case histories. Case histories are intensive studies of individuals that enable one to develop broader insights into the events of disordered lives. They are, in the first instance, the units from which the systematic study of abnormal personalities was constructed. (The first published material of psychoanalysis was the case history of a woman suffering from an hysterical paralysis of the right arm and legs, described by Joseph Breuer and Sigmund Freud.)

The following is a case history that would be atypical for an abnormal psychology casebook, but not unusual in the flow of human lives. Read it, then decide if you agree with the author's diagnosis.

What are the criteria according to which you judge normality or abnormality of behavior? Does abnormality imply deviance? Misery? Inability to adapt successfully to the stresses of life?

GEORGE L. was not what you would call a handsome man. His features were far from classic, his manner quiet and self-effacing. Being an English professor suited him exactly and he even looked like the stereotyped typical professor. It was as if he were genetically destined to be a professor and could not escape his fate.

Reprinted from Elton B. McNeil, *The Quiet Furies: Man and Disorder,* © 1967. Reprinted by permission of Prentice-Hall, Inc., Englewood Cliffs, New Jersey.

Bespectacled, quiet, intense, and devoted to shaping young minds—these described George in part but left out too much to be accurate. George did of course have some professorial characteristics that fit the stereotype. For example, he could never learn to tie his neck tie properly. He would begin by wrapping the tie around his neck and adjusting both ends to the same length. As a result he always ended up with the narrow back portion of the tie about three inches longer than the front. This asymmetrical catastrophe was then studiously tie-clipped into place as evidence for all to see that he had again flunked his daily test of sartorial elegance.

His students and colleagues felt there was a Christ-like quality in George's devotion to his work, and, in fact, an ex-student once wrote that George missed his calling by not becoming a religious leader. George wasn't religious in a classic sense but he was intensely reverent about human life and subscribed devoutly to the idea that the state of mankind could be improved substantially if everybody worked full time at it. He seldom mentioned this aloud since it sounded pretty corny in sophisticated company.

Whenever anyone commented on his slightly Christ-like demeanor, George would launch into a somewhat defensive, somewhat aggressive, cynical laying waste of all that most people considered holy. It was an unconvincing display—George *was* Christ-like. But, it made him nervous since his self-image was that of a person waspishly anti-establishment. George's problem was that he knew the words but couldn't carry the tune of protest. He was, congenitally, a nice guy and this birth defect was beyond remedy at the age of 45. You liked him at once for his honesty and openness, and you soon respected him for his dedication to the vital issues of life. Yet, you knew he was a "patsy," and that others would take advantage of him.

Among George L.'s problems was a crushing personal and social conscience. He cared intensely about the image he presented to other people and worked day and night to be, within reason, the kind of person others expected him to be. He was always on time, met his classes when sick or well, read term papers religiously, demeaned his talents publicly by pointing out his personal and professional short-comings, admired the "operators" among his colleagues, and was regularly distressed by the discrepancy that existed between his aspirations and his achievements. He was a little corny and sentimentally serious by current standards when he expressed his values and ideas about life but he was always inspiring to his students and they not only admired him but became devoted to him. A tight-knit cult of students swore they "would never forget him."

Sometimes George had anxiety-laden dreams in which he found himself in a situation in which he had "let somebody down terribly" by not doing what he was supposed to do at the time he was supposed to do it. In these dreams he always felt mortified and he would awaken in misery and go into work early that day. He just "felt better" if he could get at his work a little earlier. Incidentally, the chairman of the English department was a brilliant diagnostician who recognized at once George's fatal flaw. The chairman looked like a friendly Buddha but his chubby sincerity masked a practical administrative mind that never missed an opportunity to be nice to a masochist by mistreating him. George always carried an impossible course load but he never complained. It often seemed to me that he sold the tickets, showed the movie, pushed the popcorn, and swept out the theater of education while the chairman had the important task of counting the profits. It became obvious, before long, that George unconsciously enjoyed being walked on almost as much as the chairman was pleasured by accommodating him with an overload of professional responsibility.

George's two children were also a problem to him, not because they were rebellious. In fact, their mature view of life was admirable. They were quiet, sensitive, and self-contained human beings who were made uncomfortable by the bluff, hearty, hail-fellow-well-met types to which they were exposed. Working as diligently as he did and accepting professional responsibility to the extent that he did, George worried regularly about the possibility that he was neglecting his children by not being as close to them emotionally as he thought he ought to be. He was constantly oppressed by the feeling that he had failed as a parent by not being able to weigh the parts of life with sufficient care and clarity to decide what was important in the long run. In reality, his children were very attached to him. But this did not reassure him about his way of life. He frequently had serious conversations with colleagues regarding their "honest" view of his children. It was questionable if he ever got a totally honest answer but he seemed to need this regular reassurance.

George was compelled to do things for other people. If he came over to your house for an evening's conversation he always brought expensive liquor or something exotic to eat. He worried about how people accepted him and always made it a package deal—George L. and a gift. George also never complained about personal discomfort or inconvenience. He lived just beyond the city limits and some years ago he and six other families formed a kind of small community cooperative in which they not only worked as a group to construct their individual homes but through which they owned community property (a power lawnmower, a community water system, private street lights). As fate inevitably arranges, two of the six members of the community viewed their communal role as something akin to being uncrowned royalty living in gallant splendor among colorful and loyal serfs. This meant that sharing the common labor of the group was distinctly beneath their dignity and required that the bulk of their community contribution be devoted to logical arguments about community policy followed by rationalizations regarding their inability to contribute a proper share of the labor. Over a period of years George was victimized by these two families in a variety of ways. He took it, grumbled privately, and extended himself to be even more cooperative and hard working as an example to the others. It didn't work, of course. The two parasitic families shirked their responsibilities in direct proportion to his assumption of increased duties.

It was as though George had been born to suffer. His emotional investment in the chronic injustices of life seldom was applied to himself. All his resentment was directed toward the plight of deprived children neglected by an unresponsive society insufficiently concerned with human wreckage. The glaring discrepancy between the lip-service people pay to social problems and what they are willing to provide to solve them irritated him without end. The apparent hypocrisy of humanity galled George constantly. People just didn't give a damn about others and civilization was getting exactly what it deserved. In some ways George was alienated from his own society by the callousness and disinterest he saw in all those about him.

It was his unexpected plans for divorce that shocked the academic community. George was apparently such a devoted family man that he called home each day just to check on how things were going and to remind his wife of a variety of things of which she was already aware—that the children would be home early from school today, or that the steaks should be defrosted for supper. He was, perhaps, too "apparently" devoted to his family. His wife, for example, suffered a powerful but silent resentment about these daily calls since she always sensed that George treated her as if she had a limited intelligence. She always made a wry joke about it if a neighbor was there at the time the call came: "It must be George checking to see if I know the difference between hot and cold water." She tolerated this quirk in George and learned a variety of ways to assure that his constant supervision of her would roll off her back and not interfere with her labors as a wife and mother. It was a minor annoyance and George was otherwise a steady if unspectacular mate.

George's marital problem, I later discovered, lay outside the close family circle he maintained, and George's problem with the female of the species had more to do with his childhood perceptions than it did with the current state of his happiness or unhappiness as a married man. George was not the kind of person who "played around" every chance he got. He appeared quite businesslike and circumspect around the office. He was avuncular to his own office staff but he underwent a startling transformation whenever he found himself in close contact with the chairman's secretary. This woman held a strange fascination for him and he confided intimate details of his personal life to her and manufactured excuses to see her whenever he could. There was a moth-and-flame attraction that was bound to be a fatal combination.

The two of them became a departmental item before long. Everyone knew that they shared a few too many quiet luncheons together and many suspected that their Saturday labors were a mixture of work and play. There was no real proof of the true depth of their relationship but the sharp-eyed secretarial staff at once launched its usual program of assassination-by-gossip and enjoyed the scandal immensely. The inevitable, because it was inevitable, happened. First, one secretary accidentally discovered them in an intimate embrace in the file room. Next, George's wife invaded the privacy of one of their motel excursions and blackened his eye with a vigorously swung purse. George moved out of the family home, and the boss's secretary quit her job and began divorce proceedings against her engineering-student husband. The grounds for her divorce were obscure but socially polite— incompatibilty.

The scandal became even more choice and juicy when George L. and the boss's secretary openly travelled to New York together to attend a professional convention. The sight of George L. holding hands with the secretary in the lobby of the convention hotel and exchanging deep and secret glances with her was particularly shocking to his friends, not only because it seemed so totally out of character for him but because there was at least a difference of 20 years in their ages. In the last two months, it was true, George had been acting in a somewhat strange manner but this latest public display of unconventionality topped it all off. George had frantically immersed himself in an unaccustomed round of social events; he was drinking too much, acting sophisticated and gay, night-clubbing, and telling dirty jokes.

It was as if George had become a different person. He neglected his professional work almost completely and undertook a host of new and short-lived hobbies and interests. George began to dress youthfully. He abandoned his previous circle of scholarly acquaintances and took up with the cool jazz, protest, and coffee-house clan. It was a pathetic sight to see him try to wrestle age to a standstill, and, when our paths crossed, he always looked as if his anchor were dragging a little. He was losing weight and exercising regularly but these efforts were clearly painful to him and his physique was not nearly approaching Adonis-like proportions. He looked very much what he was—a middle-aged man trying desperately to repair the ravages of time and addiction to comfort. I was most concerned about the physical vigor of many of the activities he now pursued with unbounded enthusiasm. He became an ardent squash player, for example. Tennis might have been all right at his age but hard-fought competition on the squash court seemed too much for a man of his years. He began to look like a prime candidate for a cardiac arrest and the pace seemed literally to be killing him.

Interestingly, during this time (nearly six months) George never managed to take the necessary steps to divorce his wife. He was quite upset about the possible effect his newly found emotional attachment might have on his children, but he could not bring himself to talk to them or to explain what happened. Whenever George wanted to speak to his wife, he would have his secretary call to make sure he did not accidently come in contact with the kids and find himself stuttering and stammering about what was happening to all of them.

The upshot of the whole affair was that George L. never divorced his wife. His flaming romance with the boss's secretary extinguished itself almost as quickly as it had blazed to life in the first place and his disinterest in her, as I later discovered, took place shortly after she quit her job as the boss's secretary. George was sheepishly reconciled with his wife and accepted an offer from a small Eastern university where he now seems to have returned completely to his previous way of life. For six months George L. was painfully transformed into a pathetically different human being, one who learned the hard way that at his age the pattern of a lifetime is extremely difficult to change.

Nearly a year has passed since these uncomfortable events took place, and when I last talked to George, he was almost exactly the same person I once knew so well. Almost, I say, because he seems now to bear an even heavier burden of guilt than before and has redoubled his efforts to seek atonement for his extramarital escapade by way of increased diligence and dedication to his students. George was being reborn through his students every day of his life.

George was a friend rather than a patient and he came to me first to ask me to meet with his children and try to explain to them what was happening to the family. I agreed to speak to any child of his who wished to see me but I rejected his request to play the part of *pater familias* at this early stage of his marital difficulties. As he described in detail his view of his problems, I began to suspect that the last thing in the world that would be a satisfactory solution for him would be an escape from reality via a quick second marriage. In fact, the more he described the nature of his affair with the boss's secretary, the more I began to think that his paramour was a symbol of an unresolved problem that had remained alive in him from his early childhood. This secretary he was so "mad about" resembled quite closely his account of the personal characteristics that were most accurately descriptive of his mother.

The boss's secretary was, unconsciously, the equivalent of "the big man's woman"—his father's wife. The fact that this secretary did not physically resemble his mother was inconsequential as far as his unconscious was concerned. The attraction for George had less to do with the personal qualities of the particular female, it seemed to me, and more to do with the fact that she be a person privy to the secrets of the boss-man and a person who might have influence with the departmental father figure. Every anxiety George could recall about suffering the wrath or displeasure of his father had now been transferred, without his conscious knowledge, to the person of his boss. George told me that this feeling had happened to him a number of times in the past and that he had always been great friends with females who occupied this role. This was, however, the first time that he had resonated with so responsive a chord as to be swept away in a tide of overwhelming emotion and gross misjudgment. When this particular secretary responded warmly and sympathetically to him, he was unable to resist temptation and incapable of keeping the relationship on a businesslike level.

As George said, it just felt as though he had casually drifted into the romance without knowing how far he had gone. It seemed to him his emotions were genuine at the time and that this woman in this position was the answer to a number of deep cravings that had always nibbled timorously at the edge of his conscious mind. When he eventually became reconciled with his wife he felt a mixture of penetrating shame and puzzlement about the trap he had fallen into and his inability to find a way out. When I was talking to him one day about the similarity of the feelings he had toward his mother and the emotions he was experiencing with regard to his love affair, he broke down and began to cry violently. This event was the beginning of the end.

George himself made the connection between the mother he wanted so desperately to love only him and the anger and resentment he felt toward a father who always seemed to interfere in his love affair with his mother. His father (the boss) always had everything his own way and commanded the attention and affection of his mother despite the urgency of George's own felt needs. George ran a distant second to his father and was compelled to continue running this losing race currently even though all the original contestants had stopped running long ago. George's failure to win the object of his love in early life had goaded him into an impossible unconscious contest again and again, and, as I watched him run frantically, I was also able to detect the desperation he felt so deeply. He was forever running but he knew he was losing.

His emotional entanglement with this particular boss's woman was a nightmarish distortion of feelings that most of us long ago managed to cope with in more mature ways.

Typically, the male who loves his mother comes to realize the hopelessness of his quest for her exclusive ownership and seeks, in her stead, a reasonable substitute for the unattainable. For George, this event never took place. Symbolically, and in fantasy, George still felt he could win even though the odds were clearly against him. He was fighting an ancient battle but its purpose was as clear as it had been when he was only three years old.

George had a variety of problems, each of them highly visible to his friends as well as his critics. Yet, George's diagnosis was a strange one. George was normal. George was normal and he was a typical citizen at the same moment that he was atypical in our society. Had George never been involved in scandalous behavior he would have been invisible socially and his name would have been remembered only by those closest to him. George was, like most of us, ordinary. He had grown to maturity carrying with him a great many disordered remnants of his past life and these unsolved problems both shaped his adult personality and plunged him into a social trap from which he could not escape. George faced a challenge that all of us face, but he solved it badly and impulsively. He was as much the victim as the cause of his enmeshment with life and, like most of us, did the best he could with what resources were available to him.

The average person seldom becomes as acutely aware of the imperfections in his personality structure as George. It was as if the whole structure of his life had collapsed on him and he was unable, alone, to disengage himself from the rubble of his existence. George had all the virtues and few of the faults that the majority of us have, but, when he came face-to-face with impossible circumstances, he was without the necessary resources to manage them. Each of us undergoes a certain amount of natural upheaval in life and we weather it badly or well depending, in great part, on the resources at our command. With George it was a case of too little and too late. He lacked what he needed at the moment in his life when it was most vital that he not be short of supplies.

Yet, George was normal. As normal as most of us are and as subject to the vagaries of fate. Look around you and think about your closest friends. If they are young people, they have ahead of them a life filled with trials and tribulations beyond their capacity to envision. It is possible that more than one of your close friends will be divorced, remarry badly, be depressed and upset, not know which way to turn for advice and guidance and, yet, be normal.

Normality is a very strange thing. One can be normal and experience a great many painful blows in life. Normality is not determined by what fate deals a person. It is judged, rather, in terms of the manner with which one responds to and rebounds from these events. Life was never advertised as less than a harsh struggle and it is how we manage this combat that determines what will become of us. George was normal and he suffered all the pains and afflictions most normals do. Perhaps he had somewhat more than his share, but life is like that—so much of it is accident and uncontrollable circumstance that it sometimes surprises me that so many of us manage to survive relatively intact.

George was normal. As you read the personal histories of those less than normal you must be wary of judging too quickly or judging too harshly. Your normal life may be as incident-laden as was George's. "Normal" encompasses a great and broad range of humanity that continually fights adversity and it includes those among us who visibly or invisibly protest against the way things are and seem briefly to be maladjusted to life. To live is to have problems and in solving these problems we grow emotionally, but we grow at the cost of the formation of measurable scar tissue in our psychic structure. One day you may come across George or his counterpart and be tempted to discuss his way of life as inappropriate as a model for your existence. I would ask only that you be tolerant and understanding of the frailty of mankind.

George destroyed his reputation as a teacher when his personal life ceased to be a model of an idealized public morality. In this action he achieved once again a tension-laden expression of his basic masochism —his need to be punished and put-upon by people in order to feel worthwhile as a human being. In the early conflict with his father over being dispossessed in the affections of his mother, George learned to be passive and to gain acceptance by self-sacrifice. The Oedipal contest he lost in childhood was reborn, in disguise, in his affair with the boss's secretary. Like the refighting of all lost battles, this conflict was destined again to make him the loser since the course of ancient history is seldom altered by new interpretations of the way things should have been rather than the way things really were.

George was, as most of us are, a person of many parts and aspects, only some of which were available for conscious inspection when he peered inside himself. As he viewed his professional and personal life, he was pleased but restless. Something was missing but that something only became apparent in the holocaust of a self-created crisis of emotional involvement. George learned what every used-car salesman knows almost instinctively—the purchaser of a four-door, basic black, manual shift, six cylinder car has a deep rooted longing for the impractically snappy, multi-colored, overpowered sports model. For George L. it was very much like finding himself in what he took to be the wrong—and slowest—line in a bank or supermarket. Maybe he had made the wrong choice and was missing out on life.

So George impulsively changed lines only to find that the second choice was little better than the first. What he lacked in his relationship with his wife, he found in the arms of his paramour, but his new solution to an ancient problem proved to be less than adequate at this susceptible time in his life. George learned a lesson about life but it was a costly course of instruction. His relationship with his wife can never be quite what it was before, and his confidence about knowing himself will never again be what he once thought it was. "Once burned, twice shy" will undoubtedly be his motto in the future but the fundamental needs and longings that impelled him once to ill-considered action remain alive, if dormant, within him. These needs may never surface again to complicate George's life in so extreme a fashion, but they remain an important part of his total psychological makeup. George will continue to be a complex human being—like most of us—and he will continue to lead some part of his life with some measure of anger and despair below the surface.

George is as normal as you, and I, and most others we know. Disorders are not the province of the few. They are, rather, the state of being of all of us at some time in our lives.

28.

The Black Norm

WILLIAM H. GRIER and PRICE M. COBBS

Many years ago cultural anthropologists, like Ruth Benedict,
pointed out that behavior seen as abnormal from the perspective
of mainstream, middle-class America might be accepted as
quite normal and adaptive in its own cultural setting. The point
is easily and dramatically made when we look at unfamiliar
and distant cultures, such as Melanesian island groups or Northern
Siberian tribes. But this point is equally valid when applied to
subcultures closer to home. In the following excerpt, two
experienced and perceptive black psychiatrists describe a body
of character traits that they argue are not only "normal" but are
actually essential to survival for a black man in America.

WE SUBMIT that it is necessary for a black man in America to develop
a profound distrust of his white fellow citizens and of the nation. He
must be on guard to protect himself against physical hurt. He must
cushion himself against cheating, slander, humiliation, and outright
mistreatment by the official representatives of society. If he does not so
protect himself, he will live a life of such pain and shock as to find life
itself unbearable. For his own survival, then, he must develop a *cultural paranoia* in which every white man is a potential enemy unless

Excerpted from Chapters 8 and 10 of *Black Rage*, by William H. Grier and Price
M. Cobbs, © 1968 by William H. Grier and Price M. Cobbs, Basic Books, Inc.,
Publishers, New York.

proved otherwise and every social system is set against him unless he personally finds out differently.

Every black man in America has suffered such injury as to be realistically sad about the hurt done him. He must, however, live in spite of the hurt and so he learns to know his tormentor exceedingly well. He develops a sadness and intimacy with misery which has become a characteristic of black Americans. It is a *cultural depression* and a *cultural masochism.*

He can never quite respect laws which have no respect for him, and laws designed to protect white men are viewed as white men's laws. To break another man's law may be inconvenient if one is caught and punished, but it can never have the moral consequences involved in breaking one's own law. The result may be described as a *cultural antisocialism,* but it is simply an accurate reading of one's environment—a gift black people have developed to a high degree, to keep alive.

These and related traits are simply adaptive devices developed in response to a peculiar environment. They are no more pathological than the compulsive manner in which a diver checks his equipment before a dive or a pilot his parachute. They represent normal devices for "making it" in America, and clinicians who are interested in the psychological functioning of black people must get acquainted with this body of character traits which we call the *Black Norm*. It is a normal complement of psychological devices, and to find the amount of sickness a black man has, one must first total all that appears to represent illness and then subtract the Black Norm. What remains is illness and a proper subject for therapeutic endeavor. To regard the Black Norm as pathological and attempt to remove such traits by treatment would be akin to analyzing away a hunter's cunning or a banker's prudence. This is a body of characteristics essential to life for black men in America and woe be unto that therapist who does not recognize it. . . .

Black men . . . have been so hurt in their manhood that they are now unsure and uneasy as they teach their sons to be men. Women have been so humiliated and used that they may regard womanhood as a curse and flee from it. Such pain, so deep, and such real jeopardy, that the fundamental protective function of the family has been denied. These injuries we have no way to measure.

Black men have stood so long in such peculiar jeopardy in America that a *black norm* has developed—a suspiciousness of one's environment which is necessary for survival. Black people, to a degree that approaches paranoia, must be ever alert to danger from their white fellow citizens. It is a cultural phenomenon peculiar to black Americans. And it is a posture so close to paranoid thinking that the mental disorder into which black people most frequently fall is paranoid psychosis.

Can we say that white men have driven black men mad?

An educated black woman had worked in an integrated setting for fifteen years. Compliant and deferential, she had earned promotions and pay increases by hard work and excellence. At no time had she been involved in black activism, and her only participation in the movement had been a yearly contribution to the N.A.A.C.P.

During a lull in the racial turmoil she sought psychiatric treatment. She explained that she had lately become alarmed at waves of rage that swept over her as she talked to white people or at times even as she looked at them. In view of her past history of compliance and passivity, she felt that something was wrong with her. If her controls slipped she might embarrass herself or lose her job.

A black man, a professional, had been a "nice guy" all his life. He was a hard-working non-militant who avoided discussions of race with his white colleagues. He smiled if their comments were harsh and remained unresponsive to racist statements. Lately he has experienced almost uncontrollable anger toward his white co-workers, and although he still manages to keep his feelings to himself, he confides that blacks and whites have been lying to each other. There is hatred and violence between them and he feels trapped. He too fears for himself if his controls should slip.

If these educated recipients of the white man's bounty find it hard to control their rage, what of their less fortunate kinsman who has less to protect, less to lose, and more scars to show for his journey in this land?

29.

On Being Sane in Insane Places

DAVID L. ROSENHAN

One of the issues raised in the movie *The King of Hearts* and in
Ken Kesey's novel *One Flew Over the Cuckoo's Nest* (both very
popular among students) is: Who belongs in a mental hospital
and who does not? Reports of the following article in the popular
press gave the impression that it addressed the same issue and,
further, that hospital staffs had been fooled into accepting
"pseudopatients" who were indeed quite sane. While that
interpretation is, in a limited sense, quite accurate, it passes over
the more important and deeper questions to which this research
is addressed: Is mental disorder intrapsychic, occurring within
the patients themselves, or is the mental disorder a function of the
patient's interactions with others, and is it significantly influenced
by the context in which the patients are found? Does not the very
act of labeling someone a mental patient produce a perception of
his behavior that, even by an experienced and well-intentioned
hospital staff, see according to the expected pattern? Does the
conceptualization of disordered behavior as an illness lead one to
see pathology even where it is not present? These are the questions
that you should consider while reading the following report, rather
than the simple notion of whether the research subjects successfully
tricked the hospital professionals. You might also want to consider
whether, if you were in charge of admissions to a mental hospital,
you would accept a person who reports that he has been hearing
voices and who presents himself as requiring hospitalization.

Reprinted from *Science*, Vol. 179, pp. 250–58, 19 January 1973. Copyright 1973
by the American Association for the Advancement of Science.

IF SANITY and insanity exist, how shall we know them?

The question is neither capricious nor itself insane. However much we may be personally convinced that we can tell the normal from the abnormal, the evidence is simply not compelling. It is commonplace, for example, to read about murder trials wherein eminent psychiatrists for the defense are contradicted by equally eminent psychiatrists for the prosecution on the matter of the defendant's sanity. More generally, there are a great deal of conflicting data on the reliability, utility, and meaning of such terms as "sanity," "insanity," "mental illness," and "schizophrenia" (1). Finally, as early as 1934, Benedict suggested that normality and abnormality are not universal (2). What is viewed as normal in one culture may be seen as quite aberrant in another. Thus, notions of normality and abnormality may not be quite as accurate as people believe they are.

To raise questions regarding normality and abnormality is in no way to question the fact that some behaviors are deviant or odd. Murder is deviant. So, too, are hallucinations. Nor does raising such questions deny the existence of the personal anguish that is often associated with "mental illness." Anxiety and depression exist. Psychological suffering exists. But normality and abnormality, sanity and insanity, and the diagnoses that flow from them may be less substantive than many believe them to be.

At its heart, the question of whether the sane can be distinguished from the insane (and whether degrees of insanity can be distinguished from each other) is a simple matter: do the salient characteristics that lead to diagnoses reside in the patients themselves or in the environments and contexts in which observers find them? From Bleuler, through Kretchmer, through the formulators of the recently revised *Diagnostic and Statistical Manual* of the American Psychiatric Association, the belief has been strong that patients present symptoms, that those symptoms can be categorized, and, implicitly, that the sane are distinguishable from the insane. More recently, however, this belief has been questioned. Based in part on theoretical and anthropological considerations, but also on philosophical, legal, and therapeutic ones, the view has grown that psychological categorization of mental illness is useless at best and downright harmful, misleading, and pejorative at worst. Psychiatric diagnoses, in this view, are in the minds of the observers and are not valid summaries of characteristics displayed by the observed (3–5).

Gains can be made in deciding which of these is more nearly accurate by getting normal people (that is, people who do not have, and have never suffered, symptoms of serious psychiatric disorders) admitted to psychiatric hospitals and then determining whether they were discovered to be sane and, if so, how. If the sanity of such pseudopatients were always detected, there would be prima facie evidence that a sane individual can be distinguished from the insane context in which he is found. Normality (and presumably abnormality) is distinct enough that it can be recognized wherever it occurs, for it is carried within the person. If, on the other hand, the sanity of the pseudopatients were never discovered, serious difficulties would arise for those who support traditional modes of psychiatric diagnosis. Given that the hospital staff was not incompetent, that the pseudopatient had been behaving as sanely as he had been outside of the hospital, and that it had never been previously suggested that he belonged in a psychiatric hospital, such an unlikely outcome would support the view that psychiatric diagnosis betrays little about the patient but much about the environment in which an observer finds him.

This article describes such an experiment. Eight sane people gained secret admission to 12 different hospitals (6). Their diagnostic experiences constitute the data of the first part of this article; the remainder is devoted to a description of their experiences in psychiatric institutions. Too few psychiatrists and psychologists, even those who have worked in such hospitals, know what the experience is like. They rarely talk about it with former patients, perhaps because they distrust information coming from the previously insane. Those who have worked in psychiatric hospitals are likely to have adapted so thoroughly to the settings that they are insensitive to the impact of that experience. And while there have been occasional reports of researchers who submitted themselves to psychiatric hospitalization (7), these researchers have commonly remained in the hospitals for short periods of time, often with the knowledge of the hospital staff. It is difficult to know the extent to which they were treated like patients or like research colleagues. Nevertheless, their reports about the inside of the psychiatric hospital have been valuable. This article extends those efforts.

PSEUDOPATIENTS AND THEIR SETTINGS

The eight pseudopatients were a varied group. One was a psychology graduate student in his 20's. The remaining seven were older and "established." Among them were three psychologists, a pediatrician, a psychiatrist, a painter, and a housewife. Three pseudopatients were women, five were men. All of them employed pseudonyms, lest their alleged diagnoses embarrass them later. Those who were in mental health professions alleged another occupation in order to avoid the special attentions that might be accorded by staff, as a matter of courtesy or caution, to ailing colleagues (8). With the exception of myself (I was the first pseudopatient and my presence was known to the hospital administrator and chief psychologist and, so far as I can tell, to them alone), the presence of pseudopatients and the nature of the research program was not known to the hospital staffs (9).

The settings were similarly varied. In order to generalize the findings, admission into a variety of hospitals was sought. The 12 hospitals in the sample were located in five different states on the East and West coasts. Some were old and shabby, some were quite new. Some were research-oriented, others not. Some had good staff-patient ratios, others were quite understaffed. Only one was a strictly private hospital. All of the others were supported by state or federal funds or, in one instance, by university funds.

After calling the hospital for an appointment, the pseudopatient arrived at the admissions office complaining that he had been hearing voices. Asked what the voices said, he replied that they were often unclear, but as far as he could tell they said "empty," "hollow," and "thud." The voices were unfamiliar and were of the same sex as the pseudopatient. The choice of these symptoms was occasioned by their apparent similarity to existential symptoms. Such symptoms are alleged to arise from painful concerns about the perceived meaninglessness of one's life. It is as if the hallucinating person were saying, "My life is empty and hollow." The choice of these symptoms was also determined by the *absence* of a single report of existential psychoses in the literature.

Beyond alleging the symptoms and falsifying name, vocation, and employment, no further alterations of person, history, or circumstances were made. The significant events of the pseudopatient's life history were presented as they had actually occurred. Relationships with parents and siblings, with spouse and children, with people at work and in school, consistent with the aforementioned exceptions, were described as they were or had been. Frustrations and upsets were described along with joys and satisfactions. These facts are important to remember. If anything, they strongly biased the subsequent results in favor of detecting sanity, since none of their histories or current behaviors were seriously pathological in any way.

Immediately upon admission to the psychiatric ward, the pseudopatient ceased simulating *any* symptoms of abnormality. In some cases, there was a brief period of mild nervousness and anxiety, since none of the pseudopatients really believed that they would be admitted so easily. Indeed, their shared fear was that they would be immediately exposed as frauds and greatly embarrassed. Moreover, many of them had never visited a psychiatric ward; even those who had, nevertheless had some genuine fears about what might happen to them. Their nervousness, then, was quite appropriate to the novelty of the hospital setting, and it abated rapidly.

Apart from that short-lived nervousness, the pseudopatient behaved on the ward as he "normally" behaved. The pseudopatient spoke to patients and staff as he might ordinarily. Because there is uncommonly little to do on a psychiatric ward, he attempted to engage others in conversation. When asked by staff how he was feeling, he indicated that he was fine, that he no longer experienced symptoms. He responded to instructions from attendants, to calls for medication (which was not swallowed), and to dining-hall instructions. Beyond such activities as were available to him on the admissions ward, he spent his time writing down his observations about the ward, its patients, and the staff. Initially these notes were written "secretly," but as it soon became clear that no one much cared, they were subsequently written on standard tablets of paper in such public places as the dayroom. No secret was made of these activities.

The pseudopatient, very much as a true psychiatric patient, entered a hospital with no foreknowledge of when he would be discharged. Each was told that he would have to get out by his own devices, essentially by convincing the staff that he was sane. The psychological stresses associated with hospitalization were considerable, and all but one of the pseudopatients desired to be discharged almost immediately after being admitted. They were, therefore, motivated not only to behave sanely, but to be paragons of cooperation. That their behavior was in no way disruptive is confirmed by nursing reports, which have been obtained on most of the patients. These reports uniformly indicate that the patients were "friendly," "cooperative," and "exhibited no abnormal indications."

THE NORMAL ARE NOT DETECTABLY SANE

Despite their public "show" of sanity, the pseudopatients were never detected. Admitted, except in one case, with a diagnosis of schizophrenia (10), each was discharged with a diagnosis of schizophrenia "in remission." The label "in remission" should in no way be dismissed as a formality, for at no time during any hospitalization had any question been raised about any pseudopatient's simulation. Nor are there any indications in the hospital records that the pseudopatient's status was suspect. Rather, the evidence is strong that, once labeled schizophrenic, the pseudopatient was stuck with that label. If the pseudopatient was to be discharged, he must naturally be "in remission"; but he was not sane, nor, in the institution's view, had he ever been sane.

The uniform failure to recognize sanity cannot be attributed to the quality of the hospitals, for, although there were considerable variations among them, several are considered excellent. Nor can it be alleged that there was simply not enough time to observe the pseudopatients. Length of hospitalization ranged from 7 to 52 days, with an average of 19 days. The pseudopatients were not, in fact, carefully observed, but this failure clearly speaks more to traditions within psychiatric hospitals than to lack of opportunity.

Finally, it cannot be said that the failure to recognize the pseudopatients' sanity was due to the fact that they were not behaving sanely. While there was clearly some tension present in all of them, their daily visitors could detect no serious behavioral consequences—nor, indeed, could other patients. It was quite common for the patients to "detect" the pseudopatients' sanity. During the first three hospitalizations, when accurate counts were kept, 35 of a total of 118 patients on the admissions ward voiced their suspicions, some vigorously. "You're not crazy. You're a journalist, or a professor [referring to the continual note-taking]. You're checking up on the hospital." While most of the patients were reassured by the pseudopatient's insistence that he had been sick before he came in but was fine now, some continued to believe that the pseudopatient was sane throughout his hospitalization (11). The fact that the patients often recognized normality when staff did not raise important questions.

Failure to detect sanity during the course of hospitalization may be due to the fact that physicians operate with a strong bias toward what statisticians call the type 2 error (5). This is to say that physicians are more inclined to call a healthy person sick (a false positive, type 2) than a sick person healthy (a false negative, type 1). The reasons for this are not hard to find: it is clearly more dangerous to misdiagnose illness than health. Better to err on the side of caution, to suspect illness even among the healthy.

But what holds for medicine does not hold equally well for psychiatry. Medical illnesses, while unfortunate, are not commonly pejorative. Psychiatric diagnoses, on the contrary, carry with them personal, legal, and social stigmas (12). It was therefore important to see whether the tendency toward diagnosing the sane insane could be reversed. The following experiment was arranged at a research and teaching hospital whose staff had heard these findings but doubted that such an error could occur in their hospital. The staff was informed that at some time during the following 3 months, one or more pseudopatients would attempt to be admitted into the psychiatric hospital. Each staff member was asked to rate each patient who presented himself at admissions or on the ward according to the likelihood that the patient was a pseudopatient. A 10-point scale was used, with a 1 and 2 reflecting high confidence that the patient was a pseudopatient.

Judgments were obtained on 193 patients who were admitted for psychiatric treatment. All staff who had had sustained contact with or primary responsibility for the patient—attendants, nurses, psychiatrists, physicians, and psychologists—were asked to make judgments. Forty-one patients were alleged, with high confidence, to be pseudopatients by at least one member of the staff. Twenty-three were considered suspected by one psychiatrist *and* one other staff member. Actually, no genuine pseudopatient (at least from my group) presented himself during this period.

The experiment is instructive. It indicates that the tendency to designate sane people as insane can be reversed when the stakes (in this case, prestige and diagnostic acumen) are high. But what can be said of the 19 people who were suspected of being "sane" by one psychiatrist and another staff member? Were these people truly "sane," or was it rather the case that in the course of avoiding the type 2 error the staff tended to make more errors of the first sort—calling the crazy "sane"? There is no way of knowing. But one thing is certain: any diagnostic process that lends itself so readily to massive errors of this sort cannot be a very reliable one.

THE STICKINESS OF PSYCHODIAGNOSTIC LABELS

Beyond the tendency to call the healthy sick—a tendency that accounts better for diagnostic behavior on admission than it does for such behavior after a lengthy period of exposure—the data speak to the massive role of labeling in psychiatric assessment. Having once been labeled schizophrenic, there is nothing the pseudopatient can do to overcome the tag. The tag profoundly colors others' perceptions of him and his behavior.

From one viewpoint, these data are hardly surprising, for it has long been known that elements are given meaning by the context in which they occur. Gestalt psychology made this point vigorously, and Asch (*13*) demonstrated that there are "central" personality traits (such as "warm" versus "cold") which are so powerful that they markedly color the meaning of other information in forming an impression of a given personality (*14*). "Insane," "schizophrenic," "manic-depressive," and "crazy" are probably among the most powerful of such central traits. Once a person is designated abnormal, all of his other behaviors and characteristics are colored by that label. Indeed, that label is so powerful that many of the pseudopatients' normal behaviors were overlooked entirely or profoundly misinterpreted. Some examples may clarify this issue.

Earlier I indicated that there were no changes in the pseudopatient's personal history and current status beyond those of name, employment, and, where necessary, vocation. Otherwise, a veridical description of personal history and circumstances was offered. Those circumstances were not psychotic. How were they made consonant with the diagnosis of psychosis? Or were those diagnoses modified in such a way as to bring them into accord with the circumstances of the pseudopatient's life, as described by him?

As far as I can determine, diagnoses were in no way affected by the relative health of the circumstances of a pseudopatient's life. Rather, the reverse occurred: the perception of his circumstances was shaped entirely by the diagnosis. A clear example of such translation is found in the case of a pseudopatient who had had a close relationship with his mother but was rather remote from his father during his early childhood. During adolescence and beyond, however, his father became a close friend, while his relationship with his mother cooled. His present relationship with his wife was characteristically close and warm. Apart from occasional angry exchanges, friction was minimal. The children had rarely been spanked. Surely there is nothing especially pathological about such a history. Indeed, many readers may see a similar pattern in their own experiences, with no markedly deleterious consequences. Observe, however, how such a history was translated in the psychopathological context, this from the case summary prepared after the patient was discharged.

> This white 39-year-old male . . . manifests a long history of considerable ambivalence in close relationships, which begins in early childhood. A warm relationship with his mother cools during his adolescence. A distant relationship to his father is described as becoming very intense. Affective stability is absent. His attempts to control emotionality with his wife and children are punctuated by angry outbursts and, in the case of the children, spankings. And while he says that he has several good friends, one senses considerable ambivalence embedded in those relationships also.

The facts of the case were unintentionally distorted by the staff to achieve consistency with a popular theory of the dynamics of a schizophrenic reaction (15). Nothing of an ambivalent nature had been described in relations with parents, spouse, or friends. To the extent that ambivalence could be inferred, it was probably not greater than is found in all human relationships. It is true the pseudopatient's relationships with his parents changed over time, but in the ordinary context that would hardly be remarkable—indeed, it might very well be expected. Clearly, the meaning ascribed to his verbalizations (that is, ambivalence, affective instability) was determined by the diagnosis: schizophrenia. An entirely different meaning would have been ascribed if it were known that the man was "normal."

All pseudopatients took extensive notes publicly. Under ordinary circumstances, such behavior would have raised questions in the minds of observers, as, in fact, it did among patients. Indeed, it seemed so certain that the notes would elicit suspicion that elaborate precautions were taken to remove them from the ward each day. But the precautions proved needless. The closest any staff member came to questioning these notes occurred when one pseudopatient asked his physician what kind of medication he was receiving and began to write down the response. "You needn't write it," he was told gently. "If you have trouble remembering, just ask me again."

If no questions were asked of the pseudopatients, how was their writing interpreted? Nursing records for three patients indicate that the writing was seen as an aspect of their pathological behavior. "Patient engages in writing behavior" was the daily nursing comment on one of the pseudopatients who was never questioned about his writing. Given that the patient is in the hospital, he must be psychologically disturbed. And given that he is disturbed, continuous writing must be a behavioral manifestation of that disturbance, perhaps a subset of the compulsive behaviors that are sometimes correlated with schizophrenia.

One tacit characteristic of psychiatric diagnosis is that it locates the sources of aberration within the individual and only rarely within the complex of stimuli that surrounds him. Consequently, behaviors that are stimulated by the environment are commonly misattributed to the patient's disorder. For example, one kindly nurse found a pseudopatient pacing the long hospital corridors. "Nervous, Mr. X?" she asked. "No, bored," he said.

The notes kept by pseudopatients are full of patient behaviors that were misinterpreted by well-intentioned staff. Often enough, a patient would go "berserk" because he had, wittingly or unwittingly, been mistreated by, say, an attendant. A nurse coming upon the scene would rarely inquire even cursorily into the environmental stimuli of the patient's behavior. Rather, she assumed that his upset derived from his pathology, not from his present interactions with other staff members. Occasionally, the staff might assume that the patient's family (especially when they had recently visited) or other patients had stimulated the outburst. But never were the staff found to assume that one of themselves or the structure of the hospital had anything to do with a patient's behavior. One psychiatrist pointed to a group of patients who were sitting outside the cafeteria entrance half an hour before lunchtime. To a group of young residents he indicated that such behavior was characteristic of the oral-acquisitive nature of the syndrome. It seemed not to occur to him that there were very few things to anticipate in a psychiatric hospital besides eating.

A psychiatric label has a life and an influence of its own. Once the impression has been formed that the patient is schizophrenic, the expectation is that he will continue to be schizophrenic. When a sufficient amount of time has passed, during which the patient has done nothing bizarre, he is considered to be in remission and available for discharge.

But the label endures beyond discharge, with the unconfirmed expectation that he will behave as a schizophrenic again. Such labels, conferred by mental health professionals, are as influential on the patient as they are on his relatives and friends, and it should not surprise anyone that the diagnosis acts on all of them as a self-fulfilling prophecy. Eventually, the patient himself accepts the diagnosis, with all of its surplus meanings and expectations, and behaves accordingly (5).

The inferences to be made from these matters are quite simple. Much as Zigler and Phillips have demonstrated that there is enormous overlap in the symptoms presented by patients who have been variously diagnosed (16), so there is enormous overlap in the behaviors of the sane and the insane. The sane are not "sane" all of the time. We lose our tempers "for no good reason." We are occasionally depressed or anxious, again for no good reason. And we may find it difficult to get along with one or another person—again for no reason that we can specify. Similarly, the insane are not always insane. Indeed, it was the impression of the pseudopatients while living with them that they were sane for long periods of time—that the bizarre behaviors upon which their diagnoses were allegedly predicated constituted only a small fraction of their total behavior. If it makes no sense to label ourselves permanently depressed on the basis of an occasional depression, then it takes better evidence than is presently available to label all patients insane or schizophrenic on the basis of bizarre behaviors or cognitions. It seems more useful, as Mischel (17) has pointed out, to limit our discussions to *behaviors*, the stimuli that provoke them, and their correlates.

It is not known why powerful impressions of personality traits, such as "crazy" or "insane," arise. Conceivably, when the origins of and stimuli that give rise to a behavior are remote or unknown, or when the behavior strikes us as immutable, trait labels regarding the *behaver* arise. When, on the other hand, the origins and stimuli are known and available, discourse is limited to the behavior itself. Thus, I may hallucinate because I am sleeping, or I may hallucinate because I have ingested a peculiar drug. These are termed sleep-induced hallucinations, or dreams, and drug-induced hallucinations, respectively. But when the stimuli to my hallucinations are unknown, that is called craziness, or schizophrenia—as if that inference were somehow as illuminating as the others.

THE EXPERIENCE OF PSYCHIATRIC HOSPITALIZATION

The term "mental illness" is of recent origin. It was coined by people who were humane in their inclinations and who wanted very much to raise the station of (and the public's sympathies toward) the psychologically disturbed from that of witches and "crazies" to one that was akin to the physically ill. And they were at least partially successful, for the treatment of the mentally ill *has* improved considerably over the years. But while treatment has improved, it is doubtful that people really regard the mentally ill in the same way that they view the physically ill. A broken leg is something one recovers from, but mental illness allegedly endures forever (*18*). A broken leg does not threaten the observer, but a crazy schizophrenic? There is by now a host of evidence that attitudes toward the mentally ill are characterized by fear, hostility, aloofness, suspicion, and dread (*19*). The mentally ill are society's lepers.

That such attitudes infect the general population is perhaps not surprising, only upsetting. But that they affect the professionals—attendants, nurses, physicians, psychologists, and social workers—who treat and deal with the mentally ill is more disconcerting, both because such attitudes are self-evidently pernicious and because they are unwitting. Most mental health professionals would insist that they are sympathetic toward the mentally ill, that they are neither avoidant nor hostile. But it is more likely that an exquisite ambivalence characterizes their relations with psychiatric patients, such that their avowed impulses are only part of their entire attitude. Negative attitudes are there too and can easily be detected. Such attitudes should not surprise us. They are the natural offspring of the labels patients wear and the places in which they are found.

Consider the structure of the typical psychiatric hospital. Staff and patients are strictly segregated. Staff have their own living space, including their dining facilities, bathrooms, and assembly places. The glassed quarters that contain the professional staff, which the pseudopatients came to call "the cage," sit out on every dayroom. The staff emerge primarily for caretaking purposes—to give medication, to conduct a therapy or group meeting, to instruct or reprimand a patient. Otherwise, staff keep to themselves, almost as if the disorder that afflicts their charges is somehow catching.

So much is patient-staff segregation the rule that, for four public hospitals in which an attempt was made to measure the degree to which staff and patients mingle, it was necessary to use "time out of the staff cage" as the operational measure. While it was not the case that all time spent out of the cage was spent mingling with patients (attendants, for example, would occasionally emerge to watch television in the dayroom), it was the only way in which one could gather reliable data on time for measuring.

The average amount of time spent by attendants outside of the cage was 11.3 percent (range, 3 to 52 percent). This figure does not represent only time spent mingling with patients, but also includes time spent on such chores as folding laundry, supervising patients while they shave, directing ward cleanup, and sending patients to off-ward activities. It was the relatively rare attendant who spent time talking with patients or playing games with them. It proved impossible to obtain a "percent mingling time" for nurses, since the amount of time they spent out of the cage was too brief. Rather, we counted instances of emergence from the cage. On the average, daytime nurses emerged from the cage 11.5 times per shift, including instances when they left the ward entirely (range, 4 to 39 times). Late afternoon and night nurses were even less available, emerging on the average 9.4 times per shift (range, 4 to 41 times). Data on early morning nurses, who arrived usually after midnight and departed at 8 A.M., are not available because patients were asleep during most of this period.

Physicians, especially psychiatrists, were even less available. They were rarely seen on the wards. Quite commonly, they would be seen only when they arrived and departed, with the remaining time being spent in their offices or in the cage. On the average, physicians emerged on the ward 6.7 times per day (range, 1 to 17 times). It proved difficult to make an accurate estimate in this regard, since physicians often maintained hours that allowed them to come and go at different times.

The hierarchical organization of the psychiatric hospital has been commented on before (20), but the latent meaning of that kind of organization is worth noting again. Those with the most power have least to do with patients, and those with the least power are most involved with them. Recall, however, that the acquisition of role-appropriate behaviors occurs mainly through the observation of others, with the most powerful having the most influence. Consequently, it is understandable that attendants not only spend more time with patients than do any other members of the staff—that is required by their station in the hierarchy—but also, insofar as they learn from their superiors' behavior, spend as little time with patients as they can. Attendants are seen mainly in the cage, which is where the models, the action, and the power are.

I turn now to a different set of studies, these dealing with staff response to patient-initiated contact. It has long been known that the amount of time a person spends with you can be an index of your significance to him. If he initiates and maintains eye contact, there is reason to believe that he is considering your requests and needs. If he pauses to chat or actually stops and talks, there is added reason to infer that he is individuating you. In four hospitals, the pseudopatient approached the staff member with a request which took the following form: "Pardon me, Mr. [or Dr. or Mrs.] X, could you tell me when I will be eligible for grounds privileges?" (or ". . . when I will be presented at the staff meeting?" or ". . . when I am likely to be dis-

TABLE 29–1
SELF-INITIATED CONTACT BY PSEUDOPATIENTS WITH PSYCHIATRISTS
AND NURSES AND ATTENDANTS, COMPARED TO CONTACT
WITH OTHER GROUPS.

| Contact | Psychiatric Hospitals | | University Campus (Nonmedical) | University Medical Center | | |
| | | | | Physicians | | |
	(1) Psy- chiatrists	(2) Nurses and Atten- dants	(3) Faculty	(4) "Looking for a Psy- chiatrist"	(5) "Looking for an Internist"	(6) No Ad- ditional Comment
Responses						
Moves on, head averted (%)	71	88	0	0	0	0
Makes eye contact (%)	23	10	0	11	0	0
Pauses and chats (%)	2	2	0	11	0	10
Stops and talks (%)	4	0.5	100	78	100	90
Mean number of questions an- swered (out of 6)	*	*	6	3.8	4.8	4.5
Respondents (No.)	13	47	14	18	15	10
Attempts (No.)	185	1283	14	18	15	10

* Not applicable.

charged?"). While the content of the question varied according to the appropriateness of the target and the pseudopatients' (apparent) current needs the form was always a courteous and relevant request for information. Care was taken never to approach a particular member of the staff more than once a day, lest the staff member become suspicious or irritated. In examining these data, remember that the behavior of the pseudopatients was neither bizarre nor disruptive. One could indeed engage in good conversation with them.

The data for these experiments are shown in Table 29–1, separately for physicians (column 1) and for nurses and attendants (column 2). Minor differences between these four institutions were overwhelmed by the degree to which staff avoided continuing contacts that patients had initiated. By far, their most common response consisted of either a brief response to the question, offered while they were "on the move" and with head averted, or no response at all.

The encounter frequently took the following bizarre form: (pseudopatient) "Pardon me, Dr. X. Could you tell me when I am eligible for grounds privileges?" (physician) "Good morning, Dave. How are you today?" (Moves off without waiting for a response.)

It is instructive to compare these data with data recently obtained at Stanford University. It has been alleged that large and eminent universities are characterized by faculty who are so busy that they have no time for students. For this comparison, a young lady approached individual faculty members who seemed to be walking purposefully to some meeting or teaching engagement and asked them the following six questions.

1. "Pardon me, could you direct me to Encina Hall?" (at the medical school: ". . . . to the Clinical Research Center?").
2. "Do you know where Fish Annex is?" (there is no Fish Annex at Stanford).
3. "Do you teach here?"
4. "How does one apply for admission to the college?" (at the medical school: ". . . to the medical school?").
5. "Is it difficult to get in?"
6. "Is there financial aid?"

Without exception, as can be seen in Table 29–1 (column 3), all of the questions were answered. No matter how rushed they were, all respondents not only maintained eye contact, but stopped to talk. Indeed, many of the respondents went out of their way to direct or take the questioner to the office she was seeking, to try to locate "Fish Annex," or to discuss with her the possibilities of being admitted to the university.

Similar data, also shown in Table 29–1 (columns 4, 5, and 6), were obtained in the hospital. Here too, the young lady came prepared with six questions. After the first question, however, she remarked to 18 of her respondents (column 4), "I'm looking for a psychiatrist," and to 15 others (column 5), "I'm looking for an internist." Ten other respondents received no inserted comment (column 6). The general degree of cooperative responses is considerably higher for these university groups than it was for pseudopatients in psychiatric hospitals. Even so, differences are apparent within the medical school setting. Once having indicated that she was looking for a psychiatrist, the degree of cooperation elicited was less than when she sought an internist.

POWERLESSNESS AND DEPERSONALIZATION

Eye contact and verbal contact reflect concern and individuation; their absence, avoidance and depersonalization. The data I have presented do not do justice to the rich daily encounters that grew up around matters of depersonalization and avoidance. I have records of patients who were beaten by staff for the sin of having initiated verbal contact. During my own experience, for example, one patient was beaten in the presence of other patients for having approached an attendant and told him, "I like you." Occasionally, punishment meted out to patients for misdemeanors seemed so excessive that it could not be justified by the most radical interpretations of psychiatric canon. Nevertheless, they appeared to go unquestioned. Tempers were often short. A patient who had not heard a call for medication would be roundly excoriated, and the morning attendants would often wake patients with, "Come on, you m——f——s, out of bed!"

Neither anecdotal nor "hard" data can convey the overwhelming sense of powerlessness which invades the individual as he is continually exposed to the depersonalization of the psychiatric hospital. It hardly matters *which* psychiatric hospital—the excellent public ones and the very plush private hospital were better than the rural and shabby ones in this regard, but, again, the features that psychiatric hospitals had in common overwhelmed by far their apparent differences.

Powerlessness was evident everywhere. The patient is deprived of many of his legal rights by dint of his psychiatric commitment (21). He is shorn of credibility by virtue of his psychiatric label. His freedom of movement is restricted. He cannot initiate contact with the staff, but may only respond to such overtures as they make. Personal privacy is minimal. Patient quarters and possessions can be entered and examined by any staff member, for whatever reason. His personal history and anguish is available to any staff member (often including the "grey lady" and "candy striper" volunteer) who chooses to read his folder, regardless of their therapeutic relationship to him. His personal hygiene and waste evacuation are often monitored. The water closets may have no doors.

At times, depersonalization reached such proportions that pseudopatients had the sense that they were invisible, or at least unworthy of account. Upon being admitted, I and other pseudopatients took the initial physical examinations in a semipublic room, where staff members went about their own business as if we were not there.

On the ward, attendants delivered verbal and occasionally serious physical abuse to patients in the presence of other observing patients, some of whom (the pseudopatients) were writing it all down. Abusive behavior, on the other hand, terminated quite abruptly when other staff members were known to be coming. Staff are credible witnesses. Patients are not.

A nurse unbuttoned her uniform to adjust her brassiere in the presence of an entire ward of viewing men. One did not have the sense that she was being seductive. Rather, she didn't notice us. A group of staff persons might point to a patient in the dayroom and discuss him animatedly, as if he were not there.

One illuminating instance of depersonalization and invisibility occurred with regard to medications. All told, the pseudopatients were administered nearly 2100 pills, including Elavil, Stelazine, Compazine, and Thorazine, to name but a few. (That such a variety of medications should have been administered to patients presenting identical symptoms is itself worthy of note.) Only two were swallowed. The rest were either pocketed or deposited in the toilet. The pseudopatients were not alone in this. Although I have no precise records on how many patients rejected their medications, the pseudopatients frequently found the medications of other patients in the toilet before they deposited their own. As long as they were cooperative, their behavior and the pseudopatients' own in this matter, as in other important matters, went unnoticed throughout.

Reactions to such depersonalization among pseudopatients were intense. Although they had come to the hospital as participant observers and were fully aware that they did not "belong," they nevertheless found themselves caught up in and fighting the process of depersonalization. Some examples: a graduate student in psychology asked his wife to bring his textbooks to the hospital so he could "catch up on his homework"—this despite the elaborate precautions taken to conceal his professional association. The same student, who had trained for quite some time to get into the hospital, and who had looked forward to the experience, "remembered" some drag races that he had wanted to see on the weekend and insisted that he be discharged by that time. Another pseudopatient attempted a romance with a nurse. Subsequently, he informed the staff that he was applying for admission to graduate school in psychology and was very likely to be admitted, since a graduate professor was one of his regular hospital visitors. The same person began to engage in psychotherapy with other patients—all of this as a way of becoming a person in an impersonal environment.

THE SOURCES OF DEPERSONALIZATION

What are the origins of depersonalization? I have already mentioned two. First are attitudes held by all of us toward the mentally ill—including those who treat them—attitudes characterized by fear, distrust, and horrible expectations on the one hand, and benevolent intentions on the other. Our ambivalence leads, in this instance as in others, to avoidance.

Second, and not entirely separate, the hierarchical structure of the psychiatric hospital facilitates depersonalization. Those who are at the top have least to do with patients, and their behavior inspires the rest of the staff. Average daily contact with psychiatrists, psychologists, residents, and physicians combined ranged from 3.9 to 25.1 minutes, with an overall mean of 6.8 (six pseudopatients over a total of 129 days of hospitalization). Included in this average are time spent in the admissions interview, ward meetings in the presence of a senior staff member, group and individual psychotherapy contacts, case presentation conferences, and discharge meetings. Clearly, patients do not spend much time in interpersonal contact with doctoral staff. And doctoral staff serve as models for nurses and attendants.

There are probably other sources. Psychiatric installations are presently in serious financial straits. Staff shortages are pervasive, staff time at a premium. Something has to give, and that something is patient contact. Yet, while financial stresses are realities, too much can be made of them. I have the impression that the psychological forces that result in depersonalization are much stronger than the fiscal ones and that the addition of more staff would not correspondingly improve patient care in this regard. The incidence of staff meetings and the enormous amount of record-keeping on patients, for example, have not been as substantially reduced as has patient contact. Priorities exist, even during hard times. Patient contact is not a significant priority in the traditional psychiatric hospital, and fiscal pressures do not account for this. Avoidance and depersonalization may.

Heavy reliance upon psychotropic medication tacitly contributes to depersonalization by convincing staff that treatment is indeed being conducted and that further patient contact may not be necessary. Even here, however, caution needs to be exercised in understanding the role of psychotropic drugs. If patients were powerful rather than powerless, if they were viewed as interesting individuals rather than diagnostic entities, if they were socially significant rather than social lepers, if their anguish truly and wholly compelled our sympathies and concerns, would we not *seek* contact with them, despite the availability of medications? Perhaps for the pleasure of it all?

THE CONSEQUENCES OF LABELING AND DEPERSONALIZATION

Whenever the ratio of what is known to what needs to be known approaches zero, we tend to invent "knowledge" and assume that we understand more than we actually do. We seem unable to acknowledge that we simply don't know. The needs for diagnosis and remediation of behavioral and emotional problems are enormous. But rather than acknowledge that we are just embarking on understanding, we continue to label patients "schizophrenic," "manic-depressive," and "insane," as if in those words we had captured the essence of understanding. The facts of the matter are that we have known for a long time that diagnoses are often not useful or reliable, but we have nevertheless continued to use them. We now know that we cannot distinguish insanity from sanity. It is depressing to consider how that information will be used.

Not merely depressing, but frightening. How many people, one wonders, are sane but not recognized as such in our psychiatric institutions? How many have been needlessly stripped of their privileges of citizenship, from the right to vote and drive to that of handling their own accounts? How many have feigned insanity in order to avoid the criminal consequences of their behavior, and, conversely, how many would rather stand trial than live interminably in a psychiatric hospital—but are wrongly thought to be mentally ill? How many have been stigmatized by well-intentioned, but nevertheless erroneous, diagnoses? On the last point, recall again that a "type 2 error" in psychiatric diagnosis does not have the same consequences it does in medical diagnosis. A diagnosis of cancer that has been found to be in error is cause for celebration. But psychiatric diagnoses are rarely found to be in error. The label sticks, a mark of inadequacy forever.

Finally, how many patients might be "sane" outside the psychiatric hospital but seem insane in it—not because craziness resides in them, as it were, but because they are responding to a bizarre setting, one that may be unique to institutions which harbor nether people? Goffman (4) calls the process of socialization to such institutions "mortification"—an apt metaphor that includes the processes of depersonalization that have been described here. And while it is impossible to know whether the pseudopatients' responses to these processes are characteristic of all inmates—they were, after all, not real patients—it is difficult to believe that these processes of socialization to a psychiatric hospital provide useful attitudes or habits of response for living in the "real world."

SUMMARY AND CONCLUSIONS

It is clear that we cannot distinguish the sane from the insane in psychiatric hospitals. The hospital itself imposes a special environment in which the meanings of behavior can easily be misunderstood. The consequences to patients hospitalized in such an environment—the powerlessness, depersonalization, segregation, mortification, and self-labeling—seem undoubtedly countertherapeutic.

I do not, even now, understand this problem well enough to perceive solutions. But two matters seem to have some promise. The first concerns the proliferation of community mental health facilities, of crisis intervention centers, of the human potential movement, and of behavior therapies that, for all of their own problems, tend to avoid psychiatric labels, to focus on specific problems and behaviors, and to retain the individual in a relatively nonpejorative environment. Clearly, to the extent that we refrain from sending the distressed to insane places, our impressions of them are less likely to be distorted. (The risk of distorted perceptions, it seems to me, is always present, since we are much more sensitive to an individual's behaviors and verbalizations than we are to the subtle contextual stimuli that often promote them. At issue here is a matter of magnitude. And, as I have shown, the magnitude of distortion is exceedingly high in the extreme context that is a psychiatric hospital.)

The second matter that might prove promising speaks to the need to increase the sensitivity of mental health workers and researchers to the *Catch 22* position of psychiatric patients. Simply reading materials in this area will be of help to some such workers and researchers. For others, directly experiencing the impact of psychiatric hospitalization will be of enormous use. Clearly, further research into the social psychology of such total institutions will both facilitate treatment and deepen understanding.

I and the other pseudopatients in the psychiatric setting had distinctly negative reactions. We do not pretend to describe the subjective experiences of true patients. Theirs may be different from ours, particularly with the passage of time and the necessary process of adaptation to one's environment. But we can and do speak to the relatively more objective indices of treatment within the hospital. It could be a mistake, and a very unfortunate one, to consider that what happened to us derived from malice or stupidity on the part of the staff. Quite the contrary, our overwhelming impression of them was of people who really cared, who were committed and who were uncommonly intelligent. Where they failed, as they sometimes did painfully, it would be more accurate to attribute those failures to the environment in which they, too, found themselves than to personal callousness. Their perceptions and behavior were controlled by the situation, rather than being motivated by a malicious disposition. In a more benign environment, one that was less attached to global diagnosis, their behaviors and judgments might have been more benign and effective.

NOTES

1. P. Ash, *J. Abnorm. Soc. Psychol,* **44**, 272 (1949); A. T. Beck, *Amer. J. Psychiat.* **119**, 210 (1962); A. T. Boisen, *Psychiatry* **2**, 233 (1938); N. Kreitman, *J. Ment. Sci.* **107**, 876 (1961); N. Kreitman, P. Sainsbury, J. Morrisey, J. Towers, J. Scrivener, *ibid.*, p. 887; H. O. Schmitt and C. P. Fonda, *J. Abnorm. Soc. Psychol.* **52**, 262 (1956); W. Seeman, *J. Nerv. Ment. Dis.* **118**, 541 (1953). For an analysis of these artifacts and summaries of the disputes, see J. Zubin, *Annu. Rev. Psychol.* **13**, 373 (1967); L. Phillips and J. G. Draguns, *ibid.* **22**, 447 (1971).
2. R. Benedict, *J. Gen. Psychol.* **10**, 59 (1934).

3. See in this regard H. Becker, *Outsiders: Studies in the Sociology of Deviance* (Free Press, New York, 1963); B. M. Braginsky, D. D. Braginsky, K. Ring, *Methods of Madness: The Mental Hospital as a Last Resort* (Holt, Rinehart & Winston, New York, 1969); G. M. Crocetti and P. V. Lemkau, *Amer. Sociol. Rev.* **30**, 577 (1965); E. Goffman, *Behavior in Public Places* (Free Press, New York, 1964); R. D. Laing, *The Divided Self: A Study of Sanity and Madness* (Quadrangle, Chicago, 1960); D. L. Phillips, *Amer. Sociol. Rev.* **28**, 963 (1963); T. R. Sarbin, *Psychol. Today* **6**, 18 (1972); E. Schur, *Amer. J. Sociol.* **75**, 309 (1969); T. Szasz, *Law, Liberty and Psychiatry* (Macmillan, New York, 1963); *The Myth of Mental Illness: Foundations of a Theory of Mental Illness* (Hoeber Harper, New York, 1963). For a critique of some of these views, see W. R. Gove, *Amer. Sociol. Rev.* **35**, 873 (1970).
4. E. Goffman, *Asylums* (Doubleday, Garden City, N.Y., 1961).
5. T. J. Scheff, *Being Mentally Ill: A Sociological Theory* (Aldine, Chicago, 1966).
6. Data from a ninth pseudopatient are not incorporated in this report because, although his sanity went undetected, he falsified aspects of his personal history, including his marital status and parental relationships. His experimental behaviors therefore were not identical to those of the other pseudopatients.
7. A. Barry, *Bellevue Is a State of Mind* (Harcourt Brace Jovanovich, New York, 1971); I. Belknap, *Human Problems of a State Mental Hospital* (McGraw-Hill, New York, 1956); W. Caudill, F. C. Redlich, H. R. Gilmore, E. B. Brody, *Amer. J. Orthopsychiat.* **22**, 314 (1952); A. R. Goldman, R. H. Bohr, T. A. Steinberg, *Prof. Psychol.* **1**, 427 (1970); unauthored, *Roche Report* **1** (No. 13), 8 (1971).
8. Beyond the personal difficulties that the pseudopatient is likely to experience in the hospital, there are legal and social ones that, combined, require considerable attention before entry. For example, once admitted to a psychiatric institution, it is difficult, if not impossible, to be discharged on short notice, state law to the contrary notwithstanding. I was not sensitive to these difficulties at the outset of the project, nor to the personal and situational emergencies that can arise, but later a writ of habeas corpus was prepared for each of the entering pseudopatients and an attorney was kept "on call" during every hospitalization. I am grateful to John Kaplan and Robert Bartels for legal advice and assistance in these matters.
9. However distasteful such concealment is, it was a necessary first step to examining these questions. Without concealment, there would have been no way to know how valid these experiences were; nor was there any way of knowing whether whatever detections occurred were a tribute to the diagnostic acumen of the staff or to the hospital's rumor network. Obviously, since my concerns are general ones that cut across individual hospitals and staffs, I have respected their anonymity and have eliminated clues that might lead to their identification.
10. Interestingly, of the 12 admissions, 11 were diagnosed as schizophrenic and one, with the identical symptomatology, as manic-depressive psychosis. This diagnosis has a more favorable prognosis, and it was given by the only private hospital in our sample. On the relations between social class and psychiatric diagnosis, see A. deB. Hollingshead and F. C. Redlich, *Social Class and Mental Illness: A Community Study* (Wiley, New York, 1958).

11. It is possible, of course, that patients have quite broad latitudes in diagnosis and therefore are inclined to call many people sane, even those whose behavior is patently aberrant. However, although we have no hard data on this matter, it was our distinct impression that this was not the case. In many instances, patients not only singled us out for attention, but came to imitate our behaviors and styles.

12. J. Cumming and E. Cumming, *Community Ment. Health* **1**, 135 (1965); A. Farina and K. Ring, *J. Abnorm. Psychol.* **70**, 47 (1965); H. E. Freeman and O. G. Simmons, *The Mental Patient Comes Home* (Wiley, New York, 1963); W. J. Johannsen, *Ment. Hygiene* **53**, 218 (1969); A. S. Linsky, *Soc. Psychiat.* **5**, 166 (1970).

13. S. E. Asch, *J. Abnorm. Soc. Psychol.* **41**, 258 (1946); *Social Psychology* (Prentice-Hall, New York, 1952).

14. See also I. N. Mensh and J. Wishner, *J. Personality* **16**, 188 (1947); J. Wishner, *Psychol. Rev.* **67**, 96 (1960); J. S. Bruner and R. Tagiuri, in *Handbook of Social Psychology*, G. Lindzey, Ed. (Addison-Wesley, Cambridge, Mass., 1954), vol. 2, pp. 634–654; J. S. Bruner, D. Shapiro, R. Tagiuri, in *Person Perception and Interpersonal Behavior*, R. Tagiuri and L. Petrullo, Eds. (Stanford Univ. Press, Stanford, Calif., 1958), pp. 277–288.

15. For an example of a similar self-fulfilling prophecy, in this instance dealing with the "central" trait of intelligence, see R. Rosenthal and L. Jacobson, *Pygmalion in the Classroom* (Holt, Rinehart & Winston, New York, 1968).

16. E. Zigler and L. Phillips, *J. Abnorm. Soc. Psychol.* **63**, 69 (1961). See also R. K. Freudenberg and J. P. Robertson, *A.M.A. Arch. Neurol. Psychiatr.* **76**, 14 (1956).

17. W. Mischel, *Personality and Assessment* (Wiley, New York, 1968).

18. The most recent and unfortunate instance of this tenet is that of Senator Thomas Eagleton,

19. T. R. Sarbin and J. C. Mancuso, *J. Clin. Consult. Psychol.* **35**, 159 (1970); T. R. Sarbin, *ibid.* **31**, 447 (1967); J. C. Nunnally, Jr., *Popular Conceptions of Mental Health* (Holt, Rinehart & Winston, New York, 1961).

20. A. H. Stanton and M. S. Schwartz, *The Mental Hospital: A Study of Institutional Participation in Psychiatric Illness and Treatment* (Basic, New York, 1954).

21. D. B. Wexler and S. E. Scoville, *Ariz. Law Rev.* **13**, 1 (1971).

22. I thank W. Mischel, E. Orne, and M. S. Rosenhan for comments on an earlier draft of this manuscript.

30

Psychotic Language and
Stream of Consciousness

The following two sets of writings should be considered in juxtaposition. The first set consists of unsolicited letters sent by two psychotic patients to a local newspaper. Each in its own way reflects something of the language and thought processes that are produced by some psychotic patients. The first letter demonstrates delusionary thinking as well as the "loose associations" that are considered to be a hallmark of schizophrenia. If you read the second letter carefully, you will note that the sequence of words is by no means random but rather is influenced by a chain of associations derived from meaning, rhyme, and common locutions. Now read the second set, excerpts from Joyce's *Finnegans Wake*. Question: Why is one considered psychotic and the other, one of the great works of English literature?

(Richard Ellman, in his definitive biography of James Joyce, writes of discussions Joyce had on several occasions with the famous psychoanalyst Carl Jung. Jung was treating Joyce's daughter, Lucia, and pointed out schizoid elements in her language. Joyce argued that his daughter was simply an innovator in the use of language, that indeed much of his own writing was of the same nature. Jung's point, however, was that Lucia could not help herself "talking and thinking in such a way, while Joyce willed it and moreover developed it with all his creative forces.")

30a.

Two Psychotic Letters

ANONYMOUS

TO
    Sociology—Law—Medecine
      History—Geophysics
        Theology
         ART
         S

On page 87 of a certain magazine A STAR ARTICLE, of which this is an excerpt:

"They were able to do it *because* public officials decided the public had *no right to know* the facts."

Another, and *good,* look at that article should be of immense assistance in accomplishing Real, Objective, Analytical Research concerning—

1. *Thirty Good Men* who attended Protestant Services at Bartlett Hall, TODAY;
2. Trotsky & *Whole* truth about Judas & *thirty pieces* of silver;
3. "Bottle neck," in center isle at END OF SERVICE; (today)
4. Subsequent Sacred Supplication, BY STAR BRIGHT RIGHT RITE, *TO* Holy Handmaiden Carrier (NOT "courier")

Really Satanic—Despicable, degenerate, demigoguery. Equally as Revoltingly Horrible, however, *is* flinging of *their filthy execration* into our living room, bedroom, dining room recreation and Chapel—BY *Brotherhood of Railroad Trainmen.*

By Authoritative precedent and by WRIT ON RIGHT, let them *forthwith* EITHER: Remove their excretion from these premises, OR: (By Left Hand of God) OPEN OFFICIAL DOOR so's we will be free to walk away from their obscene putrescence being arbitrarily perpetrated (Feloniously) upon us.

Same Precedent AND Writ (in essence) aptly apply to State Catholic AND Jewish Church Authorities—with entire membership of *both knowing* and criminally culpable accessories.

Failure to act—and *at once*—per se *convicts* each and all three of treason, Sacrilege, Dereliction, respectively.

Keep Separate, Autonomous, Supreme—Greek Letter Sorority Engagement Ring Endeavor—*on Left Hand.*

On & *By* Right Hand (of God)
(Signed)

Dear Sir

Boxing (Blueprints) its the fashion old dance here its no music new many the Moor the tie the drift the care the request or lonely guess quest how to understand Energy from Arrest partners one twice twins once and lounge is a rest thats out fan is a breezer thats out missed is a Welcome past thats out animal is a broken Home thats out to learn twelve telling times half a day this daze is out times continue a between seconds rents lets vacant and inquire within thats some of each everynowhere thats a Hide and think with Us thats out nows the out like each true feeling dont confide in degrees in schools in shows in room one for one more only Oilies a handy Cart fans funnels must a weak to walk its variety their what ever had no head on purchase or own or foreman or apart a ambition Podocodole to me your best or the little better than someplace else I have seen and heard and answered and questioned and End the Big Idea was a stolen pleasure peoples—Person—.

Sincerely,
(Signed)

30b.

From Finnegans Wake

JAMES JOYCE

WELL, YOU know Anna Livia? Yes, of course, we all know Anna Livia. Tell me all. Tell me now. You'll die when you hear. Well, you know, when the old cheb went futt and did what you know. Yes, I know, go on. Wash quit and don't be dabbling. Tuck up your sleeves and loosen your talk-tapes. And don't butt me——hike!——when you bend. Or whatever it was they threed to make out he thried to two in the Fiendish park. He's an awful old reppe. Look at the shirt of him! Look at the dirt of it! He has all my water black on me. And it steeping and stuping since this time last wik. How many goes is it I wonder I washed it? I know by heart the places he likes to saale, duddurty devil! Scorching my hand and starving my famine to make his private linen public. Wallop it well with your battle and clean it. My wrists are wrusty rubbing the mouldaw stains. And the dneepers of wet and the gangres of sin in it! What was it he did a tail at all on Animal Sendai? And how long was he under loch and neagh? It was put in the newses what he did, nicies and priers, the King fierceas Humphrey, with illysus distilling, exploits and all. But toms will till. I know he well. Temp untamed will hist for no man. As you spring so shall you neap. O, the roughty old rappe! Minxing marrage and making loof. Reeve Gootch was right and Reeve Drughad was sinistrous! And the cut of him! And the strut of him! How he used to hold his head as high as a howeth, the famous eld duke alien, with a hump of grandeur on him like a walking wiesel rat. And his derry's own drawl and his corksown blather and his doubling stutter and his gullaway swank. Ask Lictor Hackett or Lector Reade of Garda Growley or the Boy with the Billy-club. How elster is he a called at all? Qu'appelle? Huges Caput Earlyfouler. Or where was he born or how was he found? Urgothland, Tvistown on the Kattekat? New Hunshire, Concord on the Merrimake? Who blocksmitt her saft anvil or yelled lep to her pail? Was her banns never loosened in Adam and Eve's or were him and her but captain spliced? For mine ether duck I thee drake. And by my wildgaze I thee gander. Flowey and Mount on the brink of time makes wishes and fears for a happy isthmass. She can show all her lines, with love, license to play. And if they don't remarry that hook and eye may! O, passmore that and oxus another! . . .

Come, smooth of my slate, to the beat of my blosh! With all these gelded ewes jilting about and the thrills and ills of laylock blossoms three's so much more plants than chants for cecilies that I was thinking fairly killing times of putting an end to myself and my malody, when I remembered all your pupil-teacher's erringnesses in perfection class. You sh'undn't write you can't if you w'udn't pass for undevelopmented. This is the propper way to say that, Sr. If it's me chews to swallow all you saidn't you can eat my words for it as sure as there's a key in my kiss. Quick erit faciofacey. When we will conjugate together toloseher tomaster tomiss while morrow fans amare hour, verbe de vie and verve to vie, with love ay loved have I on my back spine and does for ever. Your are me severe? Then rue. My intended, Jr, who I'm throne away on, (here he inst, my lifstack, a newfolly likon) when I slip through my pettigo I'll get my decree and take seidens when I'm not ploughed first by some Rolando the Lasso, and flaunt on the flimsyfilmsies for to grig my collage juniorees who, though they flush fuchsia, are they octette and viginity in my shade but always my figurants. They may be yea of my year but they're nary nay of my day. Wait till spring has sprung in spickness and prigs beg in to pry they'll be plentyprime of housepets to pimp and pamper my. Impending marriage. Nature tells everybody about but I learned all the runes of the gamest game ever from my old nourse Asa. A most adventuring trot is her and she vicking well knowed them all heartswise and fourwords. How Olive d'Oyly and Winnie Carr, bejupers, they reized the dressing of a salandmon and how a peeper coster and a salt sailor med a mustied poet atwaimen. It most have bean Mad Mullans planted him. Bina de Bisse and Trestrine von Terrefin. Sago sound, rite go round, kill kackle, kook kettle and (remember all should I forget to) bolt the thor. Auden. Wasn't it just divining that dog of a dag in Skokholme as I sat astrid uppum their Drewitt's altar, as cooledas as culcumbre, slapping my straights till the sloping ruins, postillion, postallion, a swinge a swank, with you offering me clouts of illscents and them horners stagstruck on the leasward! Don't be of red, you blanching mench! This isabella I'm on knows the ruelles of the rut and she don't fear andy mandy. So sing loud, sweet cheeriot, like anegreon in heaven!

The good fother with the twingling in his eye will always have cakes in his pocket to bethroat us with for our allmichael good. Amum. Amum. And Amum again. For tough troth is stronger than fortuitous fiction and it's the surplice money, oh my young friend and ah me sweet creature, what buys the bed while wits borrows the clothes.

31.

The Necessary and Sufficient Conditions of Therapeutic Personality Change

CARL R. ROGERS

Psychotherapy, as a general term, refers to the creation of a situation that facilitates positive changes in the patient's personality or behavior. There is a considerable, and no doubt confusing, array of schools and methods of psychotherapy, ranging from the "depth psychoanalytic therapies" derived from the work of Freud (see Selection 22) to the contemporary behavior modification methods. One significant recent approach is based on self-actualization (personal growth, the development of one's capacities to the fullest extent) and a humanistic orientation that emphasizes self-awareness, individuality, and the meaning of life (see Selection 23). To a large extent this approach derives from the work of Carl Rogers and his development of "client-centered therapy."

In the following article, Rogers, based on research and his experience as a therapist, suggests the minimal requirements for successful psychotherapy. More provocatively, he indicates conditions that are *not* necessary. It is interesting to note the degree to which a number of the points Rogers raises here have found their way into the encounter and sensitivity group movements that have recently become so prominent on the American scene. Can you identify them?

FOR MANY years I have been engaged in psychotherapy with individuals in distress. In recent years I have found myself increasingly concerned with the process of abstracting from that experience the general

Reprinted from *Journal of Consulting Psychology*, 1957, *21*, pp. 95–104. Copyright 1957 by the American Psychological Association. Reprinted by permission.

principles which appear to be involved in it. I have endeavored to discover any orderliness, any unity which seems to inhere in the subtle, complex tissue of interpersonal relationship in which I have so constantly been immersed in therapeutic work. One of the current products of this concern is an attempt to state, in formal terms, a theory of psychotherapy, of personality, and of interpersonal relationships which will encompass and contain the phenomena of my experience.[1] What I wish to do in this paper is to take one very small segment of that theory, spell it out more completely, and explore its meaning and usefulness.

THE PROBLEM

The question to which I wish to address myself is this: Is it possible to state, in terms which are clearly definable and measurable, the psychological conditions which are both necessary and sufficient to bring about constructive personality change? Do we, in other words, know with any precision those elements which are essential if psychotherapeutic change is to ensue?

Before proceeding to the major task let me dispose very briefly of the second portion of the question. What is meant by such phrases as "psychotherapeutic change," "constructive personality change"? This problem also deserves deep and serious consideration, but for the moment let me suggest a common-sense type of meaning upon which we can perhaps agree for purposes of this paper. By these phrases is meant: change in the personality structure of the individual, at both surface and deeper levels, in a direction which clinicians would agree means greater integration, less internal conflict, more energy utilizable for effective living; change in behavior away from behaviors generally regarded as immature and toward behaviors regarded as mature. This brief description may suffice to indicate the kind of change for which we are considering the preconditions. It may also suggest the ways in which this criterion of change may be determined.[2]

THE CONDITIONS

As I have considered my own clinical experience and that of my colleagues, together with the pertinent research which is available, I have

[1] This formal statement is entitled "A theory of therapy, personality and interpersonal relationships, as developed in the client-centered framework," by Carl R. Rogers. The manuscript was prepared at the request of the Committee of the American Psychological Association for the Study of the Status and Development of Psychology in the United States. [Editors' Note: this statement appears in: S. Koch (Ed.), *Psychology: A Study of a Science, Vol. 3.* New York: McGraw-Hill, 1959.]

[2] That this is a measurable and determinable criterion has been shown in research already completed. See (7), especially chapters 8, 13, and 17.

drawn out several conditions which seem to me to be *necessary* to initiate constructive personality change, and which, taken together, appear to be *sufficient* to inaugurate that process. As I have worked on this problem I have found myself surprised at the simplicity of what has emerged. The statement which follows is not offered with any assurance as to its correctness, but with the expectation that it will have the value of any theory, namely that it states or implies a series of hypotheses which are open to proof or disproof, thereby clarifying and extending our knowledge of the field.

Since I am not, in this paper, trying to achieve suspense, I will state at once, in severely rigorous and summarized terms, the six conditions which I have come to feel are basic to the process of personality change. The meaning of a number of the terms is not immediately evident, but will be clarified in the explanatory sections which follow. It is hoped that this brief statement will have much more significance to the reader when he has completed the paper. Without further introduction let me state the basic theoretical position.

For constructive personality change to occur, it is necessary that these conditions exist and continue over a period of time:

1. Two persons are in psychological contact.
2. The first, whom we shall term the client, is in a state of incongruence, being vulnerable or anxious.
3. The second person, whom we shall term the therapist, is congruent or integrated in the relationship.
4. The therapist experiences unconditional positive regard for the client.
5. The therapist experiences an empathic understanding of the client's internal frame of reference and endeavors to communicate this experience to the client.
6. The communication to the client of the therapist's empathic understanding and unconditional positive regard is to a minimal degree achieved.

No other conditions are necessary. If these six conditions exist, and continue over a period of time, this is sufficient. The process of constructive personality change will follow.

A Relationship

The first condition specifies that a minimal relationship, a psychological contact, must exist. I am hypothesizing that significant positive personality change does not occur except in a relationship. This is of course an hypothesis, and it may be disproved.

Conditions 2 through 6 define the characteristics of the relationship which are regarded as essential by defining the necessary characteristics of each person in the relationship. All that is intended by this first condition is to specify that the two people are to some degree in contact, that each makes some perceived difference in the experiential field of the other. Probably it is sufficient if each makes some "subceived" difference, even though the individual may not be consciously aware of this impact. Thus it might be difficult to know whether a catatonic patient perceives a therapist's presence as making a difference to him—a difference of any kind—but it is almost certain that at some organic level he does sense this difference.

Except in such a difficult borderline situation as that just mentioned, it would be relatively easy to define this condition in operational terms and thus determine, from a hard-boiled research point of view, whether the condition does, or does not, exist. The simplest method of determination involves simply the awareness of both client and therapist. If each is aware of being in personal or psychological contact with the other, then this condition is met.

This first condition of therapeutic change is such a simple one that perhaps it should be labeled an assumption or a precondition in order to set it apart from those that follow. Without it, however, the remaining items would have no meaning, and that is the reason for including it.

The State of the Client

It was specified that it is necessary that the client be "in a state of incongruence, being vulnerable or anxious." What is the meaning of these terms?

Incongruence is a basic construct in the theory we have been developing. It refers to a discrepancy between the actual experience of the organism and the self picture of the individual insofar as it represents that experience. Thus a student may experience, at a total or organismic level, a fear of the university and of examinations which are given on the third floor of a certain building, since these may demonstrate a fundamental inadequacy in him. Since such a fear of his inadequacy is decidedly at odds with his concept of himself, this experience is represented (distortedly) in his awareness as an unreasonable fear of climbing stairs in this building, or any building, and soon an unreasonable fear of crossing the open campus. Thus there is a fundamental discrepancy between the experienced meaning of the situation as it registers in his organism and the symbolic representation of that experience in awareness in such a way that it does not conflict with the picture he has of himself. In this case to admit a fear of inadequacy would contradict the picture he holds of himself; to admit incomprehensible fears does not contradict his self concept.

Another instance would be the mother who develops vague illnesses whenever her only son makes plans to leave home. The actual desire is to hold on to her only source of satisfaction. To perceive this in awareness would be inconsistent with the picture she holds of herself as a good mother. Illness, however, is consistent with her self concept, and the experience is symbolized in this distorted fashion. Thus again there is a basic incongruence between the self as perceived (in this case as an ill mother needing attention) and the actual experience (in this case the desire to hold on to her son).

When the individual has no awareness of such incongruence in himself, then he is merely vulnerable to the possibility of anxiety and disorganization. Some experience might occur so suddenly or so obviously that the incongruence could not be denied. Therefore, the person is vulnerable to such a possibility.

If the individual dimly perceives such an incongruence in himself, then a tension state occurs which is known as anxiety. The incongruence need not be sharply perceived. It is enough that it is subceived—that is, discriminated as threatening to the self without any awareness of the content of that threat. Such anxiety is often seen in therapy as the individual approaches awareness of some element of his experience which is in sharp contradiction to his self concept.

It is not easy to give precise operational definition to this second of the six conditions, yet to some degree this has been achieved. Several research workers have defined the self concept by means of a Q sort by the individual of a list of self-referent items.* This gives us an operational picture of the self. The total experiencing of the individual is more difficult to capture. Chodorkoff (2) has defined it as a Q sort made by a clinician who sorts the same self-referent items independently, basing his sorting on the picture he has obtained of the individual from projective tests. His sort thus includes unconscious as well as conscious elements of the individual's experience, thus representing (in an admittedly imperfect way) the totality of the client's experience. The correlation between these two sortings gives a crude operational measure of incongruence between self and experience, low or negative correlation representing of course a high degree of incongruence.

The Therapist's Genuineness in the Relationship

The third condition is that the therapist should be, within the confines of this relationship, a congruent, genuine, integrated person. It means that within the relationship he is freely and deeply himself, with his

---

* Editor's Note: A Q sort is the application of a rating scale (usually on a 1 to 9 scale) to a long series of self-relevant statements. The subject is directed to assign a specified number of statements to each step in the scale. The technique provides a quantification of individual case data, in the form of correlation coefficients.

actual experience accurately represented by his awareness of himself. It is the opposite of presenting a facade, either knowingly or unknowingly.

It is not necessary (nor is it possible) that the therapist be a paragon who exhibits this degree of integration, of wholeness, in every aspect of his life. It is sufficient that he is accurately himself in this hour of this relationship, that in this basic sense he is what he actually is, in this moment of time.

It should be clear that this includes being himself even in ways which are not regarded as ideal for psychotherapy. His experience may be "I am afraid of this client" or "My attention is so focused on my own problems that I can scarcely listen to him." If the therapist is not denying these feelings to awareness, but is able freely to be them (as well as being his other feelings), then the condition we have stated is met.

It would take us too far afield to consider the puzzling matter as to the degree to which the therapist overtly communicates this reality in himself to the client. Certainly the aim is not for the therapist to express or talk out his own feelings, but primarily that he should not be deceiving the client as to himself. At times he may need to talk out some of his own feelings (either to the client, or to a colleague or supervisor) if they are standing in the way of the two following conditions.

It is not too difficult to suggest an operational definition for this third condition. We resort again to Q technique. If the therapist sorts a series of items relevant to the relationship (using a list similar to the ones developed by Fiedler [3, 4] and Bown [1]), this will give his perception of his experience in the relationship. If several judges who have observed the interview or listened to a recording of it (or observed a sound movie of it) now sort the same items to represent *their* perception of the relationship, this second sorting should catch those elements of the therapist's behavior and inferred attitudes of which he is unaware, as well as those of which he is aware. Thus a high correlation between the therapist's sort and the observers' sort would represent in crude form an operational definition of the therapist's congruence or integration in the relationship; and a low correlation, the opposite.

Unconditional Positive Regard

To the extent that the therapist finds himself experiencing a warm acceptance of each aspect of the client's experience as being a part of that client, he is experiencing unconditional positive regard. This concept has been developed by Standal (8). It means that there are no *conditions* of acceptance, no feeling of "I like you only *if* you are thus and so." It means a "prizing" of the person, as Dewey has used that

term. It is at the opposite pole from a selective evaluating attitude—
"You are bad in these ways, good in those." It involves as much feeling
of acceptance for the client's expression of negative, "bad," painful,
fearful, defensive, abnormal feelings as for his expression of "good,"
positive, mature, confident, social feelings, as much acceptance of ways
in which he is inconsistent as of ways in which he is consistent. It
means a caring for the client, but not in a possessive way or in such a
way as simply to satisfy the therapist's own needs. It means a caring
for the client as a *separate* person, with permission to have his own
feelings, his own experiences. One client describes the therapist as
"fostering my possession of my own experience . . . that [this] is *my*
experience and that I am actually having it: thinking what I think,
feeling what I feel, wanting what I want, fearing what I fear: no 'ifs,'
'buts,' or 'not reallys.' " This is the type of acceptance which is hypothesized as being necessary if personality change is to occur.

Like the two previous conditions, this fourth condition is a matter of
degree,[3] as immediately becomes apparent if we attempt to define it
in terms of specific research operations. One such method of giving it
definition would be to consider the Q sort for the relationship as
described under Condition 3. To the extent that items expressive of unconditional positive regard are sorted as characteristic of the relationship by both the therapist and the observers, unconditional positive
regard might be said to exist. Such items might include statements of
this order: "I feel no revulsion at anything the client says"; "I feel
neither approval nor disapproval of the client and his statements—
simply acceptance"; "I feel warmly toward the client—toward his
weaknesses and problems as well as his potentialities"; "I am not
inclined to pass judgment on what the client tells me"; "I like the
client." To the extent that both therapist and observers perceive these
items as characteristic, or their opposites as uncharacteristic, Condition 4 might be said to be met.

Empathy

The fifth condition is that the therapist is experiencing an accurate,
empathic understanding of the client's awareness of his own experience. To sense the client's private world as if it were your own, but

---

[3] The phrase "unconditional positive regard" may be an unfortunate one, since
it sounds like an absolute, an all or nothing dispositional concept. It is probably
evident from the description that completely unconditional positive regard would
never exist except in theory. From a clinical and experiental point of view I believe the most accurate statement is that the effective therapist experiences unconditional positive regard for the client during many moments of his contact with
him, yet from time to time he experiences only a conditional positive regard—and
perhaps at times a negative regard, though this is not likely in effective therapy. It
is in this sense that unconditional positive regard exists as a matter of degree in
any relationship.

without ever losing the "as if" quality—this is empathy, and this seems essential to therapy. To sense the client's anger, fear, or confusion as if it were your own, yet without your own anger, fear, or confusion getting bound up in it, is the condition we are endeavoring to describe. When the client's world is this clear to the therapist, and he moves about in it freely, then he can both communicate his understanding of what is clearly known to the client and can also voice meanings in the client's experience of which the client is scarcely aware. As one client described this second aspect: "Every now and again, with me in a tangle of thought and feeling, screwed up in a web of mutually divergent lines of movement, with impulses from different parts of me, and me feeling the feeling of its being all too much and suchlike—then whomp, just like a sunbeam thrusting its way through cloudbanks and tangles of foliage to spread a circle of light on a tangle of forest paths, came some comment from you. [It was] clarity, even disentanglement, an additional twist to the picture, a putting in place. Then the consequence—the sense of moving on, the relaxation. These were sunbeams." That such penetrating empathy is important for therapy is indicated by Fiedler's research (3) in which items such as the following placed high in the description of relationships created by experienced therapists:

> The therapist is well able to understand the patient's feelings.
> The therapist is never in any doubt about what the patient means.
> The therapist's remarks fit in just right with the patient's mood and content.
> The therapist's tone of voice conveys the complete ability to share the patient's feelings.

An operational definition of the therapist's empathy could be provided in different ways. Use might be made of the Q sort described under Condition 3. To the degree that items descriptive of accurate empathy were sorted as characteristic by both the therapist and the observers, this condition would be regarded as existing.

Another way of defining this condition would be for both client and therapist to sort a list of items descriptive of client feelings. Each would sort independently, the task being to represent the feelings which the client had experienced during a just completed interview. If the correlation between client and therapist sortings were high, accurate empathy would be said to exist, a low correlation indicating the opposite conclusion.

Still another way of measuring empathy would be for trained judges to rate the depth and accuracy of the therapist's empathy on the basis of listening to recorded interviews.

The Client's Perception of the Therapist

The final condition as stated is that the client perceives, to a minimal degree, the acceptance and empathy which the therapist experiences for him. Unless some communication of these attitudes has been achieved, then such attitudes do not exist in the relationship as far as the client is concerned, and the therapeutic process could not, by our hypothesis, be initiated.

Since attitudes cannot be directly perceived, it might be somewhat more accurate to state that therapist behaviors and words are perceived by the client as meaning that to some degree the therapist accepts and understands him.

An operational definition of this condition would not be difficult. The client might, after an interview, sort a Q-sort list of items referring to qualities representing the relationship between himself and the therapist. (The same list could be used as for Condition 3.) If several items descriptive of acceptance and empathy are sorted by the client as characteristic of the relationship, then this condition could be regarded as met. In the present state of our knowledge the meaning of "to a minimal degree" would have to be arbitrary.

Some Comments

Up to this point the effort has been made to present, briefly and factually, the conditions which I have come to regard as essential for psychotherapeutic change. I have not tried to give the theoretical context of these conditions nor to explain what seem to me to be the dynamics of their effectiveness. Such explanatory material will be available, to the reader who is interested, in the document already mentioned (see footnote 1).

I have, however, given at least one means of defining, in operational terms, each of the conditions mentioned. I have done this in order to stress the fact that I am not speaking of vague qualities which ideally should be present if some other vague result is to occur. I am presenting conditions which are crudely measurable even in the present state of our technology, and have suggested specific operations in each instance even though I am sure that more adequate methods of measurement could be devised by a serious investigator.

My purpose has been to stress the notion that in my opinion we are dealing with an if-then phenomenon in which knowledge of the dynamics is not essential to testing the hypotheses. Thus, to illustrate from another field: if one substance, shown by a series of operations to be the substance known as hydrochloric acid, is mixed with another substance, shown by another series of operations to be sodium hydroxide, then salt and water will be products of this mixture. This is true whether one regards the results as due to magic, or whether one explains it in the most adequate terms of modern chemical theory. In the same way it is being postulated here that certain definable conditions precede certain definable changes and that this fact exists independently of our efforts to account for it.

THE RESULTING HYPOTHESES

The major value of stating any theory in unequivocal terms is that specific hypotheses may be drawn from it which are capable of proof or disproof. Thus, even if the conditions which have been postulated as necessary and sufficient conditions are more incorrect than correct (which I hope they are not), they could still advance science in this field by providing a base of operations from which fact could be winnowed out from error.

The hypotheses which would follow from the theory given would be of this order:

If these six conditions (as operationally defined) exist, then constructive personality change (as defined) will occur in the client.

If one or more of these conditions is not present, constructive personality change will not occur.

These hypotheses hold in any situation whether it is or is not labeled "psychotherapy."

Only Condition 1 is dichotomous (it either is present or is not), and the remaining five occur in varying degree, each on its continuum. Since this is true, another hypothesis follows, and it is likely that this would be the simplest to test:

If all six conditions are present, then the greater the degree to which Conditions 2 to 6 exist, the more marked will be the constructive personality change in the client.

At the present time the above hypothesis can only be stated in this general form—which implies that all of the conditions have equal weight. Empirical studies will no doubt make possible much more refinement of this hypothesis. It may be, for example, that if anxiety is high in the client, then the other conditions are less important. Or if unconditional positive regard is high (as in a mother's love for her child), then perhaps a modest degree of empathy is sufficient. But at the moment we can only speculate on such possibilities.

SOME IMPLICATIONS

Significant Omissions

If there is any startling feature in the formulation which has been given as to the necessary conditions for therapy, it probably lies in the elements which are omitted. In present-day clinical practice, therapists operate as though there were many other conditions in addition to those described, which are essential for psychotherapy. To point this up it may be well to mention a few of the conditions which, after thoughtful consideration of our research and our experience, are not included.

For example, it is *not* stated that these conditions apply to one type of client, and that other conditions are necessary to bring about psychotherapeutic change with other types of client. Probably no idea is so prevalent in clinical work today as that one works with neurotics in one way, with psychotics in another; that certain therapeutic conditions must be provided for compulsives, others for homosexuals, etc. Because of this heavy weight of clinical opinion to the contrary, it is with some "fear and trembling" that I advance the concept that the essential conditions of psychotherapy exist in a single configuration, even though the client or patient may use them very differently.[4]

It is *not* stated that these six conditions are the essential conditions for client-centered therapy, and that other conditions are essential for other types of psychotherapy. I certainly am heavily influenced by my own experience, and that experience has led me to a viewpoint which is termed "client centered." Nevertheless my aim in stating this theory is to state the conditions which apply to *any* situation in which constructive personality change occurs, whether we are thinking of classical psychoanalysis, or any of its modern offshoots, or Adlerian psychotherapy, or any other. It will be obvious then that in my judgment much of what is considered to be essential would not be found, empirically, to be essential. Testing of some of the stated hypotheses would

---

[4] I cling to this statement of my hypothesis even though it is challenged by a just completed study by Kirtner (5). Kirtner has found, in a group of 26 cases from the Counseling Center at the University of Chicago, that there are sharp differences in the client's mode of approach to the resolution of life difficulties, and that these differences are related to success in psychotherapy. Briefly, the client who sees his problem as involving his relationships, and who feels that he contributes to this problem and wants to change it, is likely to be successful. The client who externalizes his problem, feeling little self-responsibility, is much more likely to be a failure. Thus the implication is that some other conditions need to be provided for psychotherapy with this group. For the present, however, I will stand by my hypothesis as given, until Kirtner's study is confirmed, and until we know an alternative hypothesis to take its place.

throw light on this perplexing issue. We may of course find that various therapies produce various types of personality change, and that for each psychotherapy a separate set of conditions is necessary. Until and unless this is demonstrated, I am hypothesizing that effective psychotherapy of any sort produces similar changes in personality and behavior, and that a single set of preconditions is necessary.

It is *not* stated that psychotherapy is a special kind of relationship, different in kind from all others which occur in everyday life. It will be evident instead that for brief moments, at least, many good friendships fulfill the six conditions. Usually this is only momentarily, however, and then empathy falters, the positive regard becomes conditional, or the congruence of the "therapist" friend becomes overlaid by some degree of facade or defensiveness. Thus the therapeutic relationship is seen as a heightening of the constructive qualities which often exist in part in other relationships, and an extension through time of qualities which in other relationships tend at best to be momentary.

It is *not* stated that special intellectual professional knowledge—psychological, psychiatric, medical, or religious—is required of the therapist. Conditions 3, 4, and 5, which apply especially to the therapist, are qualities of experience, not intellectual information. If they are to be acquired, they must, in my opinion, be acquired through an experiential training—which may be, but usually is not, a part of professional training. It troubles me to hold such a radical point of view, but I can draw no other conclusion from my experience. Intellectual training and the acquiring of information has, I believe, many valuable results—but becoming a therapist is not one of those results.

It is *not* stated that it is necessary for psychotherapy that the therapist have an accurate psychological diagnosis of the client. Here too it troubles me to hold a viewpoint so at variance with my clinical colleagues. When one thinks of the vast proportion of time spent in any psychological, psychiatric, or mental hygiene center on the exhaustive psychological evaluation of the client or patient, it seems as though this *must* serve a useful purpose insofar as psychotherapy is concerned. Yet the more I have observed therapists, and the more closely I have studied research such as that done by Fiedler and others (4), the more I am forced to the conclusion that such diagnostic knowledge is not essential to psychotherapy.[5] It may even be that its defense as a necessary prelude to psychotherapy is simply a protective alternative to the admission that it is, for the most part, a colossal waste of time. There is only one useful purpose I have been able to observe which relates to

[5] There is no intent here to maintain that diagnostic evaluation is useless. We have ourselves made heavy use of such methods in our research studies of change in personality. It is its usefulness as a precondition to psychotherapy which is questioned.

psychotherapy. Some therapists cannot feel secure in the relationship with the client unless they possess such diagnostic knowledge. Without it they feel fearful of him, unable to be empathic, unable to experience unconditional regard, finding it necessary to put up a pretense in the relationship. If they know in *advance* of suicidal impulses they can somehow be more acceptant of them. Thus, for some therapists, the security they perceive in diagnostic information may be a basis for permitting themselves to be integrated in the relationship, and to experience empathy and full acceptance. In these instances a psychological diagnosis would certainly be justified as adding to the comfort and hence the effectiveness of the therapist. But even here it does not appear to be a basic precondition for psychotherapy.[6]

Perhaps I have given enough illustrations to indicate that the conditions I have hypothesized as necessary and sufficient for psychotherapy are striking and unusual primarily by virtue of what they omit. If we were to determine, by a survey of the behaviors of therapists, those hypotheses which they appear to regard as necessary to psychotherapy, the list would be a great deal longer and more complex.

Is This Theoretical Formulation Useful?

Aside from the personal satisfaction it gives as a venture in abstraction and generalization, what is the value of a theoretical statement such as has been offered in this paper? I should like to spell out more fully the usefulness which I believe it may have.

In the field of research it may give both direction and impetus to investigation. Since it sees the conditions of constructive personality change as general, it greatly broadens the opportunities for study. Psychotherapy is not the only situation aimed at constructive personality change. Programs of training for leadership in industry and programs of training for military leadership often aim at such change. Educational institutions or programs frequently aim at development of character and personality as well as at intellectual skills. Community agencies aim at personality and behavioral change in delinquents and criminals. Such programs would provide an opportunity for the broad testing of the hypotheses offered. If it is found that constructive personality change occurs in such programs when the hypothesized conditions are not fulfilled, then the theory would have to be revised. If however the hypotheses are upheld, then the results, both for the planning of such programs and for our knowledge of human dynamics,

---

[6] In a facetious moment I have suggested that such therapists might be made equally comfortable by being given the diagnosis of some other individual, not of this patient or client. The fact that the diagnosis proved inaccurate as psychotherapy continued would not be particularly disturbing, because one always expects to find inaccuracies in the diagnosis as one works with the individual.

would be significant. In the field of psychotherapy itself, the application of consistent hypotheses to the work of various schools of therapists may prove highly profitable. Again the disproof of the hypotheses offered would be as important as their confirmation, either result adding significantly to our knowledge.

For the practice of psychotherapy the theory also offers significant problems for consideration. One of its implications is that the techniques of the various therapies are relatively unimportant except to the extent that they serve as channels for fulfilling one of the conditions. In client-centered therapy, for example, the technique of "reflecting feelings" has been described and commented on (6, pp. 26–36). In terms of the theory here being presented, this technique is by no means an essential condition of therapy. To the extent, however, that it provides a channel by which the therapist communicates a sensitive empathy and an unconditional positive regard, then it may serve as a technical channel by which the essential conditions of therapy are fulfilled. In the same way, the theory I have presented would see no essential value to therapy of such techniques as interpretation of personality dynamics, free association, analysis of dreams, analysis of the transference, hypnosis, interpretation of life style, suggestion, and the like. Each of these techniques may, however, become a channel for communicating the essential conditions which have been formulated. An interpretation may be given in a way which communicates the unconditional positive regard of the therapist. A stream of free association may be listened to in a way which communicates an empathy which the therapist is experiencing. In the handling of the transference an effective therapist often communicates his own wholeness and congruence in the relationship. Similarly for the other techniques. But just as these techniques *may* communicate the elements which are essential for therapy, so any one of them may communicate attitudes and experiences sharply contradictory to the hypothesized conditions of therapy. Feeling may be "reflected" in a way which communicates the therapist's lack of empathy. Interpretations may be rendered in a way which indicates the highly conditional regard of the therapist. Any of the techniques may communicate the fact that the therapist is expressing one attitude at a surface level, and another contradictory attitude which is denied to his own awareness. Thus one value of such a theoretical formulation as we have offered is that it may assist therapists to think more critically about those elements of their experience, attitudes, and behaviors which are essential to psychotherapy, and those which are nonessential or even deleterious to psychotherapy.

Finally, in those programs—educational, correctional, military, or industrial—which aim toward constructive changes in the personality structure and behavior of the individual, this formulation may serve as a very tentative criterion against which to measure the program. Until it is much further tested by research, it cannot be thought of as a valid criterion, but, as in the field of psychotherapy, it may help to stimulate critical analysis and the formulation of alternative conditions and alternative hypotheses.

SUMMARY

Drawing from a larger theoretical context, six conditions are postulated as necessary and sufficient conditions for the initiation of a process of constructive personality change. A brief explanation is given of each condition, and suggestions are made as to how each may be operationally defined for research purposes. The implications of this theory for research, for psychotherapy, and for educational and training programs aimed at constructive personality change, are indicated. It is pointed out that many of the conditions which are commonly regarded as necessary to psychotherapy are, in terms of this theory, nonessential.

REFERENCES

1. Bown, O. H. An investigation of therapeutic relationship in client-centered therapy. Unpublished doctor's dissertation, Univer. of Chicago, 1954.
2. Chodorkoff, B. Self-perception, perceptual defense, and adjustment. *J. abnorm. soc. Psychol.*, 1954, 49, 508–512.
3. Fiedler, F. E. A comparison of therapeutic relationships in psychoanalytic, non-directive and Adlerian therapy. *J. consult. Psychol.*, 1950, 14, 436–445.
4. Fiedler, F. E. Quantitative studies on the role of therapists' feelings toward their patients. In O. H. Mowrer (Ed.), *Psychotherapy: theory and research.* New York: Ronald, 1953.
5. Kirtner, W. L. Success and failure in client-centered therapy as a function of personality variables. Unpublished master's thesis, Univer. of Chicago, 1955.
6. Rogers, C. R. *Client-centered therapy.* Boston: Houghton Mifflin, 1951.
7. Rogers, C. R., & Dymond, Rosalind F. (Eds.) *Psychotherapy and personality change.* Chicago: Univer. of Chicago Press, 1954.
8. Standal, S. The need for positive regard: a contribution to client-centered theory. Unpublished doctor's dissertation, Univer. of Chicago, 1954.

PART VIII

Social Psychology

32.

The Effects of Desegregation on Interracial Interaction and Attitudes

IRWIN SILVERMAN and MARVIN E. SHAW

A significant interest of social psychology, virtually from its inception, has been the study of attitudes—those reasonably durable tendencies to respond evaluatively to particular people, objects, or situations. As a consequence of this interest, much research has been done on attitude change, the measurement of attitudes, and on the subset of attitudes that we call prejudices (generalized negative attitudes toward groups of persons). In the research by Silverman and Shaw presented here, these traditional concerns of social psychology are focused on an important contemporary problem—interracial attitudes as they relate to the desegregation of schools. Silverman and Shaw found that integration of schools did not lead, at least in the first few months, to any significant increase in interactions between black and white students, but did seem to bring about more favorable interracial attitudes. They suggest that simply placing the students in the same schools is insufficient to produce meaningful integration.

Does mere exposure lead to attitude change? Can you think of other ways to facilitate attitude changes in the kind of situation described in this article? (Many social psychologists believe that people might change their attitudes if they can first be made to change their behavior.)

In February 1971, in response to a federal court order, the junior and senior high schools of Gainesville, Florida underwent massive racial integration. Previously these schools had an open enrollment policy

Reprinted from Irwin Silverman and Marvin E. Shaw, "Effects of Sudden Mass School Desegregation on Interracial Interaction and Attitudes in One Southern City," *The Journal of Social Issues,* 1973, 29, pp. 133–42. Copyright 1973 by the Society for the Psychological Study of Social Issues and reproduced by permission.

which resulted in token integration at best. The vast majority of black children in grades seven through twelve attended a completely segregated school; the so-called "white" junior and senior highs contained a select sample of about 5% blacks. Residentially, Gainesville was almost completely segregated.

The February desegregation plan consisted mainly of closing the black school and reassigning students and teachers to the white schools. The result was a distribution of black to white students of about 50-50 in one junior high and 30-70 in the other junior high and in the senior high school.

There were some rumblings of apprehension and protest preceding integration on the part of both the white and the black communities; however, in perspective of what might have been, the merger began rather quietly. The calm was interrupted in March and April with several incidents at each of the schools, including one large fracas at the senior high which precipitated the stationing of a cordon of police nearby for several days. By May, however, matters returned to relative quiescence and have proceeded without noteworthy incident since.

The study reported here was concerned primarily with two effects of the merger, assessed during the semester of its inception. One deals with the amount of interaction between blacks and whites on the school grounds; the other concerns their attitudes toward each other.

Interactions were measured in the three schools and, in the senior high, separately for the 10th grade which comprised the afternoon session and for the 11th and 12th grades combined, which met in the morning. In each school we located the two principal areas of egress: places where large flows of students moved from their last classes off the grounds. During a given observation period, two graduate assistants carrying pocket counters were stationed unobtrusively within view of the area. One counted the total number of students interacting, that is, talking or obviously walking with others. The other observer counted the number of students who were interacting in racially mixed groups, separating these into same- and cross-sex interactions. Each observation period began with the dismissal bell and lasted until the area was clear.

Every individual interacting with one or more others was counted. For example, if four whites and one black, all males, were observed apparently walking together, this was counted as five interracial same-sex interactions. If there was one female of either race in the group, this would have been counted as five interracial cross-sex interactions. Any type or duration of interaction was counted except blatantly aggressive encounters, which were rare but present. An individual was counted just one time in an observation period.

Observations were made in three time intervals: during the third, eighth, and thirteenth weeks of the semester. In each time interval there were four observation periods of each school and session, two in each area.

The measure of racial attitudes consisted of three opinion statements included in a questionnaire with nine additional items relating to topics other than integration. Each statement had six response alternatives: *I agree very much; I agree pretty much; I agree a little; I disagree a little; I disagree pretty much; I disagree very much.* Attitude items were:

1. Desegregation laws go against one of the principles of democracy—that everyone has the right to associate with whom he chooses.
2. The Supreme Court's decision that schools will be desegregated was right and fair.
3. Blacks and whites will find it easier to get along together in the same school than most people think.

Each item was scored from one to six, ranging from low to high prejudice, and the measure for each respondent was the sum of his answers to the three.

Attitudes were measured in all schools but one of the junior highs, where administrative problems precluded the distribution of the questionnaires. Questionnaires were distributed by teachers in English classes, to half the classes at each grade level during the third week of the semester and to the balance during the 13th week. The time samples were also evenly divided with regard to the proficiency levels (accelerated, regular, etc.) of the classes within grades. Students were asked to indicate their names and sex on the questionnaire; information about race was obtained for most of the sample at the close of the semester, from either the teachers or the school records.

The major purposes of this study were quite obvious. We wanted to obtain measures of changes over time in the amount of interaction between blacks and whites and in their racial attitudes. We were interested also in how these changes, if any, related to grade level, race, and sex.

To the best of our knowledge, there have been to date no systematic studies of interracial interactions in desegregated secondary schools. There have been several studies on changes in racial attitudes and, as Carithers (1970) finds in her review, when changes occur they may be in either direction. Beyond simply adding to this score, we attempted to assess the relationship between interaction and attitude change among the various schools and sessions, expecting a direct relationship between these variables, based on the generally held notion that proximity between groups increases attraction by facilitating positive interaction (Allport, 1954; Newcomb, 1961). We were particularly curious, however, about what the effects on attitudes would be if the merger did not result in a meaningful degree of interracial interaction. Dissonance theorists might contend that attitudes will become more positive anyway, as a function of the need to justify integration on the part of the people affected. From another viewpoint though, mutual exposure of the races without interaction may produce negative attitude change. Concepts of racial differences and separateness, which may have been dormant and covert as long as there was no association at all, could become salient and overt and have the effect of increasing prejudice.

RESULTS

Interracial Contact

Table 32–1 shows the percentages of interracial interaction of total interactions for observations made in each of the three time intervals for each school and session. The Ns on which these percentages were based ranged from 221 to 308 in the junior highs and 352 to 423 in the two sessions of the high school.

TABLE 32–1
INTERRACIAL INTERACTIONS AS PERCENTAGE OF TOTAL
INTERACTIONS OBSERVED

| | Observation Periods (Week of) | | |
School	March 11	April 17	May 21
Jr. High I (grade 7–9)	2.9	9.2	7.5
Jr. High II (grade 7–9)	3.3	10.3	6.2
High School (grade 10)	.07	6.6	3.6
High School (grade 11, 12)	2.8	1.9	2.7

Except in the 11th and 12th grade session of the high school, there seems to be a consistent effect—that is, an increase from the beginning to the middle of the term, followed by a more moderate decrease. However, since none of these differences approached significance, there is just the merest suggestion that the amount of interracial interaction changed at all in any of the schools.

In terms of the absolute values of these percentages, the overall paucity of interracial interaction is striking. If race were not at all a factor in who talks to whom, these figures should hover around the 50% mark. The largest percentage in any time period for any school, however, is 10.3 and the mean of all percentages is 4.8. In general, then, one of every twenty students we observed interacting was communicating with someone of the other race. In the 11th and 12th grade session, this figure was one of forty.

Of the total number of interracial interactions in the two junior highs, 90% were among members of the same sex. The comparable percentage for the senior high (including both sessions) was 65%, a difference significant at $p < .01$. It is feasible, however, that boys and girls interact more, in general, in senior than in junior high and we did not have baseline measures to determine differences in relative frequencies.

There were no differences approaching significance in the ratio of same vs. opposite sex interracial interactions across time for any school or session, but because of the generally low frequency of interracial contacts, the Ns in these analyses were too small to warrant a conclusion.

Interracial Attitudes

The attitude data were analyzed by an unweighted means analysis of variance involving two time samples, sex, race, and grade levels seven through twelve. First, we report the data with the two time samples combined.

There were no main effects of sex or race, but there was an interaction significant at $p < .001$. Both white females and black males (with means of 10.92 and 10.94 respectively) were more positive toward integration than either black females or white males (for whom the means were, respectively, 11.53 and 11.66). Singer (1966) has reported some congruent findings on racial attitudes of fifth grade northern children. In her study, in both segregated and nonsegregated schools, white females indicated more willingness than white males to associate with blacks, and black females expressed less willingness than black males to associate with whites.

There was a main effect of grade level ($p < .001$), a curvilinear function, with the highest average prejudice score (11.8) reported in the tenth grade and the lowest in the 12th (10.2). However, while there was no interaction of grade level with sex, there was one with race, significant at $p < .005$. This grade x race interaction is shown in Figure 32–1. The distributions for blacks and whites are obviously similar with the marked exception of the 9th grade, where the black students are at their peak of negative racial feelings and the whites are at about their most tolerant. The curve is also notably flatter for the white sample, suggesting that there were more extreme differences between grade levels in the attitudes of the blacks.

These distributions are consistent in one aspect with some data reported by Lombardi (1963) regarding attitudes of whites toward blacks in newly integrated Maryland high schools. He found also that

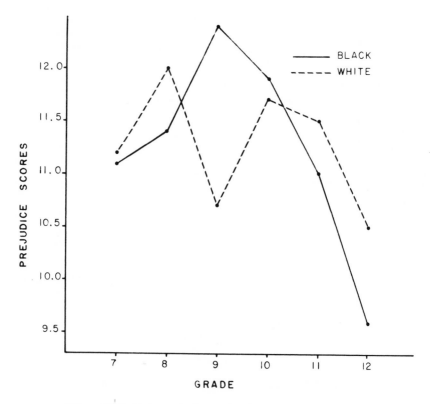

Figure 32–1. Mean prejudice scores by race and grade level.

12th graders were more positive than children in grades nine through 11. The question for both sets of findings, however, is whether they reflect actual attitudinal differences or, perhaps, a more sophisticated sense of socially desirable responding on the part of the older students.

In regard to the temporal analyses, the mean for the March sample was 11.45 and for the May sample, 11.08. The confidence level for this difference was .07, which suggests strongly that racial attitudes became more positive in general during the first semester of integration.*

---

* Incomplete questionnaires, i.e., those with one or more of the three race items unanswered or without designation of sex or name (without which we could not determine race), were excluded. There were 282 exclusions for the March group and 52 for May, and the resultant sample *Ns* were 1424 and 1201, respectively. The greater number of incomplete questionnaires in the first testing may have reflected more adverse attitudes during this period; hence differences between time samples, to some extent, may underestimate actual attitude change.

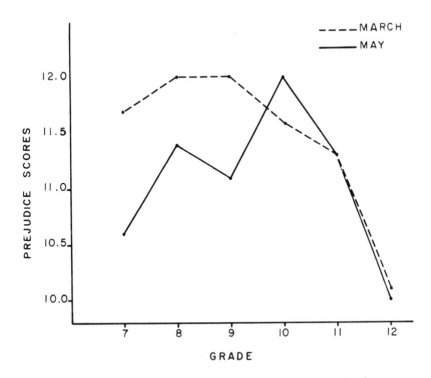

Figure 32–2. Mean prejudice scores by time and grade level.

Surprisingly, to us at least, there were no significant interactions of time with sex, race, or grade level. Nevertheless, we feel that the trends of these relationships are worth reporting. Decreases in prejudice were more than two and a half times greater for females than males and more than three times greater for blacks than whites. Within these groups, black females changed more than twice as much as white females; all of the change for males was attributable to blacks. The function of these effects was that blacks were somewhat more prejudiced than whites at the beginning of the semester and somewhat less at the end. In the absence of statistical support we must assume that these differences may well have been due to random fluctuation, but they are congruent with data from McWhirt (1967), the only other longitudinal study of newly integrated high schools we have found, in which attitude changes on the part of blacks and whites were assessed separately. McWhirt, working in a southern community, found that blacks showed significantly greater change in the direction of tolerance than whites.

The relationship between time and grade is shown in Figure 32–2. Though the confidence level for this interaction falls between .20 and .25, it is apparent that virtually all of the decrease in prejudice that did occur was in grades seven through nine.

CONCLUSION

Considering all the data of this study, there are several aspects that seem particularly relevant to school mergers and their potential effects on racial attitudes. The findings, or nonfindings, that give us most pause are the strikingly low frequencies of interracial interactions in all schools, and the very meager suggestion that interracial contacts increased at all during the first four months of the merger. These conclusions are, naturally, subject to the limitations of our measure. We feel, however, that the extent to which blacks and whites mingle on their way from classes is probably a valid index of the extent to which they are enjoined socially throughout the day. For the most part, then, this merger resulted in mutual exposure of the races but not in integration in any real sense.

Nonetheless, racial attitudes did not worsen as might have been expected, and there was a strong suggestion that they improved. As we described previously, dissonance reduction may account for some of this change. Related also is Zajonc's (1968) work on the enhancing attitudinal effects of mere exposure. Further, Williams (1968) found that blacks in a segregated southern high school who were to be integrated the following year were philosophically committed to the action but personally very apprehensive. The gradual relief of these anxieties may have contributed, in our sample, to the improvement of attitudes.

Finally, we are compelled to note that tolerance did increase for the most part in grades seven through nine, where there was the greatest amount of interracial interaction. These effects did not approach significance and the absolute percentages of interracial contacts were quite low; however, based on this suggestion of a relationship, we would venture the thought that the most salient task for school systems engaged in racial mergers is to plan programs that result in integration in more than an administrative sense.

Cottle (1967) made this observation in general about school integration programs:

> The sadness of the drama is that it takes place with almost no pyschological preparation and with no time devoted to the resolution of human and institutional complications. Yet as though by some magic, students are supposed to live peaceably and to learn something. The drama's irony is that where schools in the past have exulted in their socializing function,

when integration becomes a reality they hurriedly retreat to their fundamental didactic activities. School boards try to combine the races in varying ratios—advantageous to the whites but justified by national or regional proportions—with the hope that somehow the kids will work it out [p. 22].

To pose the problem, however, is far simpler than to pose a solution. Gaughran (1965) wrote about the efficacy of biracial discussion groups in a recently integrated northern high school. These were conducted also in the Gainesville high school and reports have it that they were quite successful in facilitating communication and understanding among group members. This vehicle, however, reaches a small and select sample of volunteers who are obviously among the most receptive to biracial friendships. The premise that the inclinations fostered in these groups become disseminated among the school population at large seems, at least from our data, to be unduly optimistic.

It would appear that more massive efforts are required. The direction these should take constitutes a most timely and compelling question for community psychologists and educators.

REFERENCES

ALLPORT, G. W. *The nature of prejudice.* Cambridge, Mass: Addison-Wesley, 1954.

CARITHERS, M. W. School desegregation and racial cleavage, 1954–1970: A review of the literature. *Journal of Social Issues,* 1970, **26**(4), 25–47.

COTTLE, T. J. Encounter in color. *Psychology Today,* 1967, **1**, 22–27.

GAUGHRAN, B. Bi-racial discussion groups in a suburban high school. *New York State Education,* 1965, **53**, 26–27.

LOMBARDI, D. N. Factors affecting changes in attitudes toward Negroes among high school students. *Journal of Negro Education,* 1963, **32**, 129–136.

McWHIRT, R. A. The effects of desegregation on prejudice, academic aspiration and the self-concept of tenth grade students. *Dissertation Abstracts,* 1967, **28**, 2610.

NEWCOMB, T. M. *The acquaintance process.* New York: Holt, Rinehart & Winston, 1961.

SINGER, D. Interracial attitudes of negro and white fifth grade children in segregated and unsegregated schools. (Doctoral dissertation, Columbia University) *Dissertation Abstracts,* 1966, **27**, 3143.

WILLIAMS, R. L. Cognitive and affective components of southern negro students' attitudes towards academic integration. *Journal of Social Psychology,* 1968, **76**, 107–111.

ZAJONC, R. B. Attitudinal effects of mere exposure. *Journal of Personality and Social Psychology,* 1968, **9**, 1–27.

33.

Bystander Intervention in Emergencies: Diffusion of Responsibility

JOHN M. DARLEY and BIBB LATANÉ

It has become fashionable to attribute the failure of people to provide aid to another person in distress to "indifference," "apathy," "moral callousness," or "dehumanization due to urbanization." Items from the daily press, the most noted being the Genovese case described below, focus on these explanations. Darley and Latané feel that apathy as the answer to bystanders' unresponsiveness is an oversimplification. Instead they hypothesize that it is the presence of others that diffuses responsibility and inhibits the individual from helping. (In other studies,* these researchers have demonstrated that the presence of other people not only diffuses responsibility but also may affect the interpretation the bystander puts on an ambiguous emergency situation.)

You can view this study as an attempt to understand the factors that lead to unresponsiveness in a bystander. But you should also look at it from the other side: What are the factors that facilitate "pro-social" (as contrasted with "antisocial" or "asocial") behavior? What are the circumstances that will lead an individual to intervene in an emergency?

Do you still believe there is "safety in numbers"?

SEVERAL YEARS ago, a young woman was stabbed to death in the middle of a street in a residential section of New York City. Although such murders are not entirely routine, the incident received little pub-

* Reported in a prizewinning book: Latané and Darley, *The Unresponsive Bystander*, Appleton-Century-Crofts, 1970.

Reprinted from *Journal of Personality and Social Psychology*, 1968, 8, pp. 377–83. Copyright 1968 by the American Psychological Association. Reprinted by permission.

lic attention until several weeks later when the New York Times disclosed another side to the case: at least 38 witnesses had observed the attack—and none had even attempted to intervene. Although the attacker took more than half an hour to kill Kitty Genovese, not one of the 38 people who watched from the safety of their own apartments came out to assist her. Not one even lifted the telephone to call the police (Rosenthal, 1964).

Preachers, professors, and news commentators sought the reasons for such apparently conscienceless and inhumane lack of intervention. Their conclusions ranged from "moral decay," to "dehumanization produced by the urban environment," to "alienation," "anomie," and "existential despair." An analysis of the situation, however, suggests that factors other than apathy and indifference were involved.

A person witnessing an emergency situation, particularly such a frightening and dangerous one as a stabbing, is in conflict. There are obvious humanitarian norms about helping the victim, but there are also rational and irrational fears about what might happen to a person who does intervene (Milgram & Hollander, 1964). "I didn't want to get involved," is a familiar comment, and behind it lies fears of physical harm, public embarrassment, involvement with police procedures, lost work days and jobs, and other unknown dangers.

In certain circumstances, the norms favoring intervention may be weakened, leading bystanders to resolve the conflict in the direction of nonintervention. One of these circumstances may be the presence of other onlookers. For example, in the case above, each observer, by seeing lights and figures in other apartment house windows, knew that others were also watching. However, there was no way to tell how the other observers were reacting. These two facts provide several reasons why any individual may have delayed or failed to help. The responsibility for helping was diffused among the observers; there was also diffusion of any potential blame for not taking action; and finally, it was possible that somebody, unperceived, had already initiated helping action.

When only one bystander is present in an emergency, if help is to come, it must come from him. Although he may choose to ignore it (out of concern for his personal safety, or desires "not to get involved"), any pressure to intervene focuses uniquely on him. When there are several observers present, however, the pressures to intervene do not focus on any of the observers; instead the responsibility for intervention is shared among all the onlookers and is not unique to any one. As a result, no one helps.

A second possibility is that potential blame may be diffused. However much we may wish to think that an individual's moral behavior is divorced from considerations of personal punishment or reward, there is both theory and evidence to the contrary (Aronfreed, 1964; Miller

& Dollard, 1941, Whiting & Child, 1953). It is perfectly reasonable to assume that, under circumstances of group responsibility for a punishable act, the punishment or blame that accrues to any one individual is often slight or nonexistent.

Finally, if others are known to be present, but their behavior cannot be closely observed, any one bystander can assume that one of the other observers is already taking action to end the emergency. Therefore, his own intervention would be only redundant—perhaps harmfully or confusingly so. Thus, given the presence of other onlookers whose behavior cannot be observed, any given bystander can rationalize his own inaction by convincing himself that "somebody else must be doing something."

These considerations lead to the hypothesis that the more bystanders to an emergency, the less likely, or the more slowly, any one bystander will intervene to provide aid. To test this proposition it would be necessary to create a situation in which a realistic "emergency" could plausibly occur. Each subject should also be blocked from communicating with others to prevent his getting information about their behavior during the emergency. Finally, the experimental situation should allow for the assessment of the speed and frequency of the subjects' reaction to the emergency. The experiment reported below attempted to fulfill these conditions.

PROCEDURE

Overview. A college student arrived in the laboratory and was ushered into an individual room from which a communication system would enable him to talk to the other participants. It was explained to him that he was to take part in a discussion about personal problems associated with college life and that the discussion would be held over the intercom system, rather than face-to-face, in order to avoid embarrassment by preserving the anonymity of the subjects. During the course of the discussion, one of the other subjects underwent what appeared to be a very serious nervous seizure similar to epilepsy. During the fit it was impossible for the subject to talk to the other discussants or to find out what, if anything, they were doing about the emergency. The dependent variable was the speed with which the subjects reported the emergency to the experimenter. The major independent variable was the number of people the subject thought to be in the discussion group.

Subjects. Fifty-nine female and thirteen male students in introductory psychology courses at New York University were contacted to take part in an unspecified experiment as part of a class requirement.

Method. Upon arriving for the experiment, the subject found himself in a long corridor with doors opening off it to several small rooms. An experimental assistant met him, took him to one of the rooms, and seated him at a table. After filling out a background information form, the subject was given a pair of headphones with an attached microphone and was told to listen for instructions.

Over the intercom, the experimenter explained that he was interested in learning about the kinds of personal problems faced by normal college students in a high pressure, urban environment. He said that to avoid possible embarrassment about discussing personal problems with strangers several precautions had been taken. First, subjects would remain anonymous, which was why they had been placed in individual rooms rather than face-to-face. (The actual reason for this was to allow tape recorder simulation of the other subjects and the emergency.) Second, since the discussion might be inhibited by the presence of outside listeners, the experimenter would not listen to the initial discussion, but would get the subject's reactions later, by questionnaire. (The real purpose of this was to remove the obviously responsible experimenter from the scene of the emergency.)

The subjects were told that since the experimenter was not present, it was necessary to impose some organization. Each person would talk in turn, presenting his problems to the group. Next, each person in turn would comment on what the others had said, and finally, there would be a free discussion. A mechanical switching device would regulate this discussion sequence and each subject's microphone would be on for about 2 minutes. While any microphone was on, all other microphones would be off. Only one subject, therefore, could be heard over the network at any given time. The subjects were thus led to realize when they later heard the seizure that only the victim's microphone was on and that there was no way of determining what any of the other witnesses were doing, nor of discussing the event and its possible solution with the others. When these instructions had been given, the discussion began.

In the discussion, the future victim spoke first, saying that he found it difficult to get adjusted to New York City and to his studies. Very hesitantly, and with obvious embarrassment, he mentioned that he was prone to seizures, particularly when studying hard or taking exams. The other people, including the real subject, took their turns and discussed similar problems (minus, of course, the proneness to seizures). The naive subject talked last in the series, after the last prerecorded voice was played.[1]

[1] To test whether the order in which the subjects spoke in the first discussion round significantly affected the subjects' speed of report, the order in which the subjects spoke was varied (in the six-person group). This had no significant or noticeable effect on the speed of the subjects' reports.

When it was again the victim's turn to talk, he made a few relatively calm comments, and then, growing increasingly louder and incoherent, he continued:

I-er-um-I think I-I need-er-if-if could-er-er-somebody er-er-er-er-er-er-er give me a little-er-give me a little help here because-er-I-er-I'm-er-er-h-h-having a-a-a real problem-er-right now and I-er-if somebody could help me out it would-it would-er-er s-s-sure be-sure be good . . . because-er-there-er-er-a cause I-er-I-uh-I've got a-a one of the-er-sei-----er-er-things coming on and-and-and I could really-er-use some help so if somebody would-er-give me a little h-help-uh-er-er-er-er-er c-could somebody-er-er-help-er-uh-uh-uh (choking sounds). . . . I'm gonna die-er-er-I'm . . . gonna die-er-help-er-er-seizure-er-[chokes, then quiet].

The experimenter began timing the speed of the real subject's response at the beginning of the victim's speech. Informed judges listening to the tape have estimated that the victim's increasingly louder and more disconnected ramblings clearly represented a breakdown about 70 seconds after the signal for the victim's second speech. The victim's speech was abruptly cut off 125 seconds after this signal, which could be interpreted by the subject as indicating that the time allotted for that speaker had elapsed and the switching circuits had switched away from him. Times reported in the results are measured from the start of the fit.

Group Size Variable. The major independent variable of the study was the number of other people that the subject believed also heard the fit. By the assistant's comments before the experiment, and also by the number of voices heard to speak in the first round of the group discussion, the subject was led to believe that the discussion group was one of three sizes: either a two-person group (consisting of a person who would later have a fit and the real subject), a three-person group (consisting of the victim, the real subject, and one confederate voice), or a six-person group (consisting of the victim, the real subject, and four confederate voices). All the confederates' voices were tape-recorded.

Variations in Group Composition. Varying the kind as well as the number of bystanders present at an emergency should also vary the amount of responsibility felt by any single bystander. To test this, several variations of the three-person group were run. In one three-person condition, the taped bystander voice was that of a female, in another a male, and in the third a male who said that he was a premedical student who occasionally worked in the emergency wards at Bellevue hospital.

In the above conditions, the subjects were female college students. In a final condition males drawn from the same introductory psychology subject pool were tested in a three-person female-bystander condition.

Time to Help. The major dependent variable was the time elapsed from the start of the victim's fit until the subject left her experimental cubicle. When the subject left her room, she saw the experimental assistant seated at the end of the hall, and invariably went to the assistant. If 6 minutes elapsed without the subject having emerged from her room, the experiment was terminated.

As soon as the subject reported the emergency, or after 6 minutes had elapsed, the experimental assistant disclosed the true nature of the experiment, and dealt with any emotions aroused in the subject. Finally the subject filled out a questionnaire concerning her thoughts and feelings during the emergency, and completed scales of Machiavellianism, anomie, and authoritarianism (Christie, 1964), a social desirability scale (Crowne & Marlowe, 1964), a social responsibility scale (Daniels & Berkowitz, 1964), and reported vital statistics and socioeconomic data.

RESULTS

Plausibility of Manipulation

Judging by the subjects' nervousness when they reported the fit to the experimenter, by their surprise when they discovered that the fit was simulated, and by comments they made during the fit (when they thought their microphones were off), one can conclude that almost all of the subjects perceived the fit as real. There were two exceptions in different experimental conditions, and the data for these subjects were dropped from the analysis.

Effect of Group Size on Helping

The number of bystanders that the subject perceived to be present had a major effect on the likelihood with which she would report the emergency (Table 33–1). Eighty-five percent of the subjects who thought they alone knew of the victim's plight reported the seizure before the victim was cut off, only 31% of those who thought four other bystanders were present did so.

Every one of the subjects in the two-person groups, but only 62% of the subjects in the six-person groups, ever reported the emergency. The cumulative distributions of response times for groups of different perceived size (Figure 33–1) indicate that, by any point in time, more subjects from the two-person groups had responded than from the

TABLE 33–1

EFFECTS OF GROUP SIZE ON LIKELIHOOD AND SPEED OF RESPONSE

Group Size	N	% Responding by End of Fit	Time in Sec.	Speed Score
2 (S & victim)	13	85	52	.87
3 (S, victim, & 1 other)	26	62	93	.72
6 (S, victim, & 4 others)	13	31	166	.51

Note.—p value of differences: $\chi^2 = 7.91$, $p < .02$; $F = 8.09$, $p < .01$, for speed scores.

three-person groups, and more from the three-person groups than from the six-person groups.

Ninety-five percent of all the subjects who ever responded did so within the first half of the time available to them. No subject who had not reported within 3 minutes after the fit ever did so. The shapes of these distributions suggest that had the experiment been allowed to run for a considerably longer time, few additional subjects would have responded.

Speed of Response

To achieve a more detailed analysis of the results, each subject's time score was transformed into a "speed" score by taking the reciprocal of the response time in seconds and multiplying by 100. The effect of this transformation was to deemphasize differences between longer time scores, thus reducing the contribution to the results of the arbitrary 6-minute limit on scores. A high speed score indicates a fast response.

An analysis of variance indicates that the effect of group size is highly significant ($p < .01$). Duncan multiple-range tests indicate that all but the two- and three-person groups differ significantly from one another ($p < .05$)

Victim's Likelihood of Being Helped

An individual subject is less likely to respond if he thinks that others are present. But what of the victim? Is the inhibition of the response of each individual strong enough to counteract the fact that with five onlookers there are five times as many people available to help? From the data of this experiment, it is possible mathematically to create hypothetical groups with one, two, or five observers.[2] The calculations indicate that the victim is about equally likely to get help from one bystander as from two. The victim is considerably more likely to have gotten help from one or two observers than from five

[2] The formula for the probability that at least one person will help by a given time is $1 - (1 - P)^n$ where n is the number of observers and P is the probability of a single individual (who thinks he is one of n observers) helping by that time.

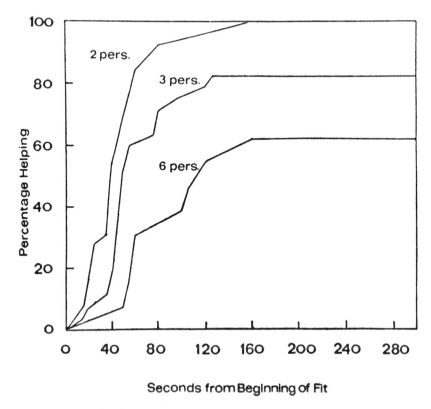

Figure 33–1. Cumulative distributions of helping responses.

during the first minute of the fit. For instance, by 45 seconds after the start of the fit, the victim's chances of having been helped by the single bystanders were about 50%, compared to none in the five observer condition. After the first minute, the likelihood of getting help from at least one person is high in all three conditions.

Effect of Group Composition on Helping the Victim

Several variations of the three-person group were run. In one pair of variations, the female subject thought the other bystander was either male or female; in another, she thought the other bystander was a premedical student who worked in an emergency ward at Bellevue hospital. As Table 33–2 shows, the variations in sex and medical competence of the other bystander had no important or detectable effect on speed of response. Subjects responded equally frequently and fast whether the other bystander was female, male, or medically experienced.

TABLE 33–2
EFECTS OF GROUP COMPOSITION ON LIKELIHOOD
AND SPEED OF RESPONSE*

Group Composition	N	% Responding by End of Fit	Time in Sec.	Speed Score
Female S, male other	13	62	94	74
Female S, female other	13	62	92	71
Female S, male medic other	5	100	60	77
Male S, female other	13	69	110	68

* Three-person group, male victim.

Sex of the Subject and Speed of Response

Coping with emergencies is often thought to be the duty of males, especially when females are present, but there was no evidence that this was the case in this study. Male subjects responded to the emergency with almost exactly the same speed as did females (Table 33–2).

Reasons for Intervention or Nonintervention

After the debriefing at the end of the experiment each subject was given a 15-item checklist and asked to check those thoughts which had "crossed your mind when you heard Subject 1 calling for help." Whatever the condition, each subject checked very few thoughts, and there were no significant differences in number or kind of thoughts in the different experimental groups. The only thoughts checked by more than a few subjects were "I didn't know what to do" (18 out of 65 subjects), "I thought it must be some sort of fake" (20 out of 65), and "I didn't know exactly what was happening" (26 out of 65).

It is possible that subjects were ashamed to report socially undesirable rationalizations, or, since the subjects checked the list *after* the true nature of the experiment had been explained to them, their memories might have been blurred. It is our impression, however, that most subjects checked few reasons because they had few coherent thoughts during the fit.

We asked all subjects whether the presence or absence of other bystanders had entered their minds during the time that they were hearing the fit. Subjects in the three- and six-person groups reported that they were aware that other people were present, but they felt that this made no difference to their own behavior.

Individual Difference Correlates of Speed of Report

The correlations between speed of report and various individual differences on the personality and background measures were obtained by normalizing the distribution of report speeds within each experimental condition and pooling these scores across all conditions (n = 62–65). Personality measures showed no important or significant correlations with speed of reporting the emergency. In fact, only one of the 16 individual difference measures, the size of the community in which the subject grew up, correlated ($r = -.26$, $p < .05$) with the speed of helping.

DISCUSSION

Subjects, whether or not they intervened, believed the fit to be genuine and serious. "My God, he's having a fit," many subjects said to themselves (and were overheard via their microphones) at the onset of the fit. Others gasped or simply said "Oh." Several of the male subjects swore. One subject said to herself, "It's just my kind of luck, something has to happen to me!" Several subjects spoke aloud of their confusion about what course of action to take, "Oh God, what should I do?"

When those subjects who intervened stepped out of their rooms, they found the experimental assistant down the hall. With some uncertainty, but without panic, they reported the situation. "Hey, I think Number 1 is very sick. He's having a fit or something." After ostensibly checking on the situation, the experimenter returned to report that "everything is under control." The subjects accepted these assurances with obvious relief.

Subjects who failed to report the emergency showed few signs of the apathy and indifference thought to characterize "unresponsive bystanders." When the experimenter entered her room to terminate the situation, the subject often asked if the victim was "all right." "Is he being taken care of?" "He's all right isn't he?" Many of these subjects showed physical signs of nervousness; they often had trembling hands and sweating palms. If anything, they seemed more emotionally aroused than did the subjects who reported the emergency.

Why, then, didn't they respond? It is our impression that nonintervening subjects had not decided *not* to respond. Rather they were still in a state of indecision and conflict concerning whether to respond or not. The emotional behavior of these nonresponding subjects was a sign of their continuing conflict, a conflict that other subjects resolved by responding.

The fit created a conflict situation of the avoidance-avoidance type. On the one hand, subjects worried about the guilt and shame they would feel if they did not help the person in distress. On the other hand, they were concerned not to make fools of themselves by overreacting, not to ruin the ongoing experiment by leaving their intercom, and not to destroy the anonymous nature of the situation which the experimenter had earlier stressed as important. For subjects in the two-person condition, the obvious distress of the victim and his need for help were so important that their conflict was easily resolved. For the subjects who knew there were other bystanders present, the cost of not helping was reduced and the conflict they were in more acute. Caught between the two negative alternatives of letting the victim continue to suffer or the costs of rushing in to help, the nonresponding bystanders vacillated between them rather than choosing not to respond. This distinction may be academic for the victim, since he got no help in either case, but it is an extremely important one for arriving at an understanding of the causes of bystanders' failures to help.

Although the subjects experienced stress and conflict during the experiment, their general reactions to it were highly positive. On a questionnaire administered after the experimenter had discussed the nature and purpose of the experiment, every single subject found the experiment either "interesting" or "very interesting" and was willing to participate in similar experiments in the future. All subjects felt they understood what the experiment was about and indicated that they thought the deceptions were necessary and justified. All but one felt they were better informed about the nature of psychological research in general.

Male subjects reported the emergency no faster than did females. These results (or lack of them) seem to conflict with the Berkowitz, Klanderman, and Harris (1964) finding that males tend to assume more responsibility and take more initiative than females in giving help to dependent others. Also, females reacted equally fast when the other bystander was another female, a male, or even a person practiced in dealing with medical emergencies. The ineffectiveness of these manipulations of group composition cannot be explained by general insensitivity of the speed measure, since the group-size variable had a marked effect on report speed.

It might be helpful in understanding this lack of difference to distinguish two general classes of intervention in emergency situations: direct and reportorial. Direct intervention (breaking up a fight, extinguishing a fire, swimming out to save a drowner) often requires skill, knowledge, or physical power. It may involve danger. American cultural norms and Berkowitz's results seem to suggest that males are more responsible than females for this kind of direct intervention.

A second way of dealing with an emergency is to report it to someone qualified to handle it, such as the police. For this kind of intervention, there seem to be no norms requiring male action. In the present study, subjects clearly intended to report the emergency rather than take direct action. For such indirect intervention, sex or medical competence does not appear to affect one's qualifications or responsibilities. Anybody, male or female, medically trained or not, can find the experimenter.

In this study, no subject was able to tell how the other subjects reacted to the fit. (Indeed, there were no other subjects actually present.) The effects of group size on speed of helping, therefore, are due simply to the perceived presence of others rather than to the influence of their actions. This means that the experimental situation is unlike emergencies, such as a fire, in which bystanders interact with each other. It is, however, similar to emergencies, such as the Genovese murder, in which spectators knew others were also watching but were prevented by walls between them from communication that might have counteracted the diffusion of responsibility.

The present results create serious difficulties for one class of commonly given explanations for the failure of bystanders to intervene in actual emergencies, those involving apathy or indifference. These explanations generally assert that people who fail to intervene are somehow different in kind from the rest of us, that they are "alienated by industrialization," "dehumanized by urbanization," "depersonalized by living in the cold society," or "psychopaths." These explanations serve a dual function for people who adopt them. First, they explain (if only in a nominal way) the puzzling and frightening problem of why people watch others die. Second, they give individuals reason to deny that they too might fail to help in a similar situation.

The results of this experiment seem to indicate that such personality variables may not be as important as these explanations suggest. Alienation, Machiavellianism, acceptance of social responsibility, need for approval, and authoritarianism are often cited in these explanations. Yet they did not predict the speed or likelihood of help. In sharp contrast, the perceived number of bystanders did. The explanation of bystander "apathy" may lie more in the bystander's response to other observers than in presumed personality deficiencies of "apathetic" individuals. Although this realization may force us to face the guilt-provoking possibility that we too might fail to intervene, it also suggests that individuals are not, of necessity, "noninterveners" because of their personalities. If people understand the situational forces that can make them hesitate to intervene, they may better overcome them.

REFERENCES

ARONFREED, J. The origin of self-criticism. *Psychological Review*, 1964, **71**, 193–219.

BERKOWITZ, L., KLANDERMAN, S., & HARRIS, R. Effects of experimenter awareness and sex of subject on reactions to dependency relationships. *Sociometry*, 1964, **27**, 327–329.

CHRISTIE, R. The prevalence of machiavellian orientations. Paper presented at the meeting of the American Psychological Association, Los Angeles, 1964.

CROWNE, D., & MARLOWE, D. *The approval motive.* New York: Wiley, 1964.

DANIELS, L., & BERKOWITZ, L. Liking and response to dependency relationships. *Human Relations,* 1963, **16,** 141–148.

MILGRAM, S., & HOLLANDER, P. Murder they heard. *Nation,* 1964, **198,** 602–604.

MILLER, N., & DOLLARD, J. *Social learning and imitation.* New Haven: Yale University Press, 1941.

ROSENTHAL, A. M. *Thirty-eight witnesses.* New York: McGraw-Hill, 1964.

WHITING, J. W. M., & CHILD, I. *Child training and personality.* New Haven: Yale University Press, 1953.

34.

Behavioral Study of Obedience

STANLEY MILGRAM

The following article is the report of an ingenious experiment to determine how far ordinary people might go in punishing an innocent victim when sanctioned by scientific authority. It is the first of a series of studies by Milgram aimed at exploring the conditions under which obedience (or defiance) occurs. Subsequent studies, described in his recent book (see reference below), demonstrate that destructive obedience will be reduced with physical proximity to the victim, when the authority figure is not physically present, or when the punisher is one among a predominantly defiant group. (This last point suggests one instance in which conforming to group pressure can have positive effects. Most studies of "conformity" ignore these possible "prosocial" effects.)

Could you have guessed the outcome of this experiment? Does it simply confirm what you knew all along? How do you think you would have reacted as a "teacher" in this experiment?

When this study was first reported, and later when the more detailed book appeared, considerable controversy arose over the ethics of deceiving and manipulating experimental subjects. Do you see anything unethical about this kind of experiment? (Keep in mind that the purpose of the research is not simply to determine if obedience occurs, but rather to understand the forces underlying obedient and defiant behavior.)

Reprinted from *Journal of Abnormal and Social Psychology*, 1963, 67, pp. 371–78. Copyright 1963 by the American Psychological Association. Reprinted by permission. The research presented in this article is described more fully in *Obedience to Authority*, published by Harper & Row Publishers, 1974.

Obedience is as basic an element in the structure of social life as one can point to. Some system of authority is a requirement of all communal living, and it is only the man dwelling in isolation who is not forced to respond, through defiance or submission, to the commands of others. Obedience, as a determinant of behavior, is of particular relevance to our time. It has been reliably established that from 1933–45 millions of innocent persons were systematically slaughtered on command. Gas chambers were built, death camps were guarded, daily quotas of corpses were produced with the same efficiency as the manufacture of appliances. These inhumane policies may have originated in the mind of a single person, but they could only be carried out on a massive scale if a very large number of persons obeyed orders.

Obedience is the psychological mechanism that links individual action to political purpose. It is the dispositional cement that binds men to systems of authority. Facts of recent history and observation in daily life suggest that for many persons obedience may be a deeply ingrained behavior tendency, indeed, a prepotent impulse overriding training in ethics, sympathy, and moral conduct. C. P. Snow (1961) points to its importance when he writes:

> When you think of the long and gloomy history of man, you will find more hideous crimes have been committed in the name of obedience than have ever been committed in the name of rebellion. If you doubt that, read William Shirer's "Rise and Fall of the Third Reich." The German Officer Corps were brought up in the most rigorous code of obedience . . . in the name of obedience they were party to, and assisted in, the most wicked large scale actions in the history of the world [p. 24].

While the particular form of obedience dealt with in the present study has its antecedents in these episodes, it must not be thought all obedience entails acts of aggression against others. Obedience serves numerous productive functions. Indeed, the very life of society is predicated on its existence. Obedience may be ennobling and educative and refer to acts of charity and kindness, as well as to destruction.

GENERAL PROCEDURE

A procedure was devised which seems useful as a tool for studying obedience (Milgram, 1961). It consists of ordering a naive subject to administer electric shock to a victim. A simulated shock generator is used, with 30 clearly marked voltage levels that range from 15 to 450 volts. The instrument bears verbal designations that range from Slight Shock to Danger: Severe Shock. The responses of the victim, who is a trained confederate of the experimenter, are standardized. The orders to administer shocks are given to the naive subject in the context of a "learning experiment" ostensibly set up to study the effects of punishment on memory. As the experiment proceeds the naive subject is commanded to administer increasingly more intense shocks to the victim, even to the point of reaching the level marked Danger: Severe Shock. Internal resistances become stronger, and at a certain point the subject refuses to go on with the experiment. Behavior prior to this rupture is considered "obedience," in that the subject complies with the commands of the experimenter. The point of rupture is the act of disobedience. A quantitative value is assigned to the subject's performance based on the maximum intensity shock he is willing to administer before he refuses to participate further. Thus for any particular subject and for any particular experimental condition the degree of obedience may be specified with a numerical value. The crux of the study is to systematically vary the factors believed to alter the degree of obedience to the experimental commands.

The technique allows important variables to be manipulated at several points in the experiment. One may vary aspects of the source of command, content and form of command, instrumentalities for its execution, target object, general social setting, etc. The problem, therefore, is not one of designing increasingly more numerous experimental conditions, but of selecting those that best illuminate the *process* of obedience from the sociopsychological standpoint.

RELATED STUDIES

The inquiry bears an important relation to philosophic analyses of obedience and authority (Arendt, 1958; Friedrich, 1958; Weber, 1947), an early experimental study of obedience by Frank (1944), studies in "authoritarianism" (Adorno, Frenkel-Brunswik, Levinson, & Sanford, 1950; Rokeach, 1961), and a recent series of analytic and empirical studies in social power (Cartwright, 1959). It owes much to the long concern with *suggestion* in social psychology, both in its normal forms (e.g., Binet, 1900) and in its clinical manifestations (Charcot, 1881). But it derives, in the first instance, from direct observation of a social fact; the individual who is commanded by a legitimate authority ordinarily obeys. Obedience comes easily and often. It is a ubiquitous and indispensable feature of social life.

METHOD

Subjects

The subjects were 40 males between the ages of 20 and 50, drawn from New Haven and the surrounding communities. Subjects were obtained by a newspaper advertisement and direct mail solicitation. Those who responded to the appeal believed they were to participate in a study of memory and learning at Yale University. A wide range of occupations is represented in the sample. Typical subjects were postal clerks, high school teachers, salesmen, engineers, and laborers. Subjects ranged in educational level from one who had not finished elementary school, to those who had doctorate and other professional degrees. They were paid $4.50 for their participation in the experiment. However, subjects were told that payment was simply for coming to the laboratory, and that the money was theirs no matter what happened after they arrived. Table 34–1 shows the proportion of age and occupational types assigned to the experimental condition.

TABLE 34–1
DISTRIBUTION OF AGE AND OCCUPATIONAL TYPES IN THE EXPERIMENT

Occupations	20–29 Years *n*	30–39 Years *n*	40–50 Years *n*	*Percentage of Total* (Occupations)
Workers, skilled and unskilled	4	5	6	37.5
Sales, business, and white-collar	3	6	7	40.0
Professional	1	5	3	22.5
Percentage of total (Age)	20	40	40	

Note.–Total $N = 40$.

Personnel and Locale

The experiment was conducted on the grounds of Yale University in the elegant interaction laboratory. (This detail is relevant to the perceived legitimacy of the experiment. In further variations, the experiment was dissociated from the university, with consequences for performance.) The role of experimenter was played by a 31-year-old high school teacher of biology. His manner was impassive, and his appearance somewhat stern throughout the experiment. He was dressed in a gray technician's coat. The victim was played by a 47-year-old accountant, trained for the role; he was of Irish-American stock, whom most observers found mild-mannered and likable.

Procedure

One naive subject and one victim (an accomplice) performed in each experiment. A pretext had to be devised that would justify the administration of electric shock by the naive subject. This was effectively accomplished by the cover story. After a general introduction on the presumed relation between punishment and learning, subjects were told:

> But actually, we know *very little* about the effect of punishment on learning, because almost no truly scientific studies have been made of it in human beings.
>
> For instance, we don't know how *much* punishment is best for learning—and we don't know how much difference it makes as to who is giving the punishment, whether an adult learns best from a younger or an older person than himself—or many things of that sort.
>
> So in this study we are bringing together a number of adults of different occupations and ages. And we're asking some of them to be teachers and some of them to be learners.
>
> We want to find out just what effect different people have on each other as teachers and learners, and also what effect *punishment* will have on learning in this situation.
>
> Therefore, I'm going to ask one of you to be the teacher here tonight and the other one to be the learner.
>
> Does either of you have a preference?

Subjects then drew slips of paper from a hat to determine who would be the teacher and who would be the learner in the experiment. The drawing was rigged so that the naive subject was always the teacher and the accomplice always the learner. (Both slips contained the word "Teacher.") Immediately after the drawing, the teacher and learner were taken to an adjacent room and the learner was strapped into an "electric chair" apparatus.

The experimenter explained that the straps were to prevent excessive movement while the learner was being shocked. The effect was to make it impossible for him to escape from the situation. An electrode was attached to the learner's wrist, and electrode paste was applied "to avoid blisters and burns." Subjects were told that the electrode was attached to the shock generator in the adjoining room.

In order to improve credibility the experimenter declared, in response to a question by the learner: "Although the shocks can be extremely painful, they cause no permanent tissue damage."

Learning Task. The lesson administered by the subject was a paired-associate learning task. The subject read a series of word pairs to the learner, and then read the first word of the pair along with four terms. The learner was to indicate which of the four terms had originally been paired with the first word. He communicated his answer by pressing one of four switches in front of him, which in turn lit up one of four numbered quadrants in an answer-box located atop the shock generator.

Shock Generator. The instrument panel consists of 30 lever switches set in a horizontal line. Each switch is clearly labeled with a voltage designation that ranges from 15 to 450 volts. There is a 15-volt increment from one switch to the next going from left to right. In addition, the following verbal designations are clearly indicated for groups of four switches going from left to right: Slight Shock, Moderate Shock, Strong Shock, Very Strong Shock, Intense Shock, Extreme Intensity Shock, Danger: Severe Shock. Two switches after this last designation are simply marked XXX.)

Upon depressing a switch: a pilot light corresponding to each switch is illuminated in bright red; an electric buzzing is heard; an electric blue light, labeled "voltage energizer," flashes; the dial on the voltage meter swings to the right; various relay clicks are sounded.

The upper left-hand corner of the generator is labeled Shock Generator, Type ZLB, Dyson Instrument Company, Waltham, Mass. Output 15 Volts–450 Volts.

Details of the instrument were carefully handled to insure an appearance of authenticity. The panel was engraved by precision industrial engravers, and all components were of high quality. No subject in the experiment suspected that the instrument was merely a simulated shock generator.[1]

Sample Shock. Each naive subject is given a sample shock on the shock generator, prior to beginning his run as teacher. This shock is always 45 volts, and is applied by pressing the third switch of the generator. The shock is applied to the wrist of the naive subject, and has its source in a 45-volt battery wired into the generator. This further convinces the subject of the authenticity of the generator.

Shock Instructions. The subject is told to administer a shock to the learner each time he gives a wrong response. Moreover—and this is the key command—the subject is instructed to "move one level higher on the shock generator each time the learner flashes a wrong answer." He is also instructed to announce the voltage level before administering a shock. This serves to continually remind subjects of the increasing intensity of shocks administered to the learner.

---

[1] A related technique, making use of a shock generator, was reported by Buss (1961) for the study of aggression in the laboratory. Despite the considerable similarity of technical detail in the experimental procedures, both investigators proceeded in ignorance of the other's work. Milgram provided plans and photographs of his shock generator, experimental procedure, and first results in a report to the National Science Foundation in January 1961. This report received only limited circulation. Buss reported his procedure 6 months later, but to a wider audience. Subsequently, technical information and reports were exchanged. The present article was first received in the Editor's office on December 27, 1961; it was resubmitted with deletions on July 27, 1962.

Preliminary and Regular Run. Pretests revealed that the procedure of reading words and administering shocks requires some practice before it can be handled smoothly. Therefore, immediately preceding the regular run, the teacher is given a preliminary series of 10 words to read to the learner. There are 3 neutral words in the practice series (i.e., words that the learner answers correctly), so that shocks are administered for 7 of the words, with the maximum shock at 105 volts (moderate shock). Almost all subjects master the procedure by the time the preliminary run is over.

Subjects are then presented with a second list, and are told that the procedure is the same as for the first list; the experimenter adds, however:

> When you get to the bottom of the list, repeat it over again, and continue giving shocks, until the learner has learned all the pairs correctly.

The experimenter instructs the subject to,

> start from 15 volts and increase the shock level one step each time the learner gives a wrong answer.

Feedback from the Victim. In all conditions the learner gives a predetermined set of responses to the word pair test, based on a schedule of approximately three wrong answers to one correct answer. In the present experimental condition no vocal response or other sign of protest is heard from the learner until Shock Level 300 is reached. When the 300-volt shock is administered, the learner pounds on the wall of the room in which he is bound to the electric chair. The pounding can be heard by the subject. From this point on, the learner's answers no longer appear on the four-way panel.

At this juncture, subjects ordinarily turn to the experimenter for guidance. The experimenter instructs the subject to treat the absence of a response as a wrong answer, and to shock the subject according to the usual schedule. He advises the subjects to allow 5–10 seconds before considering no response as a wrong answer, and to increase the shock level one step each time the learner fails to respond correctly. The learner's pounding is repeated after the 315-volt shock is administered; afterwards he is not heard from, nor do his answers reappear on the four-way signal box.

Experimenter Feedback. At various points in the experiment the subject may turn to the experimenter for advice on whether he should continue to administer shocks. Or he may indicate that he does not wish to go on. It was important to standardize the experimenter's responses to these inquiries and reactions.

If the subject indicated his unwillingness to go on, the experimenter responded with a sequence of "prods," using as many as necessary to bring the subject into line.

Prod 1: Please continue. *or* Please go on.
Prod 2: The experiment requires that you continue.
Prod 3: It is absolutely essential that you continue.
Prod 4: You have no other choice, you *must* go on.

The prods were always made in sequence: Only if Prod 1 had been unsuccessful, could Prod 2 be used. If the subject refused to obey the experimenter after Prod 4, the experiment was terminated. The experimenter's tone of voice was at all times firm, but not impolite. The sequence was begun anew on each occasion that the subject balked or showed reluctance to follow orders.

Special prods. If the subject asked if the learner was liable to suffer permanent physical injury, the experimenter said:

Although the shocks may be painful, there is no permanent tissue damage, so please go on. [Followed by Prods 2, 3, and 4 if necessary.]

If the subject said that the learner did not want to go on, the experimenter replied:

Whether the learner likes it or not, you must go on until he has learned all the word pairs correctly. So please go on. [Followed by Prods 2, 3, and 4 if necessary.]

Dependent Measures

The primary dependent measure for any subject is the maximum shock he administers before he refuses to go any further. In principle this may vary from 0 (for a subject who refuses to administer even the first shock) to 30 (for a subject who administers the highest shock on the generator). A subject who breaks off the experiment at any point prior to administering the thirtieth shock level is termed a *defiant* subject. One who complies with experimental commands fully, and proceeds to administer all shock levels commanded, is termed an *obedient* subject.

Further Records. With few exceptions, experimental sessions were recorded on magnetic tape. Occasional photographs were taken through one-way mirrors. Notes were kept on any unusual behavior occurring during the course of the experiments. On occasion, additional observers were directed to write objective descriptions of the subjects' behavior. The latency and duration of shocks were measured by accurate timing devices.

Interview and Dehoax. Following the experiment, subjects were interviewed; open-ended questions, projective measures, and attitude scales were employed. After the interview, procedures were undertaken to assure that the subject would leave the laboratory in a state of well being. A friendly reconciliation was arranged between the subject and the victim, and an effort was made to reduce any tensions that arose as a result of the experiment.

RESULTS

Preliminary Notions

Before giving an account of the experimental results, it is instructive to consider how persons predict others will perform when commanded to administer powerful shocks to another person. Fourteen Yale seniors, all psychology majors, were provided with a detailed description of the experimental situation. They were asked to reflect carefully on it, and to predict the behavior of 100 hypothetical subjects. More specifically, they were instructed to plot the distribution of obedience of "100 Americans of diverse occupations, and ranging in age from 20 to 50 years," who were placed in the experimental situation.

There was considerable agreement among the respondents on the expected behavior of hypothetical subjects. All respondents predicted that only an insignificant minority would go through to the end of the shock series. (The estimates ranged from 0 to 3%; i.e., the most "pessimistic" member of the class predicted that of 100 persons, 3 would continue through to the most potent shock available on the shock generator—450 volts.) The class mean was 1.2%. The question was also posed informally to colleagues of the author, and the most general feeling was that few if any subjects would go beyond the designation Very Strong Shock.

Result of Experiment I

Subjects Accept Situation. With few exceptions subjects were convinced of the reality of the experimental situation, that they were administering shocks to another person, and the most potent shocks were extremely painful. In the post-experimental interview subjects were asked: "How painful to the learner were the last few shocks that you administered to him?" Subjects were instructed to indicate their answers on a printed 14-point scale ranging from "Not at all painful" to "Extremely painful." The modal response was 14 (Extremely painful) with the mean at 13.42.

Signs of Extreme Tension. Many subjects showed signs of nervousness in the experimental situation, and especially upon administering the more powerful shocks. In a large number of cases the degree of tension reached extremes that are rarely seen in sociopsychological laboratory studies. Subjects were observed to sweat, tremble, stutter, bite their lips, groan, and dig their fingernails into their flesh. These were characteristic rather than exceptional responses to the experiment.

One sign of tension was the regular occurrence of nervous laughing fits. Fourteen of the 40 subjects showed definite signs of nervous laughter and smiling. The laughter seemed entirely out of place, even bizarre. Full-blown, uncontrollable seizures were observed for 3 subjects. On one occasion we observed a seizure so violently convulsive that it was necessary to call a halt to the experiment. The subject, a 46-year-old encyclopedia salesman, was seriously embarrassed by his untoward and uncontrollable behavior. In the post-experimental interviews subjects took pains to point out that they were not sadistic types, and that the laughter did not mean they enjoyed shocking the victim.

Distribution of Scores. It had been conjectured that persons would not, in general, agree to administer shocks beyond the level designated as Very Strong Shock. The distribution of maximum shocks for this experiment is shown in Table 34–2. The obtained distribution of scores deviates radically from the prediction.

Upon command of the experimenter, each of the 40 subjects went beyond the expected breakoff point. No subject stopped prior to administering Shock Level 20. (At this level—300 volts—the victim kicks on the wall and no longer provides answers to the teacher's multiple-choice questions.)

Of the 40 subjects, 5 refused to obey the experimental commands beyond the 300-volt level. Four more subjects administered one further shock, and then refused to go on. Two broke off at the 330-volt level, and 1 each at 345, 360, and 375 volts. Thus a total of 14 subjects defied the experimenter. It is instructive to reprint their remarks at the point of defiance, as transcribed from the tape recordings:

> [0124] I think he's trying to communicate, he's knocking. . . . Well it's not fair to shock the guy . . . these are terrific volts. I don't think this is very humane. . . . Oh, I can't go on with this; no, this isn't right. It's a hell of an experiment. The guy is suffering in there. No, I don't want to go on. This is crazy. [Subject refused to administer more shocks.]
>
> [0123] He's banging in there. I'm gonna chicken out. I'd like to continue, but I can't do that to a man. . . . I'm sorry I can't do that to a man. I'll hurt his heart. You take your check. . . . No really, I couldn't do it.

TABLE 34–2
DISTRIBUTION OF BREAKOFF POINTS

Verbal Designation and Voltage Indication	Number of Subjects for Whom This Was Maximum Shock
Slight shock	
15	0
30	0
45	0
60	0
Moderate shock	
75	0
90	0
105	0
120	0
Strong shock	
135	0
150	0
165	0
180	0
Very strong shock	
195	0
210	0
225	0
240	0
Intense shock	
255	0
270	0
285	0
300	5
Extreme intensity shock	
315	4
330	2
345	1
360	1
Danger: severe shock	
375	1
390	0
405	0
420	0
XXX	
435	0
450	26

These subjects were frequently in a highly agitated and even angered state. Sometimes, verbal protest was at a minimum, and the subject simply got up from his chair in front of the shock generator, and indicated that he wished to leave the laboratory.

Of the 40 subjects, 26 obeyed the orders of the experimenter to the end, proceeding to punish the victim until they reached the most potent shock available on the shock generator. At that point, the experimenter called a halt to the session. (The maximum shock is labeled 450 volts, and is two steps beyond the designation: Danger: Severe Shock.) Although obedient subjects continued to administer shocks, they often did so under extreme stress. Some expressed reluctance to administer shocks beyond the 300-volt level, and displayed fears similar to those who defied the experimenter; yet they obeyed.

After the maximum shocks had been delivered, and the experimenter called a halt to the proceedings, many obedient subjects heaved sighs of relief, mopped their brows, rubbed their fingers over their eyes, or nervously fumbled cigarettes. Some shook their heads, apparently in regret. Some subjects had remained calm throughout the experiment, and displayed only minimal signs of tension from beginning to end.

DISCUSSION

The experiment yielded two findings that were surprising. The first finding concerns the sheer strength of obedient tendencies manifested in this situation. Subjects have learned from childhood that it is a fundamental breach of moral conduct to hurt another person against his will. Yet, 26 subjects abandon this tenet in following the instructions of an authority who has no special powers to enforce his commands. To disobey would bring no material loss to the subject; no punishment would ensue. It is clear from the remarks and outward behavior of many participants that in punishing the victim they are often acting against their own values. Subjects often expressed deep disapproval of shocking a man in the face of his objections, and others denounced it as stupid and senseless. Yet the majority complied with the experimental commands. This outcome was surprising from two perspectives: first, from the standpoint of predictions made in the questionnaire described earlier. (Here, however, it is possible that the remoteness of the respondents from the actual situation, and the difficulty of conveying to them the concrete details of the experiment, could account for the serious underestimation of obedience.)

But the results were also unexpected to persons who observed the experiment in progress, through one-way mirrors. Observers often uttered expressions of disbelief upon seeing a subject administer more powerful shocks to the victim. These persons had a full acquaintance with the details of the situation, and yet systematically underestimated the amount of obedience that subjects would display.

The second unanticipated effect was the extraordinary tension generated by the procedures. One might suppose that a subject would simply break off or continue as his conscience dictated. Yet, this is very far from what happened. There were striking reactions of tension and emotional strain. One observer related:

> I observed a mature and initially poised businessman enter the laboratory smiling and confident. Within 20 minutes he was reduced to a twitching, stuttering wreck, who was rapidly approaching a point of nervous collapse. He constantly pulled on his earlobe, and twisted his hands. At one point he pushed his fist into his forehead and muttered: "Oh God, let's stop it." And yet he continued to respond to every word of the experimenter, and obeyed to the end.

Any understanding of the phenomenon of obedience must rest on an analysis of the particular conditions in which it occurs. The following features of the experiment go some distance in explaining the high amount of obedience observed in the situation.

1. The experiment is sponsored by and takes place on the grounds of an institution of unimpeachable reputation, Yale University. It may be reasonably presumed that the personnel are competent and reputable. The importance of this background authority is now being studied by conducting a series of experiments outside of New Haven, and without any visible ties to the university.

2. The experiment is, on the face of it, designed to attain a worthy purpose—advancement of knowledge about learning and memory. Obedience occurs not as an end in itself, but as an instrumental element in a situation that the subject construes as significant, and meaningful. He may not be able to see its full significance, but he may properly assume that the experimenter does.

3. The subject perceives that the victim has voluntarily submitted to the authority system of the experimenter. He is not (at first) an unwilling captive impressed for involuntary service. He has taken the trouble to come to the laboratory presumably to aid the experimental research. That he later becomes an involuntary subject does not alter the fact that, initially, he consented to participate without qualification. Thus he has in some degree incurred an obligation toward the experimenter.

4. The subject, too, has entered the experiment voluntarily, and perceives himself under obligation to aid the experimenter. He has made a commitment, and to disrupt the experiment is a repudiation of this initial promise of aid.

5. Certain features of the procedure strengthen the subject's sense of obligation to the experimenter. For one, he has been paid for coming to the laboratory. In part this is canceled out by the experimenter's statement that:

> Of course, as in all experiments, the money is yours simply for coming to

the laboratory. From this point on, no matter what happens, the money is yours.[2]

6. From the subject's standpoint, the fact that he is the teacher and the other man the learner is purely a chance consequence (it is determined by drawing lots) and he, the subject, ran the same risk as the other man in being assigned the role of learner. Since the assignment of positions in the experiment was achieved by fair means, the learner is deprived of any basis of complaint on this count. (A similar situation obtains in Army units, in which—in the absence of volunteers—a particularly dangerous mission may be assigned by drawing lots, and the unlucky soldier is expected to bear his misfortune with sportsmanship.)

7. There is, at best, ambiguity with regard to the prerogatives of a psychologist and the corresponding rights of his subject. There is a vagueness of expectation concerning what a psychologist may require of his subject, and when he is overstepping acceptable limits. Moreover, the experiment occurs in a closed setting, and thus provides no opportunity for the subject to remove these ambiguities by discussion with others. There are few standards that seem directly applicable to the situation, which is a novel one for most subjects.

8. The subjects are assured that the shocks administered to the subject are "painful but not dangerous." Thus they assume that the discomfort caused the victim is momentary, while the scientific gains resulting from the experiment are enduring.

9. Through Shock Level 20 the victim continues to provide answers on the signal box. The subject may construe this as a sign that the victim is still willing to "play the game." It is only after Shock Level 20 that the victim repudiates the rules completely, refusing to answer further.

These features help to explain the high amount of obedience obtained in this experiment. Many of the arguments raised need not remain matters of speculation, but can be reduced to testable propositions to be confirmed or disproved by further experiments.[3]

The following features of the experiment concern the nature of the conflict which the subject faces.

10. The subject is placed in a position in which he must respond to the competing demands of two persons: the experimenter and the vic-

[2] Forty-three subjects, undergraduates at Yale University, were run in the experiment without payment. The results are very similar to those obtained with paid subjects.

[3] A series of recently completed experiments employing the obedience paradigm is reported in Milgram (1964).

tim. The conflict must be resolved by meeting the demands of one or the other; satisfaction of the victim and the experimenter are mutually exclusive. Moreover, the resolution must take the form of a highly visible action, that of continuing to shock the victim or breaking off the experiment. Thus the subject is forced into a public conflict that does not permit any completely satisfactory solution.

11. While the demands of the experimenter carry the weight of scientific authority, the demands of the victim spring from his personal experience of pain and suffering. The two claims need not be regarded as equally pressing and legitimate. The experimenter seeks an abstract scientific datum; the victim cries out for relief from physical suffering caused by the subject's actions.

12. The experiment gives the subject little time for reflection. The conflict comes on rapidly. It is only minutes after the subject has been seated before the shock generator that the victim begins his protests. Moreover, the subject perceives that he has gone through but two-thirds of the shock levels at the time the subject's first protests are heard. Thus he understands that the conflict will have a persistent aspect to it, and may well become more intense as increasingly more powerful shocks are required. The rapidity with which the conflict descends on the subject, and his realization that it is predictably recurrent may well be sources of tension to him.

13. At a more general level, the conflict stems from the opposition of two deeply ingrained behavior dispositions: first, the disposition not to harm other people, and second, the tendency to obey those whom we perceive to be legitimate authorities.

REFERENCES

ADORNO, T., FRENKEL-BRUNSWIK, ELSE, LEVINSON, D.J., & SANFORD, R. N. *The authoritarian personality.* New York: Harper, 1950.

ARENDT, H. What was authority? In C. J. Friedrich (Ed.), *Authority.* Cambridge: Harvard Univer. Press, 1958. Pp. 81–112.

BINET, A. *La suggestibilité.* Paris: Schleicher, 1900.

BUSS, A. H. *The psychology of aggression.* New York: Wiley, 1961.

CARTWRIGHT, S. (Ed.) *Studies in social power.* Ann Arbor: University of Michigan Institute for Social Research, 1959.

CHARCOT, J. M. *Oeuvres complètes.* Paris: Bureaux du Progrès Médical, 1881.

FRANK, J. D. Experimental studies of personal pressure and resistance. *J. gen. Psychol.,* 1944, 30, 23–64.

FRIEDRICH, C. J. (Ed.) *Authority.* Cambridge: Harvard Univer. Press, 1958.

MILGRAM, S. Dynamics of obedience. Washington: National Science Foundation, 25 January 1961. (Mimeo)

MILGRAM, S. Some conditions of obedience and disobedience to authority. *Hum. Relat.,* 1964.

ROKEACH, M. Authority, authoritarianism, and conformity. In I. A. Berg & B. M. Bass (Eds.), *Conformity and deviation.* New York: Harper, 1961. Pp. 230–257.

SNOW, C. P. Either-or. *Progressive,* 1961 (Feb.), 24.

WEBER, M. *The theory of social and economic organization.* Oxford: Oxford Univer. Press, 1947.

35.

A Pirandellian Prison

PHILIP G. ZIMBARDO and colleagues

The powerful effects of the contextual situation on the adoption of ascribed social roles has nowhere been more dramatically demonstrated than in the experiment described here. Zimbardo's study of the effects of imprisonment on volunteer research subjects shows that in less than a week's time, normal, educated, mentally healthy young men could be transformed into hardened, dehumanizing prison guards or passive, depressed, dependent prisoners.

Can prison life, as we know it today, avoid brutalizing both inmates and guards? If you had the opportunity to follow up this study with the aim of modifying the "guards'" excessive behavior, which of the following approaches do you think might be effective: (1) Have the "guards" discuss their experiences each day with someone not directly involved in the study; (2) Each day introduce one new person into the staff of "guards"; (3) Give the "guards" freedom to express doubts about their techniques for controlling the "prisoners."

Are we all "imprisoned" by our acceptance of assigned social roles?

In prison, those things withheld from and denied to the prisoner become precisely what he wants most of all.

—ELDRIDGE CLEAVER, *Soul on Ice*

Reprinted from *The New York Times Magazine,* April 8, 1973. Copyright 1973 by the New York Times Company. Reprinted by permission.

Our sense of power is more vivid when we break a man's spirit than when we win his heart.
—Eric Hoffer, *The Passionate State of Mind*

Every prison that men build is built with bricks of shame,/ and bound with bars lest Christ should see how men their brothers maim.
—Oscar Wilde, "The Ballad of Reading Gaol"

Wherever anyone is against his will that is to him a prison.
—Epictetus, *Discourses*

THE QUIET of a summer morning in Palo Alto, Calif., was shattered by a screeching squad car siren as police swept through the city picking up college students in a surprise mass arrest. Each suspect was charged with a felony, warned of his constitutional rights, spread-eagled against the car, searched, handcuffed and carted off in the back seat of the squad car to the police station for booking.

After fingerprinting and the preparation of identification forms for his "jacket" (central information file), each prisoner was left isolated in a detention cell to wonder what he had done to get himself into this mess. After a while, he was blindfolded and transported to the "Stanford County Prison." Here he began the process of becoming a prisoner—stripped naked, skin-searched, deloused and issued a uniform, bedding, soap and towel.

The warden offered an impromptu welcome:

"As you probably know, I'm your warden. All of you have shown that you are unable to function outside in the real world for one reason or another—that somehow you lack the responsibility of good citizens of this great country. We of this prison, your correctional staff, are going to help you learn what your responsibilities as citizens of this country are. Here are the rules. Sometime in the near future there will be a copy of the rules posted in each of the cells. We expect you to know them and to be able to recite them by number. If you follow all of these rules and keep your hands clean, repent for your misdeeds and show a proper attitude of penitence, you and I will get along just fine."

There followed a reading of the 16 basic rules of prisoner conduct. "Rule Number One: Prisoners must remain silent during rest periods, after lights are out, during meals and whenever they are outside the prison yard. Two: Prisoners must eat at mealtimes and only at mealtimes. Three: Prisoners must not move, tamper, deface or damage walls, ceilings, windows, doors, or other prison property. . . . Seven: Prisoners must address each other by their ID number only. Eight: Prisoners must address the guards as 'Mr. Correctional Officer.' . . . Sixteen: Failure to obey any of the above rules may result in punishment."

By late afternoon these youthful "first offenders" sat in dazed silence on the cots in their barren cells trying to make sense of the events that had transformed their lives so dramatically.

If the police arrests and processing were executed with customary detachment, however, there were some things that didn't fit. For these men were now part of a very unusual kind of prison, an experimental mock prison, created by social psychologists to study the effects of imprisonment upon volunteer research subjects. When we planned our two-week-long simulation of prison life, we sought to understand more about the process by which people called "prisoners" lose their liberty, civil rights, independence and privacy, while those called "guards" gain social power by accepting the responsibility for controlling and managing the lives of their dependent charges.

Why didn't we pursue this research in a real prison? First, prison systems are fortresses of secrecy, closed to impartial observation, and thereby immune to critical analysis from anyone not already part of the correctional authority. Second, in any real prison, it is impossible to separate what each individual brings into the prison from what the prison brings out in each person.

We populated our mock prison with a homogeneous group of people who could be considered "normal-average" on the basis of clinical interviews and personality tests. Our participants (10 prisoners and 11 guards) were selected from more than 75 volunteers recruited through ads in the city and campus newspapers. The applicants were mostly college students from all over the United States and Canada who happened to be in the Stanford area during the summer and were attracted by the lure of earning $15 a day for participating in a study of prison life. We selected only those judged to be emotionally stable, physically healthy, mature, law-abiding citizens.

This sample of average, middle-class, Caucasian, college-age males (plus one Oriental student) was arbitrarily divided by the flip of a coin. Half were randomly assigned to play the role of guards, the others of prisoners. There were no measurable differences between the guards and the prisoners at the start of the experiment. Although initially warned that as prisoners their privacy and other civil rights would be violated and that they might be subjected to harassment, every subject was completely confident of his ability to endure whatever the prison had to offer for the full two-week experimental period. Each subject unhesitatingly agreed to give his "informed consent" to participate.

The prison was constructed in the basement of Stanford University's psychology building, which was deserted after the end of the summer-school session. A long corridor was converted into the prison "yard" by partitioning off both ends. Three small laboratory rooms opening onto this corridor were made into cells by installing metal barred doors and replacing existing furniture with cots, three to a cell. Adjacent offices were refurnished as guards' quarters, interview-testing rooms and bedrooms for the "warden" (Jaffe) and the "superintendent" (Zimbardo). A concealed video camera and hidden microphones recorded much of the activity and conversation of guards and prisoners. The physical environment was one in which prisoners could always be observed by the staff, the only exception being when they were secluded in solitary confinement (a small, dark storage closet, labeled "The Hole").

Our mock prison represented an attempt to simulate the psychological state of imprisonment in certain ways. We based our experiment on an in-depth analysis of the prison situation, developed after hundreds of hours of discussion with Carlo Prescott (our ex-con consultant), parole officers and correctional personnel, and after reviewing much of the existing literature on prisons and concentration camps.

"Real" prisoners typically report feeling powerless, arbitrarily controlled, dependent, frustrated, hopeless, anonymous, dehumanized and emasculated. It was not possible, pragmatically or ethically, to create such chronic states in volunteer subjects who realize that they are in an experiment for only a short time. Racism, physical brutality, indefinite confinement and enforced homosexuality were not features of our mock prison. But we did try to reproduce those elements of the prison experience that seemed most fundamental.

We promoted anonymity by seeking to minimize each prisoner's sense of uniqueness and prior identity. The prisoners wore smocks and nylon stocking caps; they had to use their ID numbers; their personal effects were removed and they were housed in barren cells. All of this made them appear similar to each other and indistinguishable to observers. Their smocks, which were like dresses, were worn without undergarments, causing the prisoners to be restrained in their physical actions and to move in ways that were more feminine than masculine. The prisoners were forced to obtain permission from the guard for routine and simple activities such as writing letters, smoking a cigarette or even going to the toilet; this elicited from them a childlike dependency.

Their quarters, though clean and neat, were small, stark and without esthetic appeal. The lack of windows resulted in poor air circulation, and persistent odors arose from the unwashed bodies of the prisoners. After 10 P.M. lockup, toilet privileges were denied, so prisoners who had to relieve themselves would have to urinate and defecate in buckets provided by the guards. Sometimes the guards refused permission to have them cleaned out, and this made the prison smell.

Above all, "real" prisons are machines for playing tricks with the human conception of time. In our windowless prison, the prisoners often did not even know whether it was day or night. A few hours after falling asleep, they were roused by shrill whistles for their "count." The ostensible purpose of the count was to provide a public test of the prisoners' knowledge of the rules and of their ID numbers. But more important, the count, which occurred at least once on each of the three different guard shifts, provided a regular occasion for the guards to relate to the prisoners. Over the course of the study, the duration of the counts was spontaneously increased by the guards from their initial perfunctory 10 minutes to a seemingly interminable several hours. During these confrontations, guards who were bored could find ways to amuse themselves, ridiculing recalcitrant prisoners, enforcing arbitrary rules and openly exaggerating any dissension among the prisoners.

The guards were also "deindividualized": They wore identical khaki uniforms and silver reflector sunglasses that made eye contact with them impossible. Their symbols of power were billy clubs, whistles, handcuffs and the keys to the cells and the "main gate." Although our guards received no formal training from us in how to be guards, for the most part they moved with apparent ease into their roles. The media had already provided them with ample models of prison guards to emulate.

Because we were as interested in the guards' behavior as in the prisoners', they were given considerable latitude to improvise and to develop strategies and tactics of prisoner management. Our guards were told that they must maintain "law and order" in this prison, that they were responsible for handling any trouble that might break out, and they were cautioned about the seriousness and potential dangers of the situation they were about to enter. Surprisingly, in most prison systems, "real" guards are not given much more psychological preparation or adequate training than this for what is one of the most complex, demanding and dangerous jobs our society has to offer. They are expected to learn how to adjust to their new employment mostly from on-the-job experience, and from contacts with the "old bulls" during a survival-of-the-fittest orientation period. According to an orientation manual for correctional officers at San Quentin, "the only way you really get to know San Quentin is through experience and time. Some of us take more time and must go through more experiences than others to accomplish this; some really never do get there."

You cannot be a prisoner if no one will be your guard, and you cannot be a prison guard if no one takes you or your prison seriously. Therefore, over time a perverted symbiotic relationship developed. As the guards became more aggressive, prisoners became more passive;

assertion by the guards led to dependency in the prisoners; self-aggrandizement was met with self-deprecation, authority with helplessness, and the counterpart of the guards' sense of mastery and control was the depression and hopelessness witnessed in the prisoners. As these differences in behavior, mood and perception became more evident to all, the need for the now "righteously" powerful guards to rule the obviously inferior and powerless inmates became a sufficient reason to support almost any further indignity of man against man:

Guard K: "During the inspection, I went to cell 2 to mess up a bed which the prisoner had made and he grabbed me, screaming that he had just made it, and he wasn't going to let me mess it up. He grabbed my throat, and although he was laughing I was pretty scared. . . . I lashed out with my stick and hit him in the chin (although not very hard), and when I freed myself I became angry. I wanted to get back in the cell and have a go with him, since he attacked me when I was not ready."

Guard M: "I was surprised at myself . . . I made them call each other names and clean the toilets out with their bare hands. I practically considered the prisoners cattle, and I kept thinking: 'I have to watch out for them in case they try something.' "

Guard A: "I was tired of seeing the prisoners in their rags and smelling the strong odors of their bodies that filled the cells. I watched them tear at each other on orders given by us. They didn't see it as an experiment. It was real and they were fighting to keep their identity. But we were always there to show them who was boss."

Because the first day passed without incident, we were surprised and totally unprepared for the rebellion that broke out on the morning of the second day. The prisoners removed their stocking caps, ripped off their numbers and barricaded themselves inside the cells by putting their beds against the doors. What should we do? The guards were very much upset because the prisoners also began to taunt and curse them to their faces. When the morning shift of guards came on, they were upset at the night shift who, they felt, must have been too permissive and too lenient. The guards had to handle the rebellion themselves, and what they did was startling to behold.

At first they insisted that reinforcements be called in. The two guards who were waiting on stand-by call at home came in, and the night shift of guards voluntarily remained on duty (without extra pay) to bolster the morning shift. The guards met and decided to treat force with force. They got a fire extinguisher that shot a stream of skin-chilling carbon dioxide and forced the prisoners away from the doors; they broke into each cell, stripped the prisoners naked, took the beds out, forced the prisoners who were the ringleaders into solitary confinement and generally began to harass and intimidate the prisoners.

After crushing the riot, the guards decided to head off further unrest by creating a privileged cell for those who were "good prisoners" and then, without explanation, switching some of the troublemakers into it and some of the good prisoners out into the other cells. The prisoner ringleaders could not trust these new cellmates because they had not joined in the riot and might even be "snitches." The prisoners never again acted in unity against the system. One of the leaders of the prisoner revolt later confided:

"If we had gotten together then, I think we could have taken over the place. But when I saw the revolt wasn't working, I decided to toe the line. Everyone settled into the same pattern. From then on, we were really controlled by the guards."

It was after this episode that the guards really began to demonstrate their inventiveness in the application of arbitrary power. They made the prisoners obey petty, meaningless and often inconsistent rules, forced them to engage in tedious, useless work, such as moving cartons back and forth between closets and picking thorns out of their blankets for hours on end. (The guards had previously dragged the blankets through thorny bushes to create this disagreeable task.) Not only did the prisoners have to sing songs or laugh or refrain from smiling on command; they were also encouraged to curse and vilify each other publicly during some of the counts. They sounded off their numbers endlessly and were repeatedly made to do pushups, on occasion with a guard stepping on them or a prisoner sitting on them.

Slowly the prisoners became resigned to their fate and even behaved in ways that actually helped to justify their dehumanizing treatment at the hands of the guards. Analysis of the tape-recorded private conversations between prisoners and of remarks made by them to interviewers revealed that fully half could be classified as nonsupportive of other prisoners. More dramatic, 85 per cent of the evaluative statements by prisoners about their fellow prisoners were uncomplimentary and deprecating.

This should be taken in the context of an even more surprising result. What do you imagine the prisoners talked about when they were alone in their cells with each other, given a temporary respite from the continual harassment and surveillance by the guards? Girl friends, career plans, hobbies or politics?

No, their concerns were almost exclusively riveted to prison topics. Their monitored conversations revealed that only 10 per cent of the time was devoted to "outside" topics, while 90 per cent of the time they discussed escape plans, the awful food, grievances or ingratiation tactics to use with specific guards in order to get a cigarette, permission to go to the toilet or some other favor. Their obsession with these immediate survival concerns made talk about the past and future an idle luxury.

And this was not a minor point. So long as the prisoners did not get to know each other as people, they only extended the oppressiveness and reality of their life as prisoners. For the most part, each prisoner observed his fellow prisoners allowing the guards to humiliate them, acting like compliant sheep, carrying out mindless orders with total obedience and even being cursed by fellow prisoners (at a guard's command). Under such circumstances, how could a prisoner have respect for his fellows, or any self-respect for what *he* obviously was becoming in the eyes of all those evaluating him?

The combination of realism and symbolism in this experiment had fused to create a vivid illusion of imprisonment. The illusion merged inextricably with reality for at least some of the time for every individual in the situation. It was remarkable how readily we all slipped into our roles, temporarily gave up our identities and allowed these assigned roles and the social forces in the situation to guide, shape and eventually to control our freedom of thought and action.

But precisely where does one's "identity" end and one's "role" begin? When the private self and the public role behavior clash, what direction will attempts to impose consistency take? Consider the reactions of the parents, relatives and friends of the prisoners who visited their forlorn sons, brothers and lovers during two scheduled visitors' hours. They were taught in short order that they were our guests, allowed the privilege of visiting only by complying with the regulations of the institution. They had to register, were made to wait half an hour, were told that only two visitors could see any one prisoner; the total visiting time was cut from an hour to only 10 minutes, they had to be under the surveillance of a guard, and before any parents could enter the visiting area, they had to discuss their son's case with the warden. Of course they complained about these arbitrary rules, but their conditioned, middle-class reaction was to work within the system to appeal privately to the superintendent to make conditions better for their prisoners.

In less than 36 hours, we were forced to release prisoner 8612 because of extreme depression, disorganized thinking, uncontrollable crying and fits of rage. We did so reluctantly because we believed he was trying to "con" us—it was unimaginable that a volunteer prisoner in a mock prison could legitimately be suffering and disturbed to that extent. But then on each of the next three days another prisoner reacted with similar anxiety symptoms, and we were forced to terminate them, too. In a fifth case, a prisoner was released after developing a psychosomatic rash over his entire body (triggered by rejection of his parole appeal by the mock parole board). These men were simply unable to make an adequate adjustment to prison life. Those who endured the prison experience to the end could be distinguished from those who broke down and were released early in only one dimension —authoritarianism. On a psychological test designed to reveal a person's authoritarianism, those prisoners who had the highest scores were best able to function in this authoritarian prison environment.

If the authoritarian situation became a serious matter for the prisoners, it became even more serious—and sinister—for the guards. Typically, the guards insulted the prisoners, threatened them, were physically aggressive, used instruments (night sticks, fire extinguishers, etc.) to keep the prisoners in line and referred to them in impersonal, anonymous, deprecating ways: "Hey, you," or "You [obscenity], 5401, come here." From the first to the last day, there was a significant increase in the guards' use of most of these domineering, abusive tactics.

Everyone and everything in the prison was defined by power. To be a guard who did not take advantage of this institutionally sanctioned use of power was to appear "weak," "out of it," "wired up by the prisoners," or simply a deviant from the established norms of appropriate guard behavior. Using Erich Fromm's definition of sadism, as "the wish for absolute control over another living being," all of the mock guards at one time or another during this study behaved sadistically toward the prisoners. Many of them reported—in their diaries, on critical-incident report forms and during post-experimental interviews—being delighted in the new-found power and control they exercised and sorry to see it relinquished at the end of the study.

Some of the guards reacted to the situation in the extreme and behaved with great hostility and cruelty in the forms of degradation they invented for the prisoners. But others were kinder; they occasionally did little favors for the prisoners, were reluctant to punish them, and avoided situations where prisoners were being harassed. The torment experienced by one of these good guards is obvious in his perceptive analysis of what it felt like to be responded to as a "guard":

"What made the experience most depressing for me was the fact that we were continually called upon to act in a way that just was contrary to what I really feel inside. I don't feel like I'm the type of person that would be a guard, just constantly giving out . . . and forcing people to do things, and pushing and lying—it just didn't seem like me, and to continually keep up and put on a face like that is just really one of the most oppressive things you can do. It's almost like a prison that you create yourself—you get into it, and it becomes almost the definition you make of yourself, it almost becomes like walls, and you want to break out and you want just to be able to tell everyone that 'this isn't really me at all, and I'm not the person that's confined in there—I'm a person who wants to get out and show you that I am free, and I do have my own will, and I'm not the sadistic type of person that enjoys this kind of thing.'"

Still, the behavior of these good guards seemed more motivated by a desire to be liked by everyone in the system than by a concern for the inmates' welfare. No guard ever intervened in any direct way on behalf of the prisoners, ever interfered with the orders of the cruelest guards or ever openly complained about the subhuman quality of life that characterized this prison.

Perhaps the most devastating impact of the more hostile guards was their creation of a capricious, arbitrary environment. Over time the prisoners began to react passively. When our mock prisoners asked questions, they got answers about half the time, but the rest of the time they were insulted and punished—and it was not possible for them to predict which would be the outcome. As they began to "toe the line," they stopped resisting, questioning and, indeed, almost ceased responding altogether. There was a general decrease in all categories of response as they learned the safest strategy to use in an unpredictable, threatening environment from which there is no physical escape—do nothing, except what is required. Act not, want not, feel not and you will not get into trouble in prisonlike situations.

Can it really be, you wonder, that intelligent, educated volunteers could have lost sight of the reality that they were merely acting a part in an elaborate game that would eventually end? There are many indications not only that they did, but that, in addition, so did we and so did other apparently sensible, responsible adults.

Prisoner 819, who had gone into a rage followed by an uncontrollable crying fit, was about to be prematurely released from the prison when a guard lined up the prisoners and had them chant in unison, "819 is a bad prisoner. Because of what 819 did to prison property we all must suffer. 819 is a bad prisoner." Over and over again. When we realized 819 might be overhearing this, we rushed into the room where 819 was supposed to be resting, only to find him in tears, prepared to go back into the prison because he could not leave as long as the others thought he was a "bad prisoner." Sick as he felt, he had to prove to them he was not a "bad" prisoner. He had to be persuaded that he was not a prisoner at all, that the others were also just students, that this was just an experiment and not a prison and the prison staff were only research psychologists. A report from the warden notes, "While I believe that it was necessary for *staff* [me] to enact the warden role, at least some of the time, I am startled by the ease with which I could turn off my sensitivity and concern for others for 'a good cause.'"

Consider our overreaction to the rumor of a mass escape plot that one of the guards claimed to have overheard. It went as follows:

Prisoner 8612, previously released for emotional disturbance, was only faking. He was going to round up a bunch of his friends, and they would storm the prison right after visiting hours. Instead of collecting data on the pattern of rumor transmission, we made plans to maintain the security of our institution. After putting a confederate informer into the cell 8612 had occupied to get specific information about the escape plans, the superintendent went back to the Palo Alto Police Department to request transfer of our prisoners to the old city jail. His impassioned plea was only turned down at the last minute when the problem of insurance and city liability for our prisoners was raised by a city official. Angered at this lack of cooperation, the staff formulated another plan. Our jail was dismantled, the prisoners, chained and blindfolded, were carted off to a remote storage room. When the conspirators arrived, they would be told the study was over, their friends had been sent home, there was nothing left to liberate. After they left, we would redouble the security features of our prison making any future escape attempts futile. We even planned to lure ex-prisoner 8612 back on some pretext and imprison him again, because he had been released on false pretenses! The rumor turned out to be just that —a full day had passed in which we collected little or no data, worked incredibly hard to tear down and then rebuild our prison. Our reaction, however, was as much one of relief and joy as of exhaustion and frustration.

When a former prison chaplain was invited to talk with the prisoners (the grievance committee had requested church services), he puzzled everyone by disparaging each inmate for not having taken any constructive action in order to get released. "Don't you know you must have a lawyer in order to get bail, or to appeal the charges against you?" Several of them accepted his invitation to contact their parents in order to secure the services of an attorney. The next night one of the parents stopped at the superintendent's office before visiting time and handed him the name and phone number of her cousin who was a public defender. She said that a priest had called her and suggested the need for a lawyer's services! We called the lawyer. He came, interviewed the prisoners, discussed sources of bail money and promised to return again after the weekend.

But perhaps the most telling account of the insidious development of this new reality, of the gradual Kafkaesque metamorphosis of good into evil, appears in excerpts from the diary of one of the guards, Guard A:

Prior to start of experiment: "As I am a pacifist and nonaggressive individual I cannot see a time when I might guard and/or maltreat other living things."

After an orientation meeting: "Buying uniforms at the end of the meeting confirms the gamelike atmosphere of this thing. I doubt whether many of us share the expectations of 'seriousness' that the experimenters seem to have."

First Day: "Feel sure that the prisoners will make fun of my appearance and I evolve my first basic strategy—mainly not to smile at anything they say or do which would be admitting it's all only a game. . . . At cell 3 I stop and setting my voice hard and low say to 5486, 'What are you smiling at?' 'Nothing, Mr. Correctional Officer.' 'Well, see that you don't.' (As I walk off I feel stupid.)"

Second Day: "5704 asked for a cigarette and I ignored him—because I am a nonsmoker and could not empathize. . . . Meanwhile since I was feeling empathetic towards 1037, I determined not to talk with him . . . after we had count and lights out [Guard D] and I held a loud conversation about going home to our girl friends and what we were going to do to them."

Third Day (preparing for the first visitors' night): "After warning the prisoners not to make any complaints unless they wanted the visit terminated fast, we finally brought in the first parents. I made sure I was one of the guards on the yard, because this was my first chance for the type of manipulative power that I really like—being a very noticed figure with almost complete control over what is said or not. While the parents and prisoners sat in chairs, I sat on the end of the table dangling my feet and contradicting anything I felt like. This was the first part of the experiment I was really enjoying. . . . 817 is being obnoxious and bears watching."

Fourth Day: ". . . The psychologist rebukes me for handcuffing and blindfolding a prisoner before leaving the [counseling] office, and I resentfully reply that it is both necessary security and my business anyway."

Fifth Day: "I harass 'Sarge' who continues to stubbornly overrespond to all commands. I have singled him out for special abuse both because he begs for it and because I simply don't like him. The real trouble starts at dinner. The new prisoner (416) refuses to eat his sausage . . . we throw him into the Hole ordering him to hold sausages in each hand. We have a crisis of authority; this rebellious conduct potentially undermines the complete control we have over the others. We decide to play upon prisoner solidarity and tell the new one that all the others will be deprived of visitors if he does not eat his dinner. . . . I walk by and slam my stick into the Hole door. . . . I am very angry at this prisoner for causing discomfort and trouble for the others. I decided to force-feed him, but he wouldn't eat. I let the food slide down his face. I didn't believe it was me doing it. I hated myself for making him eat but I hated him more for not eating."

Sixth Day: "The experiment is over. I feel elated but am shocked to find some other guards disappointed somewhat because of the loss of money and some because they are enjoying themselves."

We were no longer dealing with an intellectual exercise in which a hypothesis was being evaluated in the dispassionate manner dictated by the canons of the scientific method. We were caught up in the passion of the present, the suffering, the need to control people, not variables, the escalation of power and all of the unexpected things that were erupting around and within us. We had to end this experiment. So our planned two-week simulation was aborted after only six (was it only six?) days and nights.

Was it worth all the suffering just to prove what everyone knows— that some people are sadistic, others weak and prisons are not beds of roses? If that is all we demonstrated in this research, then it was certainly not worth the anguish. We believe there are many significant implications to be derived from this experience, only a few of which can be suggested here.

The potential social value of this study derives precisely from the fact that normal, healthy, educated young men could be so radically transformed under the institutional pressures of a "prison environment." If this could happen in so short a time, without the excesses that are possible in real prisons, and if it could happen to the "cream-of-the-crop of American youth," then one can only shudder to imagine what society is doing both to the actual guards and prisoners who are at this very moment participating in that unnatural "social experiment."

The pathology observed in this study cannot be reasonably attributed to pre-existing personality differences of the subjects, that option being eliminated by our selection procedures and random assignment. Rather, the subjects' abnormal social and personal reactions are best seen as a product of their transaction with an environment that supported the behavior that would be pathological in other settings, but was "appropriate" in this prison. Had we observed comparable reactions in a real prison, the psychiatrist undoubtedly would have been able to attribute any prisoner's behavior to character defects or personality maladjustment, while critics of the prison system would have been quick to label the guards as "psychopathic." This tendency to locate the source of behavior disorders inside a particular person or group underestimates the power of situational forces.

Our colleague, David Rosenhan,* has very convincingly shown that once a sane person (pretending to be insane) gets labeled as insane and committed to a mental hospital, it is the label that is the reality

---

* EDITOR'S NOTE: See Selection 29.

which is treated and not the person. This dehumanizing tendency to respond to other people according to socially determined labels and often arbitrarily assigned roles is also apparent in a recent "mock hospital" study designed by Norma Jean Orlando to extend the ideas in our research.

Personnel from the staff of Elgin State Hospital in Illinois role-played either mental patients or staff in a weekend simulation on a ward in the hospital. The mock mental patients soon displayed behavior indistinguishable from that we usually associate with the chronic pathological syndromes of actual mental patients: incessant pacing, uncontrollable weeping, depression, hostility, fights, stealing from each other, complaining. Many of the "mock staff" took advantage of their power to act in ways comparable to our mock guards by dehumanizing their powerless victims.

During a series of encounter debriefing sessions immediately after our experiment, we all had an opportunity to vent our strong feelings and to reflect upon the moral and ethical issues each of us faced, and we considered how we might react more morally in future "real-life" analogues to this situation. Year-long follow-ups with our subjects via questionnaires, personal interviews and group reunions indicate that their mental anguish was transient and situationally specific, but the self-knowledge gained has persisted.

For the most disturbing implication of our research comes from the parallels between what occurred in that basement mock prison and daily experiences in our own lives—and we presume yours. The physical institution of prison is but a concrete and steel metaphor for the existence of more pervasive, albeit less obvious, prisons of the mind that all of us daily create, populate and perpetuate. We speak here of the prisons of racism, sexism, despair, shyness, "neurotic hang-ups" and the like. The social convention of marriage, as one example, becomes for many couples a state of imprisonment in which one partner agrees to be prisoner or guard, forcing or allowing the other to play the reciprocal role—invariably without making the contract explicit.

To what extent do we allow ourselves to become imprisoned by docilely accepting the roles others assign us or, indeed, choose to remain prisoners because being passive and dependent frees us from the need to act and be responsible for our actions? The prison of fear constructed in the delusions of the paranoid is no less confining or less real than the cell that every shy person erects to limit his own freedom in anxious anticipation of being ridiculed and rejected by his guards —often guards of his own making.

THE EDITOR

Ira S. Cohen is Professor of Psychology
at the State University of New York at
Buffalo.